PINSTRIPE PATRONAGE

By the Authors

*A World Ignited: How Apostles of Ethnic, Religious and Racial Hatred Torch the
    Globe*
Glass Houses: Congressional Ethics and the Politics of Venom
Selling Our Security: The Erosion of America's Assets
Buying Into America: How Foreign Money Is Changing the Nation
Dismantling America: The Rush to Deregulate
Clout: Womanpower and Politics
To the Victor: Political Patronage from the Club House to the White House

By Susan J. Tolchin

The Angry American: How Voter Rage Is Changing the Nation
Women in Congress: 1917–1976

PINSTRIPE PATRONAGE

POLITICAL FAVORITISM
FROM THE CLUBHOUSE TO THE WHITE HOUSE AND BEYOND

BY MARTIN AND
SUSAN J. TOLCHIN

Paradigm Publishers
Boulder • London

Copyright © 2011 Paradigm Publishers

Published in the United States by Paradigm Publishers, 2845 Wilderness Place, Suite 200, Boulder, CO 80301 USA.

Paradigm Publishers is the trade name of Birkenkamp & Company, LLC, Dean Birkenkamp, President and Publisher.

Library of Congress Cataloging-in-Publication Data

Tolchin, Martin.
  Pinstripe patronage : political favoritism from the clubhouse to the White house and beyond / Martin and Susan J. Tolchin.
       p. cm.
  Includes bibliographical references and index.
  ISBN 978-1-59451-592-7 (hardcover : alk. paper)
  1. Patronage, Political—United States. 2. United States—Politics and government. I. Tolchin, Susan J. II. Title.
  JK736.T648 2010
  306.20973—dc22

                                                                  2010013788

Printed and bound in the United States of America on acid-free paper that meets the standards of the American National Standard for Permanence of Paper for Printed Library Materials.

Designed and Typeset by Straight Creek Bookmakers.

14 13 12 11 10   1 2 3 4 5

To Charles Tolchin DeMarchi,
Thomas DeMarchi,
and Karen Tolchin

CONTENTS

PREFACE

Pinstripe Patronage: From the Clubhouse to the White House and Beyond examines the financial rewards bestowed upon those involved in politics and how they have changed in the last quarter century. We found that the biggest rewards now go to those more at home in the boardroom than on the assembly line, as the Christmas turkey has been replaced by billion-dollar contracts. We were intrigued by the strategies created by politicians to circumvent five Supreme Court decisions, beginning in 1976, which severely restricted political patronage: the discretionary favors of government awarded to political supporters.

Each of those Supreme Court decisions cited our earlier book, *To the Victor: Political Patronage from the Clubhouse to the White House,* which originated at a 1968 meeting of *The New York Times* political reporters conducted by Arthur Gelb, the newspaper's legendary metropolitan editor, who later became managing editor. Gelb asked the assembled reporters why people risked their reputations by going into politics. Veteran reporters said that most of them had made their fortunes and wanted to "give back" to their fellow citizens.

This view was not universally shared, however. Martin, then a metropolitan reporter, had just returned from an interview with Stanley Steingut, Brooklyn Democratic leader and Speaker of the New York State Assembly. During the interview, Steingut had received several telephone calls, and Steingut's end of the conversation went as follows: "Yes, Max, you get the plumbing, but Harry gets the electrical work, Morris gets the engineering, Sam gets the cafeteria." Subsequent calls from Harry, Morris, and Sam elicited a similar recital. Eventually, Martin asked Steingut if the contracts related to a public or private building. His response: "Does it really matter?"

The inference was clear: Financial rewards awaited those involved in politics. Gelb assigned Martin to ferret out the many ways in which politicians enrich themselves and their political allies. The resulting articles led to a book written with Susan (a professor of political science) and published in 1971. In that effort, we also were guided by an extraordinarily creative editor, Jason Epstein, at Random House. *To the Victor* was the first of our eight books, many of which took 180 turns from their original premises. Initially, we considered patronage somewhat sleazy, the coin of the realm of political machines, whose bosses did well to stay one jump ahead of the sheriff. Reams of articles and books focused on patronage in terms of corruption, party building, and illicit exchanges of campaign contributions for political rewards. But we shifted our opinions after scores of interviews in dozens of towns, cities, and visits to Washington, D.C., to talk to members of Congress, the judiciary and the executive branch, as well as to key figures in city halls and statehouses. We concluded that despite its considerable baggage, patronage continued to be a necessary tool of government, and that those who disdained its practices often proved ineffective public servants. The conundrum continues to this day: how to succeed in politics and retain one's integrity?

All our subsequent books returned to our initial theme: the back story of politics in America reverted to the theme of government patronage. Although it appears today in many different guises—such as outsourcing, privatization, and earmarks—it all comes down to the rewards that hold political organizations together.

Our interviews with public officials persuaded us to abandon our initial view that patronage consisted mainly of jobs. We were told that key constituents often wanted favors ranging from a photograph with a mayor, governor, or president to display on an office wall; to zoning variances, bank deposits, earmarks, contracts, tax exemptions, guardianships, refereeships—in other words, a host of rewards available only from those in power. *Pinstripe Patronage* reflects the fact that political favoritism has been taken to a new and loftier level and affects every facet of government, even foreign policy and intelligence.

Our collaboration of journalist and political scientist dismayed many of our colleagues. In the world of academe, there is no more pejorative epithet than "journalistic." To the cognoscenti, that is often code for superficial, anecdotal, and unreliable. Yet at the same time, academics rely very heavily for their own research on what they call "secondary sources," which are often the very print media articles or blogs they have previously disdained. Similarly, working journalists hurl their own insults at the academic world, at times labeling research "academic." Translation: ivory tower, poorly written, and, worst of all, irrelevant. On the other hand, journalists often quote academics to lend credibility to their articles. We aimed for the best of both worlds: extensive reporting enriched by insights and perspective. Journalism brings a fresh and innovative approach to solving the mysteries of political life; the academic approach affords the advantages of time and reflection, free from the burdens of daily deadlines and word limits. In sum, this book is a collaborative effort in many ways, in addition to the obvious one of a "husband-wife team." It builds on the thoughts, insights, and scholarship of generations of forefathers and foremothers to produce its very own way of looking at the world, and we hope that it benefits from both approaches.

Since *To the Victor* was published nearly forty years ago, the U.S. Supreme Court severely restricted both the hiring and firing of public employees on the basis of their party affiliation, and the awarding of contracts on the basis of campaign contributions. We decided to explore the impact of those Supreme Court decisions. Were they definitive? Did they end the hiring and firing of political supporters? Did they affect the way politicians awarded public contracts? Did they undermine political machines? Did they improve the quality of elected officials? Did they produce accountability and a fairer, more equitable, and more efficient form of government?

To find the answers, we retraced our steps and interviewed scores of current mayors and governors, as well as members of Congress, the judiciary, and the executive branch. Some were more forthcoming than others, but taken together they produced a rich tapestry of contemporary politics. They were partners in our endeavor to explore the often neglected underpinnings of politics and government, in the hope of illuminating how public policy decisions are really made. We hope we've broken new ground in describing how patronage works today, how it affects the nation's politics and government, and its impact around the world.

Susan's professional home at the School of Public Policy at George Mason University has been consistently supportive of her research efforts. Her students and colleagues have offered many ideas and critical perspectives. Special thanks to Dean Kingsley Haynes, Associate Dean James Finkelstein, Provost Peter Stearns, President Alan Merten, and Associate Ph.D. Public Policy Director Elizabeth Eck for providing an encouraging academic atmosphere and furnishing resources for research assistance.

At George Mason University, Susan's research assistants provided extraordinary skills at checking facts, tracking down leads, constructing charts, editing, and solving computer mysteries. They are Ha Vu and Carol Whitney, both of whom did yeoman service in bringing this manuscript to fruition.

We also are grateful to the Woodrow Wilson International Center for Scholars, and especially Lee Hamilton and Mike Van Dusen, for providing Martin with an intellectual home, resources, and support. Many of our observations are the result of the collegial give-and-take for which the center is justly renowned. The center's librarian, Janet Spikes, and her assistants Michelle Kamalich and Dagne Gizaw, were unflaggingly helpful; as were the center's program directors Kent Hughes, Don Wolfensberger, Philippa Strum, and David Klaus; research assistants John Morrill and John Bohrer-Yardley; and fellow scholars, especially

Kate Lavelle, Samer Shehata, and Vladimir Tismaneanu. Elizabeth Byers provided all-around help. We also want to thank Diane Barry, archivist at the Ronald Reagan Presidential Library, and James Cornelius, archivist at the Abraham Lincoln Presidential Library. We also are indebted to Ray Scheppach and his staff at the National Governors Association, and Tom Cochran and his staff at the U.S. Conference of Mayors.

All the direct quotes in the book that are not cited as footnotes are drawn from interviews. We interviewed more than 200 people in researching this book and benefited from their insights. Especially helpful were Gary Ackerman, Scott Amey, David Anderson, Nan Aron, Michael Barbaro, Evan Bayh, James Blanchard, Michael Bloomberg, John Boffa, Richard Brown, David Burnham, Lou Cannon, Paul Charlton, Mary Cheh, David Chen, Pat Choate, Joseph Crowley, Mitch Daniels, Chet Culver, Anne Donahue, Jim Douglas, Ken Duberstein, Alan Ehrenhalt, Albert Eisele, Jack Evans, Alvin S. Felzenberg, Dan Glickman, Vincent Gray, Phyllis Hanfling, Robert Hanfling, John Hilley, Charles Hynes, David Keene, Marcy Kaptur, Robert Katzmann, Tom Kean, Colbert King, Ed Koch, Natasha Korecki, Kevin Kosar, John Koskinen, Madeline Kunin, Joe Manchin, Deborah Markowitz, Matt Mezzanotte, Abner Mikva, Ruth Ann Minner, Jedd Moscowitz, Peter Nickles, James Oberstar, Bob Packwood, Joyce Purnick, Ralph Regula, Donald Ritchie, Renee Roth, Warren Rudman, William Safire, Carol Schwartz, Michael Schenkler, Dick Simpson, Gaye Symington, Vladimir Tismaneaunu, Henry Waxman, and David Yassky.

Many of our friends and colleagues read selected chapters of the book—some even plowed though the entire manuscript—and were especially helpful in sharing their criticism and insights: Pat Choate, Thomas DeMarchi, A. Lee Fritschler, Kent Hughes, James Pfiffner, Karen Tolchin, Janine Wedel, Don Wolfensberger, and Carol Whitney. Linda Cashdan deserves special mention for lending her gimlet eye and editing skills to the manuscript.

Finally, we must express our gratitude to our editor, Jennifer Knerr. This is the third book we've done together, and her vision and professionalism have guided us throughout. We think she's the best in the business. Our thanks also to Nancy Sixsmith, copy editor par excellence, and Candace English, who skillfully shepherded this book through production.

All the sources and critics mentioned here have contributed mightily to our endeavor to produce a book on how government really works. Any errors are, of course, our own.

Susan J. Tolchin and Martin Tolchin
Washington, D.C.
Warren, Vermont

CHAPTER ONE
"THE ONLY WAY TO RUN A GOVERNMENT"

"Politics is the art of putting people under obligation to you."
Jacob Arvey, Illinois Democratic leader

"Some people, when they want something from somebody, walk up and hit them with a two by four. I walk up and give them hugs and kisses."
Michael Bloomberg, Mayor, New York City

Justice William Brennan and Speaker Thomas P. "Tip" O'Neill Jr., both liberal Irish Catholics, arrived in Washington in the 1950s and played major roles in shaping late twentieth century America. But during their forty years as powerful public officials in the nation's capital, they never met except for handshakes at public events. Once they retired, however, they wanted to get to know one another. After several attempts that failed because of their various health problems, the great Supreme Court jurist and the consummate politician finally lunched together at Washington's Cosmos Club.

Tip was in rare form. The old Boston "pol" regaled the self-effacing Justice with his successful effort, on behalf of President Bill Clinton, to persuade seventeen House Democrats to support NAFTA, the North American Free Trade Agreement. Tip recalled that when he was Speaker, President Jimmy Carter sought his help in passing an energy bill during a crisis Carter had called "the moral equivalent of war." To obtain congressional votes, Tip said, he had urged Carter to "Call the fellows in, see what they want—a highway, a bridge, a veteran's hospital, a post office." But Carter considered himself above such mundane, pork barrel politics. He paid the price and obtained an energy bill that only vaguely resembled what he had sought.

When Tip offered the same advice to President Clinton to help round up congressional votes for NAFTA, he recalled, "Clinton understood." Clinton bartered away highways, bridges, hospitals, post offices, and almost anything else he could get his hands on, and still the bill barely passed. Mary Brennan, the Justice's conservative wife, was appalled. "Tip," she said, "that's a hell of a way to run a government." The former Speaker beamed his most benign smile and told her, "Mary darling, that's the *only* way to run a government."

Political patronage, awarding the discretionary favors of government in exchange for political support—is alive and well in twenty-first century America. The enormous growth of government in the last century created a concurrent expansion of the discretionary powers of political leaders. Welcomed equally by Democrats and Republicans, these new patronage powers increased their ability to reward constituents and remained the lifeblood of politics and government. Jake Arvey, the late Illinois Democratic leader who fostered Adlai Stevenson's political career, said there were many definitions of politics, including "the art of the possible" and "the art of compromise." "But my definition," he said, "is that politics is the art of putting people under obligation to you."

Politicians put people under obligation to them through patronage, which cements loyalty up and down the political ladder. Former Michigan Governor Jim Blanchard, appointed ambassador to Canada by President Clinton, was not surprised when his phone rang at the start of the 2008 presidential primary season, and a raspy voice intoned "Mr. Ambassador, we need your help." How could he refuse Bill Clinton? Blanchard explained, "I've had a 20-year relationship with the Clintons," adding, "I'm intensely loyal." Blanchard became a strong advocate for Hillary Clinton's campaign for the Democratic nomination for president and even represented her before the Democratic Party's Rules Committee. Another Democrat, Governor Ed Rendell of Pennsylvania, also rallied his troops on behalf of Hillary Clinton during the hotly contested 2008 Democratic primary. Rendell, previously mayor of Philadelphia, had received President Clinton's support for revitalizing the Philadelphia Naval Shipyard and for federal funds to put more police officers on the street. President Clinton also appointed Rendell's wife, Marjorie O. Rendell, to the district court in 1994 and to the Court of Appeals in 1997 and named Rendell chairman of the Democratic National Committee during the 2000 election. But some people are less loyal than others. Bill Richardson, whom Clinton appointed UN ambassador and Energy Secretary, and Robert Reich, his Labor Secretary, jumped ship and supported Barack Obama. Richardson evoked the scorn of Clinton attack dog and strategist James Carville, who denounced him as a "Judas."

New York's billionaire mayor, Michael Bloomberg, used both his private fortune and government perks to achieve his political goals. "Some people, when they want something from somebody, walk up and hit them with a two by four," Bloomberg said. "I walk up and give them hugs and kisses."

This is the way the world works—usually—in politics and government, the business community, and even in families. The goal is to use favors to deprive recipients of their ability to make independent decisions. In government, those favors come in many forms—from a mayor's attendance at a wedding, to a governor's speech at a private dinner, to a president's invitation to spend a night in the Lincoln bedroom. More substantial favors include zoning variances, tax exemptions, judgeships, refereeships, appointments to boards and commissions, guardianships, insurance contracts, and bank deposits, as well as jobs and billion-dollar defense contracts.

In addition to traditional patronage, the new landscape now includes "pinstripe patronage"—billions of dollars in outsourcing, the privatization of services previously conducted by government. Pinstripe patronage also includes earmarks, which are government grants specified for the use of an individual, corporation, or community; and the highly-paid salaries for top executives and board members of hybrid agencies such as Fannie Mae and Freddie Mac, which are public-private partnerships.

It is called pinstripe patronage because it usually benefits those more at home in a boardroom than on an assembly line, who reciprocate by giving politicians the ever-increasing funds needed to conduct their political campaigns. Pinstripe patronage has replaced the Christmas turkey and snow removal jobs that politicians gave the less fortunate and includes billions of dollars in noncompetitive contracts for Halliburton, Blackwater, and other companies whose executives have given megabucks to both political parties. Their work in Iraq has made these companies American representatives on the world stage, where they have embarrassed America in the eyes of the world.

To critics, political patronage represents the dark underbelly of American politics, whose practitioners are fortunate to keep one step ahead of the sheriff. They believe that patronage breeds corruption, incompetence, and waste. They cite billions in wasted dollars spent on unneeded projects to win political support and the withholding of needed projects to punish political foes. The late Representative John Murtha, Pennsylvania Democrat and the powerful chairman of the House Appropriations Subcommittee on Defense, obtained $150 million in federal payments for the John Murtha Airport in Johnstown, which has an average of fewer than 30 passengers per day. The airport has an $8.5 million, taxpayer-funded radar system that has never been used and is less than a two-hour drive from the Pittsburgh airport.[1] A highly decorated ex-Marine, Murtha represented the twelfth district of Pennsylvania. The committee he chaired oversees appropriations for the Department of Defense, which includes the Air Force, Army, Marine Corps, Navy, and intelligence community.

To its practitioners, however, patronage is an essential ingredient of effective government, and those who disdain its use often find themselves unable to enact and implement their programs. They acknowledge the waste, fraud, and abuse inherent in some traditional patronage practices, but say that they represent the costs of living in a democracy, where people have freedom of choice.

On its most basic level, patronage cements political loyalty; politicians are loyal to those above them who bestow favors upon them, while receiving the loyalty of subordinates who in turn depend on them for favors. A district leader will usually be loyal to a county leader, who will be loyal to a state leader, who will be loyal to a national leader. Thus, a member of Congress often defers to his party leaders and committee chairmen, as well as to the political, business, and labor leaders back home that fund his campaigns.

But other factors sometimes come into play. Representative Bill Brewster, an Oklahoma Republican who served on the board of the National Rifle Association (NRA), switched his NAFTA vote for a promise that President Clinton would go duck hunting with him as a visible sign of support for the NRA. In 1993, two days after Christmas and five weeks after the NAFTA vote, Clinton and Brewster, clad in full hunting regalia, went duck hunting in Oklahoma in sixteen-degree weather. Photographs of the two men in their hunting gear, holding their shotguns, later appeared on the cover of the NRA's magazine.[2]

Movers and shakers have long used patronage to achieve their goals. President Franklin Delano Roosevelt created a raft of alphabet agencies, which became patronage havens. Instead, he could have placed these agencies in existing cabinet departments whose employees were subject to the civil service laws. In New York, the unelected power broker, Robert Moses (who was appointed to chair state park commissions and bridge and highway authorities), granted thousands of favors—including selecting general contractors for the building of highways, bridges, parks, and government buildings; hiring white- and blue-collar workers recommended by city councilmen, state assemblymen, and state senators; awarding architecture, engineering, underwriting, and insurance contracts to the politically connected; and placing toll receipts in banks owned by politicians. That's how Moses consolidated decades of his control over the shaping of both the city and state of New York. His favors included moving the Manhattan entrance of the Triboro Bridge from 96th Street to 125th Street to accommodate the media tycoon William Randolph Hearst, who owned real estate between the two streets.[3]

Indeed, as Tip O'Neill noted, patronage is an essential tool of governing. Those who turn up their noses, like President Carter, often have a difficult time achieving their policy goals. But patronage is also extremely susceptible to corruption—extortion, kickbacks, fraud, and waste, including "no-show" jobs and unnecessary services and projects.

There are so many legitimate ways for politicians to enrich themselves that those who resort to such behavior betray a poverty of imagination. Nevertheless, it sometimes seems that election to high office puts a politician on a glide path to a prison cell. Three former governors of Illinois, representing both parties, were convicted of corruption, and a fourth has been indicted for extortion and fraud. Three successive secretaries of state in New Jersey, also from both parties, wound up with convictions for fraud. Judges, senators, and House members have served time behind bars. A total of more than 20,000 public officials and private citizens were convicted of public corruption in the last two decades, totaling an average of 1,000 per year.[4] Many have given a bad name to what so many consider an essential tool of government; indeed, it is surprising that with so many politicians behind bars, there hasn't been more political support for prison reform.

"The Jacksonian ideal was that patronage was efficient," said Prof. Alvin S. Felzenberg of the University of Pennsylvania. "It ensured accountability because public dissatisfaction with the delivery of services inevitably led to a politician's vulnerability at the polls." President George W. Bush's mishandling of Hurricane Katrina, for example, was traced to the Federal Emergency Management Administration (FEMA), which was riddled with inept political appointees. "Human nature suggests you can't run government without patronage," Felzenberg added, and when there is incompetence or corruption, "the fault isn't patronage, but those who abuse it, and the purposes for which it is used."

The tools of patronage have changed since the glory days of the old political machines, whose leaders happily dispensed food for the poor and jobs for ward heelers, those on the lowest level of the political ladder. But as money continues to flow into political campaigns despite major reform efforts, politicians continue to reward supporters despite five decisions by the U.S. Supreme Court that placed severe restrictions on hiring, firing, and promoting government employees, as well as awarding government contracts, on the basis of party affiliation and political support. The Court ignored warnings from many quarters that patronage was the lifeblood of politics and government. Nature abhors a vacuum, and despite all the new laws against "politics as usual," the empty spaces were quickly filled. In other words, patronage didn't go away; it just took new forms.

In the first of those cases, in 1976, the court ruled in *Elrod v. Burns*[5] in 1976 that the newly elected Cook County (Illinois) sheriff, a Democrat, could not discharge non–civil service employees because they were Republicans. Such discharges violated the First and Fourteenth Amendments' guarantees of freedom of speech and association, as well as various statutes including the Civil Rights Act of 1871, concluded Justice William Brennan, who wrote the court's decision. In the second case, in 1980,[6] Justice John Paul Stevens ruled in *Branti v. Finkel* that the public defender in Rockland County, New York, a Democrat, could not discharge assistant public defenders who had been satisfactorily performing their jobs solely because they were Republicans. The third case was handed down later, in 1990: *Rutan v. Republican Party of Illinois*.[7] At this time, the court ruled that Governor James Thompson of Illinois, a Republican, could not base hiring and promotions on financial contributions and service to the Republican Party. "To the victor belong only those spoils that may be constitutionally obtained," Justice Brennan wrote. Using political affiliation as a basis for hiring and firing, he added, is unconstitutional because it places "burdens on free speech and association." This protection was finally extended to government contractors in the fourth case, in 1996. Justice Sandra Day O'Connor, who delivered the court's opinion in *Board of County Commissioners, Wabaunsee County, Kansas v. Umbehr*,[8] ruled that a county could not terminate a contract to haul trash because the contractor was an outspoken critic of the Board of County Commissioners. The court held that the First Amendment protected independent contractors from governmental retaliation against their speech. This opinion was echoed in the fifth case, *O'Hare Truck Service vs. City of Northlake*,[9] in a decision by Justice Kennedy delivered the same day.[10]

Many assumed that these decisions would have sounded the death knell of political patronage. Not so. In Illinois, New Jersey New York, Louisiana, and Kentucky, among other locales, old-fashioned patronage practices—such as placing supporters in non-exempt government jobs—were thriving well into the twenty-first century. Indeed, examples of political patronage can be found in every state. Although some of its practitioners have recently wound up behind bars, many experts believe that the system is deeply embedded in the culture of many communities and continues to thrive.

But patronage lives on, often in disguise, thanks to soaring government budgets and the phenomenal increase of earmarks on the local, state, and federal level for everything from the arts and sciences to the infamous "Bridge to Nowhere." At the same time, there has been a great increase in privatization, outsourcing everything from state hospitals, prisons, and transportation to the war in Iraq. Both earmarks and privatization have provided grist for the patronage mill. There were more contract employees in Iraq, for example, than there were military personnel.

The Supreme Court decisions also coincided with the rise of television, with its increased use in political campaigns. In addition to volunteers needed to obtain signatures on petitions to place a candidate's name on the ballot and escort voters to the polls, candidates needed megabucks to underwrite their increasingly expensive campaigns. A decision by the U.S. Supreme Court in early 2010 added even more fuel to the controversy. *Citizens United v. Federal Election Commission* gave corporations carte blanche in financing elections: to restrict them, said the court, was tantamount to violating the free speech clause of the First Amendment of the

U.S. Constitution. In effect, the Court declared vital sections of the McCain-Feingold law on campaign finance unconstitutional and opened the floodgates to corporate money. The decision reversed decades of precedent.[11]

The cost of television commercials escalated, especially as contests became increasingly negative. Big donors were often rewarded with pinstripe patronage such as lucrative contracts to provide government services and other highly imaginative forms of "boodle"—an old-fashioned word for political patronage. Mayors, governors and even presidents could then call on these contractors to employ political supporters in private sector, nongovernment jobs, thus circumventing the Supreme Court's restrictions on government employment.

Efforts at privatization and contracting out government services affected local, state, and federal governments. Today it is estimated that more than 50 percent of all federal functions are "contracted out," most of them without competitive bidding. In fiscal 2006, the U.S. government spent more than $415 billion on contracts with 176,172 companies. About one-quarter of that total, $100 billion, went to only six companies. More than 60 percent of these contracts, most of them with the Department of Defense, were awarded without competitive bidding. "The rapid growth in no-bid and limited competition contracts has made full and open competition the exception, not the rule," reported Robert O'Harrow.[12] State and local governments followed suit, with soaring budgets for both privatization and "earmarks" that all too often rewarded political supporters. Defense Department contracts dwarf those awarded by state and local government.

To politicians, government remains the spender of first resort. When James Willmot, a contractor, was unable to sell condos or cooperatives, or even rent several high-rise apartment buildings he had built in his native Rochester, New York in 1976, he sought federal rent subsidies. The fact that he was also chairman of the Democratic National Committee's Finance Committee meant that help was only a phone call away. Tip O'Neill badgered Carla Hills, Secretary of Housing and Urban Development in the Ford administration, on the status of Willmot's application for $2.2 million in federal funds. "What's the status of the subsidies?" O'Neill asked in numerous telephone calls to Hills. Willmot got his subsidies. For exactly one year, O'Neill shunned *New York Times* reporter Martin Tolchin, who broke the story and then finally granted an interview. At the end of the session, O'Neill leaned back in his chair and said, "You know, Marty, I'm Irish, and we Irish never carry grudges." Tolchin replied, "The thought never occurred to me, Mr. Speaker." O'Neill then retorted, "But that article you wrote was such a piece of s____." But the incident was an example of access, influence, and the perks enjoyed by the chairman of the Democratic Party's Finance Committee.

At times, a politician will block a patronage request to settle a score. When Senator Warren Rudman, a New Hampshire Republican, was about to graduate from Syracuse University, he was outraged to learn that there was an $8 diploma fee. He refused to pay the fee, and when he marched onto the stage of the auditorium he received an empty cylinder. He did, however, receive his Second Lieutenant's bars as a result of serving in the ROTC, and shortly after graduation found himself leading a platoon in Korea. One night, in a brief respite in a mountain foxhole, he wrote to the university president describing his perilous position and asked that the diploma be sent to his parents. The president responded by saying that the university would gladly send his parents the diploma, after receiving the diploma fee. Rudman declined. After his election to the Senate, a Republican colleague, Senator Alfonse M. D'Amato of New York, sought a multimillion-dollar grant for a new facility at Syracuse University. Despite the personal pleas of both D'Amato and the university president, Rudman blocked the appropriation each of the twelve years he served in the Senate. You don't have to construct a cost-benefit scale to weigh an $8 diploma fee against a multimillion-dollar federal grant!

A president's vast patronage powers explain why he almost always controls his party. Barring an overriding national issue, patronage powers, usually vested in party elders, explain why politics is usually oriented more to the past than to current movements, and more toward conservative than to innovative programs. Congress especially rewards longevity with power, allowing those with long service to collect numerous IOUs and to obtain the lion's share of new ones. Even those members motivated by ideological commitment quickly discover, in the words of the legendary Speaker of the House Sam Rayburn of Texas, "To get along, you have to go along." Mr. Rayburn never expected a congressman to vote against the interests of his constituents, but often advised members that "anyone should find a way to go along with his leaders 70 percent of the time." Although the cards are stacked against them, it is sometimes possible for those who seek significant change to prevail and bypass party elders.

The patronage system thrives as one of the occupational hazards of government, in both democracies and authoritarian regimes. But in a land where most people have freedom of choice, incentives are often required to bestir them to public action. Patronage also ensures that ideology plays a relatively small role in the decisions of government, because soaring rhetoric often conceals the hard, cold, unemotional realities of political ambitions meshing into place.

Not surprisingly, the ideological approach to politics and government is encouraged by the politicians themselves, who would much rather portray themselves as motivated more by principle than by the quest for power or personal profit. The ideological approach to government also receives sustenance from the mass media, which finds it easier, less costly, and infinitely safer to report campaign speeches or depict members of Congress standing toe-to-toe in angry debate than to learn, for example, why a lawmaker changed a vote during a closed committee meeting, or to predict the financial crisis of 2008–2009. These theatrics, especially beloved by the electronic media, often obscure the patronage system of debts incurred and IOUs held, accompanied by the silent but overriding theme of political ambition.

Patronage power is defended as a necessary and legitimate extension of the power of elected officials, who must overcome inertia, powerful interest groups, and recalcitrant legislators. A president is not a general whose orders must be obeyed; on the contrary, his greatest power, according to presidential scholar Richard Neustadt (who had been an aide to President Truman) was the power to persuade. Patronage is a potent tool in that arsenal, with the American people and their elected representatives the obvious targets. When the late Mike Mansfield (who had been Senate majority leader) was ambassador to Japan, large photographs of congressional leaders hung on his office walls. He explained that many Japanese believed that the president had the authority to make unilateral decisions. That's why Mansfield showed his guests the faces of those a president must convince to translate his wishes into laws.

Patronage defenders claim that their system is more humane than a meritocracy in which individuals are appointed on more neutral criteria and have little investment in the success or failure of an administration. Who has not been frustrated by clerks at a city's tax or licensing bureau, who seem to spend most of their time chatting with their colleagues, oblivious of the long lines at their desks? This leads to the argument that patronage encourages conscientious work habits because poor performance by public officials could lead to public outrage that brings down their patrons, and could cost them their jobs. In addition, in many places the "merit system" can also be phony; only the names are changed: from patronage to "mentor, network, or protégé."

The good news is that patronage drives public policy. The bad news is that patronage drives public policy. And the worst news is that patronage is beginning to drive U.S. foreign policy in ways that undermine America's stature in the world. Private corporations that represent the U.S. in Iraq and Afghanistan have committed abuses that have outraged the local citizenry and undermined the nation's ability to win the hearts and minds that are so vital to our success in that region.

Patronage has long been a two-edged sword. It has been used to enact healthcare legislation and prolong wars, prohibit smoking in public places and end term limits, enact programs for the poor, and deprive opponents of jobs. Unquestionably, patronage distorts government priorities, and one's view of this distortion depends on how one feels about the policy involved. If one supported NAFTA, Clinton's use of patronage was a worthy use of presidential prerogatives. But Representative Marcy Kaptur, an Ohio Democrat, was in tears on the House floor during the vote, when she discovered that many colleagues who had pledged to support her opposition to NAFTA had yielded to the White House's blandishments.

But the kind of pork Clinton provided to win enactment of NAFTA was assailed in 2009 by the Tea Party movement. Its members, alarmed by the soaring deficits created by congressional earmarks, placed fiscal stability and tax reduction above the need for the wide-ranging projects. Although the nation's infrastructure was crumbling with collapsing bridges and deteriorating highways, and despite the need for hospitals, schools, and other government services, Tea Party members set their sights on both Republican and Democratic congressmen who had prided themselves on bringing home the bacon. Their early victims included Senator Bob Bennett of (R-Utah), an unquestioned conservative whose grandfather was a president of the Mormon Church, and Representative Alan Mollohan, (D-West Virginia), both members of congressional appropriations committees. The Tea Party also succeeded in gaining a victory in Kentucky for Rand Paul, who easily defeated Trey Grayson, the establishment candidate in the Republican primary for U.S. Senate.

The major problem with patronage is not that it builds political empires or private fortunes, but that it encourages public officials to compromise the public interest for private gain and to sacrifice the interests of citizens on the altar of a politician's needs. Why should a neighborhood lose a playground because it voted against a mayor or elected a councilman who refuses to bow to a mayor's wishes? How much of the soaring military budgets ($663.8 billion in 2010) are actually needed to protect the country, for example, and how much is allocated to reward political supporters? The late Jamie Whitten, a Mississippi Democrat who chaired the Defense Appropriations Subcommittee, once testified, "I am convinced that defense is only one of the factors that enter into our determination for defense spending."[13] In 2008, hearings conducted by the House Government Operations Committee confirmed that such skepticism remains well-founded; in fact, many military contractors in Iraq were chosen less for their expertise and professionalism and more for their financial and political support of the administration.[14] One wonders how long the Iraq war would have continued if it were *against* the patronage interests of the nation's political leaders, or if it imposed hardships, such as substantially increased taxes and fees. Indeed, former Chief Justice Earl Warren explained why the Vietnam War protest was led by young people: "So long as youth carry the burden of the war while their elders seem in no hurry to end it, and, indeed, seem to profit financially from it, they have a right to complain."[15] Unlike Vietnam, the Iraq and Afghanistan wars were fought by a volunteer army instead of draftees. America's middle class remained largely untouched by military service or additional taxes, which partly explained why the nation was reluctant to end both conflicts.

Patronage also plays a crucial role in determining the quality of the nation's public officials, an interesting balancing act between the forces of obligation and the interests of professionalism. A spirited defense of judicial mediocrity was made by the late Senator Roman L. Hruska, Nebraska Republican, who defended President Nixon's nomination of G. Harrold Carswell as a Supreme Court Justice by arguing, "Even if he were mediocre, there are a lot of mediocre judges and people and lawyers. They are entitled to a little representation, aren't they, and a little chance?"[16]

Patronage powers also give politicians the power to determine the quality of law enforcement, one of the most coveted powers of government. The discretionary aspects often surface when a new administration prosecutes public officials who previously enjoyed immunity while their own party controlled the administration. Few presidents have used these powers in a more partisan manner than George W. Bush, whose attorney general fired prosecutors considered overly aggressive in pursuing Republican officials and too sluggish in prosecuting Democrats. The Bush Justice Department prosecuted a former Alabama governor who was a leader of the state's Democratic Party. Dozens of state attorneys general of both parties expressed outrage over the case.[17]

Patronage affects the quality of life of most Americans. Even neighborhood projects, such as parks, playgrounds, and traffic lights, which seem apolitical on the surface, can be used to reward supporters and punish opponents. Mayor Adrian Fenty of Washington, D.C. openly rewards his supporters among the city council members with projects in their districts, while withholding them from districts represented by political opponents. After his reelection in 1973, Mayor John Lindsay of New York jokingly denied being a practitioner of this strategy. At the 1974 dinner of the Inner Circle, a group of political reporters, he said, "How can Queens (a county that voted for his opponent) complain that I haven't given them any new facilities? My new budget clearly shows plans to build a sewage treatment plant there." Of course, a sewage treatment plant is not exactly the kind of public works project sought by most neighborhoods.

A voter who fails to vote his conscience in a general election out of gratitude to a party official for a personal favor, or a traffic light, or a playground can hardly be critical of the councilman, state legislator, or congressman who fails to "vote his conscience" on an issue, but instead goes along with his party's leadership out of gratitude for past favors and the expectation of new ones. It may be argued, however, that a voter who supports a congressional candidate who has solved his problems with a federal agency is at least acting on the basis of concrete performance, whereas a candidate's position on Iraq or tax reform may be a good deal less dependable.

Many patronage practices have changed very little. The successful patronage seeker is well aware that government must bank its money, insure its property, and construct office buildings—all on a noncompetitive basis because bank and insurance rates are uniform and there are no objective standards for architecture, engineering, and (often) construction contracts. This means that officers of the bank that was "selected" can expect to be called upon for future campaign contributions, and were probably selected in the first place for their past generosity. Most important, city and state controllers reap political power by deciding where to invest government funds. Government buildings need furniture, stationery, plumbing systems, heating, wiring and vending machines—franchises often worth millions of dollars to the recipients of this patronage.

Politicians today have opportunities undreamed of by George Washington Plunkitt, the colorful turn-of-the-century Tammany boss, and his political heirs. Today's Plunkitts can choose among a vast array of favors for loyalists. Through privatization, a public official is freed from the judicial constraints on his ability to reward supporters with government jobs and noncompetitive contracts. A mayor can pick up a telephone and find a job for a supporter in a sanitation or engineering company that he has given a lucrative contract. Plunkitt defined the difference between what he called "dishonest graft" (bribery and extortion) and "honest graft" (availing oneself of inside information and political networking). With a verve that does honor to the politicians of his day, Mr. Plunkitt noted that he had made a fortune in politics by purchasing real estate with the advance knowledge that a new subway line would soon enhance its value. "I seen my opportunities and I took 'em," boasted Plunkitt, in the best definition to date of honest graft. Although some reformers tend to regard all patronage as "dishonest graft" because it grants favors on the basis of favoritism, not merit, orthodox politicians consider patronage the vehicle that balances the pressures and interests on which a democracy rests. They are well aware that a politician whose patronage is so inflexible that he cannot accommodate rising new interest groups may find himself displaced by them at election time. The successful politician relies not only on his ability to satisfy organized local pressure groups but also on his sensitivity to the political desires of the broad base of constituents who are not organized.

To protect their patronage, politicians have often searched out and nominated outstanding candidates to head their tickets: Franklin D. Roosevelt was enthusiastically supported by Ed Flynn's Bronx machine, Harry S Truman was the protégé of the Thomas Pendergast machine in Kansas City, and Adlai Stevenson was handpicked by the powerful Chicago Democratic machine led by Jacob Arvey. A distinguished, popular candidate at the top of the ticket often carries into office the judges, sheriffs, and local legislators who are the lifeblood of a machine. Hymie Shorenstein, a Brooklyn district leader nearly a century ago, was once confronted by a worried Assembly candidate who had not received the funds he needed to campaign effectively. Shorenstein calmed him: "You see the ferryboats come in?" Shorenstein asked. "You see them pull into the slip? You see the water suck in behind? And when the water sucks in behind the ferry-boat, all kinds of dirty garbage comes smack into the slip with the ferryboat? Go home. Al Smith [the candidate for New York governor] is the ferryboat. This year, you're the garbage."

With the advent of television, which enables politicians to speak directly to voters, members of Congress, governors, and mayors might seem to need fewer troops to get out the vote. In fact, however, some of the mightiest machines are run by members of Congress, governors, and mayors.

Conventional wisdom holds that political machines are obsolete. As is often the case, conventional wisdom is wrong. Today's political machines provide would-be candidates with access to the ballot. They continue to have much to say about which candidates are on the top of the ticket, as well as the selection of judges. They are more businesslike than their predecessors, whose bosses had colorful nicknames like John "Bath House" Coughlin, "Red Mike" Hylan, Michael "Hinky Dink" Kenna, "Slippery Dick" Connolly, "Old King Cole," "King" James McManes, and "Iz" Durham.[18]

Ward bosses sometimes took credit they didn't deserve. In the late 1980s, John Boffa, now a successful businessman in Washington, D.C., decided to run for the city council in Albany, New York. Boffa rang doorbells to introduce him-self to the voters, and as a courtesy, shared his experience with Nicholas Sacca, the Democratic leader of the Center Square neighborhood adjoining the state capital. One of the things Boffa learned was that there were many burned-out street lights in the district. Sacca checked the registration of those who lived in houses near the street lights, and had Niagara Power replace those near houses that belonged to Democrats. When Boffa offered to call Niagara Power, he was informed that only the ward boss would make those calls and take credit for restoring the street lights in the process. Without the support of Sacca, Boffa was defeated.

Also defeated in a race for city council was Phyllis Hanfling, who sought vainly to gain the support of Arthur T. Barbieri, Democratic leader of New Haven, Con-necticut "Why do you want to run?" Barbieri asked. "I believe in good govern-ment," Hanfling replied. "We don't want any 'goo goos,'" said Barbieri, who later installed Bartholomew Guida, who ran a gas station, as the city's mayor.

In the last several decades, as whites fled to the suburbs, African Americans and Hispanics have entered the inner-city machines long dominated by Irish and Italian politicians. These machines have proven every bit as venal as their ethnic ancestors. They also have become more personal, with elected officials often creating their own machines. In addition to Newark and Detroit, African American politicians have developed machines in most major cities. Harlem's Herman "Denny" Farrell is a Manhattan Democratic leader, and Maxine Waters has developed a formidable machine in Los Angeles. Also, under old-style ethnic leadership, the suburbs continue to have some of the strongest political machines.

Voters still know only those candidates at the top of the ticket and usually have little knowledge of the dozens of judges, commissioners, council, board members, propositions, referenda, and amendments at the bottom of the ticket. How did they get there? Usually, through the good offices of political machines, which provide the manpower to get the thousands of signatures needed to get on the ballot. Lawyers continue to dominate the political arena because of the many rewards they can reap, from clerkships to executorships, trusteeships, and judgeships. These rewards are usually distributed by political bosses.

Political machines assure that in the last century little has changed in the selection of judges. A *New York Times* editorial lamented that "New York's Supreme Court judges—who are trial level judges, not members of the state's highest court, the Court of Appeals—are nominated through an archaic system of judicial conventions. These conventions are dominated by delegates handpicked by party bosses, who vote however the bosses tell them." Was this editorial written in the 1930s, 1950s, or 1970s? No, it was the lead editorial on Oct. 2, 2007, and entitled "Real Judicial Elections."[19] Similarly, the *Washington Post*[20] lamented an administration that "increasingly emphasized partisan political ties over expertise in selecting the judges who decide the fate of hundreds of thousands of immigrants, despite laws that preclude such considerations." The 1800s? The 1900s? No. The article described the administration of President George W. Bush.

Another newspaper article[21] lamented that a big city mayor built a political machine through cult of personality. Was it referring to Jimmy Walker, Richard J. Daley, or Carmine DeSapio? No, the article described former Mayor Sharpe James of Newark, New Jersey. James was found guilty of defrauding the city by selling a lady friend nine parcels of city land for $46,000, which she quickly resold for $665,000. "This was among the mayor's many stark examples of the greed and arrogance of unchecked power," said U.S. Attorney Christopher J. Christie. James was convicted of fraud and conspiracy and sentenced to twenty-seven months in prison. That same year, Detroit Mayor Kwame Kilpatrick, who built a formidable patronage machine, pleaded guilty to fraud, corruption, and obstruction of justice. He resigned as part of a plea agreement that also brought him four months in jail and a $100,000 fine. Other recent political machines, including the Richard M. Daley machine in Chicago, the Jim Dimora machine in Cleveland, and the George Norcross machine in New Jersey, have also run afoul of the law.

The president governs from the apex of the political structure and makes the ultimate decisions on federal judgeships (subject to Senate approval), commissions, boards, contracts, and executive positions. One of a president's most coveted discretionary powers, an absolute constitutional power unchecked by Congress or the courts, is his ability to grant pardons. Public outrage followed President Clinton's pardon, on his last night in office, of Marc Rich, a fugitive financier who had jumped bail in the United States and was living a luxurious life in Switzerland. Rich's wife, Denise, was a major financial contributor as well as fundraiser for Clinton's White House campaigns, which could explain, but not justify, Clinton's "midnight" pardon. Mayors and governors control billions of dollars in contracts for political supporters. Cities and states have privatized prisons, hospitals, transportation, sanitation, and other facilities and services, often putting taxpayers' monies into the pockets of their political leaders' allies. There is an upside, however. In some cases, new prisons would not have been built, and existing prisons would remain overcrowded, if not for the private sector. Similarly, many city and county hospitals would have closed had they not been bought by private corporations. But still, these facilities remain a lucrative source of revenue for the companies involved.

Mayors and governors of financially hard-pressed cities and states found that selling off public assets was both lucrative and politically rewarding. So much so, in fact, that they began selling off anything that wasn't nailed down, and at times even so-called permanent fixtures. One example: leasing public highways to private investors. Governor Mitch Daniels of Indiana, a Republican who once headed the Office of Management and Budget at the White House, has sold long-term leases of sections of the state's highways to private investors, who will reap profits via toll booths on taxpayer-financed roads. The Indiana toll road was leased to Macquarie, a large Australian investment banking firm, which partnered with the Spanish firm Cintra Concesiones de Infraestructuras de Transport, S.A. The two companies also sought a fifty-year lease of Texas state highway 121 outside Dallas.

Patronage exists at all levels of government, including school boards, county commissions, city and state administrations, Congress, the judiciary, and the White House. Who gets to underwrite the bonds for a new school, highway, or prison? Who receives the insurance contracts on government buildings? Who receives the architectural, engineering, and building contracts? Which lawyers receive the guardianships and refereeships, lucrative judicial patronage when someone dies without a will? For that matter, who becomes a judge?

As Tip O'Neill suggested, despite the abuses, patronage is an essential tool used by successful politicians to build the kind of support that enables them to succeed in public life. Truly, there is no Democratic or Republican way to pick up the garbage, design a building, or provide food services for U.S. troops in Iraq. Congress rewards political supporters with billions of dollars in earmarks—11,514 earmarks totaling $16.5 billion in fiscal 2008, according to the

Office of Management and Budget—expressly directed to specific projects and services. Some lawmakers have transmuted that largesse into tangible rewards, with many of them charged with felonies in the process.[22]

In addition to earmarks, which allocate federal funds to specific projects, members of Congress also earn the gratitude of their voters by providing constituent services—to help with dealing with the federal bureaucracy. These services have proven so effective in cementing the loyalty of voters to lawmakers that for many years, more members of Congress were indicted or convicted than defeated for reelection. Governors and mayors also use earmarks as bargaining chips, supporting projects sought by a state legislator or city councilman in exchange for support of a governor's or mayor's policy initiative.

Patronage, then, is an inextricable part of the texture of democratic politics. It is a tool that can be used for good or ill, for progress or repression. Those who would change society—in ways large or small—are advised to pay close attention to the patronage networks, which usually tell far more than political rhetoric about how governments really operate. Those networks have extended beyond traditional boundaries into the international arena. Patronage practices also reveal that cooperation plays a greater role in political life than confrontation, the theme most often emphasized by the media. Political ideology and persuasion can be effective in those relatively rare moments when an idea's hour has come, but its importance has been exaggerated.

Patronage exists because of human nature and the universal desire for self-betterment. It is both an extension of the electoral process, providing public officials with the tools to govern, and a diminution of the electoral process, robbing legislators of the ability to decide issues solely on their merits. Finally, it is a totally integrated system, in which favors granted by politicians can have profound effects upon the selection of our national leaders, the goals they achieve, and the future of the nation. With pinstripe patronage, the stakes have soared, with an impact felt around the world.

CHAPTER TWO
PATRONAGE POLITICS AT THE GRASS ROOTS

"Only the newly arrived or the terminally naïve thought merit determined who got a city job here."
Chicago Tribune editorial, July 7, 2006

"Things haven't changed very much with the Queens [New York] Democratic Party since I came on the scene in the late 1970s."
Michael Schenkler, publisher, the *Queens Tribune*

When Abner Mikva was a student at the University of Chicago Law School, he recalled, he wanted to volunteer in Adlai Stevenson's presidential campaign. Mikva went to the local Democratic Party office and was interviewed by the ward boss. "Who sent you?" the ward boss asked. "Nobody sent me," Mikva replied. "We don't want nobody nobody sent," the ward boss said, and ushered Mikva out the door.

One might think that a thirty-year-old United States Supreme Court decision that drove a stake through the heart of traditional patronage would end that practice, and that political machines would be a thing of the past. But a 1976 decision that banned as unconstitutional the firing of non-exempt government employees on the basis of their party affiliation has been largely ignored in certain traditional patronage precincts.[1]

So have four additional Supreme Court decisions (in 1980, 1990, and 1996) that expanded that ban to include the hiring of government employees, as well as awarding and rescinding government contracts on the basis of political support.[2]

Chicago, the temple of patronage, with 37,000 exempt city jobs and 18,000 exempt Cook County jobs, regarded the Supreme Court decisions the same way many drivers regard traffic signals—as mere suggestions. Patronage remained alive and well, so much so that on July 5, 2006, a full thirty years after the first Supreme Court decision, Robert A. Sorich, 43, nominally Chicago's director of Intergovernmental Affairs but actually Mayor Richard M. Daley's patronage chief, was convicted of facilitating jobs and promotions to politically supportive candidates and campaign workers. The underlying charges included fraud, "theft of honest services," and misusing his position.

Federal prosecutors claimed that Sorich and two aides had created "blessed lists" of preselected winners for certain jobs and promotions based on political work or union sponsorship. There was evidence of 5,000 names on a so-called "Clout List" of preferred applicants since the 1990s, although Sorich was accused of placing only 300 campaign workers in jobs. Campaign coordinators would give Sorich lists of campaign workers and volunteers, whose names he would then send to the heads of various city departments—Aviation, Streets and Sanitation, Sewers, Water, and so on—for jobs. The scheme involved sham interviews, falsified ratings forms, and the destruction of personnel files. Sorich contended that he had only made "recommendations," and not given orders, when he provided the names of candidates to fill job vacancies. The fraud consisted of maintaining false official records that concealed the true nature of Chicago's employment process.[3]

The actions violated a thirty-year-old federal court order, known as the Shakman decree, which prohibited political considerations in hiring and promotions for city and county employees. "I think what we saw in this case was the revealing of the Chicago machine, the inner workings of the Chicago machine," said S. Jay Olshansky, the jury foreman. "There clearly is one. It has been in existence for quite some time."[4] The Chicago Democratic machine over the years was a personal machine, presided over (before the Elrod decision) by Mayor Richard J. Daley; his son, Richard M. Daley, has been the mayor since 1989, making him Chicago's longest-serving mayor.

On November 20, 2006, Sorich was sentenced to forty-six months in prison. The city created a $12 million fund for those who claimed they had been discriminated against because they lacked the clout to get a job, promotion, transfer, or overtime wages.[5] In addition, Cook County agreed to pay $3.5 million to patronage victims. "Even before this criminal chapter in Chicago's history, only the newly arrived or the terminally naïve thought merit determined who got a city job here," the *Chicago Tribune* editorialized.[6]

Although the Sorich case showed that patronage and a political machine still thrive in the Windy City, "there's less patronage now," said Mikva, who mentored President Barack Obama and had served four terms in Congress before being appointed a federal appellate judge. Mikva ultimately rose to Chief Judge of the U.S. Court of Appeals for the District of Columbia and also served as White House Counsel to President Bill Clinton from 1994–1995. "It's not like the old days, when you couldn't get any kind of job without machine support," Mikva said, noting that the Daley organization once controlled tens of thousands of jobs in the private sector. One reason for the decline of the Democratic machine was that in some parts of the city, volunteers no longer collect signatures on petitions or escort people to the polls. "People don't answer their doorbells in the areas that used to be dominated by the machine for fear of crime. But in the suburbs, machines still exist." Asked why Daley wasn't implicated in the Sorich case, because Sorich was Daley's patronage dispenser, Mikva explained, "Daley, like his father, kept his hands off. You didn't call the mayor if you wanted a job." Patronage was totally administered by subordinates.

The "Shakman Decree," the basis of the case against Sorich, originated in 1969 with efforts by Michael Shakman, a young, newly minted lawyer, to become a candidate for delegate to the state's constitutional convention. Shakman found that his candidacy was futile because even though he was running as an independent in liberal Hyde Park, his opponents were backed by the Democratic machine. "Many people with city jobs told me they would gladly vote for me, but they couldn't. They had to support the party choices and work for them. They weren't free."[7] Shakman and a friend, Paul M. Lurie, challenged the constitutionality of Chicago's patronage system. The case was initially dismissed by a Daley-supported federal judge, but was reversed on appeal. The parties then engaged in a prolonged negotiation that ended in a consent decree banning all politically motivated firing. After some judicial ups and downs on the state and local levels, the Supreme Court decisions in Elrod and Branti held sway, and a final decree, known as Shakman III, was ordered in 1983, which eliminated—at least on paper—political sponsorship from influencing the hiring process. As part of the order, the city of Chicago was required to provide public notice of all job openings and post a notice where job applicants gathered, declaring "HIRING MUST NOT BE BASED UPON OR AFFECTED BY THE PROSPECTIVE EMPLOYEE'S POLITICAL AFFILIATION, POLITICAL SUPPORT OR ACTIVITY, POLITICAL FINANCIAL CONTRIBUTION, OR PROMISES OF SUCH POLITICAL SUPPORT, ACTIVITY OR FINANCIAL CONTRIBUTION."[8] It was this order that Sorich was convicted of violating.

Has the Sorich case ended the city's tradition of providing jobs for the mayor's political supporters? Natasha Korecki, a reporter who covered the trial for the *Chicago Sun-Times,* has her doubts. "I'm pretty certain that it still goes on," she said.

Shakman, now in his late sixties, agrees. "Political patronage is deeply embedded in our culture," Shakman said. "It's hard to change the culture." And

Professor Dick Simpson, who chairs the Political Science Department at the University of Illinois at Chicago and who has extensively studied Chicago politics, believes, "It will take several decades to curb patronage and the Chicago machine."

A Two-Edged Sword

Cities are big business. The 2009 New York City budget totaled $59 billion, Los Angeles $23 billion, and Chicago $7.5 billion. As with the federal budget, the vast majority of the funds are spoken for: City budgets provide funds for public safety, education, transportation, healthcare, social services, community and economic revitalization, and environmental protection. But that still leaves millions for discretionary spending.

Mayoral patronage transcends jobs. It also includes lucrative municipal contracts, earmarks, zoning variances, bank deposits, insurance policies, and architectural and engineering contracts. A mayor controls schools and hospitals; police, courts, and jails; sanitation; parks and beaches; playground construction and renovation; street pavings and closings. He also has a role in inner-city transportation—buses, light rail, subways—sometimes directly and at times through appointments to a governing authority. In addition, mayors share with governors and presidents the power to appoint judges, commissioners, and board members, and also find private-sector jobs and contracts for political supporters. Mayors can smooth the way for those seeking municipal services or throw roadblocks in their path. The most powerful mayors can deliver the votes of local members of Congress to congressional leaders, as well as the votes of state legislators to governors and legislative leaders. In return, the mayors are rewarded with congressional and state patronage.[9] County executives share many of these powers involving services and facilities under their jurisdiction.

Mayoral patronage is not just about corruption. It also has benefited the nation's cities. Patronage has been used to convert city streets into pedestrian malls, and to build urban parks and inner-city swimming pools, libraries, and senior citizen centers. New York's Mayor Michael Bloomberg used patronage to overcome the opposition of owners of restaurants and bars and persuade the city council to ban cigarette, cigar, and pipe smoking in public places. But he also used patronage to persuade the city council to rescind a two-term limit that would have barred him from seeking reelection. Washington's Mayor Adrian Fenty used patronage to wrest control of education from a powerful but moribund school board. But he also used patronage to deprive political opponents of needed projects in their neighborhoods. Chicago's Mayor Richard M. Daley used patronage to obtain funds to build a 24.5-acre urban park and otherwise beautify the city, but also to suppress dissent. When Joseph Alioto was mayor of San Francisco, he granted Warner Brothers the right to film the motion picture *Bullitt* in the city, including extensive filming at the airport, in exchange for a $50,000 swimming pool in the city's Hunter's Point ghetto. Alioto also "influenced" the builders of Rockefeller Center West, a five-block area in downtown San Francisco, to construct theaters by telling them: "We'll close a street in the area if you build theaters." Unless induced by specific compensations, builders shirk the construction of legitimate theaters, which in their view often amount to economic liabilities.[10]

Patronage has also been used by political leaders to attract and retain businesses. Mayor Jerry Cavanaugh of Detroit was able to help the auto industry, which he equated with the general health of his city, when he used his powers over land use to rezone lands "adjacent to the Ternstadt Plant of General Motors from residential to commercial purposes in order to keep the company from moving out of the city."[11]

In New York City, Mayor John Lindsay insisted that real estate developers given zoning variances in lower Manhattan be "required to give something back to the city." The U.S. Steel Corporation and Uris Brothers gave urban parks to the city and were responsible for their maintenance and upkeep. At Lincoln Center, pedestrian malls were built as the *quid pro quo* for being allowed to build in the area. Permission to close the streets used by the World Trade Center was not approved until the Port of New York Authority agreed to increase the taxes it paid to the city.[12]

But Lindsay also was among the first mayors to engage in the major privatization of previously public functions, including consulting contracts for firms that had been helpful in his campaigns. Despite a large municipal workforce filled with hundreds of experts who took city jobs during the Great Depression, Lindsay awarded McKinsey and Company $1.5 million in consulting contracts. Those contracts often provided the mayor with the rationale to do what he wanted to do in the first place. A McKinsey employee noted, "There is a problem when the consultant is assumed to be more objective than a civil servant or academic, or more knowledgeable than a political hack. We are not more objective, we have our own biases. We become eligible for contracts because we are the right social people, we have the right values, and we're trustworthy, just as other kinds of people, who wear different clothes and have different values, receive their contracts from the clubhouse."[13]

Today's political leaders are even more anxious to translate their power for the public good—as long as their good works are publicized and they receive full credit. In Prince George's County, Maryland, business leaders who won development contracts from the county were required to donate hundreds of thousands of dollars ($450,000 dollars, to be exact) to local charities (charities, that is, that were approved by county officials). Lest they forget, arrangements for these donations were specified in the contracts, and included the Laurel Boys and Girls Club, the Family Crisis Center of Prince George's County, and the Tabernacle Church. It was a sound idea, but because the county did not follow through to find out whether the funds were collected, none of the charities received any money. There were donations, to be sure, but they went directly to politicians, not to charities. Several of the developers who held fundraisers for county officials and contributed to their campaigns had one thing in common: ties to County Executive Jack B. Johnson. Johnson was able to sell county-owned land at cut-rate prices to his developer friends, some of whom had no development experience and were "fortunate" enough to win no-bid contracts.[14]

The Good Old Days

Patronage traditions go back to biblical days but were perfected more than half a century ago by the nation's most powerful mayor, Richard J. Daley of Chicago, father of the city's present mayor. Ruling over the patronage capital of the country, Mayor Daley reputedly wielded control over an estimated 30,000–35,000 city and county jobs, as well as another 30,000 jobs in the private sector. The Cook County Democratic organization (Chicago's population makes up more than half the county) determined who got apartments in public housing, the distribution of welfare checks, and hospital clinic appointments—in addition to the many jobs at the machine's disposal. At the time, other big city mayors publicly reviled Daley; they considered him an old-line party machine hack whose style was passé. But they secretly envied him his vast power; his ability to forge alliances with Washington and with the state capital, Springfield; and most of all, his network of local supporters and bankrollers who virtually guaranteed his political longevity.[15] They also envied him the perception of Chicago as a city that works. Today, his son, Richard M. Daley, governs through a more modified patronage system, but he clearly absorbed his father's political lessons. The $475 million Millennium Park, an ambitious urban development project completed in 2004, was financed by private benefactors including business leaders. So was the city's unsuccessful bid for the 2016 Olympics, among other projects. But the mayor has shown that he knows how to reward his benefactors. Companies connected to Daley through friendship or campaign contributions have been accused of making inflated profits on contracts like street paving and newsstands. A company chosen to clean up after a city-sponsored food festival appeared to have won the contract because it donated tens of thousands of dollars to a political committee that supported the mayor.[16] Other scandals involved airport franchises in which friends and political allies of the mayor acted as lobbyists and brokers, and a fraudulent private trucking firm contracted for trucks not needed by the city. "A complete list of scandals in the Richard M. Daley administration would require a separate paper, if not an entire book, but the general pattern is clear—family friends, campaign contributors, and political insiders have the inside track in obtaining very lucrative city contracts and franchises," observed five political scientists at the University of Illinois at Chicago. "Thus the old-fashioned corruption that has characterized the various forms of machine politics in Chicago for 150 years continues."[17]

In Daley Sr.'s time, other big-city mayors were forced to use their imaginations to reward supporters and punish their enemies. Mayor John V. Lindsay of New York denounced the "power brokers," but still used every bit of patronage available to him. One striking example involved the removal of long-promised projects from neighborhoods that had voted against him, while projects were awarded to neighborhoods that had supported him. "The Midwood section of Brooklyn, a middle-class neighborhood that had supported the mayor, was awarded one of two new high schools, although the neighborhood was not among those listed by the Board of Education as among the 15 most in need of a new high school."[18] County, state, and federal budgets are still a good place to look for rewards for political friends and their projects.

Lindsay also tapped into a long tradition of using his power over land use to reward his allies, even when the impact of those decisions threatened community safety. One zoning change accompanied the sale of St. Joseph's Convent in Flushing, Queens, triggering an emotionally charged zoning battle. The convent, which was located in a residential section of Queens, was sold to private developers who planned to build a shopping mall on its grounds. Because a shopping mall promised fatter profits than a nunnery, the selling price was doubled—to the delight of the church and the buyers. Everyone was happy. Everyone, that is, except the community, which protested that the ensuing traffic would endanger those who used facilities located directly across the street: two churches, a school, a synagogue, and a library. "Quite a place to build a shopping center, wouldn't you say?" said Beverly Moss Spatt, a member of the New York City Planning Commission, "With children darting in and out of the traffic." Community groups asked, "Would you build a shopping center in the middle of Central Park?" So why do it in the first place? "We wanted to do something for the Catholic Church," said Mayor Lindsay, explaining the zoning variance that raised the density from residential to commercial usage; he wanted to cement his newly developed relationship with Cardinal Cooke.[19] The zoning variance was approved, the church benefited from the additional profit, and the mayor developed a new source of political support. The action also showed the enormous financial power of the mayor, who was able to increase the value of land exponentially, merely by changing its zoning designation. Ever wonder why real estate developers are major contributors to mayoral campaigns?

With notable exceptions, land use and zoning favors usually remain in the shadows of local politics, too obscure to get the public aroused—even when the community turns out to be the big loser. In the meantime, nothing has changed; if anything, the process has gained momentum. In February 2009, *The New York Times* reported that candidates for city council were "awash" in real estate cash, attracting contributions at a rate three to four times the amounts they had raised in the past. This despite the fact that the election was more than nine months away, and the country was in the grip of the worst recession since the Great Depression. It came as no surprise that Melinda Katz, who chairs the powerful Land Use Committee on the council, raised the most money: $196,266 from 25 firms.[20]

All kinds of contracts provide patronage opportunities. Architectural contracts and engineering and consulting contracts still prove to be useful rewards for political supporters, regardless of the waste to the taxpayer. Most are awarded without competition. One especially dubious consulting contract in New York City, for example, concluded that traffic was particularly heavy entering the city during the morning hours and leaving the city in the late afternoon and early evening.

As mayors increasingly turn to the privatization of city services, allowing them to proudly report a reduction in the number of city employees, they can exploit a whole host of patronage opportunities: garbage collection; police and fire protection; health and hospital services; and even some judicial functions, such as mediation. These services attract public attention only when they go awry, or impose excessive costs, but most of the time they fall under the radar. They have long since replaced the Christmas turkey as viable, lucrative, and important new sources of political patronage. In fact, they mirror the lavish defense contracts freely awarded on the national level by friends, supporters, and allies of the president, influential members of Congress, and other political leaders.

The End of an Era?

The *Elrod v. Burns* decision was supposed to end all that. But as Mark Twain once commented, "reports of my death are greatly exaggerated." So was the obituary for patronage and political machines. Although Elrod and four successive cases sought to end traditional practices, patronage remains alive and well—reappearing when it is least expected. (The *Elrod v. Burns* and *Branti v. Finkel* cases will hereinafter be referred to as "Elrod" and "Branti.")

In Elrod, the U.S. Supreme Court ruled against job patronage in Cook County, Illinois, on the grounds that the practice violated the First and Fourteenth Amendments' protections of free speech and association. In this case, the sheriff of Cook County, Richard J. Elrod, on instruction from Mayor Richard J. Daley of Chicago, had dismissed Republican appointees in the sheriff's office and replaced them with Democrats. The Democrats had just won an election and expected, following the custom, to reap the spoils of office. At the time, Mayor (Richard J.) Daley occupied virtually every significant Democratic office, including the presidency of the Democratic Organization of Cook County and the chairmanship of the Democratic County Central Committee of Cook County.

Because none of the plaintiffs had civil service protection, the District Court ruled in favor of the Daley organization. The court found that the plaintiffs had not suffered "irreparable" injuries, they had no right to expect to keep their jobs; in other words, why challenge political tradition? The Court of Appeals reversed the lower court's decision and was eventually upheld by the U.S. Supreme Court. Political patronage, the court said, was unconstitutional. "Patronage dismissals," concluded Justice William J. Brennan (writing for the majority) "severely restrict political belief and association … and government may not … force a public employee to relinquish his right to political association as the price of holding a public job." In response to the argument that party homogeneity brings about more efficiency in government, Brennan countered: "The inefficiency resulting from wholesale replacement of public employees on a change of administration belies the argument that employees not of the same political persuasion as the controlling party will not be motivated to work effectively; nor is it clear that patronage appointees are more qualified than those they replace." In other words, no one has yet proven that political appointees are more loyal or efficient than nonpolitical ones except at the very top levels of government—which the sheriff's office certainly was not.

The Elrod case dug deeply into the farthest recesses of the patronage system on the local level and challenged some of its most accepted beliefs. Americans accept a system that gives executives a great deal of leeway in the appointment of policymaking officials, in marked contrast to other democracies in the industrialized world. Today, U.S. citizens take for granted an executive branch that gives the president about 1,100 subcabinet and cabinet posts to fill among a total of 7,000 appointments, in keeping with the idea that because the president is elected by a majority of the citizenry, he deserves a team that will carry out his mandate. In parliamentary systems—such as Great Britain, Germany, and Japan—political appointees are few: They usually number under 100 appointments, and in many cases, far fewer than that.

Is it legitimate to view the sheriff's office in a policy-making category? Perhaps. In a sense, every police officer frequently makes policy decisions, or at least judgment calls. Many of us have benefited from a state trooper who gives us a lecture but no ticket for speeding. Similarly, police attitudes toward misdemeanors and felonies can be idiosyncratic. But whether or not law enforcement, or any job category for that matter, should be classified as policymaking really didn't matter to the court, which was more concerned with the effects of patronage on the system, and particularly on the "restraint it places on freedoms of belief and association."[21] Additional party obligations, wrote Brennan, may also impinge on individual rights, including "financial and campaign assistance," being forced to work for the election of another party, or "pledging allegiance to that party." Most damaging, he added, was the fact that job patronage "tips the electoral process in favor of the incumbent party."[22]

Successive cases built on the Elrod decision and extended the restrictions on patronage. *Branti v. Finkel,* decided four years later, in 1980, also involved Republicans who were suing Democrats for job losses. This time the two Republican plaintiffs were dismissed from jobs in the Rockland County, New York, public defender's office following a Democratic election victory.[23] The Branti case was similar to Elrod, but it addressed one of its important omissions: namely, the two-layer American political system that divides policy versus nonpolicy positions at all levels of government. The Branti case strengthened the First Amendment's restrictions on patronage hiring by putting the burden of proof on employers to show whether the jobs in question qualified for the policy exemption: Specifically, were the jobs sufficiently "policymaking" or "confidential" to justify appointments based on party affiliation? The Court also held that First and Fourteenth Amendment protections also applied to employees in a merit-based system.[24] Many legal scholars accorded more credit to the Branti decision than to Elrod because Justice John Paul Stevens's decision in Branti picked up an additional vote (the court ruled 6–3 in favor of the plaintiffs); Brennan's opinion in Elrod, on the other hand, was joined by two other justices, while two justices disagreed with some of the specifics of his argument and wrote concurring opinions.

Ironically, both the Branti and Elrod decisions involved complaints from patronage recipients challenging the legitimacy of the very system from which they had benefited! They initially won their jobs through the patronage system, only to reverse direction when it worked against them. Only half the employees in the sheriff's office in the Elrod case, for example, were covered by civil service protections; the rest were party appointees. And in Rockland County, assistant public defenders get their jobs from the public defender, who was appointed in the Branti case by the newly-elected Democratic majority in the county legislature. The decisions also threw the patronage system open to legal challenges by virtually anyone who felt disadvantaged. Some critics argued that the two decisions were flawed, in that they neglected to show which specific jobs could be considered patronage jobs and which could not. They also failed to define "effective performance," downplayed vital state interests that justified political control of the bureaucracy, and ignored the positive contributions that political parties made to government.[25] No one questions the president's appointment of an intelligence director or secretary of state: These are clearly policy positions. But the chief of the Newark Department of Sanitation? The town dog catcher? The Court left open the question of how many jobs were involved; what jobs would remain exempt; and where the line should be drawn between civil service protection and party loyalty.

In the final analysis, the decisions threw the patronage system out without sufficiently recognizing its benefits or replacing it with a substitute. In his dissent in Branti, for example, Justice Lewis F. Powell Jr. argued that patronage provided considerable benefits to the state and that individual jurisdictions should have the right to decide if a patronage "system serves their needs" or not.[26]

Ten years went by before the Supreme Court once again took up the question of patronage, this time involving the constitutionality of related patronage practices on the state level. In *Rutan v. Republican Party of Illinois*,[27] the court was asked to decide the constitutionality of whether promotion, transfer, recall, and hiring decisions involving low-level employees should be based on party affiliation and support. After his election in 1980, Governor Jim Thompson, a Republican, ordered state officials not to hire, promote, or recall new employees without approval from his office, which based its personnel decisions on—no surprise—service, support, and loyalty to the Republican Party of Illinois. Written by Justice Brennan, the Court held, this time in a 5–4 decision, that Governor Thompson's practice was unconstitutional because it violated the plaintiffs' First Amendment rights. Brennan cited the precedents of the Elrod and Branti cases.

The final cases reaffirmed the principles laid down by their three predecessors and went beyond job patronage to contracts—the newest form of patronage. In *Board of County Commissioners, Wabaunsee County, Kansas v. Umbehr*,[28] the court, in a 7–2 decision, extended First Amendment protections to independent contractors. Delivering the opinion of the Court, Justice Sandra Day O'Connor wrote that contractors could not be dismissed at will in retaliation for their exercise of free speech. The case involved a trash hauler, Umbehr, who lost his county business after he openly criticized the county commissioners by speaking out at commission meetings and writing letters and editorials accusing them of wasting taxpayers' money. The Umbehr case closed the patronage loop by including the lucrative practice of government contracting. But Umbehr stopped at the county line: No significant challenges have been taken up subsequently by the U.S. Supreme Court, leaving patronage at all levels open to past practices and to the creativity of party leaders. Delivered the same day as the Umbehr decision was the Court's decision in *O'Hare Truck Service, et al. v. City of Northlake et al.*[29] This involved another independent contractor, O'Hare Truck Service, Inc., which was removed by the city of Northlake, Illinois, from a list of companies that provided towing services because its owner opposed the mayor's election. In a 7–2 decision written by Justice Kennedy, the Court held that the protections of Branti and Elrod extended to contractors and providers of services. Only Justices Antonin Scalia and Clarence Thomas dissented, as they had in all the previous cases.

The trajectory between the first decision, in Elrod, which was decided by a vote of 5–4, and the last two decisions, Umbehr and O'Hare, which were decided by votes of 7–2, suggests a hardening of the Court's antipatronage stance. So does the extension of patronage restrictions to include private contractors and providers of services, in addition to city employees.

"Expediters" and Patronage Politics in the Nation's Capital

From the time he was four years old, Matt Mezzanotte practiced to become a concert violinist. He studied at the Peabody School of Music and performed as a soloist with orchestras including the National Symphony Orchestra and Leopold Stokowski's Hollywood Bowl orchestra. But he switched careers when he was thirty, after realizing that he could never achieve the greatness of his idol, Jascha Heifetz. Instead, Mezzanotte, who is short, balding, and now in his late eighties, became a builder in his hometown of Washington, D.C. He built office buildings and apartment houses, and owned and renovated two hotels in the district, the Savoy in upper Georgetown and the Carlyle near Dupont Circle.

Mezzanotte found that when Marion Barry became mayor, the city's approval of work licenses, which previously took a few hours, began to take up to four weeks. Mezzanotte recalled that he would go to City Hall to obtain a work permit for a plumber or electrician, or approval of a building design. The city clerk would tell him that there was no problem, but it would take a month to obtain the permit. "But I've got a crew standing by," Mezzanotte would explain, adding that every idle hour would cost him a great deal of money. The clerk would respond, "Then you may want to think about getting an expediter." What's an expediter? It is someone, usually a retiree from a city agency, who could obtain a permit in twenty-four hours, for a fee of $5,000. Mezzanotte had no choice. "This is something the city should have provided," he said. The practice continued under mayors Anthony Williams and Adrian Fenty, Mezzanotte noted. Why should it cost a builder $5,000 for permits from a city government, especially one with pretensions of "reform," to do the administrative work it should be doing all along? Who were the ultimate recipients of the $5,000? And what percentage of that $5,000 did the "expediters" give back to the party, the organization, the mayor, and/or the individual who "recommended" the expediter in the first place?

Mayor Adrian Fenty, who presides over this system, declined to discuss the issue, but his aides said he was trying to reform the system and had initiated an "Ambassador" program to "help" megaprojects, such as a stadium or convention center, without charge. A tall, athletically built man who sports a shaved head, Fenty is regarded by some on the city council as remote—even imperious. Fenty has developed a habit, for example, of closely holding decisions, with scant input from the twelve-member council on which he previously served—decisions such as the appointment of Michele Rhee as superintendent of schools, and the reorganization of the police department. On the school closings, he met with council members only the day before; the police reorganization also came as a surprise. "At eleven at night the phone rings, and I'm invited to a press conference the next day on police reorganization," a council member complained.

But the mayor gets credit for being a doer in a city government known for being lackadaisical. "He has a sense of urgency," said Council Chairman Vincent Gray, a psychologist who worked with children and later challenged Fenty in the 2010 mayoral primary. "He's willing to take on the system. He doesn't accept bureaucratic answers." The downside, Gray added, was the mayor's "desire to be in control of anything and everything."

The capital city's patronage system began long before the residents controlled their political fortunes. For decades, the city's politicians had authority only on matters of education; before home rule was instituted in 1973, the Board of Education was the only elected body in the District of Columbia. Indeed, Marion Barry got his start in politics as a board member, well before his election to the council and the mayoralty. This left Washington's schools as the city's only major patronage outlet—with disastrous, albeit predictable results. With thousands of well-paying jobs, the schools became a patronage paradise. The quality of the schools plummeted as appointments were made on the basis of political support instead of competence.

As mayor, Barry hired tens of thousands of Washingtonians for his summer jobs program. "There wasn't a family in Washington that didn't have some member—a son, daughter, brother, or sister—in the summer jobs program, and that includes my kids," said Carol Schwartz, an ebullient woman who for many years before her defeat in 2008 was the only Republican member of the city council.

This experience suggests that in a one-party city with an exceptionally small voter turnout (council members win the all-important Democratic primary with a total of between 1,000 and 2,500 votes each out of a population of

600,000), public officials do not have to worry about broad accountability, but only with satisfying the needs of a miniscule base. Nor are Washington's elites overly concerned about the public schools—most of their children go to private schools. "There are very few people with a stake in the school system," said Colbert King, who writes a highly regarded column on city government in the *Washington Post*.

After home rule was enacted, the entire municipal work force became a patronage dumping ground, with the same disastrous results. The Department of Motor Vehicles was notorious for its incompetence and hostility to city residents who needed driver's licenses and automobile plates. One city dweller, who moved to Washington, D.C. 12 years ago and had to register his car, was given a printed notice directing him to an inspection site on Florida Avenue. When he reached the location, he discovered the site had been closed six months earlier.

Although he wore the mantle of reform, Fenty believes in *quid pro quo* politics, according to several members of the city council who have rejected several of his nominees as incompetent. "He's probably the most political mayor we've had since Marion Barry," said Colbert King. "He knows power and how to use power. He can be prickly and difficult, and he bears grudges."

Like both his predecessors and his counterparts across the country, Fenty's payoffs usually take the form of earmarks and contracts. "It's understood, and sometimes very specific," said Council Vice Chairman Jack Evans, a corporate lawyer who is also chairman of the Finance Committee. His diverse district encompasses both poor and wealthy neighborhoods. "The mayor is appreciative. I'll tell the mayor, 'This is my list of all the things I want funded.' Then the mayor would say, 'We need help with this on the budget." One hand washes the other. Evans continued: "If you have an adverse relationship with the mayor, how do you expect to get what you want?" In 2008, Evans's wish list included $2 million for Southeastern University; $1 million each for the Washington Ballet, Washington Performing Arts Society, Duke Ellington Festival, and the expansion of a bus route that serves his constituents; $500,000 each for the Hoop Dreams Scholarship Fund, Peaceaholics, and the Woolly Mammoth Theater; $250,000 each for Tudor Place, the D.C. Jewish Community Center, and the Capital Breast Care Center; and $100,000 each for Bread for the City and the D.C. Central Kitchen. Evans got almost everything he asked for. What do the mayor and council members get out of all this largesse? "It serves their political interests," King explained. "They're looking for political support."

Evans's explanation was even more benign: "You're either in the Council because there's nothing else you can do, or you want to accomplish something," said Evans, who was a major supporter of the construction of Nationals Park, the $600 million, 42,000-seat, state-of-the-art home of the Washington Nationals, the district's new major league baseball team. "You can look at something and feel, if not for me, that wouldn't be there." Evans is forthright about his campaign fundraising. He told a meeting of Washington's Real Estate Board during his 2008 reelection campaign: "Your endorsement and a $500 check from your PAC isn't what I want. I want you to ask every one of your members for a $500 personal check, and a $500 check from your company." Evans explained, "You could run a campaign on $100,000. I'll pass $400,000 this year, which I'll use for direct mail and door-to-door campaigning."

Mary Cheh, a smart, no-nonsense law professor at George Washington University, who represents a well-heeled district in northwest Washington, also defends the use of earmarks in city government. "There's nothing intrinsically wrong with them," she said. "Who knows better than I what I need in my ward, as long as the process is open and the projects are worthy? Iona Senior Services wanted money for an arts center. A Palisades community group wanted a center for elderly services. I got each of them $25,000."

A council member explained: "I went to the mayor for earmarks, and he said, 'Make me a list,' which I did. He then said, 'I also have a list—school takeover, overhaul of fire and emergency services.' I said, 'I can't promise you a blank check, but most of the things we can work on together.' The mayor's leverage isn't as great with the four at-large council members." The reason? "They don't need anything for their wards. What can he do to them, other than derail their legislation?" Indeed, the mayor routinely punished politically independent council members Phil Mendelson, Kwame Brown, David Catania, and Carol Schwartz. All four were at-large members of the council and, therefore, did not require funds for projects for their constituents. But the mayor routinely opposed their legislation, and declined to send witnesses to their hearings. Other council members who occasionally oppose the mayor's policies are sometimes punished by a cutback in funds for projects in their districts.

This raises some serious questions about the relationship of patronage to urban policy: Is it fair to punish a neighborhood because its council member opposes the mayor's policies? Is it good public policy to deprive a neighborhood of a school, health facility, park, or community center because it is represented by a council member at odds with the mayor? "They [the community's voters] have a choice," explained a council member. "They can elect someone else." Some critics believe that with a large and growing population of poor people and a money-saving reduction in the city's police force, Washington had no business spending hundreds of millions of dollars on a new baseball stadium or the arts. They also noted that the money for earmarks was authorized after only a single day of public hearings. King noted in a column that the largest funding went to "the congressionally-chartered, Exxon-Mobil sponsored, Washington A-list-led Ford's Theatre." The theater boasts support from foundations, corporations, and generous individual donors. "Yet Ford's Theatre walked away with $10 million in taxpayer funding to be used in its Center for Education and Leadership," King noted. "I can hear you grinches: How could lawmakers approve this kind of spending when, in the same budget, they cut police funding by $2.5 million, and whittled down the fire and emergency services' budget by nearly $3 million?"[30] Not entirely coincidental is the fact that a prominent member of the theater board is the wife of Senate Democratic leader Harry Reid, who was rumored to have promised to release funds the federal government owed the city for federal programs, such as Medicaid.

Peter Nickles, attorney general for the District of Columbia and one of Fenty's closest friends and allies, said that the mayor's problems with the council stemmed from a problem of perception: Many council members, he said, could not accept their role as "legislators" and sought to usurp the mayor's power by considering themselves part of the city's "executive branch." Council members, he continued, sometimes abuse their oversight responsibility by calling hearings more to embarrass and intimidate city officials than to elicit information relevant to their legislative duties. "Some of the Council members are not conducting oversight hearings, but are simply interested in beating up somebody," Nickles said. As for the mayor's appointments to boards and commissions, "appointing executives who are supportive of the mayor's policies is simply good government policy." Nickles claimed never to have heard of expediters and was "unfamiliar" with the political use of earmarks.

Nickles ruled that the district's Housing Authority had broken the law when it failed to seek the council's approval before awarding $82 million in contracts for parks and recreation projects. Most of the work went to firms with ties to Fenty. Specifically, a firm owned by Omar Karim, Fenty's fraternity brother and a campaign contributor, was named project manager on all twelve projects. Fenty insisted that he was not involved in the selection of the contractors and that the contract process "predates my administration."[31]

Mayoral power can involve something as petty as tickets to sports events. Fenty's relations with the council were frayed in yet another patronage fracas, this one involving tickets to Washington's new baseball team, the Nationals. Each council member was entitled to two tickets to each game in the new ballpark built by the city. Fenty took control of all twenty-four council tickets, in addition to the fifteen that he was given. "He took the Nationals tickets that belonged to us," Councilwoman Schwartz complained. Council chairman Vincent Gray was so upset that he blocked consideration of all contracts for over $1 million, which must be approved by the council, until the mayor relented. In Gray's view, the baseball ticket fracas reflected Fenty's penchant for control as well as his desire "to make the legislative body subordinate to the mayor. He wanted us to come to him for the tickets," which would then be an extension of the mayor's patronage. Not surprisingly, Fenty relented.

Like Chicago, Washington has a tradition of rewarding political supporters, through contracts as well as earmarks. "Even if you do an RFP (request for proposal), you can craft it in such a way that only one company qualifies," Cheh noted. "Politicians are only human. They would like to be of more assistance to those who like them, and help them." Evans agreed, asking "Why should I help someone who hasn't helped me?"

To his credit, one of Fenty's first actions as mayor followed the lead of New York Mayor Michael Bloomberg. Fenty wrested control of the schools from the Board of Education and installed a professional educator, Michelle Rhee, to head the system. Rhee promptly fired dozens of school principals, assistant principals, and administrators she considered incompetent, as well as hundreds of teachers and teacher aides. She also closed unneeded schools and sought to use measures of competence instead of patronage as criteria for their replacements.[32]

Other city services also have improved. The Department of Motor Vehicles is no longer a source of long lines and endless frustration. Its employees have abandoned their "How Can We Not Help You" attitude and become polite and helpful. The same can be said of the Department of Consumer and Regulatory Affairs, along with many other agencies.

Patronage still thrives in the Washington suburbs. In Prince George's County, Maryland, development deals worth millions of dollars were given to builders with ties to County Executive Jack B. Johnson. Several builders received the land at cut-rate prices, had little or no development experience, or were given no-bid contracts. In his first four years in office, Johnson awarded more than fifty consulting and other contracts to fifteen of his friends and political backers and created a dozen high-profile positions that he filled with supporters and former fraternity brothers.[33]

In Fairfax County, Virginia, another Washington suburb, the chairman of the Board of Supervisors received a $5,000 campaign contribution from a prominent Washington lobbying firm less than a month before the county awarded the firm a $10,000-per-month contract. Gerald E. Connolly, the supervisor, did not vote on the hiring of Alcalde & Fay and insisted, "There's an absolute firewall between me and that [contracting] process."

Patronage and Corruption

What constitutes legitimate patronage and what is flagrant corruption? Kickbacks, fraud, and extortion were always illegal. But what's wrong with rewarding friends and supporters with jobs and contracts, as long as they are competent? Political patronage predates the founding of the Republic, and the Supreme Court's restrictions on patronage mystify many involved in politics. At times, politicians like Sorich find themselves indicted for practices that have gone either unnoticed or unremarked for decades; society has changed and they have not. Small wonder that so many politicians are totally surprised by the public disapproval that confronts them, and even more shocked when the Justice Department or the Ethics Committees in the House and Senate take up the cudgels. When former House Ways and Means Chairman Dan Rostenkowski (D-Illinois) was indicted in 1994 for using public money to buy gifts like engraved maple chairs and crystal Capitol domes for friends, and for hiring friends and relatives for no-show jobs, he never quite understood the reason; after all, these "gifts" were considered routine in Chicago politics. "I was there [in Congress] for thirty-three years," complained Rostenkowski. "They changed the rules thirty times."[34]

The problem is that traditional patronage often crosses the line into corruption because the opportunities that present themselves are often too tempting to ignore. Jobs, contracts, and all kinds of perks pervade the political process and trap many people between the proverbial rock and hard place. Mayors, county leaders—and even sewer inspectors—often reach their positions on the basis of substantial support from many groups and individuals. And many of these supporters expect some reward for their political contributions: doorbell ringing, telephone calls, street corner speeches, the "lickin' and stickin'" of political mailers, and countless hours they've worked to elect these politicians. For them, "good government" is a concept, not a reward. They expect something substantial in return for their efforts—such as job patronage, lucrative contracts, and earmarks. The problem is that in the process of building political machines, many landmines still remain. What one prosecutor considers illegal may be ignored by another; a great deal is still left to prosecutorial discretion.

The identification of corruption depends on the vigor of a prosecutor, a local newspaper's investigative reporting, or a combination of both. Did Chicago experience a real crime wave or merely a vigorous prosecutor in Patrick Fitzgerald, the U.S. attorney? Was New Jersey sunk in corruption, or did the state merely have a vigorous prosecutor in Herbert Stern? More recently, Internet blogs have proven influential. The Monica Lewinsky scandal involving President Bill Clinton originally was broken by the *Drudge Report*.

Two mayors who once were considered the hope of their cities ended up behind bars. Mayor Sharpe James of Newark, who built a patronage machine largely through the cult of personality, was found guilty of defrauding the city and sentenced to twenty-seven months in prison. In Detroit, Mayor Kwame Kilpatrick, who also had built a patronage machine and whose mother, Rep. Carolyn Kilpatrick, had been a political power, pleaded guilty to fraud, corruption, and obstruction of justice. He resigned his office, served four months in jail, and paid a $100,000 fine. A third mayor, Sheila Dixon of Baltimore, was convicted in 2009 of stealing gift cards donated to the city for needy families.[35]

It appeared that in selected cities in New Jersey, political patronage still operated according to the customs of several generations ago—traditions carried out
by Frank Hague, boss of Jersey City and Hudson County, as well as others like
Mayor Hugh Addonizio, of Newark. Recently, the mayor of Paterson was accused
by the U.S. attorney of taking $200,000 in bribes; the executive of Essex County
for also taking bribes and arranging a cover-up; and a freeholder from Hudson
County was indicted for delivering envelopes of cash to the county executive.

Is New Jersey the sewer of the Republic? Hardly, although the extent of corruption in New Jersey still seems to outdo many of its sister states. One of the
reasons is that rich industrial states like New York, New Jersey, and Illinois simply
have more riches to offer: higher-priced real estate, tax breaks, zoning variances,
lucrative jobs and contracts, and courthouse patronage. City and county leaders have construction contracts to dole out that are worth more than they are in
North Dakota, as well as contracts for the increasing numbers of privatized services on the local level. Most of the time, economic development deals don't capture the public imagination or even its interest. The worst aspect of the scandals
in New Jersey, for example, is that the public accepted these practices as politics
as usual, and aside from isolated expressions of outrage, only the federal prosecutors displayed any interest at all in stopping the nefarious activities going on all
around them. The leader of the Hudson County Democrats attended a fundraiser
for freeholder Nidia Davila-Colon, who had just been indicted for delivering
cash-stuffed envelopes to the county executive. "Nobody even asked about it [the
indictment]," scoffed Colon, who won her election in a landslide.[36]

Nearly 500 miles away, in Cleveland, similar practices flourished, indicating
how easy it is to slide into felonies from otherwise "innocent" pursuits. It also
showed the correlation between media interest and local corruption. In this
case, Cuyahoga County Commissioner Jimmy Dimora and Auditor Frank Russo
attracted 200 federal investigators from the FBI and the IRS who raided their
offices and homes seeking evidence of jobs and contracts involving thousands of
dollars that were traded to shore up a Democratic machine that ruled with an
iron fist and controlled every elected office in the county for decades. "The nearly
inseparable men built a Democratic machine by hiring friends and allies ... the
subject of a continuing [*Cleveland*] *Plain Dealer* investigative series. And the
two have helped the party control every elective office in the county for decades,
partly through Dimora's role as county Democratic Party chairman."[37]

As the turn-of-the-century Tammany Hall ward boss, George Washington
Plunkitt, proclaimed: "Men ain't in politics for nothin'. They want to get something out of it."[38]

A further sign that little has changed in the last 100 years is the use of private
contractors as a source of jobs, and municipal largesse for political supporters.
When Tammany lost an election, Plunkitt advised: "There is more than one kind

of patronage. We lost the public kind, or a greater part of it in 1901, but Tammany has an immense private patronage that keeps things goin' when it gets a setback in the polls. My men lost public jobs, but I fixed them all right. I don't know how many jobs I got for them on the surface and elevated railroads—several hundred. I placed a lot more on public works done by contractors, and no Tammany man goes hungry in my district."

Plunkitt also spoke of the reciprocity that existed between Democrats and Republicans. "Let me tell you, too, that I got jobs from Republicans in office—federal and otherwise," Plunkitt said. "When Tammany's on top I do good turns for the Republicans. When they're on top they don't forget me. Me and the Republicans are enemies just one day in the year—election day. Then we fight tooth and nail. The rest of the time it's live and let live with us ... I seen my opportunities and I took 'em." But despite his honesty and unintended witticisms so eloquently captured for posterity by William Riordan, Plunkitt was best known for his definition of patronage as he believed it should be practiced: "honest" as opposed to "dishonest" graft, a subtle but important distinction. Honest graft involved buying land and selling it at an inflated price after a politician found out—via inside information—the land would increase in value when public projects intended for it were announced. To his mind, "dishonest graft" meant that a politician bought land, used his influence to have a project built on it, and then sold the land.[39] Plunkitt was regarded as the Robin Hood of New York politics, believing that machine politics was kinder to the poor than what was offered in its place. The machine listened to their problems, provided them with jobs and loans, helped them litigate and deal with their immigration woes—in short, provided a sense of community in an otherwise grim environment. Civil service, he believed, would spell the end of government.

Local government remains a potent lure for unscrupulous politicians, such as Michael S. Carona, Sheriff of Orange County, California, who was indicted in 2007 on charges that that he, his wife, and his mistress used his office for financial gain and to reward friends and political supporters. Two men charged as co-conspirators, George Jaramilo and Donald Haidl, whom Carona appointed assistant sheriffs, pleaded guilty to paying Carona as much as $2,000 a month for years. They also gave Carona gifts, including the use of a private plane and a yacht, a vacation to Lake Tahoe, and the lease of a Mercedes-Benz. Carona's wife and mistress also were accused of accepting gifts from Haidl. Prosecutors alleged that the gifts totaled $350,000.[40] Carona was convicted of witness tampering in January, 2009, but acquitted of some of the more serious charges.

In suburban New Jersey, Joseph Ferriero, Democratic leader of Bergen County (an area immediately across the George Washington Bridge from Manhattan), was indicted in 2007 on federal charges that he arranged for municipal governments to channel work to a consulting firm he was associated with. Ferriero, who also was County Executive, had wrested the county from Republican hands. As Democratic leader, he handpicked candidates in most of the county's legislative districts and helped Governor Jon Corzine get his start in politics.[41]

These cases are unfortunately just a few examples of the numerous scandals that keep prosecutors busy and voters shaking their heads in dismay. They also demonstrate the close relationship between "party-building" and corruption, the ever-present threat of being found out, and the fear of voter retribution that inevitably comes from being found out. Also, by revealing the temptations inherent in politics, it is easy to see how quickly political leaders can succumb to those blandishments; and indeed, how some of them arrive at a state of mind in which they actually feel "entitled" to them. Sheriff Carona, for example, saw nothing wrong with accepting rides in private aircraft or luxury yachts. After all, many rich constituents owe their wealth to political officeholders, who have the power to divert a road near their warehouses, site a power plant on previously worthless land, or let a no-bid contract for garbage collection. Why not accept something in return? The use of a yacht? Free home improvements? The list goes on, increasing in length with each restriction on campaign financing. Other politicians cement loyalty by using public money for gifts for their supporters. These gifts can be as innocuous as a glass replica of the Capitol or as outrageous as $2,000 a month payments to political cronies, monetary kickbacks from jobs and contracts, and free rides in corporate aircraft.

Mayoral Patronage Redux

Michael Bloomberg sits in a small cubicle in the center of a bullpen, a large, open space surrounded by about fifty cubicles that serve as offices for his top aides. A large television screen is at one end of the room, formerly the city's Board of Estimate, and a small aquarium is at the other end, with two additional aquariums along a long wall. A large table with fruits and other nutritious refreshments is on a small dais, alongside tables that the mayor also uses for interviews. The immense white-painted room is filled with shoulder-high cubicles, which gives the mayor instant access to his aides, they to him, and to each other. With the mayor in attendance, the layout also assures a minimum of relaxation for those who work at City Hall.

"My job as a manager is to get people to work together," Bloomberg said. The mayor is frank about his approach to those he seeks to persuade. "Some people, when they want something from somebody, walk up and hit him with a two-by-four," the mayor said. "I walk up and give them hugs and kisses."

The hugs and kisses come in the form of both government perks and the use of Bloomberg's personal fortune, estimated at $17 billion. These include generous contributions to his supporters' favorite charities, golf outings at Bloomberg's private clubs, rides on his private plane to his vacation home in Bermuda, and trips to Europe and the Middle East.

But unlike Bloomberg, many rich men and women have stubbed their toes on politics and government. Clearly more than money has made Bloomberg one of the most effective mayors in New York's history. His achievements include city-wide bans on smoking and trans fats, wresting control of education from a moribund board, and turning Times Square into a pedestrian mall.

"Good management applies in both business and government," he said. "I've always hired people smarter than me. I've built loyalty and people stay with me. I have patience. I share credit, and tell people 'get rid of the words I and me,' and try using 'we and us.' When people turn me down, I ask why, and try to address their concerns. Just because something didn't work in the past doesn't mean it won't work in the future. [Albany Speaker] Shelly Silver opposed me on congestion pricing [a fee for automobiles that enter Manhattan], but two months ago Shelly proposed something much more sweeping. Albany needs the revenue."

Bloomberg wasn't in politics for the money. Or to help the local political party build up its machine. After all, he had switched parties three times, from Democrat to Republican to Independent, and had denounced political parties as archaic and unnecessary. But as the mayor of America's largest city, he had other needs and resorted to old-fashioned Tammany-style patronage to fulfill them. Specifically, Bloomberg wanted a third term. Never mind that the city's voters had twice rejected the proposal to extend a two-term limit on the mayoralty, or that Bloomberg had previously said that the voters' wishes on this issue had to be respected. Bloomberg was intent on circumventing the polls and his own promises, and persuaded the city council to extend the two-term limit on the mayoralty to three terms. To Bloomberg, the issue was not academic. The mayor had one year left on his second term. Without the extension, he'd be out of a job at the end of 2009.

The mayor had a lot of persuading to do, and naturally resorted to the time-tested strategy of political patronage, to the consternation of some good government groups. "Former aides to the mayor, elected officials, good government advocates and voters said they have become deeply disillusioned by the way Mr. Bloomberg is corralling support to rewrite the city's term limits law, which New Yorkers have endorsed twice in citywide referendums," the *New York Times* reported. "Over the last three weeks, the mayor and his aides have silenced a potential critic of his third-term bid with the promise of a plum position on a government committee, pressed groups that rely on his donations to speak on his behalf, and cajoled union leaders to appear on camera endorsing his agenda ... 'It stinks of clubhouse politics,' said one former aide."[42] The potential critic was cosmetics billionaire Ronald Lauder, who spent $4 million of his own money on campaigns opposing the term limits extension. In exchange for Lauder's silence on the issue this time around, Bloomberg promised to appoint him to a city charter revision commission. Lauder's "conversion" on this issue showed that no one, however well-heeled, escaped the blandishments offered by an imaginative patronage system. The mayor's effort to win a third term succeeded, and he was narrowly reelected in 2009.

Was the mayor's use of patronage an aberration? A mayoral aide acknowledged, "We did very similar things during other uphill battles." These included the mayor's successful effort to ban smoking in all workplaces including restaurants and bars, and his unsuccessful effort to relieve traffic congestion by charging a fee for vehicles that entered central Manhattan during business hours. The truth is that it was not unusual to use "incentives" and apply pressure when it was called for, although most political leaders, Bloomberg included, preferred incentives whenever possible—the carrot rather than the stick.

Bloomberg has often used his personal fortune to augment his political patronage. He has used his well-appointed private plane to take Albany's legislative leaders—Speaker Sheldon Silver, a Democrat, and Senate Majority Leader Joseph Bruno, a Republican—on trips to Bermuda, where he hosted their weekend of golf. He has flown Italian councilmen to Italy, Greek politicians to Greece, and Jewish politicians to Israel. "He uses his wealth to dazzle people," said Joyce Purnick, a metropolitan columnist for *The New York Times* and the author of an insightful biography of Bloomberg. "It seeds goodwill, no question about it."

Bloomberg also has contributed to charities in which politicians have an interest. "He's probably been a fine mayor, but he seems a lot better, because all the usual agitators—the groups that exist to drive a mayor crazy—have in one way or another been bought off," one Democratic political consultant theorized. "It's amazing the climate you can have when nobody is criticizing you."[43] Bloomberg spent more than $100 million of his own money in his 2009 reelection campaign.

Bloomberg demonstrated his use of both traditional patronage and his personal fortune in enlisting support from the black clergy, a critical constituency in New York. Rev. Calvin O. Butts III, the influential pastor of the Abyssinian Baptist Church in Harlem, had promised to support William Thompson in his campaign against Bloomberg. But Bloomberg contributed $1 million to the church's development corporation, with the implicit promise of more to come, and Butts ended up endorsing Bloomberg. In another case, Rev. A.R. Bernard, pastor of the Christian Cultural Center in Brooklyn, the largest church congregation in the city, was appointed to the city's Economic Development Corporation. In 2006, the administration agreed to sell parts of two streets to the Christian

Cultural Center, helping Rev. Bernard assemble a large parcel of land around the church that he planned to use for a mixed-use project of city-subsidized housing and commercial space.[44]

Like patronage, political machines are alive and well, as demonstrated by Bloomberg's campaign for a third term. The first time he was elected, Bloomberg denounced political parties as a "swamp of dysfunction" and bankrolled a campaign to eliminate them from the city's elections. But when his reelection campaign began, he started wooing them assiduously. The reason: Without a party affiliation, his name would appear in what one Republican operative called "ballot Siberia," six rows to the right—traditionally home to longtime minority parties, such as the Socialist Workers and Marijuana Reform parties, and a potential turnoff to voters. "He has so much disdain for political parties and now, all of a sudden, he needs us," said Phil Ragusa, chairman of the Queens Republican Party, still fuming over the mayor's decision to bolt the party in 2007 after twice running as a Republican.[45]

Little has changed, and indeed New York City mayors John Lindsay and Michael Bloomberg both ran as Republicans and Democrats. Bloomberg's experience shows the conundrum inherent in American politics. Among other things, political parties still slate the candidates for nomination; provide workers for campaign efforts; swell campaign coffers; and strengthen linkages between localities and the state and national capitals that sustain them. They are held together by all kinds of networks—social, economic, and ideological—but the most important relationships are those forged over time by mutual needs, such as jobs, contracts, and zoning variances. Despite all their rhetoric, mayors as well as county freeholders all stay in power on the basis of their ability to cement these relationships through concrete rewards. In fact, the party—as Plunkitt pointed out long ago—often turns out to be more democratic than the kind of personal machine that Bloomberg and others advocate. Personal political machines often end up as "cults of personality," as witness all the disastrous examples around the world: Josef Stalin, Robert Mugabe, Idi Amin, Mahmoud Ahmadinejad, and so on. Absent any viable alternatives, most Americans would rather trust their political systems to party machines that can be voted out of office, prosecuted for fraud, or influenced by the media.

"Earmarks" New York Style

By coincidence, the term-limit extension approved by New York's city council in October, 2008 also extended the terms of the council members, who have their own methods of persuasion. One highly effective strategy for co-opting voters involved stashing taxpayer dollars for later use in the names of fictitious groups.

The names sounded reform-oriented and included such mysterious groups as the Coalition of Informed Individuals and the Magic Mountain Fund.

This strategy originated after the city's charter revision of 1980, which abolished the Board of Estimate and gave sole approval over the mayor's budget to the council. The change, in a mayor-dominated system, did not give the council a great deal of new power, but it gave members the ability to dole out the discretionary funds that the mayor, seeking to smooth the passage of his spending plan, granted them. "Funds for the fictitious group represented just a tiny portion of the city's $60 billion budget—only $4.5 million, or less than six tenths of one percent. But they were critically important to the member as a way to curry favor with supporters and constituents."[46]

"It's a way for council members to reward supporters," said David Yassky, a young councilman from Brooklyn Heights. "It's a way to push money toward backers: research assistants, campaign workers, petition carriers. I am shocked and outraged at this misuse of taxpayer money.... When I started serving the council, the earmarks amounted to $35 million. Last year they were up to $170 million." Yassky tried to change the system, to no avail. "These organizations would be better off without the money," he argued. "[The money] should be transparent." One phony group with a made-up name that Yassky cited was the Coalition of Informed New Yorkers. Who could oppose a group with a name like that?

Not all groups were fictitious, but they easily blended into the larger category of "discretionary funds" that totaled $360 million in earmarks directed toward specific organizations. Yassky's earmarks included funds for the Little League, the Brooklyn Bridge Council, and the UJO (United Jewish Organizations of Willliamsburg). According to Yassky, when he told a previous speaker, Gifford Miller, that he would vote against a bill the speaker wanted, Miller said, "OK, you can do that, but we're not going to fund UJO this year." Yassky explained that the UJO was a social service agency that served a large Hasidic community, "the poorest part of my district, with lots of kids." The Hasidic Jews voted as a bloc and gave Yassky 3500 votes. "I caved," Yassky admitted, "and got a $300,000 earmark." It also pays to "go along," said Yassky, when bending on some issues leads to being more effective later. "Sometimes I trim my sails as a crusading ideologue [because] you have to have an impact on policy. I submitted a bill years ago on hybrid taxis. [My nemesis] Gifford didn't want it. A couple of years later, I got the bill passed."

Yassky's experience shows how hard it is to be a reformer, even at the lowest level of city council, in a system that marches to the beat of a different drummer. The onerous demands made on public servants were described by the late New York City Councilman Dominick Corso, a wholly owned subsidiary of the Brooklyn Democratic organization. During a heated council debate, he pointed an accusing finger at Councilman Ted Weiss, a young impassioned liberal, and said, "You young fellows think it takes guts to stand up for what you think is *right*? Let me tell you something. That doesn't take guts. What really takes guts is to stand up for what you *know* is *wrong*." Corso eventually became a judge, supported by both the Democratic and Republican Parties.

The system hasn't changed that much; if anything, it has become even stronger. Today, Council Speaker Christine C. Quinn, Yassky explained, doles out "lulus"—funds in lieu of expenses ("lieu" as in "lu")—to keep council members in line. The lulus, received by two-thirds of the council members, range from $4,000 to $29,000. Most receive $10,000, which augments their council salary of $112,500. That way, "the Speaker has the ability to effectively give people a raise or cut their salary," Yassky added. The council also plays a role in awarding large contracts, including what is called "street furniture"—bus shelters and newsstands. Companies that seek these contracts hire lobbyists who then lobby both the mayor and the council members. The money isn't inconsequential. Cemusa, the world's largest street furniture company, won a $1 billion contract to build steel and glass newsstands throughout the city.

Worse than earmarks, according to Yassky, are the "phony names the Speaker keeps in a reserve called 'mid-year contingencies.' It is a way for council members to reward supporters, and is [also] a way to push money toward backers, research assistants, campaign workers, and petition carriers. It also gives a huge amount of power to the Speaker," not to mention a huge amount of money for the Speaker's district.

Such large sums also provide the opportunity for skullduggery. The U.S. attorney's office in Manhattan and the city's Department of Investigation are examining the relationship between council members and their staffs, as well as the groups they finance through the $360 million in discretionary money the council doles out each year. The joint investigation led to the indictments of two former aides of Councilman Kendall Stewart on the charge that they embezzled more than $145,000 in city funds. It also forced the council and city agencies to impose stricter controls on discretionary spending. Surprisingly, no council members were implicated.

In 2008, the federal-city investigation also examined a community group in Queens County that had received nearly $250,000 in city funds for possible political work on behalf of Councilman Hiram Monserrate. Specifically, Libre, the group, was accused of having two dozen workers collecting signatures to help Monserrate get on the ballot in an unsuccessful campaign for the state senate. To outsiders investigating the "community" group, Libre looked like a phantom. The group could not produce paperwork to show how it spent nearly all the city's money, which the councilman had directed to it in recent years, although it was ostensibly overseen by Monserrate's chief of staff. Libre had allegedly received hundreds of thousands of dollars in discretionary funds from the councilman to provide English language instruction, job placement assistance, and other services to the immigrant and Latino communities in the Corona section of Queens. The Queens district attorney investigated allegations that the organization had spent a portion of its time promoting Monserrate's political career. From an earmark? "This is ground zero of a high-needs district," Monserrate countered. "My role is to support such groups. And yes, there are challenges. And are some of those community organizations challenged? Yes, but they do good work. Their hearts are in the right place, and I'm not backing away from that."[47]

County Patronage

Democrats handily control four of the five New York City counties, where the Democratic leaders play a key role in the selection of judges and other public officials, as well as presiding over more mundane forms of patronage. Assemblyman Herman D. "Denny" Farrell Jr. has represented the part of Manhattan that stretches above 125th Street for three decades. The Manhattan Democratic leader, Farrell also served as chairman of the New York State Democratic Party from 2001 to 2006. During that period, Farrell increased fundraising and made gains in traditional Republican strongholds. He also played a role in Eliot Spitzer's election as governor. In the Assembly, Farrell chairs the powerful Ways and Means Committee, which oversees much of the state's budget and also handles legislation dealing with taxation.

In two other counties, blacks and Latinos fought over which group would win the Democratic leadership. Like many of his predecessors, Assemblyman Vito J. Lopez, the Brooklyn Democratic leader, left little to chance. Lopez demonstrated the strength of a political machine, while insurgents complained that the group's meetings were so tightly controlled that they were undemocratic. Meetings of his Kings County Democratic Committee "are highly scripted, down to which district leader will move to, say, accept a committee report" and which members will second the motion—speakers are chosen in advance and given printed scripts. "I've never been to a more restrictive meeting in my life," said Charles Barron, a Democratic district leader. "It insults the intelligence of everyone here that you have such a scripted meeting."[48]

In the Bronx, meanwhile, Assemblyman José Rivera fought vainly to keep his position as Democratic leader. He was challenged by Assemblyman Carl E. Heastie. The dispute involved a regular meeting of the Bronx Democratic Party in September 2008, where a group loyal to Mr. Rivera took control of the lectern and reelected him by voice vote. But Heastie, who was chairman of a party committee in the Bronx, presided over a second meeting at the same time, where he was elected party leader. The State Supreme Court determined that Heastie was the new Bronx Democratic leader.[49]

Portrait of a County Leader

Representative Joseph Crowley of Queens County, New York is easily the most powerful of New York City's Democratic leaders. A man whose tall, large frame easily accommodates his 225 pounds, Crowley's soft, personable style gives the impression of a gentle giant. Crowley is the protégé of the late Representative Tom Manton, who preceded him as county leader, and who selected Crowley as his successor. Crowley grew up in a political family: His uncle, Walter Crowley, succeeded Manton on the city council. When his uncle died, Crowley, then 23, wanted to succeed him, but Manton selected his chief of staff, Walter McCaffrey. When his local assemblyman died in 1986, Crowley, then 24, ran, won the seat, and served 12 years.

The *Almanac of American Politics* describes Crowley's accession to Congress: "In 1998, Manton filed for re-election by the July 16 filing deadline. Then at 11 a.m. on July 21, he convened a meeting of the Queens Democratic committeemen, announced he was retiring and got them to vote in Crowley, 36, as the Democratic nominee. Other potential candidates were not notified ahead of time and were naturally miffed, but quickly accepted the reality." Crowley easily defeated his Republican opponent in the overwhelmingly Democratic district. In Congress, Crowley served on the Ways and Means Committee, the most powerful in the House. He is also on the leadership ladder, as House Democrats' Chief Deputy Whip, and also serves on the Foreign Affairs Committee.[50]

Crowley has two offices in Queens: his congressional office and his office as county leader. "I keep them separate," he emphasized. Asked to describe his role as county leader, Crowley said, "I'm the manager of elected officials. I'm involved with all local officials in Queens—on the Council, in the Assembly and the State Senate." He plays a key role in the selection of those officials and interviews all candidates. His candidates usually win, but not always. What he gives them, he says, is access to the ballot, both in primary and general elections. After that, he says, "it's up to them." The candidates have to raise their own money. "We provide good legal counsel and expertise," Crowley said. Once his candidates are elected, Crowley tries to get them good committee assignments.

Crowley's selection of candidates has included efforts to reflect his increasingly ethnically and racially diverse district. "I make sure diversity is involved in the political process," Crowley says. "We are politically sensitive to the needs of diverse groups." Crowley takes pride in his selection of Carmen Velazquez, elected the first Ecuadorian American on the civil court bench. He also has created "At Large" district leaders and is proud that they now include the first Sikh woman, the first Muslim, and the first Chinese American, none of whom could have amassed enough votes alone to win office.

Like the other county leaders, Crowley helps select nominees for judgeships. "I'm very much involved," he said. "I interview all the candidates." He disagrees with the *New York Times*'s opposition to the judicial conventions, which traditionally ratify the leaders' decisions.[51] Without county conventions, Crowley argued, "Lawyers from Manhattan could go to Queens and say, 'I want to be a judge in Woodside.'" Recently, he helped elevate two civil court judges to the state Supreme Court. Crowley says that no money ever changes hands. Judicial candidates are not required to contribute a year's salary "to the party," as was the case as late as the 1970s and is still the case in other political precincts. But Crowley is also involved in more mundane pursuits. He has named scores of employees of the city's Off Track Betting (OTB) parlors.

There are few Democratic clubhouses in Queens, Crowley said, and no "walk around money" given to district leaders on election day to "get out the vote." But his political clout enables him to wring concessions from public officials. These include persuading Mayor Bloomberg not to close a firehouse in the Bronx and persuading Governor George Pataki to provide funds to move City University's law school to Long Island City.

Despite Crowley's geniality, however, some political observers believe that he rules Queens in a manner reminiscent of his less-polished predecessors. Indeed, Crowley's lawyers have knocked candidates not anointed by him off the ballot. "The law firm effectively challenges petitions, ties people up in court, and exhausts their campaigns and war chests defending petitions in cases heard by judges who were given their jobs by the county organization," charged Michael Schenkler, a longtime observer of Queens politics and publisher of the *Queens Tribune*. "A review of Assemblyman Ivan Lafayette's recent withdrawal after petitions were filed shows that the organization-controlled Committee on Vacancies—headed by Crowley—named a District Leader to replace him, and then knocked the one foe off the ballot, taking it to the appellate level. There was no Republican opponent, so they named the new Assemblyman without a vote being cast. Such is the power of the county organization and Joe Crowley. Things have not changed very much with the Queens Democratic Party and its power since I came on the political scene in the late 1970s," he concluded.

Despite all its problems, the local clubhouse provides a real sense of community in addition to an array of rewards. Just as the old clubhouses brought together like-minded citizens, today's political venues take the form of community organizations, religious groups, school boards, the Internet, and a host of others, depending on the region.

Politics is still more an art than a science, and it depends on the glue of community before anything can get done—bills passed, political leaders elected, fundraisers held, and campaigns launched. The networks that emerge from all these activities are rooted in relationships, all of which still depend on a complex system of rewards. Budgets still reflect political power, as do zoning variances, jobs, and contracts. The technology of politics may have changed over time—blogs are more influential, and campaign finance has become more sophisticated—but the system remains intact.

Chapter Three
Statehouse Patronage

"You come in with 75% of the vote, you can do anything. You come in with 51%, they'll beat you like a drum. Anything in between, you use everything you've got."

Governor Joe Manchin, Democrat of West Virginia

"For many routine jobs in state or local government, once you establish a threshold of competence and character, it's no sin to consider political affiliation in filling the position."

Alan Ehrenhalt, editor, *Governing Magazine*

Governor Ned McWhorter of Tennessee lost patience with a legislator who was blocking an education bill that the governor wanted to enact. The legislator wanted the state to repave a highway in his district. The governor, a Democrat and former Speaker, called in the recalcitrant legislator and showed him a photograph of road graders. "Take a good look," McWhorter told him, "because you're not going to see one of these in your district for four years." Not surprisingly, the legislator caved.

"Sometimes you have to find a mutuality of interest," deadpanned Senator Evan Bayh of Indiana, a Democrat and former governor, who is fond of telling the McWhorter story. His choirboy looks belie a seasoned politician whose father, Birch Bayh, also represented Indiana in the U.S. Senate. Indiana had an extensive (and infamous) patronage system, going back to the 1930s, which included tithing state employees to contribute to the political parties that had doled out their jobs. The practice went back so long it even had a name: the "2% Club." "I was the first Democratic governor in 20 years, and the (patronage) expectations were high," Bayh recalled of his 1988 election. Prodded by the Supreme Court decisions, however, Bayh put a huge dent in the state's patronage practices.[1] He began by announcing the end of the 2% Club, which required all state employees to contribute 2% of their gross salaries to the governor's party. [2] The system was so blatant "there were [even] signs in all government offices" requiring the payments, Bayh added. Bayh issued an executive order that ended the practice. "There was no law," he said, "we just stopped the practice." Also ended was the practice of donating fees for personalized license plates to the party of the governor. Today, license fees are equally divided between both political parties.

"It's a whole new day because of the Supreme Court decisions," Bayh said. But although he believed that "People should support you because they believe in what you're trying to accomplish, not because they want a job," there were still opportunities to reward political supporters. Bayh sent county leaders lists of available jobs, but complied with the Supreme Court decisions by not guaranteeing that he would hire those recommended by the county leaders. To be sure, however, the lion's share of those jobs still went to Democrats. In addition to jobs, Bayh also used the fairly new but widespread practice of privatization to give state contracts to political contributors.

The give and take of politics virtually assures that presidents, governors, mayors, and other public officials will use all available resources to further their policy goals. The power of appointment "allows us to get things done," said Governor Chet Culver of Iowa, a Democrat. Mark Schweiker, a Republican former governor of Pennsylvania, said of patronage, "Without question, it's a very important instrument for legislative success. There's a lot in the tool bag." Further justification for using patronage whenever possible came from Governor Joe Manchin, Democrat of West Virginia, who explained, "[If] you come in with 75% of the vote, you can do anything. You come in with 51%, they'll beat you like a drum. Anything in-between, you use everything you've got."

"Everything you've got" means the full range of rewards—appointments to jobs, boards, commissions[3]—even appearing at weddings and bar and bat mitzvahs hosted by supportive constituents. "As governor, you find out what presses their [state legislators'] buttons," agreed former Michigan governor Jim Blanchard, a Democrat who still loves the rough and tumble of politics. One legislator who had opposed some of Blanchard's initiatives wanted a new marina in his district. "I got him the marina, and he was with me on every tough vote," Blanchard recalled. "To this day, that legislator is a dear friend."

As governor, Blanchard appointed 160 judges, including three to the state's Supreme Court and twelve to its appeals courts. Like many other governors, he had a judicial selection committee, but, he admitted, "most [committee] members were friends of mine." Translation: an "independent committee" that could be trusted to do the governor's bidding. After being appointed, these judges could neither campaign for Blanchard nor contribute to his campaigns, "but they have wives, children, and friends," Blanchard noted. "More important, word gets out that Blanchard's friends get ahead. This helps with the entire political community. But, he added, "They have to be qualified."

Nevertheless, patronage is sometimes regarded as indistinguishable from corruption, as some have learned the hard way. Alan Ehrenhalt, the editor of *Governing* magazine, was pilloried in print for suggesting that patronage had a place in state and city government. "What did I say that was so offensive?" Ehrenhalt asked. "It was that for many routine jobs in state or local government, once you establish a threshold of competence and character, it's no sin to consider political affiliation in filling the position. The idea that one applicant out of 3,000 for a county road crew is the single most deserving candidate strikes me as naïve. If the governor wants to help a person who was loyal in the campaign, instead of someone who wasn't, so what? As long as the applicant is qualified, how exactly does the public suffer?"[4]

In addition to the U.S. Supreme Court's ban on certain kinds of patronage on the state level, critics maintain that patronage is still used to deprive recipients of their independent judgment, and therefore undermines the bedrock principle of democracy: that citizens themselves can decide what is good for their city, state, and nation. As for the efficacy of political patronage, critics assume that there is a "public interest," that public officials appointed on the basis of merit are more likely to exercise judgments based on the "public interest," and that elected officials are similarly guided by "principles," and not by politics. Supporters of patronage believe, however, that political appointees are more attuned to the wishes of elected officials and to the voters who put them in office.

A governor's ability to reward supporters and punish opponents was vividly demonstrated by two New York governors, both of whom sought the support of publisher Rupert Murdoch. The longtime media tycoon's properties include the *New York Post,* an influential newspaper that enthusiastically supported the gubernatorial candidacy of Hugh Carey, a Democrat. Once elected, Carey's administration granted a multimillion-dollar contract to run the state's Keno and Lotto lottery operations to Leisure Systems Inc., whose chairman also happened to be Murdoch. Carey's successor, Mario Cuomo, also a Democrat, was strongly opposed by the *New York Post,* and it was no coincidence that when Cuomo was elected governor, the state's contracts to Leisure Systems, Inc. were promptly revoked.[5]

But statehouse patronage can also be viewed from a positive perspective. One case in point involved Delaware Governor Ruth Ann Minner. A lifelong Democrat, Minner began her statehouse career as a young file clerk and receptionist. She served eight years in the House, ten years in the Senate, and eight years as lieutenant governor before women's groups urged her to run for the top spot.

She rewarded these groups by appointing far more women judges, commissioners, and cabinet officers than had ever served in state government. She also recruited women to run for the legislature, where women now hold one-third of the seats in both the House and Senate. "The women helped me, and now I'm helping them" she said.

Patronage also provides ample opportunities for nepotism, a major issue in Missouri's 2008 gubernatorial campaign. Representative Kenny Hulshof, the Republican candidate and Attorney General Jay Nixon, a Democrat, both pledged to end the patronage system of awarding contracts to political supporters. Missouri's system had drawn the attention of the U.S. Justice Department after Governor Matt Blunt, a Republican, awarded a contract to the wife of Todd Graves, who was U.S. attorney for the Western District of Missouri. Family traditions continued for the benefit of Graves's brother-in-law, who also received a contract. Hulshof promised that he would henceforth place all contracts up for bidding, while Nixon vowed to appoint a commission to recommend a new method for awarding the contracts. Blunt also drew criticism by banning state agencies from posting openings for jobs above $40,000 without his approval, in what was interpreted as an effort to facilitate the hiring of political partisans into designated merit system positions. In a Democratic landslide year with Barack Obama at the head of the ticket, Nixon won handily, with 55 percent of the vote.[6] The Missouri election also showed how easily patronage systems can deteriorate into corruption, and how strong public opposition can correct those abuses at the polls.

Highway Handouts: Everything That Isn't Nailed Down

Governors hard-pressed for money to balance state budgets have sold or leased public property—in short, everything that wasn't nailed down, and even some things that were. In a fiscal free fall, governors have turned to private companies to take over hospitals and prisons and, more recently, have begun to lease publicly owned state highways. Some of those public hospitals, particularly those running over budget, would have closed without private intervention, argue many governors. Similarly, private prisons relieved overcrowding in some state facilities, although many private companies tended to ratchet up their charges as soon as state legislatures relaxed their oversight.

Public criticism reached new heights with the leasing of highways, which many claimed was like selling the family jewels. Critics argued that highways, built with taxpayer dollars, should remain publicly owned, and private companies should not be collecting tolls that they could raise at will. Why sell the roof to pay off the mortgage? they asked.

Grateful companies have found many ways to say "thank you," adding a new wrinkle to the patronage system. State legislators can give their votes and support, while private companies can and do offer money in the form of campaign contributions. Transurban USA, an Australian-based company, has invested $500 million in Virginia projects, including $191 million for the Pocahontas Parkway, a toll road that connects Chippenham Parkway and Interstate 95 with eastern Henrico County, near Richmond International Airport. In July, 2008, the company disclosed that it had "mistakenly" made $172,000 in illegal contributions to Virginia politicians. Recipients included Democratic Governor Tim Kaine's campaign committees, which received a total of $9,500; the leadership PAC of House Speaker William J. Howell ($12,500); the Virginia Republican Senate Leadership Trust ($12,000); and the Commonwealth Victory Fund, a Democratic Party of Virginia Committee ($10,500). Democratic organizations and legislators received a total of $73,000, and Republican legislators and organizations received $97,000 between 2005 and 2008.[7]

Similarly, Governor Edward Rendell, Democrat of Pennsylvania, announced in October 2008 that the state had agreed to sell a 75-year lease to its 532-mile turnpike for $12.8 billion to Abertis Infrastructure, S.A., Citi Infrastructure Investors and Criteria Caixa Corp., S.A. Rendell said the sale would finance billions of dollars of deferred maintenance on these roads and free the state government from figuring out how to incorporate these expenditures into its ever-tightening budget. Criteria and Abertis are Spanish companies, while Citi Infrastructure is a subsidiary of Citigroup.[8] The lease was eventually aborted because of public opposition and the resistance of state legislators, many of whom cared little about abdicating their public sector responsibilities but were reluctant to give up the patronage of toll-keeper jobs, restaurant leases, and towing service contracts to private companies.

Governor Mitch Daniels, Republican of Indiana, who had served as director of the Office of Management and Budget under President George W. Bush, was a pioneer in the practice of state highway leasing and is a staunch defender of its fiscal advantages. What made his political life easier was that he preempted the public-private issue, made sure that no favoritism was involved, and defended the long-term lease of the 157 Indiana Toll Road to private investors strictly in terms of political necessity. In 2006, Daniels negotiated a 75-year lease for $3.8 billion, earmarked for a 10-year transportation capital initiative that Daniels called "Major Moves." The road was leased to Macquarie, an Australian company, which partnered with the Spanish firm Cintra Concesiones de Infraestructuras de Transport.

"Our philosophy was utterly practical," Daniels recalled. "If a given service or facility really is necessary, we asked, 'What is the best way, the most cost-efficient way, to provide that service?'" He continued: "We had the worst child protection system in the nation, and we [had] hired 1,000 new case workers. On the other hand, we had the most expensive and worst-tasting food in the prisons, and we [had] hired a company to feed our prisoners." In his view, neither private nor public options by themselves were optimal; instead, Daniels decided to exercise his own judgment on what was best for the state in terms of cost effectiveness, efficiency, and results.

When Daniels took office, he said, he faced a $3 billion budget deficit. The annual road budget alone came to $600–700 million. "Our toll road was losing money. We hadn't increased the tolls in 25 years. The question was how to tackle our infrastructure problem. Many European cities have leased portions of their infrastructure." The legislature was reluctant to increase the tolls for political reasons. "The last toll in northwest Indiana was 15 cents. It cost us 34 cents in manpower to collect the toll. I said, 'Let's go to the honor system and put out a cigar box.'"

Daniels practiced the old rule of policy success: If you control the formulation of an issue, you will control the outcome. In this case, Daniels precluded charges of political favoritism by immediately tackling the politically charged problem of increases in tolls. Instead, Daniels billed the leased toll road as "a regulated utility—they can't raise the tolls more than inflation. We have a 300-page contract. We took a small slice of the money to continue to subsidize passenger tolls, which have had no increase. The commercial tolls increased, but not as much as inflation."

The real problems lie in the future, and in American politics even the best plans cannot be bulletproofed. There have been few independent studies of the impact of these leases on taxpayers. One of them was conducted by NW Financial Group LLC, which advises governments on public financing projects. Noting the length of the Indiana lease and the fact that the funds were to be spent in a ten-year highway improvement project, the study asked: "Where will State transportation funds come from in years 11 through 75?" and "How will the loss of state control over a statewide thoroughfare impact future economic development efforts in the state, given the critical role that transportation infrastructure plays in driving economic development and growth?"

The study concluded that "Indiana's sale of the toll road, while helping fund transportation projects for the next ten years, will result in depriving the public transportation funding network of very large and much needed future revenues in the final 65 years of the concession agreement to pay for publicly needed capital projects both on and off the toll road. Instead, these revenues are directed to private corporate profits and shareholders. If road users are willing to pay higher tolls, these funds should be captured for the public good."[9] Nevertheless, in road privatization cases, the system prevails and determines what follows, often leaving political leaders with few choices. Like some corporate executives who can't see beyond the next quarter, some government officials apparently can't see beyond their term of office and have no qualms about leaving their successors with an empty fiscal cupboard.

Was Indiana killing the goose that laid the golden egg? "There was no egg," Daniels noted. "It [state government] was laying an egg. It was being run as a patronage operation. They didn't care about the drivers." State toll road patronage includes not only jobs but contracts for restaurants, tow services, and other services. "The private companies committed to putting an additional $4 billion into the roads, and have already built a new state police station and paid for 25 extra state policemen." What's in it for Macquarie and Cintra? "Properly structured, the lease will provide a modest but reliable return of 6, 7 or 8 percent." Bottom line: "If they don't invest and make a better road, people won't use it."

Wasn't 75 years a long time for a highway lease? "Who knows if we'll even be driving in 75 years," Daniels said. "We may see technological innovations that make cars unnecessary. Meanwhile, we'll [the state will] have pocketed the money."

Some transportation experts and public officials sympathize with the pressure on governors beset with mounting costs and declining revenues. But they believe leasing state roads is not the answer and consider this strategy shortsighted. "It is a mistake as a matter of broad public policy," said Representative James Oberstar, Minnesota Democrat and chairman of the Transportation and Infrastructure Committee. "It is a quick-hit way to monetize a public asset. It is sort of like a debit card. I think the state [Indiana] made a bad mistake. Seventy-five years is tantamount to ownership." Noting that Indiana will no longer be able to collect money from tolls, Oberstar added: "If they run out of money in ten years, don't come to us. Don't expect the Federal government to bail them out. They made the choice." But the governors who are reaping the financial benefits of long-term leases won't be around when the revenue well is dry. Future governors will bear the burden of their decisions. In addition, motorists may not have any choices: Daniels's argument about drivers not using toll roads that are not well-maintained assumes that there are alternative roads—an assumption that is not always the case.

But despite Daniels's experience, patronage traditions die hard, and evidence of more ulterior motives behind road leasing began to appear in other states. Macquarie and Cintra also sought a fifty-year lease of Texas state highway 121 outside Dallas. Bracewell & Giuliani, the law firm of Rudolph Giuliani, the former New York City mayor and presidential aspirant, received handsome fees to put together and finance the legal work. Bracewell & Giuliani gave Texas Governor Rick Perry (who would be making the leasing decision) $20,000 in PAC money in the 2006 election cycle. In March 2007, Giuliani announced the sale of his investment company, Giuliani Capital Advisors, to the Macquarie Group.

The sale price was not revealed, but was estimated to be between $80–$100 million.[10]

Fearing future patronage entanglements and higher costs, public opposition has aborted three privatization attempts involving the New Jersey Turnpike, the Pennsylvania Turnpike, and a new Texas toll road. In June 2007, after months of controversy, New Jersey Governor Jon Corzine, a Democrat who had been chairman of the investment firm Goldman Sachs, declared, "New Jersey's roadways will not be sold, and they will not be leased to a for-profit or foreign operator." At Governor Rendell's request, Governor Daniels went to Harrisburg to lobby the Pennsylvania legislators but found that "the legislators loved the [highway] patronage." Texas eventually granted Cintra a concession to develop a new toll road, but it was rescinded after truck drivers banded together with the American Automobile Association and others to create a coalition that opposed the privatization of toll roads. "American consumers will pay twice: once when they drive on the roads, and again in the increased costs of the goods they consume," said Clayton Boyce, vice president of the American Trucking Association.[11] Public outrage later stopped a plan to privatize the New Jersey Turnpike.

Few studies exist today weighing the benefits and long-term costs of privatization, and most of them focus on social services. As always, the results begin with partisan clashes and end with political compromises. In Massachusetts, for example, the clash pitted a Republican governor, William Weld, eager to privatize state services, against a Democratic legislature, more responsive to state employees fearful of losing their jobs. The result was a bill establishing a process for privatization replete with checks and balances that were supposed to guarantee fairness for all involved parties.[12] A New York State study revealed an absence of competition in contracting out for social services, raising the question of why governments try to privatize services when there seems to be scant capacity in the private sector.[13] Yet another study of Medicaid "reform" in Kansas also suggested the absence of market conditions, further highlighting the gap between "reform and the reality of the contracting experience."[14]

The Soprano State: How Patronage Can Lead to Corruption

The New Jersey governor is the strongest in the nation. He appoints all judges, prosecutors, commissions, and board members. "There are thousands of commissions and licensing boards that mean a great deal to many people," said former New Jersey Governor Tom Kean, a tall, imposing patrician with an informal style and hearty laugh. "There are boards for every medical specialty, as well as for lawyers, engineering specialists, accountants, chiropractors, podiatrists, barbers, cosmeticians, electricians, plumbers, auto mechanics, restaurants, bars," to name a few. In making those appointments, he said, "It's human nature to pay a little more attention to those who have been helpful, but you have to be very careful."

Governor Kean, a Republican, had a secret three-person committee to assess the qualifications of potential judges—two former Supreme Court justices and a highly respected lawyer. "If they said someone would make a good judge, no problem. If not, no appointment, no matter what the bar association said. Warren Dumont, boss of Warren County, wanted a judge appointed who I felt was unqualified. He held up the judgeship for three years, and then realized it would be either my judge or no judge." Kean added, "If legislators recommended somebody who was qualified, no problem. Otherwise, I got into some terrific fights."

Kean discovered early in his governorship that patronage often meant merely that others often wanted to get the credit for improving the lot of their constituents, and he was only too happy to comply. "I had a bill that would have given the outstanding teacher from every school $5,000–$2,500 in cash for the teacher, and $2,500 for the teacher to use in the school," he recounted. "The Teacher's Union blocked it. Finally I submitted another bill to raise entry level salaries of teachers. Guess what? I told the Teacher's Union it would all be in the same bill. But this time I gave the Teacher's Union credit, and it moved like lightning." Later, the head of the Teacher's Union asked if he could come to an event announcing the outstanding teachers, and Kean readily agreed. Then he asked if he could sit on the platform. Kean agreed. Then he asked if he could say something. "'Of course,' I said, 'you're the head of the Teacher's Union.' When he finally spoke, he said to the crowd, 'I hope you realize that the union helped you get these awards.'"

"The lesson is, don't take credit," Kean said. "Give it to somebody else. You'll get the credit anyway. Every bill that passed, the governor got the credit. I gave ideas to Democratic legislators and then held a press conference and said, 'It was a very good idea Senator X had. I will back it to the full extent.'"

Political machines are still alive and well in New Jersey, Kean added. George Norcross III, the South Jersey Democratic boss, controls the legislature. "He controls the Speaker, who's also from Camden, and has a sufficient number of Democrats in the House and Senate. A governor can't do anything without him. He has veto power, which he uses to get the appointments he wants." In addition, local machines are still thriving in northern New Jersey, in Bergen, Essex, Middlesex, and Hudson counties.

Money remains the mother's milk of political patronage, in New Jersey and elsewhere, and along with political machines has played a major role in the state's politics. Governor Jon Corzine secured his nomination in 2005 by spreading campaign contributions among the Democratic bosses, especially to Norcross and to John Lynch, longtime Democratic leader of Middlesex County. This was part of the $100 million of his own money Corzine spent to get elected.[15]

Kean and his predecessor, Brendan Byrne, disagree on the extent of corruption in New Jersey. Kean believes New Jersey is the most corrupt state in the union, while he said Byrne thought that the state merely had more aggressive prosecutors who rooted out practices that are commonplace elsewhere. Three successive secretaries of state were indicted for shaking down contractors: Robert Burkhardt (under Democratic Governor Richard Hughes), who avoided prison because of health problems; Ed Crabiel (under Democratic Governor Byrne), who was saved by the statute of limitations; and Paul Sherwin (under Republican Governor William Cahill).

The University of Medicine and Dentistry of New Jersey, in Newark, almost lost its accreditation because many administrators and physicians were appointed more for their political connections than on the basis of their competence. But the university was more than a dumping ground for Democratic supporters. It also was the focus of a large-scale investigation of fraud, again showing how easily patronage power can be morphed into corruption. In 2005, U.S. Attorney Chris Christie gave the university's board of directors the choice of being taken over by a federal guardian or facing indictment for $4.9 million in Medicare fraud. Not surprisingly, the university chose the guardian, Herbert Stern, an aggressive prosecutor. "UMDNJ may well have been the country's most crooked institution for training doctors, dentists—and yes, nurses."[16]

The university also gave New Jersey politicians thousands of job opportunities. It employs 15,000 people at its five campuses, has 5,000 students, and spends $1.5 billion a year. "The University of Medicine and Dentistry of New Jersey (UMDNJ) is a microcosm for corruption in the rest of the Garden State. It created a system that assigned numbers (1, 2, or 3) to job applicants based on their political connections." Most shocking of all was that patronage extended to student admissions as well as to grades. Politicians pressured administrators to give passing grades to some medical students who had failed standardized tests.[17]

In another demonstration of machine power, John Lynch, Democratic boss of Middlesex County, was the major patron of Woodbridge Mayor Jim McGreevey, whom he helped catapult into the governor's mansion. Lynch's twelve years in the State Senate included stints as majority and minority leader and Senate President. Shortly after McGreevey resigned in 2005 (in a scandal involving his appointment of a top aide who was his alleged lover), Lynch pleaded guilty to mail fraud and tax evasion involving kickbacks to get approval for a Middlesex County sand company's pet project to mine state parkland. Lynch was sentenced to three years and three months in federal prison.[18]

Patronage in the Empire State and in Illinois

For better or worse, patronage is also alive and well on the state level in New York. Like its next-door neighbor, New Jersey, New York also has a strong governor, as well as strong legislative leaders. Republicans have controlled the State Senate for all but one of the last 69 years, while Democrats have controlled the Assembly since 1975. In his inaugural speech, Governor Eliot Spitzer, a Democrat, antagonized his Republican predecessor, George Pataki, as well as the state's legislative leaders, by declaring, "Like Rip Van Winkle, New York has slept through much of the past decade while the rest of the world has passed us by." He promptly lost several legislative battles, including his choice to replace Controller Alan Hevesi and a plan to issue driver's licenses to illegal immigrants. Seeking to end the Republicans' seven-decade control of the Senate, he directed his staff to make overtures to several Republican legislators, offering them jobs in his administration. Senate Majority Leader Joseph L. Bruno charged that Spitzer had been "bribing several of the members." Spitzer responded by ordering an investigation of Bruno's use of state aircraft.[19] When Spitzer later resigned as governor in 2008 in a sex scandal, few legislators came to his defense.

As Spitzer discovered, both the Senate majority leader and the Speaker of the New York legislature have enormous power, largely attributable to the patronage at their disposal. The Speaker names the heads of Assembly committees, selects their staffs, fills committee vacancies, and dispenses political favors. Each year, the Speaker and Senate majority leader dole out about $85 million in neighborhood projects known as member items, which help ensure the loyalty of legislators.[20] In fiscal 2006, Sheldon Silver, the Speaker, was the sole sponsor of $7.2 million in member items, and directed about 70 percent of that money to organizations and services in his district on the Lower East Side of Manhattan. In addition to his legislative duties, the Speaker also has a personal injury law practice, but declines to reveal either his clients or his income.

The Speaker and Senate majority leader also dole out "lulus" in denominations of $5,000 to $10,000 for extra duties that are often undemanding and sometimes nonexistent. The payments do not require an official accounting, which makes them even more desirable to lawmakers who need the extra cash but might not want to share either its origins or its final destination with constituents. The leaders also disburse their party's campaign funds, mostly to incumbents, who win more than 95 percent of their races.[21] Bruno retired in 2008 to become chief executive officer of CMA Consulting Services, an information technology company that has numerous state contracts. Although state ethics rules barred Bruno from lobbying the legislature for two years after retirement, nothing prevented him from doing other business with the state.[22] Bruno was convicted in 2009 on charges that he reaped millions of dollars from companies and labor unions seeking business from the state, capping a long-running investigation of one of the state's most powerful figures. Prosecutors said it was not a *penny ante* operation, charging Bruno with collecting more than $3 million over a thirteen-year period from a handful of companies seeking contracts and grants with the state, as well as contracts to manage pension fund investments for at least sixteen labor unions.[23] Bruno was sentenced to two years in prison in May 2010.

State legislators also have their own mini-machines. "You can't get the average voter excited about who's going to be an assemblyman or state senator," lamented the late New York State Senator Seymour R. Thaler, a Queens Democrat. "I've got two dozen people who are going to work so much harder because if I lose, they lose." What they would lose, specifically, were their jobs. Thaler, who was also a district leader, placed on the public payroll an assistant U.S. attorney, two assistant district attorneys, two marshals, associate counsels to both the Assembly Speaker and Senate minority leader, two appointees to legislative committees, an aide to a congressman, and a staff member of the city council. At election time, he cashed in these IOUs. "My best captains in the primary," he said, "are the ones who are on the payroll."[24]

Like New Jersey and New York, Illinois also has had a long history of political corruption; indeed, it is no coincidence that the lion's share of recent patronage U.S. Supreme Court decisions emanated from that state. Three former governors ended up behind bars—George Ryan, a Republican, and Otto Kerner and Dan Walker, both Democrats. And a fourth governor, Rod Blagojevich, also a Democrat, was indicted on corruption charges. Ryan, who gained renown for halting the death penalty in the state, was sentenced in November 2007 to six-and-a-half years in prison for racketeering and fraud. The charges also involved the illegal sale of government licenses, contracts, and leases. Ryan, who in forty years in public office became one of the most powerful Republicans in the Midwest, was convicted of a long list of corruption charges stemming from his tenure as secretary of state and governor. These charges included using public money for campaign work and exchanging state business for money and gifts, among them a Caribbean island vacation.

Governor Kerner, best known as Chairman of the National Advisory Commission on Civil Disobedience, was later convicted of bribery, conspiracy, perjury, and related charges involving two racetracks, sentenced to three years in federal prison, and fined $50,000. Walker's crime was committed after he was governor and involved his role in a savings and loan scandal. He was sentenced to seven years in federal prison and served eighteen months.

Meanwhile, Ryan's successor, Governor Rod Blagojevich, a Democrat who was responsible for appointing a successor to Senator Barack Obama after Obama's election as president, was indicted by a federal grand jury in April

2009 on corruption charges including an alleged conspiracy to auction off Obama's U.S. Senate seat. He became the ex-governor on January 29, 2009, after being impeached by the Illinois Statehouse and convicted by its Senate. The governor had initially been under investigation for his ties to Antoin "Tony" Rezko, the millionaire Chicago real estate developer convicted earlier that year on charges of fraud and bribery. But Blagojevich threw caution to the winds, as prosecutors recorded conversations in which he was heard on wiretaps planning to "sell or trade Illinois's United States Senate seat vacated by President-elect Obama for financial and personal benefits for himself and his wife." Prosecutors said that the wiretaps laid bare a "pay for play" culture that began shortly after Blagojevich took office in 2002. Prosecutors said that the governor and John Harris, his chief-of-staff who was also arrested, discussed withholding funding for a children's hospital project until its chief executive made campaign donations. The governor also pressured the owners of the *Chicago Tribune* to fire an editorial writer who had been critical of him if the newspaper expected state assistance for Wrigley Field, which is owned by the Tribune Company. (The governor's intervention could have saved the company more than $100 million in capital gains taxes.) Blagojevich was also being investigated for the way he hired employees for state jobs. "Governor Blagojevich has been arrested in the middle of what we can only describe as a public corruption crime spree," said U.S. Attorney Patrick J. Fitzgerald. (Blagojevich ultimately appointed Roland Burris, a career politician, to the Senate, with no money changing hands.)[25]

Some legal experts questioned whether Blagojevich's taped telephone conversations constituted a crime; did Blagojevich cross the fine line between criminality and political deal-making? Many ambassadors and cabinet appointees, for example, had donated and raised hundreds of thousands of dollars for successful presidential candidates. What was the difference? In fact, there is often a strong correlation between political contributions and those who receive earmarks and government contracts. In attempting to define the difference, U.S. Attorney Fitzgerald said, "We're not trying to criminalize people making political horse trades on policies, or that sort of thing. But it is criminal when people are doing it for their personal enrichment."

Fitzgerald was speaking of the appointers, and not the appointees. Of course, a political appointee is enriched professionally—and sometimes financially—when he or she ascends to a high government post. One job often leads to another, or to more contracts, more media attention, and greater profits. After all, even a picture of a prominent politician adorning an office wall can and often does lead to future business for an aspiring entrepreneur. At the same time these highly publicized prosecutions were taking place, there was a movement within state government to abide by the Rutan decision.[26] This meant tearing more state employees away from party patronage and drawing them into a system based more on merit than party loyalty, an effort that produced mixed results.[27]

The overriding question is whether there was a political corruption crime wave in the state of Illinois, one of the great bastions of political patronage in the United States, or simply an aggressive prosecutor who would have found similar behavior in any state he investigated. The prosecutions of Governors Ryan and Blagojevich were both conducted by U.S. Attorney Patrick Fitzgerald, well-known as an investigative bulldog, who had earlier obtained the conviction of Lewis "Scooter" Libby, Vice President Richard Cheney's chief-of-staff. Fitzgerald was also responsible for jailing *New York Times* reporter Judith Miller, in a case involving the disclosure of the CIA career of Valerie Plame.

More than 20,000 public officials and private citizens were convicted of public corruption in the last two decades, an average of 1,000 per year, according to the *Corporate Crime Reporter*. The publication listed Illinois as only the seventh most corrupt state in the nation. Louisiana led the list. Also high on the list were Pennsylvania, Florida, New Jersey, and New York. The report, published in October 2007, was based on data from the Justice Department's Public Integrity Section's 2006 report. The rankings are based on the number of public corruption convictions from 1997 to 2006 per 100,000 residents.[28]

Statehouse Loot

In the South, where "good ol' boys" traditionally divided Statehouse loot, federal investigators are also working overtime. "There is fear in the halls of the Alabama Statehouse," Adam Nossiter reported in *The New York Times*. "Your colleague may be wired. Somebody may be watching you. An indictment looms."[29] A long-running investigation into corruption within the state's system of two-year colleges has led to guilty pleas on bribery and corruption charges by one state legislator and the system's former chancellor. Nearly one-third of the 140 members of the legislature had financial ties to the college system, with most of the jobs or contracts going to lawmakers or their relatives. The vast system of junior colleges, established by Governor George Wallace, was notorious for rewarding political allies. The former chancellor, Roy Johnson, pleaded guilty in a bribery and kickback scheme, admitting that he gave $18 million worth of business to contractors in exchange for kickbacks. Another former legislator pleaded guilty to using public money to pay gambling debts. "It's very evident that it is a corrupt system and has been for a long time," said State Representative Mike Hubbard, House minority leader and chairman of the Alabama Republican Party.[30]

In Kentucky, Governor Ernie Fletcher, the state's first Republican governor in three decades, was indicted in 2006 on charges that his administration illegally rewarded political supporters with protected state jobs, forcing Democrats out of state civil service jobs and giving the jobs to political loyalists. Fourteen other members of his administration also were indicted, but Fletcher issued a blanket pardon protecting everyone in his administration but himself from prosecution. Fletcher was nevertheless reelected in 2007, and a judge ruled that Fletcher was protected by executive immunity and could not be prosecuted while in office. The state's attorney general, Greg Stumbo, a Democrat, subsequently dismissed the charges in exchange for the governor's admission that "the evidence strongly indicated wrongdoing by his administration with regard to personnel actions within the merit system."[31]

In Florida, House Speaker Ray Sansom resigned his post in 2009, saying he could not carry out his duties while he was under investigation in a corruption inquiry. On the same day he was sworn in as Speaker, Sansom took a $110,000-per-year part-time job as vice president for development and planning with Northwest Florida State College. He is alleged to have steered millions of dollars to the college while he was chairman of the House Budget Committee. A few days earlier, Salvatore Di Masi, Speaker of the Massachusetts House, resigned after his former campaign treasurer and accountant was indicted on charges of making illegal campaign contributions and illegal lobbying.[32]

But Louisiana has a tradition all its own, going back to the legendary Governor Huey Long, who was immortalized in the classic novel *All the Kings Men*, by Robert Penn Warren.[33] Known as the "Kingfish," Governor Huey Long openly bragged, "I steal money, but a lot of what I stole has spilled over in no-toll bridges, hospitals and to build [a] university [Louisiana State University]." In 1939, James Monroe Smith, appointed by Long as president of Louisiana State University (LSU), was charged with embezzling half a million dollars in an investigation that indicted twenty state officials; the scandal also enveloped Governor Richard Leche, who received a ten-year prison sentence in a kickback scheme.

Former Representative Billy Tauzin, a Democrat turned Republican, once described his home state: "Half of Louisiana is under water and the other half is under indictment." Or so it seemed. Former Governor Edwin Edwards, who served four terms from 1972 to 1996, is currently in prison for corruption. After being acquitted in two corruption trials, he ran for governor with bumper stickers urging "Elect the Crook." The colorful Edwards remarked during the campaign that the only way he could lose was "by being found in bed with a dead girl or a live boy." Since 2004, two state judges have been charged with accepting bribes. Federal officials also investigated New Orleans Mayor Marc Morial, who was accused of skimming hundreds of thousands of dollars for his personal use from city contracts. The state's Robin Hood–type corruption history goes back to the early 1800s, when pirate Jean Lafitte distributed stolen goods to the poor. In 2009 Representative William Jefferson, a Democrat, was convicted on corruption charges.[34] That's just a partial listing. Louisianans have always elected their public officials on the basis of their entertainment value as well as their political smarts. Governor Earl Long once ran for reelection against Jim McElmore, a Cadillac dealer in Baton Rouge. Long's stump speech wasn't too subtle: "I have nothing in the world against Jim McElmore. I have only the highest esteem, affection and respect for Jim McElmore. If I was going to buy a Cadillac car, no question I would go to Baton Rouge and buy my Cadillac car from Jim McElmore. Now, if I was going to buy two Cadillac cars, I don't know. That might be just too big a deal for him."

Many of these scandals show how swiftly patronage can bleed into corruption. Politicians often find the temptations of public service overwhelming; sometimes they are pressured by their colleagues. Succumbing to the temptations of politics is especially easy for politicians who visit their hometowns and watch their friends getting richer while they remain in place. This is especially galling when their neighbors' good fortune owes so much, perhaps, to a timely intervention with state bureaucrats to ignore a pesky regulation; or to twisting a road in the direction of their factory, farm, or warehouse.

Still others engage in unsavory practices on the assumption that they will not be caught. And whether they will get caught or not all too often depends on conscientious prosecutors, investigative media, or vigorous opponents. Because there is such widespread variation across the nation, leaders must depend on their own sense of right and wrong. Former Maryland Governor Parris Glendening had his own test: "Do I want to read about it on the front page of the *Washington Post*, and how would my mother feel about it?"

Show Me the Money

State financial officers, sometimes called comptrollers, controllers, or treasurers, oversee the investment and deposit of state pension funds. Mistakenly regarded by the public as glorified bookkeepers, many state financial officers have built their own power bases independent of their governors. This often makes them politically invulnerable, with patronage opportunities that often equal and at times exceed the governor's. Their selection of repositories of state funds—banks, stocks, real estate, hedge funds, and other financial instruments—is usually limited only by the requirement that they meet prudent investor standards. Because no one has defined exactly what "prudent investor standards" mean, financial officials continue to enjoy a wide range of options. The recipients of those funds show their appreciation in many ways, including contributions to a controller's election campaigns, as well as to those of his or her mentors.

The sums are vast. Thomas P. DiNapoli, the New York state comptroller, oversees the New York State Common Retirement Fund and investments totaling $122 billion as of April 2009. A former leader of the Nassau County Democratic organization, DiNapoli is a veteran of twenty years service in the State Assembly and was handpicked for his job in 2007 by Speaker Sheldon Silver. DiNapoli's appointment was approved by the legislature after the forced resignation of Alan Hevesi, who had been elected to his second term three months earlier. The sole trustee of the retirement fund, DiNapoli enjoys wide discretion. Under state law, the fund may invest up to 70 percent of its assets in equities, including 10 percent in international equities. The fund's investments in private equity, real estate in excess of 5 percent, international equities in excess of 10 percent, and absolute return strategies (hedge funds) are authorized as long as they meet the ever-nebulous "prudent investor standard."

The investments are nominally recommended by an investment committee, but controllers are invariably sensitive to the recommendations of political leaders who may determine their future. In addition, a portion of the New York State fund is set aside for community development, and local political leaders influence where the money is spent. New York's real estate investments are always made through partners. "We have a robust oversight process," said Jim Fuchs, DiNapoli's press secretary. A state controller's investment can mean the success or failure of a bank, fund, or company. When a state controller invests, he often buys hundreds of thousands of shares. "We know we're so big we can move markets," Fuchs added.

DiNapoli's fund dwarfs the $4 billion administered in 1968 by one of his illustrious predecessors, Arthur Levitt, who served four terms as state comptroller, including fifteen years as the only Democrat to hold statewide office. His success at the polls was attributed to neither his (phlegmatic) personality nor his conservative politics, but to his control over state funds. At that time, a *New York Times* reporter, Martin Tolchin, compared the investment portfolios of New York City and New York State.[35] There were great similarities, with one notable difference: The state portfolio had a great deal of R.H. Macy stock, while the city had none. The reporter asked Mario Procaccino, then the city controller, for an explanation, and was told that the following week the city planned to purchase Macy stock. The city's block purchase of several hundred thousand shares was certain to raise the price of the stock. When Tolchin returned from lunch, there were five urgent messages from Controller Procaccino, who warned that the impending stock purchase was confidential information and was not to appear in the *The New York Times,* or anywhere else, for that matter. Tolchin then realized the value of such information, which could be used to enrich politicians' spouses, friends, and relatives, and, he figured, may account for the fact that few politicians die poor.

The massive size of the state's pension fund presents an inviting target for politically connected New Yorkers. An investigation of the fund revealed that leaders of some large investment firms routinely paid fund officials to obtain pension business. These included Steven Rattner, a major Democratic fundraiser and President Obama's point man in the restructuring of the automobile industry. The Securities and Exchange Commission found that Rattner allegedly arranged for his investment firm, the Quadrangle Group, to pay more than $1 million to have the New York State fund invest $100 million in his company. While such payments are legal, they often raise questions about conflicts of interest and would be illegal if used to bribe public officials. Rattner faced no charges, although his firm paid a total of $12 million to the pension fund and to the SEC to settle allegations that his firm had paid kickbacks. His firm's investors include CalPERS[36], the Los Angeles Fire and Police Pensions, and the New Mexico Investment Council. To obtain the $100 million investment, Quadrangle hired a firm that had been run by Hank Morris, an indicted associate of former New York State Controller Alan Hevesi, to help gain business in New York, according to state and federal authorities. Quadrangle also arranged to have a subsidiary of the firm distribute a low-budget film called *Chooch*. The film was produced by a former deputy comptroller, David Loglisci, another Hevesi associate who had also been indicted.[37]

In another case, Raymond Harding, the former chairman of New York's Liberal Party, pleaded guilty to accepting more than $800,000 that prosecutors argued was a reward for doing political favors for Alan Hevesi, the former comptroller. Prosecutors also claimed that Harding collected a portion of the finder's fees paid by two investment firms for deals to manage more than $100 million for the pension fund. "They were using the fund as a piggy bank to pay people who were doing them political favors," charged Andrew Cuomo, the state's attorney general. "The brazenness is breathtaking."[38] Following a two-year investigation into the state's pension fund, Cuomo settled with four investment firms who paid the state a total of $4.5 million. The money paid by the investment firms was returned to the state pension fund, together with an agreement to stop using "placement agents," politically connected individuals who had received lucrative "management fees" for securing these funds. The firms involved were also prohibited from doing business involving pension funds with the state for two years. "This case will go a long way to cleaning up the New York State comptroller's office," said Cuomo. During Cuomo's investigation, several other private equity firms agreed privately to pay settlements and stop the practice of using "placement agents."[39]

Financial rewards remain the most neglected and under-researched area of political patronage. They continue to thrive on the state level, mostly for lack of interest and media attention. The states, like the federal government, exercise vast purchasing power—for automobiles, food, vending machines in state buildings, computers, rentals of all kinds, and materials that go into the construction of state buildings. How many of these items are competitively bid? Not many. Trying to obtain information is next to impossible, often depending on whether the issue can be effectively used as campaign fodder, or whether leading politicians are indicted in the process. It is no coincidence that politically connected companies win the most lucrative contracts, a reward for past and future campaign contributions.

No wonder public and media interest are low. Who could possibly be interested in which company gets car rental business or who delivers milk to a school cafeteria? Public and media interest remain low because of the public's aversion to numbers. Over the past quarter century, the United States has become the land of the free and the home of the deficits (trade, current account, and budget), yet public interest glazes over when discussions of deficits arise, except in those rare cases when deficits prove to be a winning political issue.[40] The rising federal deficit became a major issue in the 2010 congressional campaigns.

State contracts also get media attention when losing companies publicly complain. Are they complaining about the rigged process? Or about their own exclusion from that process? It was interesting that the strongest complaints about leasing highways to private companies came not from citizens who feared higher tolls in the future, but from politicians who protested the loss of public business that came from those highways, such as toll keeper jobs, restaurant leases, and discretionary construction contracts.

Vermont: The "Antipatronage" State

With a few notable exceptions, patronage and political machines thrive best in densely populated areas where people don't know their next-door neighbors, much less the candidates whose names appear on the ballots. Political machines often bring a human touch to those who triple-lock their front doors and stare into space on subways. But life is different in small towns and rural areas, where people know their neighbors and there are few secrets. Unlike more populated jurisdictions, voters often enjoy personal relationships with everyone on the ballot—from the governor to members of town councils and education boards. Jim Geringer, former governor of Wyoming, said, "We're a small state where everybody has to get along. The person you're mad at today may pull you out of a snow bank tomorrow." Unlike big cities, scandals are relatively rare in small rural states, possibly because the stakes are so small. "There are no really big ticket items in Vermont," reflected former Governor Madeline Kunin.

Vermont is the prototype. With a population of 624,000, it is the second least populous state; only Wyoming, with its population of 514,000, is smaller. A Justice Department study found Vermont the second least corrupt state or territory in the United States, just behind Nebraska and barely ahead of Wyoming.[41] Montpelier, Vermont's capital, a jewel of a city where the capitol's gold dome can be seen for miles, resembles a frontier town. With only 8,000 residents, Montpelier has the distinction of having the smallest population of any state capital in the nation. By comparison, Juneau, Alaska is a thriving hub, with 30,000 residents.

There is no party registration in Vermont, and most residents consider themselves independent. "Most Vermonters have met the Governor, the Senators and me," said Democrat Deborah Markowitz, a diminutive, dynamic woman, who has served ten years as Vermont's secretary of state. Among other distinctions, the state has sent Bernie Sanders, the first New York City–born, Jewish socialist to the U.S. Senate. Sanders's Republican multimillionaire opponent, Richard Tarrant, spent $7.3 million in an unsuccessful effort to portray Sanders as an out-of-touch radical who was soft on sexual predators. But the voters knew Sanders, who proclaims his views in a strong Brooklyn accent and has wildly uncombed gray hair. Sanders, an Independent who caucuses with the Democrats, had served eight terms in the House after a stint as mayor of Burlington, the state's largest city. He trounced Tarrant, winning 65 percent of the vote. But at the same time, the voters reelected Jim Douglas, a soft-spoken, moderate Republican, as governor. The state's senior senator, Patrick J. Leahy, and lone House member, Peter Welch, are both liberal Democrats. The Swiss-born Kunin, a Democrat whose family moved to the United States when she was a child, was the first Jewish woman to be elected governor of a U.S. state, serving three terms from 1985–1991. President Clinton later appointed her as ambassador to Switzerland, where she served from 1996 to 1999. The voters' choice of political leaders flies in the face of their traditional aversion to "flatlanders"—a derisive term referring to those born outside the state.

Vermont's legislators have neither offices nor staff. They do their own constituent service and public relations. The only exceptions are the Speaker and Senate majority leader, who each have offices (and a single staffer) in the capital. Although this "citizen legislature" seems attractive, one effect of being without a staff has meant that the legislators have to rely heavily on lobbyists to draft legislation. "There are more lobbyists than legislators," said Governor Douglas, who has a personal staff of six, plus clerical personnel. He added: "Lobbyists are more powerful and prominent than they used to be." But the state's ethics rules require full disclosure, even when a lobbyist takes a legislator to lunch. The legislative session runs from January to mid-May, and the legislators earn only $5,000 per year.

The Vermont governor appoints all judges, board members, and commission members. As in New York, the Speaker appoints all House committee members and chairs and decides which bills will reach the floor. Former Speaker Gaye Symington, a tall, elegant woman, said "When I made a committee appointment, I took into account, 'Can I count on this person?'" she said. "Also, 'does this person work hard? Is he or she competent? Does he or she have an agenda?'" Symington also enjoyed the benefit of a sizeable Democratic majority: The House had ninety-three Democrats, forty-nine Republicans, six Progressives, and two Independents. "I was judicious about twisting arms, except on overriding a veto where I'd say, 'This is one that really matters.'"

Personal relationships catapulted Anne Donahue into the Vermont Statehouse. A former mental patient who had been hospitalized for depression, Donahue lives in a log cabin she built from a kit. She is editor of *Counterpoint,* a state-funded periodical for mental health patients, and spent many years prior to her election lobbying the legislature on mental health issues. The magazine provided the linchpin of her exposure of a major scandal at Burlington's Fletcher Allen Hospital, which resulted in a two-year jail term for Bill Boettcher, the hospital's CEO. "I spent days digging into the files of the state's Health Care Administration," she recalled, "and fed information to the newspapers." Her role in exposing the scandal gave Donahue name recognition.

"When I made the decision to run for the legislature, my mother said, 'You'll become a crook,'" Donahue recalled. Her mother, she said, reflected the public's deeply held belief that politics is inevitably associated with corruption. But at the same time, a House Republican leader encouraged her, saying, "I think the Republican Party is ready for a candidate with a mental illness." He said the only expectation was that if I wasn't going to vote with the caucus, to let them know. I've always let them know. They also asked me not to broadcast it, but there are some things I feel passionate about. I opposed civil commitment for sex offenders, after prison time. If they were mentally ill, they shouldn't have gone to prison."

Markowitz, the secretary of state, has also been the Democratic Party's major recruiter. Markowitz had previously run a law center out of a state municipal association. With a staff of 65, her responsibilities included overseeing professional licensing, elections, and ethics laws. Far from being handpicked, "I decided to run, and introduced myself to the Democrats. I'd never been involved in Democratic politics. When I came into office, I hired people without any regard to party. I've never asked anybody what their political background was. I kept some people on who I thought were doing a fine job. One of them has become one of my very top managers."

Maxine Grad, a lawyer, was one of the Democrats Markowitz recruited to run for the state legislature. "In 2000, Deb Markowitz called me up, asked to have lunch, and asked me to consider running for the legislature. She said,

'Don't worry, you won't win.' I won." Says Markowitz: "I started a women's leadership initiative eight years ago. Women don't self-identify as leaders. We [Vermont] lead the nation in the percentage of women in the legislature, a little over one-third of the legislators are women. We help get them over the feeling of not being qualified, balancing work and family."

But Vermont has disclosure problems. It is one of three states that have no financial disclosure laws for governors or legislators; Michigan and Idaho are the other two. Nevertheless, all candidates for governor disclose their finances. "That's the expectation," said former Governor Kunin. But Speaker Symington created a flap by failing to also disclose the finances of her husband, who was the former CEO of Ben & Jerry's, a Vermont-based ice cream company.

But even in idyllic Vermont, patronage still exists, albeit in very minor forms. Kunin acknowledged that "obviously, when you fill positions on boards and commissions, a governor would consider people he knows." And, like other governors, Kunin had recourse to a tool bag of favors to help persuade recalcitrant legislators to support her policies. "It sounds silly, but one of the most powerful forms of persuasion was arranging for a low-numbered license plate," she said. She also noted that "There could be some conflicts of interest with campaign contributions from people who do business with the state," adding, "Some [people and groups] contribute to both sides."

In addition, every public official acknowledges that with no staff to speak of—the governor has only six aides—lobbyists write almost all legislation. Lobbyists provide a sense of stability to a political system that looks apolitical from the outside but, depending on the issue, accords a great deal of power to unelected and often anonymous figures. So far, the key players seem content with this system, but it still carries with it considerable potential for abuse.

Lobbyists, Patronage, and State Politics

Lobbyists, like most politicians, are not shackled by political ideology. They usually contribute to incumbents as a reward for past favors and incentives for future support. But if the incumbent loses, they then contribute to the successful challenger by helping him retire his campaign debt. In other words, lobbyists are every bit as strategic as the politicians they woo and hope to control.

As in Washington, lobbyists have descended on state capitals in record numbers. They broke the billion-dollar mark in 2005, when a total of 40,000 registered lobbyists and the companies that hired them spent $1.16 billion to influence the almost 7,400 state legislators in the nation's fifty statehouses. Some of the most influential lobbyists were the spouses and other relatives of legislators.[42]

As in Vermont, lobbyists often play a key role in drafting legislation. In Washington, they often sit down behind closed doors with administration officials and congressional leaders to hammer out deals. This policy of secrecy also includes a refusal to identify which interest groups are included in key deliberations and which are not. Vice President Richard Cheney refused, for example, to identify the lobbyists involved in drafting the Bush administration's energy policy, and the U.S. Supreme Court supported his vision of "executive privilege."[43] Secrecy has been defended as critical to negotiations on controversial legislative issues. Remember all the warnings of how important the absence of media was to the Constitutional Convention and the eventual ratification of the U.S. Constitution.

To sustain this system of reciprocal favors, politicians have concocted other schemes to pull a curtain of secrecy around lobbyists' roles. California Assembly Speaker Fabian Nuñez created an innovation in lobbyists' donations by using a small charity as a conduit to funnel almost $300,000 from companies and organizations with business in the capital to events that helped him politically. "By giving to the charity, the donors, whom Nuñez solicited, earned tax deductions for which they would not have qualified had they given directly to Nuñez's campaign accounts. They were also able to donate more than the $7,200 maximum allowed under California's campaign fundraising rules."[44]

The charity, Collective Space, Inc., received donations from Zenith Insurance Co., AT&T, Verizon Communications Inc., the California Hospital Assn., the state prison guards union, Pacific Gas & Electric Co., and Blue Cross of California, "all groups with high stakes in legislation," reported the *Los Angeles Times*. The money was used for events including "Assembly Speaker Fabian Nuñez's Toy Drive," "Assembly Speaker Fabian Nuñez's Soccerfest 2006," and "Assembly Speaker Fabian Nuñez's Inaugural Legislative Youth Conference." Nuñez insisted that his solicitation of donations was not intended to benefit himself, but said, "When you're doing good things like this, there is nothing wrong with letting people know that you worked on it or made it happen."[45]

AT&T stood to profit from Nuñez-sponsored legislation in 2006 to open the cable TV industry to phone company competition. Zenith Insurance Co., the state's biggest private sector workers' compensation carrier, benefited from Nuñez-sponsored legislation, which gave insurers, including Zenith, their biggest profits in three decades. In February 2005, the California secretary of state suspended the charity for failing to file required information. In November 2005, the Franchise Tax Board suspended Collective Space for failure to file federal tax returns. The Nuñez-directed donations began to arrive the following month.

Many lobbyists are former state legislators. More than 1,300 former state lawmakers were registered to lobby in 2005, according to the Center for Public Integrity.[46] The study found that the revolving door between the public and private service turns just as easily in the statehouse as it does in Washington, D.C. And when the former legislators became lobbyists, they emerged as some of the most powerful, well-connected statehouse operators, raking in large fees. "I can stay in the State Senate, which I've been in for 16 years, attend meetings at night and weekends, and stand for re-election at $25,000 a year with *per diem*, or I can go out in the hall and not have to go to meetings at night, only follow the legislation that my clients care about, and make $200,000 a year," said former Indiana Democratic legislator Louis Mahern, a registered lobbyist. "You can only resist that for so long. I have to start thinking about my financial future and my children's education."[47]

As in Washington, many spouses of state legislators also prosper as lobbyists. "A lawyer who marries a legislator gains access," said Drew Johnson, president of the Tennessee Center for Policy Research. He noted that in Tennessee, Betty Anderson, who married Jimmy Naifeh, Speaker of the House, was "the most powerful lobbyist in the state."[48] Similarly, Martha Miller Harriman married Senator Morril Harriman, chairman of the Arkansas Senate Rules Committee, and then became a powerful lobbyist. In 2000, her husband resigned his seat to accept a lobbying job with the Poultry Federation. The two have been ranked among the top ten lobbyists in the state by the *Arkansas Democrat-Gazette.*[49]

Sometimes the process is reversed, and lobbyists become lawmakers. State Representative Deborah Ross of North Carolina is a former lobbyist who says she uses her lobbying skills in her legislative role. "I haven't stopped approaching bills that I want to get passed [in the same way I did as a lobbyist] just because I'm a member," she said.[50] Missouri State Senator Timothy Green was term-limited out of his seat in the Assembly and subsequently took a lobbying job before he ran for the Senate. "No matter what, a legislator, if he has the experience and knowledge and he can no longer serve the public, then he can use his knowledge in the private market, so be it," Green said. Vermont's Anne Donahue, who had lobbied the legislature on mental health issues, took her lobbying inside the legislature when she was elected to Vermont's House of Representatives.

Sometimes the public and private markets get mixed when legislators become business partners of lobbyists. "Texas House Speaker Tom Craddick is in business with a lobbyist, but can't say who," the *Associated Press* reported.[51] Craddick, a Republican who wields tremendous influence in state government, revealed in disclosure filings that he and a registered lobbyist have common business interests. The law requires he list the company involved—Centro Caswell, LLC—but Craddick isn't required to name the other lobbyist. Fellow Texas Representative Sid Miller, another Republican, disclosed his lobbyist dealings, but only after someone complained. He has an interest in a political and commercial phone bank company that was founded by A-list lobbyist Todd Smith. The two men also own shares in an Internet start-up called *E-Campus Nation.*

Miller's disclosure forms don't mention Smith by name, and there's nothing in the law that requires it.

With the complexity of twenty-first century issues, state lobbyists play an increasingly critical role in the legislative process. At best, they provide the information that helps legislators make wise decisions. They gain credibility by telling legislators both the plusses and minuses of proposed legislation, regardless of their clients' interests. Successful lobbyists, like successful politicians, know that there's always another bill and another day. At worst, lobbyists provide the money and gifts intended to put legislators under obligation to them. They can be a corrupting influence that tarnishes both the legislators and the institutions they serve.

Web of Cooperation

Some patronage scholars believed that strong governors, like strong presidents, reduced political patronage and strengthened the public interest.[52] The evidence suggests the opposite. Franklin Roosevelt, when governor of New York State, showed a mastery of patronage that he also exhibited in the White House. Governors Kean of New Jersey and Rendell of Pennsylvania are among other strong executives who also found patronage to be an essential tool of governing. And where is it written that political patronage is incompatible with the public interest? It is often necessary to use patronage to achieve the public interest.

Some believe that ideally, a strong executive presides over a number of agencies coordinated efficiently by staff, all operating within budget guidelines, and populated with workers who owe their jobs to civil service commissions, not to party leaders. That sounds good in theory, but a mountain of evidence points the other way. Savvy governors help legislators in their states in a variety of ways, hoping they will remember their generosity the next time their vote is needed on a critical issue. A governor who knows how to use patronage "creatively" can generally administer the state more effectively than one who doesn't.

Many governors have used their discretionary powers over government contracts to reward their friends and punish their enemies. Even when contracts come up for competitive bidding, loopholes exist that circumvent bidding parameters, enabling one firm to receive preferential treatment over another. On the surface, fully acceptable rationales exist: Architectural and engineering contracts can't be opened to competitive bidding because architectural projects, especially, rely so heavily on current tastes, and emergencies (like wars) force speedy decisions that don't lend themselves to long, drawn-out bidding processes. "Honest graft" can be easily manipulated in this way by wording the "specs" to fit only one firm or by "leaking" advance notice to give the favored firm more time to meet the specifications or prepare the bid. Also, the governor—or any politician for that matter—does not have a monopoly on writing job descriptions to fit only one candidate; that trick is widely used by the private sector and even by some academic departments that have been known to couch descriptions for open positions in language designed specifically for the candidate they had in mind all along.

At times, governors promise more than they can deliver, often to their regret. Ross Barnett of Mississippi promised a state job to anyone who wanted one! When Barnett was sworn in, office seekers trooped into Jackson from all over the state, reminding old-timers of the days before civil service reform calmed down the job frenzy. Campaigning for reelection four years later, the governor encountered someone who couldn't understand why he didn't get a job after the first election. After all, said the voter, he had voted for Barnett and had influenced all his friends and relatives to vote for Barnett. Ever the shrewd politician, Barnett looked his adversary firmly in the eye and told him that was precisely why he was running a second time: to find jobs for everyone he couldn't hire the first time around. But the voters didn't believe him, and he was not elected to a second term. [53]

The web of mutual obligation also weaves legislators and their constituents together, reflecting similar patterns on the national level. Legislative leaders like the Speaker of the lower house in state legislatures control committee assignments, statehouse employees, budgets, and pocket money like lulus, which greatly enhance legislative salaries. The power to grant or remove lulus sways votes in much the same way a governor wields job power. One hapless legislator in Georgia was warned by the governor that his brother would lose his job in the highway department if he didn't vote for a bond issue that was coming up. The lawmaker strode to the well of the house and delivered a public message to his brother: "Dear John," he began. "You always told me to do what was right, and that's what I'm going to do. So if they fire you, John, you come on home. There's ham in the smokehouse and flour in the bin, and we'll part the hoecakes just like we always have."[54]

Although political "deals" are widely denounced, they are an essential tool in governing, and examples on the state level abound. What is the difference, for example, between a "deal" and a "bargain?" Language, primarily: A deal smacks of shady back-room secrets negotiated by cigar-smoking, fat-bellied politicians engraved in the public mind by the nineteenth-century caricatures of cartoonist Thomas Nast. A "bargain," on the other hand, conjures up a more legitimate picture of mutual obligations: understandings between lawmakers and supporters, and lawmakers and constituents. The alternatives to bargains are legislation by fiat or dictatorial powers by an all-powerful leader. Or mob rule, of the kind feared by the Founding Fathers, who fought so hard for representative democracy. In other words, the absence of patronage leads to greater extremes in politics, which is why governors and lawmakers work hard at strengthening close relationships with each other. A smart politician publicly eliminates patronage where it doesn't matter or where it deteriorates into corruption; but at the same time uses patronage power to get bills through, to obligate other lawmakers for future projects, and to govern.

The public rarely sees this web of cooperation, buried in committee rooms or on BlackBerries and iPhones. Interest rate hikes can mean millions of dollars for banks, not to mention all the other favors doled out by the state: legal work, insurance contracts, pension funds, finder's fees, bank stock, and stock tips. The conundrum keeps repeating itself: States run by powerful parties are invariably states with ample patronage at their disposal. They are also states with more than their share of politicians indicted and convicted for their role in patronage run amok.

CHAPTER FOUR
CONGRESS

THE MOTHER LODE

"Money drives this place. It cost me a chairmanship."
Representative Ralph Regula (R-Ohio)

"I didn't get elected to Congress to spend all my time fundraising."
Representative Marcy Kaptur (D-Ohio)

Ralph Regula was incensed. The soft-spoken, eighteen-term Republican from Canton, Ohio had been on the House Appropriations Committee for thirty-four of his thirty-six years in Congress. He had chaired two subcommittees and had more seniority than any other committee member. But when the chairmanship fell open in 2005, with the term-limited resignation of longtime chairman Bill Young, a Florida Republican, Regula was brushed aside in favor of Representative Jerry Lewis, a California Republican who had raised a great deal more money for Republican candidates. "The day that Jerry Lewis walked into the Republican Caucus with a $350,000 check, I knew my chances were over," said Regula. "The seniority system was a reform. Before that, they were selling chairmanships. Now it's back to selling chairmanships, and who can raise the most money. Money drives this place. It cost me a chairmanship."

Representative Lewis had been chairman of the Defense Subcommittee of the Appropriations Committee. Where did he get the money? One of his major contributors was Cerebrus Capital Management, a Republican-dominated hedge fund that is a private investment pool for wealthy individuals and private investors. Cerebrus's chairman is former Treasury Secretary John Snow, while former Vice

President Dan Quayle sits on the board, and former Defense Secretary Donald Rumsfeld is an investor. Cerebrus's subsidiaries include IAP, which obtained billions in federal contracts for Iraq, as well as a multimillion-dollar contract to renovate Walter Reed Army Medical Center.[1] One day after Cerebrus raised $110,000 for Representative Lewis's "Future Leaders Political Action Committee" at a New York City fundraiser on July 7, 2003, the House passed a defense spending bill that preserved $160 million for a Navy project critical to Cerebrus. Who protected the project? Jerry Lewis.[2] Lewis insisted that he never discussed the Navy project with Cerebrus. In fact, Cerebrus contributed about one-third of the money raised by Lewis, who acknowledged that the firm's fundraising "played a very significant role" in his winning the Appropriations Committee chairmanship. His PAC gave $408,000 to sixty-nine House candidates in the 2004 election. Lewis also invited Cerebrus executives to an April 2004 National Republican Congressional Committee fundraiser, which he chaired.[3] Carol Lam, the U.S. attorney for San Diego, was investigating allegations that Lewis delivered *quid pro quo* favors for contractors and lobbyists who contributed to his PAC when she was abruptly dismissed by the Bush administration, along with eight other U.S. attorneys.[4]

The money chase is pursued by both parties and consumes members of Congress from the day after an election until the day of the following election. "I didn't get elected to Congress to spend all my time fundraising," lamented Representative Marcy Kaptur, a fourteen-term Democrat from Toledo, Ohio. But Speaker Nancy Pelosi and the Democratic leaders had given all Democratic members of Congress fundraising goals, and woe betide the lawmaker who failed to meet them. Their fundraising affected everything from their committee assignments to committee chairmanships and leadership posts. Kaptur said that some members had decided not to run for reelection to escape the necessity of constant fundraising. With House Democrats as well as Republicans, Kaptur said, "Forget about a chairmanship if you haven't raised a lot of money." Kaptur held up a batch of telephone messages. "Look at this handful of messages," she said. "They are all from other members of Congress trying to raise money. Everything here is about money." But Representative Joe Crowley, a New York Democrat who is Queens Democratic leader, noted that much of the fundraising went to elect Democratic freshmen in order to maintain the party's majority in Congress. This fundraising, he said, was recognition that "We're all in this together."

Congressional fundraising today is a riff on Jake Arvey's maxim about politics being "the art of putting people under obligation to you."[5] By providing campaign contributions, lobbyists, corporate executives, union leaders, and association members do exactly that: They put members of Congress under obligation to *them*. At a minimum, they gain access and influence. At a maximum, they write the laws of the land.[6] Of course, lobbyists are consummate politicians and play the game at least as well as members of Congress. Many are former senators, House members, and congressional aides.

History suggests that major campaign donors are not bashful about calling in their chits. In the heat of the Democratic presidential primaries, Harvey Weinstein, the movie mogul who supported the primary campaign of Hillary Clinton, called Speaker Pelosi and threatened to cut off campaign money to congressional Democrats unless Pelosi agreed to support and finance a revote of the Democratic presidential primaries in Florida and Michigan, which would ostensibly benefit Clinton. The Speaker held firm and refused.[7] But most members of Congress respond to the siren songs of lobbyists and other major campaign contributors. The lobbyists' Political Action Committees, or PACs, customarily collect funds from a company's executives and employees. Although invented by a labor union (the AFL-CIO), PACs were copied, and surpassed, by the business community.

Former Representative Dan Glickman, a Kansas Democrat, also lamented the incessant demands on him and other members to raise money "for the Congressional Campaign Committee, for the Democratic National Committee, for PACs and for your own campaign." Glickman noted that "The new ethics rules provide that the only time a congressman can meet socially with a lobbyist was at fundraisers. All the focus is on money," he said. "We've created a system much more based on a *quid pro quo.*"

In addition to being time-consuming, Glickman said, "Money has the insidious effect of paralyzing politics. The money flow is to preserve the status quo, not to change things. The American political system has been hurt by this constant search for money." One example offered by Glickman: President Clinton and his famous "sleepovers" in the Lincoln bedroom, which rewarded big donors with overnight stays in the White House's most famous living quarters. Contrary to expectations, the public was outraged by the use of the White House for this purpose. "It's our house," many said; the president was just there temporarily and had no right to use it for such crass political purposes. Glickman served in Congress for eighteen years, after which he was appointed Agriculture Secretary by Bill Clinton. Following his years in the public service, Glickman served as president of the Motion Picture Association of America, which lobbies for the Hollywood film studios.

Glickman's years in Congress taught him that the institution operates more often on the basis of cooperation than confrontation. After Glickman voted against Speaker Tip O'Neill's request for an appropriation for Ireland, O'Neill called Glickman up to the rostrum. "Danny, why did you vote against aid to my country?" he asked. "I would never vote against aid to your country [Israel]." Glickman responded: "Mr. Speaker, I just made a serious mistake." Glickman knew that "All Tip wanted was an apology." Glickman noted that most legislation falls under the radar and evokes no public hue and cry. Most members are interested in only a handful of issues. Most important, a legislator who is against you today may be with you tomorrow.

Former congressman and governor James Blanchard, a Michigan Democrat, observed that "In Congress, people feel strongly about two or three issues. For me it was the Great Lakes and also Israel, because I had a lot of Jewish constituents. On almost all issues, there's no moral high ground." He recalled that when in Congress, Speaker Thomas P. "Tip" O'Neill once told him, "Jimmy Boy, I'm going to put on the calendar your Great Lakes bill, but I need your vote on the bill that's coming up." Blanchard observed: "It's part of the horse trading that goes back to our founding fathers. Why did they leave slavery alone for so long? Because they needed southern votes."

Glickman lost his congressional seat in the Republican landslide of 1994 and went on to become Secretary of Agriculture "because of my personal relationships." He knew Vice President Gore, White House Chief of Staff Leon Panetta, and House Democratic Leader Richard Gephardt—all had been members of the class of newly elected Democratic members of Congress in 1976. Panetta wanted to make sure the appointment was acceptable to Senator Bob Dole, Kansas Republican, who gave his okay. "The other Senator from Kansas, Pat Roberts [also a Republican], had talked me up in the press. The moral is: Never burn your bridges. I always had a good relationship with Dole, even though we disagreed on some issues."

Glickman's predecessor at the Motion Picture Association, Jack Valenti, recalled the pressure he faced not to appoint a Democrat as his successor. He had heard about the "K Street Project," reputedly the brainchild of Representative Tom DeLay (R-Texas), the majority leader. The object was to ensure that Republicans got the plum lobbying jobs on K Street, Washington's lobbying corridor, by denying Democratic lobbyists the access they previously enjoyed. Two weeks before Valenti planned to announce Glickman's appointment, he received a phone call from a friend, a Republican lobbyist, who said, "Now Jack, please understand I am just a messenger. I have been asked to tell you that if the MPAA chooses a Democrat for your job, Tom DeLay and the House leadership will not take this kindly." Valenti recalled, "My spine began to stiffen. So the K Street Project was not some phantom. It was real, and it was here right in my face." Valenti told his caller that he did not "take kindly to that kind of pressure, and Glickman's appointment was announced shortly thereafter."[8] DeLay retired from Congress in 2005 after being charged with felony money laundering and conspiracy in connection with Republican fundraising efforts. Other members brought before the bar of justice, also for overreaching their congressional patronage power, include the following:

- Senator Ted Stevens (R-Alaska), who was convicted in 2008 (overturned in 2009) on seven counts of falsely reporting hundreds of thousands of dollars' worth of services he received from an oil services company that helped renovate his home. His conviction was rescinded because of prosecutorial misconduct.
- Representative Rick Renzi (R-Arizona), charged in 2008 with extortion, wire fraud, money laundering, and other federal crimes in an Arizona land swap that authorities say helped him collect hundreds of thousands of dollars in payoffs.
- Senator Larry Craig (R-Idaho), who pleaded guilty in 2008 to charges of disorderly conduct in a bathroom sex sting at the Minneapolis airport.
- Representative William Jefferson (D-Louisiana), indicted in 2007 (and convicted in 2009) on federal charges of racketeering, soliciting bribes for gifts, and money laundering.
- Representative Bob Ney (R-Ohio), sentenced in 2007 to two-and-a-half years for trading political favors for gifts and campaign donations from lobbyist Jack Abramoff.
- Representative Randy "Duke" Cunningham (R-California), sentenced in 2006 to eight years and four months for collecting $2.4 million in homes, yachts, antique furnishings, and other bribes.
- Representative William Janklow (R-South Dakota), convicted in 2003 of vehicular homicide after his car struck and killed a motorcyclist.
- Representative James Traficant (D-Ohio), sentenced in 2001 to eight years after being convicted of racketeering and accepting bribes.

Congressional Largesse

Congress is the mother lode of political patronage. The institution survives on discretionary favors in exchange for political support—from leadership appointments of Senators and House members to committees and committee chairmanships, to a congressman's appointment of a supporter's son to the military academies of West Point or Annapolis, to the appointment of congressional pages, and to legislation that benefits only a single individual or company. An influential congressman can bring great benefits to his district and ward off even greater catastrophes. Thus, after the government bailout of the automobile companies, Representative Barney Frank (D-Massachusetts), chairman of the Financial Services committee, persuaded the government-owned General Motors not to close a factory in his suburban Boston district. Representative Jack Murtha (D-Pennsylvania), chairman of the Defense Appropriations Subcommittee, was notorious for delivering truckloads of federal funds to Johnstown, his hometown.

Even though the public has grown more sophisticated about politicians' promises, voters still expect members of Congress to bring home jobs and new projects generously larded with federal money. Not only is it expected; it also helps attract campaign contributions for money-starved legislators. In their largesse, lawmakers have far surpassed the city bosses who dispensed Christmas turkeys. The expansion of the federal government in the last half-century has greatly increased a lawmaker's ability to help or hinder an individual, company, or entire industry, earning the gratitude of grateful constituents.

In addition to this most important role as ombudsman, the many roles of a member of Congress include national legislator, local representative, constituent advocate, investigator, educator, student, local dignitary, fundraiser, staff manager, party leader, and consensus builder. "The demands on a member of Congress can be many, and the personal moments few," observed former Representative Lee Hamilton (D-Indiana).

Even weekends at home and congressional recesses leave little time for a member of Congress to enjoy family and friends. Representative David Price, a North Carolina Democrat who was a political science professor at Duke University, collapsed in his living room one Saturday evening, exhausted after a round of weddings, bar mitzvahs, and town hall meetings, at which his appearance was considered mandatory. Missing any of these events would have been considered a slight by an important constituent.

One of a lawmaker's most coveted activities is "constituent service," which includes intervention with government agencies on behalf of constituents. Having trouble getting on Social Security disability? Need a compassionate furlough from the army to attend an ailing parent? Have a farm problem that the Agriculture Department can address? These are among the thousands of requests received by members of Congress, each of whom has a team of aides that help constituents navigate their way through the growing federal bureaucracy. Constituent service is a major reason for the growth of congressional offices, from one or two aides one-half century ago to more than a dozen today. This is all in addition to weekend visits home and a round of events that members of Congress feel obliged to attend. Some critics feel that the practice of constituent service should be treated more neutrally, as recognition for performing a service, and definitely not as what it has become—a vehicle for attracting the loyalty and lucre of individuals and groups, obligating them for an indefinite period in the future.

The power of congressional leaders and members of Congress is very real to those who benefit from congressional largesse, but in reality the "favor" may be a service to which any citizen is entitled. If a constituent is not getting his Social Security checks on time and his congressional representative speeds up the process, for example, the constituent is likely to feel obligated to the lawmaker for such help. In reality, however, those checks should arrive on time, as provided by law; and sluggish bureaucracies should, in theory at least, not respond to pressure from individual members of Congress. But reality prevails: Executive agencies depend on Congress for their budgets; some slippage is inevitable in serving the public; and members of Congress welcome the opportunity to serve as ombudsmen between citizens and their government.

Nor do the members ignore the needs of their rich and powerful constituents, whom they help master the intricacies of regulatory agencies, and for whom they secure tax benefits, government contracts, and other forms of what is sometimes called "corporate welfare." In dealing with federal agencies, the members' intervention is seldom direct. It usually takes the form of a request for a "status report," as with Speaker Tip O'Neill's efforts to help Jim Wilmot, the Democratic National Committee's finance chairman, by securing housing subsidies for Wilmot's apartment buildings.[9] By merely making the request, however, a congressman indicates not just his interest, but also the preferred outcome.

Despite numerous efforts at reform, patronage politics in Congress has stayed pretty much the same. With few exceptions, the leadership on both sides of the aisle remains in full control. The power to assign committee seats remains one of the party leadership's most important discretionary favors.

By far the most powerful congressional leader is the Speaker, who controls the House agenda; the flow of legislation; committee membership; committee chairs; the party's legislative strategy; and a wide range of favors, large and small. The Speaker can refer bills to a committee or to several committees, designate the lead committee, and impose time limits for action "which may be generous or tight."[10] In addition, the Speaker can exert the power to consider legislation of "far reaching significance" under something called the "suspension of the rules," which gives her "complete discretion over ... legislation."[11] But bills that reach the floor in that manner require a super-majority of a two-thirds vote for approval.[12] Bowing to the power of party leaders in Congress, the president and his team very often direct projects to districts represented by the Speaker—Lake Texoma was a gift to Speaker Sam Rayburn (D-Texas)—as well as to key committee and subcommittee chairmen as insurance for congressional support of White House proposals.

By comparison, the Senate runs on "unanimous consent" motions. A single senator can delay action and wreak havoc on an agenda, and sixty votes are required to end a filibuster and approve anything from a procedural motion to confirmation of a presidential appointee to a major bill. Consequently, the majority leader must confer with committee chairs before appointing members of ad hoc committees, conferees, and special committees. However, Senator Lyndon Johnson (D-Texas) showed that a majority leader with great political skills can become the "Master of the Senate," in the words of one of his biographers, Robert Caro.[13]

In seeking a specific committee assignment, a senator or representative first seeks the support of the leader of his state's delegation, before making his case to the committee chairman and finally the leadership, to whom he also becomes beholden. Geographic equity is one of the criteria: Leaders seek to ensure that all sections of the country are represented on the major committees. Although considerable jockeying goes on behind the scenes, little of the politicking ever becomes public. But occasionally a disgruntled lawmaker chooses to go to the media. When the fiery Shirley Chisholm, who represented the heart of the very urban Bedford-Stuyvesant section of Brooklyn, New York, was assigned to the Agriculture Committee, she protested, "Apparently, all they [the party leaders] know about Brooklyn is that a tree grew there."[14] It was clear at the time that Chisholm was being punished for her outspoken views, her lack of "reliability," and her vocal unwillingness to go along with the "bosses."[15]

The political advantages of committee and subcommittee assignments cannot be underestimated. The Senate Finance Committee and the House Ways and Means Committee, with their far-reaching jurisdiction over tax-writing, health-care, and other financial matters, are considered the most powerful committees of the Congress, while seats on the House and Senate Appropriations committees also are coveted. The chairmen of the Appropriations subcommittees are called the "cardinals," beseeched by colleagues seeking earmarks. With the economic meltdown of 2008–2009, the House Finance Committee and Senate Banking Committee took front and center on the congressional stage. Lawmakers also seek committee assignments with special relevance to their states and districts—western lawmakers seek appointment to the Interior committees, while those who represent the nation's breadbasket hunger for the Agriculture committees.

The bulk of committee favors rest solidly with committee chairmen, whose control over committee agendas gives them a strong role in the fate of legislation. Because such a small proportion of legislation ever emerges from committees, the power over public policy closely held by a small group of party leaders is enormous. They determine which legislation will be considered, whether hearings will be held, and whether to call in their chits to pass or defeat legislation. Until the rules were changed in 1974, seniority rules determined committee leadership. But now, money—or the ability to raise money for the fundraising arms of the congressional parties—sometimes prevails over seniority in choosing chairmen. Some would-be chairmen are bypassed because they are considered too old or infirm to be effective and yield the chair to younger, more aggressive members. Representative Henry Waxman (D-California) twice ousted committee chairs by virtue of his comparative youth and vigor, and by ample contributions to his colleagues' campaigns. In 1978, Waxman ousted Representative Richardson Preyer (D-North Carolina) from the chairmanship of the Commerce Committee's Health and Environment Subcommittee in 1978; in 2008 Waxman ousted Representative John Dingell

(D-Michigan) from the chairmanship of the Energy and Commerce Committee. The Dingell ouster was all the more remarkable because Dingell was known as the "powerhouse Dean" of the House, where he has served since 1955.

What Have You Done for Me Lately?

Congressmen should not always expect gratitude for their favors to constituents. Capitol Hill veterans tell the story, probably apocryphal, of a new and overly ambitious member of the House of Representatives who had worked especially hard to get a water project for his district. Unexpectedly, he achieved the unheard-of victory of getting the project authorized by Congress during his freshman term on Capitol Hill, instead of the customary six to sixteen years usually taken to move a major project out of the maze of congressional committees and White House roadblocks. A Southern committee chairman took the starch out of his victory, however, by suggesting that he'd gone about the whole thing in the wrong way. "You never get the whole project," the chairman advised. "You get one mile, and you go home and brag about that, and then you go to the next Congress and go for another mile. That way the project is good for maybe five, six terms. You've gone ahead and spent it all in one term, and now you'll have to wait for years for another project." The chairman was right, and the lawmaker was retired by the voters after serving two terms, unable to satisfy their queries of "Yes, but what have you done for me lately?"

"A Congressman has two constituencies," the late Sam Rayburn (D-Texas), Speaker of the House longer than any other member, used to tell House freshmen. "He has his constituents at home and his colleagues here in the House. To serve his constituents at home, he must also serve his colleagues here in the House."[16]

Congressional leaders not only giveth; they also taketh away. Senator William Proxmire, a somewhat eccentric Wisconsin Democrat known for giving "Golden Fleece" awards to scientific projects he considered undeserving, alienated Senator Robert Byrd, a West Virginia Democrat who was Senate majority leader. Proxmire was in the habit of jogging to his office every morning from his home in northwest Washington and then going upstairs to the shower room. Byrd, in a fit of pique, padlocked the shower room, leaving Proxmire to find alternate ways to remove the sweat and grime accumulated during his five-mile jog.

Rayburn was famous for his advice that "To get along, you have to go along. Anybody who tries will find a way to go along with his leaders 60–70 percent of the time," and thereby obtain the favors that can make or break a congressional career. Even in the age of the Internet, when a member of Congress can go over the heads of congressional leaders and speak directly to his or her constituents, leadership support can be critical to the success of a member's legislative initiatives and also play a role in a member's ability to obtain projects for his district.

"Mr. Sam" was never reluctant to use his power. A freshman member once complained to him that the Justice Department was conducting a lengthy investigation into charges of income tax evasion. The young congressman said the protracted investigation was like water torture (it kept him awake nights and even affected his appetite) and asked Rayburn if he could find out whether the Justice Department was preparing a criminal case or merely a civil lawsuit. Rayburn told the young congressman to return at 6:00 that evening. He then summoned the attorney general to his office, told him about the case, said that he didn't care if it was a criminal or civil case, but wanted a decision by 6:00 p.m. When the young congressman returned, Rayburn told him that he had just received a call from the attorney general: It would be a civil case.

The congressman was ecstatic. "Mr. Speaker, I don't know how to thank you," he said. "Any time you need my vote it is yours." Rayburn responded: "Funny you should say that." He explained "We've got an offshore oil bill coming up next week, and I could use your vote." The young congressman promptly pledged his vote. But when he went back to his district that weekend, he discovered that a disgruntled IRS bureaucrat had contacted his local newspaper, which published a page-one story that said that the congressman had sold his vote on an offshore oil bill in exchange for getting off the hook on income tax evasion charges.

When the congressman returned to the Capitol, he told the Speaker that he was being crucified for his pending vote and that if he voted for the offshore oil bill, he would have the shortest congressional career on record. Rayburn was firm. "You promised me your vote and I expect you to keep your promise," he said. "I want you to sit in the front row during the voting, and if I need your vote, I'll nod in the affirmative, and I'll expect your vote. If I don't need your vote, I'll nod in the negative, and you can vote however you want." During the voting, the young congressman sweated bullets. Finally, two minutes before the end of the vote, the Speaker nodded that he didn't need the young congressman's vote. The freshman heaved a huge sigh of relief, only to notice two dozen other members in the front row also heaving huge sighs of relief. "That's how Sam Rayburn ran things," an admiring Tip O'Neill later recalled.

Former Representative Lee Hamilton (D-Indiana), who served 34 years in Congress, received a vivid introduction to how power works on Capitol Hill as a freshman member in 1965. "Following the lead of the president, a small group of us introduced a measure to extend the term of House members from two years to four. Given its support in the White House, we thought we had a chance for success, so we were optimistic when we approached the chairman of the House Judiciary Committee, an awesome and fearsome New Yorker named Emanuel Celler. I was designated the spokesman for the group. How, I wanted to know, did Mr. Celler stand on the bill?' 'I don't stand on it,' Celler responded. 'I'm sitting on it. It rests four-square under my fanny and will never see the light of day.' He was right. It didn't. And we learned that day something about congressional power—that some individuals have enormous power within the institution either to move legislation forward or to kill it."[17]

It is a system that rewards cooperation, not confrontation. Senator Everett Dirksen of Illinois, the Republican minority leader, visited Russell Long, the Louisiana Democrat who was chairman of the Finance Committee, with a proposal to merge the National Football League and the American Football Conference. Dirksen explained that the Chicago Bears wanted the merger. Long agreed, but told Dirksen, "Of course, this means that New Orleans will have a team." Thus was born the New Orleans Saints.

Today, many congressmen complain of a lack of collegiality, a fractious atmosphere driven by extremists on both the left and right. They are nostalgic for the "good old days," when congressmen who fought bitterly by day would go out for a drink together at night. Like much nostalgia, their recollections are rooted more in illusion than reality. There undoubtedly were fewer heated disputes fifty years ago, but that was because the leadership and committee chairmen ruled with an iron hand. The majority of those leaders and chairmen were southern bigots and reactionaries, and it was worth a member's career to stand up against them. As recently as 1973, during a debate on the Senate floor, Senator John McLellan, (D-Arkansas), chairman of the Appropriations Committee, told Senator Jacob Javits (R-New York), who was Jewish, "Mr. Javits, we don't need *your kind* in the United States Senate." One would not hear such a comment today, nor would one encounter the pervasive antiblack feeling of that era. Today's leaders and chairmen are more diverse, better educated, and, although still powerful, have nowhere near the power of their predecessors. They also are constrained by the communications revolution that enables members to communicate with their districts through television and the Internet. What Congress has lost in collegiality, it has gained in democracy.

Comity works best when issues fly below the radar, when they are either hidden from public view or the public doesn't care very much about them. When it doesn't work, there's always a reason—and that, too, is often hidden even from the members themselves. Glickman recalled one such incident: "We had a federal judge opening in Kansas. There were no Democratic senators or congressmen. On my recommendation, Carter [president] sent down the name of Patrick Kelly, a Democratic activist. Nothing happened on the Hill. The Senate Judiciary Committee did nothing. It turned out that during the nominating process, Kelly had given $1,000 to Dole's [Senator Robert Dole, R-Kansas] opponent. I told Kelly to see Dole. He did. Dole ended up supporting him, and he got the judgeship. All Dole wanted was an apology."

Another incident of bipartisan cooperation was recalled by Senator Bob Packwood, an Oregon Republican and chairman of the Finance Committee, who was forced to resign from the Senate in a sex scandal. A constituent who headed a savings and loan bank wanted an exemption from a tax bill. Packwood needed the approval of his opposite number, Representative Dan Rostenkowski, chairman of the House Ways and Means committee, who consulted an aide who advised that the amendment had no merit. Packwood returned to Rostenkowski with the same negative result. He went back a third time, and the testy House chairman asked, "Why are you bothering me with this amendment?" Packwood explained that the head of the S&L had been his biggest supporter throughout his entire political career. "I owe him," Packwood said. "He rang doorbells for me." Rostenkowski quickly asked, "Well, why didn't you say so in the first place?" The amendment was adopted.

Nostalgic for the old days, former Senator Alan K. Simpson (R-Wyoming) recalled his despair at having his 1986 immigration bill bottled up in the House. The bill had passed the Senate, but Speaker O'Neill had prevented it from coming to the House floor. He ran into Martin Tolchin in the Capitol Plaza and vented his anger at O'Neill. "Have you ever met Tip?" Martin asked. Simpson replied that he had not. Whereupon Tolchin took Simpson to O'Neill's office, introduced the two of them, and left. He knew that each man had a great sense of humor and that they would get along famously. The result, Simpson recalled, was the Simpson-Mazzoli Immigration Reform and Control Act. Simpson contrasted that experience with the partisan standoff over health reform in the spring of 2010, deploring the increasing incivility that besets both chambers today.

These lawmakers were all masters of a system that contrasts sharply with the British system—or at least what it was intended to be—whose classic tradition of representing the national interest was expounded in Edmund Burke's famous letter to his constituents back home in Bristol: "Parliament is not a congress of ambassadors from different and hostile interests ... but Parliament is a deliberative assembly of one nation, with one interest, that of the whole; where not local purposes, not local prejudices, ought to guide, but the general good, resulting from the general reason of the whole. You choose a member indeed; but when you have chosen him, he is not a member for Bristol, but he is a member of Parliament."[18] Evidently Burke's concern for the national interest didn't sit well with the voters because, not surprisingly, Burke was defeated in the next election.

Members of Congress also have a constitutional obligation to promote the economic interests of their districts. The culture of Congress was established at the Constitutional Convention, when the Founding Fathers chose not to follow the British system, but instead to elect representatives apportioned among the states. The Constitution says nothing about congressional districts, but the case for those districts was deduced from the wording of the Constitution. In

The Federalist Papers, James Madison made this interpretation even more clear. In *Federalist Paper No. 56* he wrote: "Divide the largest state into ten or twelve districts and it will be found that there will be no peculiar interests in either which will not be within the knowledge of the Representative of the district." The Founding Fathers believed that if everyone represented his constituents, together they would represent the best interests of the nation.

Congress followed its national mandates: to settle the West; to industrialize; and later on, in the twentieth century, to protect the victims of industrialization. To settle the West, Congress gave homesteaders and railroad magnates free land and gave the railroads virtual freedom from government control. In the late nineteenth century, the commitment to industrialize led Congress to grant subsidies to oil tycoons, factory owners, and mining and shipping interests and to ignore the abuses that took their toll in worker health and safety. In the twentieth century, with the nation industrialized, Congress finally focused on easing the plight of the working Americans, with prohibitions on child labor, restrictions on working hours, and improvements in workers' health and safety. Were those bills enacted in the public's interest or were they special interest legislation? It all depends on one's perspective.

Earmarks

Earmarks are nothing new; in the old days, they were called "pork." Voters still expect members of Congress to bring home jobs and new projects generously financed by federal money. The time-honored double standard has prevailed in Congress since the founding of the Republic: One man's pork is another man's judicious expenditure. If projects are close to home, they are legitimate; if not, they are wasteful and attacked as "pork barrel."

The heated debates echo the trade battles, where members of Congress were "free traders" for industries outside their districts and protectionists for those close to home. Despite Republican attacks on "tax and spend Democrats" and their claim to be the party of fiscal responsibility, the spoils are still divided on a strictly bipartisan basis. Republicans no less than Democrats have been eager to "bring home the bacon"; less cynical types call it "constituent service." Indeed, Republican-controlled Congresses during the presidency of George W. Bush outdid their Democratic colleagues in their spending on behalf of constituents and home-state projects. Conservative watchdogs were unsuccessful in their efforts to have their conservative president veto these bills.

Earmarks are everyone's favorite slab of bacon. Technically, every appropriation is an "earmark." Hidden in complex appropriations bills, earmarks are specific projects that go directly to the districts of members of Congress. They often are payoffs, intended to persuade a member of Congress to vote for an entire appropriations bill.

Barely recognizable as congressional pork, it often takes a gimlet eye to figure out the winning earmarks, be they $25,000 for a mariachi band in Las Vegas; $188,000 for a Lobster Institute in Maine; or $3 million for The First Tee, a program that encourages young people to take up golf. Or a $10 million highway. Very often, these bills are not even voted on, but inserted by staffers after the members have left. Some projects aren't even wanted by the voters! Ironically, some of the most vociferous voices in Congress *against* earmarks are still heard arguing *for* projects in (where else?) their own states and districts.[19]

Even though earmarks have finally been "discovered" by scholars and journalists who have written hundreds of critical articles about them, the practice has survived the attacks and continues, more pervasive than ever. "Virtually every appropriation is earmarked ... [including] research projects, demonstration projects, parks, laboratories, academic grants, and contracts in ... congressional districts or states for certain specified universities or other organizations.[20] In fact, the Congressional Research Service estimates that earmarks have more than doubled since 1994.[21] Earmarks increase every year, soaring 29 percent from 2007 to 2008; or in real money, from $7.7 billion to $9.9 billion, according to Taxpayers for Common Sense, a nonpartisan group that tracks pork barrel spending.[22] Another group, The Citizens Against Government Waste, publishes a book each year called *The 2008 Congressional Pig Book Summary* ("The Book Washington Doesn't Want You to Read"), which tracks hundreds of earmarked projects that quietly attach themselves to spending bills. Their sponsors staunchly defend them, arguing that earmarks produce jobs and spur industrial development in their districts and states. And despite all the criticism and bad press, Americans remain grateful for such "constituent" service, and corporations show their gratitude in the form of campaign contributions.[23] In his 2010 State of the Union address, President Barack Obama called on Republican and Democratic members of Congress to continue their efforts to trim spending by reducing their earmark requests. His solution: not to eliminate earmarks, but to publish all earmark requests on one single website in the hopes that transparency will inhibit irresponsible spending. Obama nevertheless approved earmarks in the stimulus package and healthcare reform bills.

Eager to protect the Democratic freshmen who gave the party a majority in 2006, Democratic leaders showered them with earmarks. A study of the 2007 spending package showed that Democrats gave freshmen lawmakers in politically tough districts pet projects they could boast about to voters. Topping the list were freshmen Representative Phil Hare of Illinois, who received $92 million in earmarks; Representative John Sarbanes of Maryland, $71 million; and Representative Keith Ellison of Minnesota, $69.9 million.[24]

As the late Senator Everett M. Dirksen (R-Illinois), longtime minority leader, once complained in his gravelly voice, "A billion here and a billion there, and pretty soon you're talking real money." The Congressional Research Service calculated the cost of earmarks far higher than previous estimates. Fiscal year 2006 stands out as the "pinnacle of the earmarking frenzy," with members submitting more than 33,000 project requests to the House Appropriations Committee. 10,000 were funded, totaling $29 billion, with half the cost attributed to defense projects.[25]

Lobbyists and Earmarks

Washington insiders credit Gerald S. J. Cassidy, a successful lobbyist and founder of Cassidy & Associates, with the invention of modern earmarks. A former Hill staffer, Cassidy's method begins by identifying the goals of the group seeking his help, followed by a "resource inventory" of the group. Who were the members of the group? Were there members of the board of directors who had links to members of Congress? Friendships? Campaign contributors? What local leaders were involved in projects supported by the group? No stone was left unturned, and if Cassidy and company didn't succeed at first, the firm kept on trying. Boston University benefited from $106.1 million in earmarks through its efforts, whose services did not come cheap: The firm's fee totaled $15 million. Hahnemann Hospital in Philadelphia got a $15 million earmark to build an ambulatory care research and teaching center, thanks to the firm's successful orchestration of a meeting between three senators crucial to the project: Senator Arlen Specter, then a Republican from Pennsylvania (he switched parties in 2009 and became a Democrat), the project's "champion"; Senator Bennett Johnston (D-Louisiana), then chairman of the Appropriations Committee; and Senator Mark Hatfield (D-Oregon), its ranking member.[26]

Lobbyists and members of Congress often become tied to each other through relationships based on mutual favors. These ties have become much stronger in recent years as election "reform" necessitates more and more fundraising interdependence. For example, limits on campaign contributions give Political Action Committees (PACs) attached to labor unions, corporations, law firms, and all sorts of interest groups a key role as they "bundle" small contributions into the large sums needed to win elections. Members of Congress understand that it is in their interest to vote the way the PAC wants them to vote; after all, it stands to reason that PACs tend to contribute to lawmakers who support their causes. In addition to expecting their cooperation on key votes, many groups claim they can press their "friends" in Congress into service as quasi-lobbyists. What better intelligence network than members of Congress conveying the intentions of their fellow lawmakers? It works to everyone's benefit: Lawmakers lobby their wavering colleagues; committee chairs, also anxious to please, can postpone a vote or hasten hearings on crucial bills. In return, interest groups can offer their own kinds of help: In addition to campaign contributions, they can also supply mailing lists, advice, and campaign workers.

The advent of the Obama administration signaled an effort to end the kind of lobbying Cassidy and his firm had perfected. In early 2009, President Obama issued an executive order barring appointments to public office of anyone who had previously lobbied the government. Although no one knows exactly how this will affect future congressional and executive policymaking, most specifically, the role of earmarks in the budget process, early exemptions led to sighs of relief on K Street. Three waivers were granted almost immediately for presidential appointees: one for a lobbyist from Raytheon to be Deputy Secretary of Defense, and two others for high-level White House aides. The waivers also presaged future difficulties with eliminating both earmarks and lobbyists: Both have become too ingrained in the system to disappear.

Committee Leadership and Earmarks

The chairs of the Appropriations Committees in both the House and Senate get the biggest slabs of congressional pork and collect IOUs from junior members by pushing for the projects that will help reelect these relative neophytes. In 2008, a total of $173,200,000 (in the Senate) was earmarked for twenty-five projects sponsored by Senator Daniel Inouye (D-Hawaii), chairman of the Defense Appropriations Subcommittee; while $144,624,000 was earmarked for twenty-six projects sponsored by Senator Robert Byrd, (D-West Virginia), chairman of the Appropriations Committee. Fortunately, there were plenty of earmarks left for the committee's Republicans, including $165 million for twenty-two projects sponsored by Senator Ted Stevens of Alaska, the committee's ranking Republican and former Chairman of the Appropriations Committee; Stevens also sponsored Alaska's infamous $433 million "Bridge to Nowhere" earmark.

The project actually involved two bridges, which would have connected two remote islands with Alaska's mainland. The project was eventually abandoned but became a symbol of congressional pork, as well as a striking example of the "earmark" power of an entrenched chairman. The brainchild of Senator Ted Stevens and initially supported by Alaska governor and 2008 GOP vice presidential candidate Sarah Palin, the earmark's two bridges would have benefited only a few hundred people who risked life and limb crossing to the mainland over icy waters by boat. But at what cost? Estimates ranged around the $433 million mark, not factoring in cost overruns, weather problems, and a host of other factors that threatened to increase the final cost. The project was abandoned in 2005, although the incident propelled earmarks into the political debate. The outcry continued, adding to the political troubles of Senator Stevens, who later came under federal investigation on corruption charges unrelated to the ill-fated bridges. His conviction on those charges was later dropped in 2009 by Eric Holder, in one of his first acts as attorney general, on the grounds of prosecutorial misconduct.

Subcommittee members can also benefit from earmark largesse. Ironically, party affiliation often doesn't seem to matter. Representative Bill Young (R-Florida), the term-limited former Chairman of the Appropriations Committee who then became a member of the Defense Appropriations Subcommittee, walked off with almost $93 million for forty-seven projects in 2008, including money for advanced optics, water harvesting, and battery technology. Agriculture earmarks in other congressional districts subsidized grape and wine research, a wildlife habitat project, wood utilization, and agritourism (where tourists visit farms). Energy and water projects included oyster "revitalization" in the Delaware Bay, production of metallic glass, sediment management, and "advanced green design." Earmarks run the gamut, and all of them seem worthy, particularly to their beneficiaries. Nevertheless, some questions still lurk about the use of taxpayer dollars for "renovations to ... a nine-hole public golf course" or construction of a "National Mule and Packers Museum."[27]

Indefensible Defense

By far the most lucrative favors offered by Congress still go to the defense industry. On the House side, $121,400,000 was earmarked for forty-four projects sponsored by the late Representative John Murtha (D-Pennsylvania) chairman of the Defense Appropriations Subcommittee, who was well-known among his friends, colleagues, and enemies as the "King of Pork." *Roll Call,* a Capitol Hill newspaper, noted that "Every private entity that received a special project from the Pennsylvania Democrat in last year's defense spending bill had given him political money at some point since 2005."[28] When Representative Mike Rogers (R-Michigan) moved to exclude $23 million for the National Drug Intelligence Center, an infuriated Murtha warned, "I hope you don't have any earmarks in the defense appropriations bill because they are gone and you will not get any earmarks now and forever ... That's the way I do it."[29] Many of these contracts weren't even "sought by the military or federal agencies they were intended to benefit."[30]

Defense earmarks were only part of the earmarks sponsored by Murtha, who steered a total of $192.5 million to his district, much of it for the rebuilding of Johnstown, a city famous for its flood in the late nineteenth century.[31] On the

Republican side, Representative Jerry Lewis (R-California) sponsored 32 projects worth $86 million.

Reciprocating, the Pentagon gave committee chairs and other high-ranking members of the congressional establishment a variety of rewards. For years, critics joked that the city of Charleston, South Carolina, was sinking from all the defense installations that the late L. Mendel Rivers, chairman of the powerful House Armed Services Committee, was able to procure for his district. Experienced Capitol Hill hands recalled that the Army didn't even have to go through the charade of a site selection because the Corps of Engineers began its searches in South Carolina![32]

Some of those rewards are passé in today's political environment. For example, faced with budget woes and the pressure to close bases, the armed services no longer reward powerful committee chairs by planting army bases in their districts. Quite the opposite: Fearful of voter retribution, Congress passed the buck to a commission, known as the Base Closing and Realignment Commission (BRAC), to make the hard political choices required for base closings. But closing military bases around the country doesn't mean the army still doesn't have lots of rewards to give out. How about an $11 million small-arms range in Connecticut, thanks to the efforts of Connecticut's two senators, Joseph Lieberman, an Independent, and Christopher J. Dodd, a Democrat. Or $98 million for the defense firm Northrop Grumman to develop an aircraft sensor suite; or $497 million to a consortium of defense firms, United Technologies, Lockheed Martin, and Pratt & Whitney, for "advanced procurement or line close down costs." Appropriately, the defense firms also relied on a consortium of senators, both Republican and Democrat, who lobbied together for the earmarked appropriation.[33]

Added to military patronage are the administrative costs, an obscure and generally ignored outcome of defense earmarks. Added up, these total the "costs and demands placed on executive branch agencies that are required to manage these congressional mandated projects ... [including] political, budgetary and programmatic demands on the agency."[34]

Nor are all defense earmarks linked to national security. In 2008, Representative Anthony Weiner, a New York Democrat, obtained $4.8 million for the Jamaica Bay Unit of the Gateway National Recreation Area, which describes itself as "a wealth of history, nature and recreation, from New York City's first major airport and coastal fortifications to a wildlife refuge and pristine beaches." The same 2008 Defense Appropriations bill also contained $3 million for The First Tee, secured by House Majority Whip James Clyburn of South Carolina. The purpose of The First Tee, according to its website, is "To impact the lives of young people by providing learning facilities and educational programs that promote character development and life-enhancing values through the game of golf."[35]

Midnight Maneuvers

Some earmarks are requested by only one chamber of Congress; others are not specifically authorized, are not competitively awarded, and—like Representative Murtha's airport—serve only a local or special interest. Others are inserted or altered in appropriations bills by Hill staffers in the wee hours of the morning. The Senate asked the Justice Department for a criminal investigation of a $10 million earmark, whose provisions were mysteriously altered after Congress gave final approval to a highway funding bill.

Aides to Representative Don Young, Alaska Republican and former chairman of the House Transportation and Infrastructure Committee, acknowledged that they had "corrected" the earmark just before it went to the White House for President George W. Bush's signature. The money was targeted to a proposed highway interchange project on I-95 near Naples, Florida—which couldn't be farther from Young's Alaska district. Young's critics suggested that the motive came from campaign contributions from real estate developers who owned 4,000 acres of land near the proposed interchange, which would enhance the value of their property.[36]

Presidential Favors

One needn't be in Congress to promote earmarks. Savvy presidents use earmarks all the time to influence both recalcitrant and cooperative lawmakers. President Clinton's congressional liaison aide, Howard Paster, complained that "[W]ith every good intention, at the end of the day you can't accommodate all the requests that you get." But presidents use everything in their power: "federal and judicial positions ... location of government installations, campaign support ... plane rides on Air Force One, White House access for important constituents." It all allows presidents to "amass political IOUs they can cash in later."[37]

President Carter's ignorance of the care and feeding of lawmakers began early: His aides couldn't find sufficient seats at the inauguration for Speaker O'Neill's guests. This snub, attributed to Hamilton Jordan, Carter's chief of staff, presaged a lengthy struggle between the Democratic leadership in the House and the White House, and to the appellation of "Hannibal Jerkin," the name chosen by O'Neill to refer to Jordan. President Carter thought he could treat the Congress with the indifference with which he treated the Georgia legislature. O'Neill constantly reminded him that many of those members had carried districts that Carter had lost in the general election. They owed little to Carter and were not about to rubber stamp his proposals.

President George W. Bush quickly succumbed to the traditions of congressional patronage. Although he had publicly assailed earmarks, he submitted hundreds of millions of dollars in earmarks in his 2008 budget request, including $330 million to research and eradicate plant pests like the "sirex woodwasp." But reality trumps rhetoric every time, with the Bush White House rationalizing its actions by defining earmarks as "funds provided by Congress for projects or programs where the congressional direction ... circumvents the merit-based ... allocation process."[38]

For the first time in history, earmarks became a campaign issue during the endless presidential primary season of 2007–2008. The leading candidates swore to eliminate them, but intense media scrutiny revealed that they all participated in earmarks as eagerly as their fellow politicians. Indeed, the primaries showed once again just how hard it is to run for the presidency from Congress, where every comment is on the record, every earmark unmasked, and every vote tallied for posterity. It is really an impossible challenge for candidates: to reconcile the parochial interests that got them elected with the overarching needs of the country.

The presumptive nominees soon realized that their newfound celebrity didn't vaccinate them against harsh scrutiny. Even Barack Obama, as idealistic a politician as has ever graced Washington, yielded to political and financial pressure. As a senator, Obama supported members of a local community in his state protesting a nuclear facility, owned by the Exelon Corporation, that, argued some of the residents, produced dangerous and unreported radioactive leaks. Obama then changed his mind, supported the facility, and received large campaign contributions from the plant's executives. Initially, Obama had sponsored legislation that would have increased nuclear safety for all plants around the country, but ended up virtually on the opposite side of the fence. The revised bill was watered down: It removed language that would have mandated prompt reporting and simply offered guidance to regulators, whom it charged with addressing the issue of unreported leaks. The bill ultimately died in the full Senate. Since 2003, executives and employees of Exelon, which is based in Illinois, have contributed at least $227,000 to Obama's campaigns for the Senate and for president. Two top Exelon officials, Frank M. Clark, executive vice president, and John W. Rogers, Jr., a director, were among Obama's largest fundraisers.[39]

Similarly, Senator John McCain of Arizona, Obama's Republican rival for the presidency, also pledged an end to the special interests that beset the nation's capital, but he, too, seemed to favor wealthy contributors. Known as an "independent" and a "maverick,"[40] McCain made an exception and argued on behalf of Donald R. Diamond, a wealthy Arizona real estate developer and major campaign contributor. When Diamond wanted to snap up a stretch of virgin California coast freed by the closing of Fort Ord, an army base, McCain assigned an aide who set up a meeting for Diamond at the Pentagon. McCain later stepped in to help speed up the sale. The senator also sponsored two bills in 1991 and 1994, authorizing Diamond to swap land that he owned for thousands of acres of public land that he developed at considerable profit. McCain received $250,000 in campaign contributions raised by Diamond. McCain was one of the Keating Five in the 1980s, charged with intervening with a regulatory agency on behalf of S&L tycoon Charles Keating in the 1980s. The Ethics Committee in the Senate reprimanded him for using poor judgment.[41]

Even though McCain was criticized for supporting the sale of national park-land in his state to private developers who happened to be political allies, he stood by his disdain for earmarks and refused to request any for his state in 2008. Not so one of the leading Democratic contenders for the presidency: Senator Hillary Clinton (D-New York), who was able to get $342 million in earmarks for her state in 2007, nearly four times the total of her rival, Barack Obama.[42]

Also on the 2008 presidential campaign trail, Republican vice presidential candidate and former Governor of Alaska Sarah Palin boasted about her opposition to earmarks, yet records revealed that she was an aggressive and successful advocate for her own state and city. As governor, she proposed thirty-one earmarks for Alaska in 2008, including a grant for $496,900 to study halibut harvesting, for a grand total of $197 million. Because she had requested $254 million in earmarks in 2007, she boasted the year after that she had slashed her requests. As mayor of Wasilla, she hired a Washington lobbyist, Steven Silver (a former aide to Republican Senator Ted Stevens, then chairman of the Senate Appropriations Committee), for the express purpose of attracting earmarks for her city when they had an "important federal purpose and strong citizen support." Halibut harvesting?[43]

McCain's later protestations that he did for Diamond only what he would do for any other Arizona resident recalled an old earmark story told by another Arizona politician, the late Representative Moe Udall, a Democrat. Udall reminisced about facing a wildly enthusiastic audience on an Indian reservation in his Arizona district as he unveiled a string of promises. "I'm going to bring new roads in here," he promised. "Goomwah!" cheered the crowd. "And a hospital," he added. "Goomwah!" they yelled. Carried away, Udall went on to promise new schools, dams, jobs, and projects galore. "Goomwah! Goomwah! Goomwah!" came the waves of cheers. When he finally sat down to a thundering round of applause, he fondly gazed out over a sea of voters he knew he could count on. After the speech, the Chief invited him to his tepee so that he could properly offer him the tribe's gift of a pinto pony, which stood patiently outside the tent. As they approached the tepee, the Chief warned Udall, "Be careful not to step in the goomwah."[44]

In Defense of Earmarks

The most important impact of earmarks is that they pave the way for bigger prizes. Steve Bell, chief of staff to Senator Pete Domenici (R-New Mexico), chairman of the Budget Committee, once overheard his boss rebuking a colleague after hearing him attacking the practice of earmarks. "You're not really [a fiscal conservative]," said Domenici. "because if you were, you wouldn't worry about a million here and a million there. You'd be worried about Social Security and the big entitlements." In other words, earmarks merely pave the way for bigger, multibillion-dollar programs by enlisting the cooperation of critical legislators for programs that really matter to national leaders.[45] Also, although earmarks are a favorite target of reformers, they comprise a miniscule percentage of the federal budget. Recent estimates calculate that earmarks comprise less than 1 percent of the federal budget; some estimates say they range from 1 to 2 percent. But earmarks provide a handy target, primarily because they are so easy to understand. At the same time, even 1 percent of the federal budget amounts to $38 billion.

In defense of earmarks, members of Congress also argue that earmarks can have a positive effect, particularly when they are in conflict with the president's priorities. An earmark sponsored by a Republican, Frank Wolf of Virginia, financed the Iraq Study Group, which held Bush and the Iraqi government accountable for the war in Iraq. "In my own district," wrote Rahm Emanuel (D-Illinois) in defense of earmarks, "I obtained an earmark to rebuild a bridge that not only was rated as deficient but also was identified by the Department of Homeland Security as a major evacuation route in case of a terrorist attack on Chicago. Other earmarks I've championed include money for after-school programs, computers for police patrol cars, master teacher training programs and a children's hospital facility."[46]

Years before the gene that was responsible for cystic fibrosis was discovered in 1988, the Government Affairs Committee of the Cystic Fibrosis Foundation lobbied the Congress. Through the offices of Representative Silvio Conte (R-Massachusetts), an earmark in that year's appropriations bill allotted $6 million dollars for CF research.[47] Today, researchers can count on annual appropriations in excess of $80 million, thanks to steady increases in funding each fiscal year. No money changed hands, no contributions were involved, and the victims of this dreaded disease greatly benefited from research that led to the discovery of the CF gene, as well as to improved medical treatment.

"Either we do it, or the bureaucrats downtown do it," wrote Senator Mark Andrews (R-North Dakota) justifying earmarks in general—and specifically an $18 million bridge in his home state. Earmarks, he added, "have been done for years, long before I came to this body and I think it is a preferable way to do it."[48]

Also, in their defense, Representative Barney Frank (D-Massachusetts) argued that earmarks were the price of democracy: "If you don't want politics in this process, you probably shouldn't be handing it over to 535 politicians. That's democracy." Frank noted that public perceptions played a role in the fate of legislation. "On Monday, the politically expedient vote was to vote no. By Friday, it wasn't clear what the politically expedient thing was to do."[49]

"A Billion Here and a Billion There . . . "

Earmarks took front row center in the landmark $700 billion bailout bill that passed the House of Representatives on October 3, 2008, having failed five days before by a vote of 228–205. No less than $107 billion in tax breaks ($149 over ten years) managed to "convince" some recalcitrant legislators to switch their votes, and the bill finally passed 263–171. In the 2009 bailout bill Democratic senators were always on board, but many of the "incentives" helped them as well. The Obama administration sought to make the bailout a bipartisan bill, but no Republicans voted for it in the House. Senator Arlen Specter, a Pennsylvania Republican who switched parties and became a Democrat shortly thereafter, insisted on a $10 billion increase in the National Institutes of Health budget as the price of his vote. He got it. Fellow Republicans Olympia Snowe and Susan Collins, both of Maine, also supported the bill. Just as the bailout bill changed its name to a "rescue package," similar euphemisms labeled earmarks "sweeteners," "tax incentives," "rebates," and "credits."

But make no mistake, those "euphemisms" were more powerful than Treasury Secretary Henry Paulson's pleadings and stronger than other "good of the country" arguments in terms of changing votes. They included such items as tax breaks for NASCAR, the organization in control of auto racing; manufacturers of wooden arrows for children; rum manufacturers in Puerto Rico and the Virgin Islands; and producers of renewable energy sources.[50]

A Patronage Puzzle

One of the more controversial earmarks set aside $1.95 million secured by Representative Charles Rangel, a nineteen-term New York Democrat who chairs the Ways and Means Committee. The money was destined to fund a library and archives at the Charles B. Rangel Center for Public Service at the City College of New York. The project was challenged on the House floor on July 19, 2007 by second-term Representative, John Campbell (R-California), who said, "You don't agree with me or see any problem with us, as members, sending taxpayer funds in the creation of things named after ourselves while we're still here?" Rangel responded, "I would have a problem if *you* did it, because I don't think *you've* been around long enough" ... to "inspire a building" or a "school."

Rangel's fundraising for the Rangel Center included obtaining a $5 million pledge from a foundation controlled by Maurice R. Greenberg, former chief executive of American International Group (AIG), the insurance giant. Defending his use of congressional stationery to solicit the pledge, Rangel said, "I can't think of one piece of legislation that impacts them, and there has never been a time that they've raised any legislation to me." He told the House Ethics Committee, "So far as I am aware, none of those whom I wrote had any pending requests into my office, lobbied me regarding any legislation before my committee, or asked me for assistance on legislation in which they had a special interest." But a company spokesman said that less than a month after Rangel met with AIG officials, the company urged his support for a provision of a tax bill that would save AIG millions of dollars per year. Rangel, who had initially opposed the tax change, ultimately allowed it to be added to a bill he sponsored. He said that he had made this decision before soliciting the pledge.[51] In September 2008, the company received an $85 billion federal bailout to stave off impending bankruptcy.

Rangel's intervention with AIG was not an isolated incident. Congressional records showed that in 2007 Rangel was instrumental in preserving a lucrative tax loophole that benefited an oil-drilling company, while at the same time its chief executive had pledged $1 million to the Charles B. Rangel School of Public Service at CCNY.[52] The company, Nabors Industries, was one of four corporations based in the United States that were widely criticized for opening offices in the Caribbean to reduce their tax payments. Rangel initially opposed those offshore moves and pushed successfully for legislation to make the companies pay more taxes. But in 2007, he fought to protect them, and the tax shelter was preserved. Rangel insisted that the pledge from Nabors's chief executive, Eugene M. Isenberg, played no role in his decision. House ethics rules forbid members of Congress from asking for anything of value from a person or company with business before them.

The Senator from Wall Street

Senator Charles Schumer (D-New York) had a great afternoon job when he was a student at James Madison High School in the Flatbush section of Brooklyn. He assisted a teacher who gave tutorials on the SAT exams needed for college admission. All year long, he mimeographed the questions and answers of previous tests. When the time came for him to take his own SAT examination, he got a perfect score, graduated first in his class, and won admission to Harvard. Oh yes, the teacher was Stanley Kaplan, who went on to start a famous and lucrative SAT prep program.

Smart, hardworking, and strategic, Schumer was elected to the House in 1980 and to the Senate in 1998. He has won perfect voting scores from liberal organizations including the Americans for Democratic Action. It is, therefore, all the more remarkable that he has become Wall Street's major champion in Congress. Wall Street has rewarded him with millions of dollars in contributions for the Democratic Senatorial Campaign Committee, the fundraising arm of the Democratic Party that he chaired. Schumer raised a total of $240 million from 2004–2008 and increased Wall Street donations by 50 percent. In this role, Schumer is following the example of the late Senator Jacob K. Javits (R-New York), who also protected Wall Street's interests. After all, Wall Street is to New York what motion pictures are to California—a major industry. And senators across the nation usually protect major industries in their states.

Schumer, a member of the Finance Committee, repeatedly took steps to protect Wall Street from government oversight and tougher rules, and saved financial institutions billions of dollars in higher taxes or fees. He succeeded in limiting efforts to regulate credit-rating agencies, sponsored legislation that cut fees paid by Wall Street firms to finance government oversight, pushed to allow banks to have lower capital reserves, and called for the revision of regulations to make corporations' balance sheets more transparent. "Since the financial meltdown [in 2008 to 2009], people have been asking, 'Where was Congress? Why didn't they see this coming? Why didn't they provide better oversight?'" said Barbara Roper, director of investor protection for the Consumer Federation of America. "And the answer for some, including Senator Schumer, is that they were actually too busy pursuing a deregulatory agenda. Their focus was on how we have to lighten up regulation on Wall Street."[53]

This has translated into more campaign contributions to Senator Schumer from the securities and investment industry than to any other member of Congress except Senator John F. Kerry (D-Massachusetts). Contributors include Jamie Dimon, chief executive of JPMorgan Chase; John Mack, chief executive at Morgan Stanley; and Charles O. Prince III, the former chief executive of Citigroup. Schumer's pitch is unusually aggressive. He presses for the maximum contribution. "I need you to max out," he says; then follows up by asking that a donor's spouse and four or five friends write checks, too.[54]

When Christopher Cox, the Republican Chairman of the Securities and Exchange Commission (SEC), grew concerned over the lack of oversight of the nation's largest credit-rating agencies—Standard & Poor's and Moody's Investors Service—he asked Congress to give his agency oversight powers. Schumer couldn't stop the legislation from passing, but he managed to get the measure watered down. The amended bill explicitly prohibited the SEC from regulating the procedures and methods the agencies use to determine ratings. Although the ratings agencies were not significant campaign donors to Mr. Schumer or the Democratic campaign committee, their lobbyists and many of their clients were.

What's the difference between Schumer's and Rangel's approaches? Rangel worked for legislation that benefited individual companies, while Schumer worked to benefit an entire industry. Which approach occupies the higher moral ground? Which has done more damage to the nation?

The Polls and the Pols

The wide dichotomy in the polls between the below-sea-level rating the public gives Congress and the high esteem (and ratings) that the American public accords individual representatives has puzzled many congressional experts. Why do the American people hate the institution but love the people whom they send there? What they see relates strongly to congressional patronage: Although voters are often critical of the actions of Congress, they remain grateful to the member of Congress who has bettered their lives—with jobs that are attached to airports, profits that derive from lucrative contracts, and all sorts of other benefits that fall under the vast rubric of congressional favors.

According to the Gallup Poll, congressional ratings have steadily declined, bottoming out in 2008 with figures showing that 75 percent of the American public disapproved of Congress as an institution. When professions are scaled in surveys, Congress usually ranks at the bottom—even below funeral directors and the media. The figure continues to go down, and at last count Gallup found Congress the lowest of the sixteen institutions tested, with only 12 percent of the American people expressing confidence in Congress, the lowest percentage Gallup has measured for any institution in thirty-five years.[55]

Immediately after the 9/11 crisis in 2002, the opposite was recorded by Gallup: 84 percent of the public approved of Congress! But that was an aberrant period; even President George W. Bush drew an approval rating of more than 90 percent. Most surveys of Congress taken over the last thirty-five years have hovered in the 20–43 percent range.

But the overwhelming majority of Senators and Representatives are untouched by voter wrath; quite the contrary, voters routinely reelect their congressmen. In fact, in some years more congressmen were indicted than defeated at the polls! In a study for the Pew Center for the People and the Press taken in February 2007, more than 60 percent of the respondents told pollsters that their representatives should be reelected. These findings are borne out every two years in congressional elections, where more than 92 percent of the Congress is reelected, often including those darkened by ethical clouds. But in the 2010 midterm elections, members of Congress quaked before mounting voter resentment against Washington.

The stark contrast between these two types of surveys—the individual versus the institution—becomes clear when viewing the day-to-day job of the individual member of Congress and the reality of issue politics. Former Senator Frank Church (D-Idaho) provided a good example. Evidently, Idaho voters considered the senator too liberal for the state. But Church's constituent service was superb: He called grandmothers on their birthdays, never neglected the needs of small towns, and was instrumental in obtaining job-creating public projects for his state. But the argument is still compelling. Who is better at identifying the needs of a district than its representative in Congress? And in the long run, what is the difference between an "earmark" and "constituent service?"

Life After Congress: The Nine Lives of Patronage

In the absence of strong and enforceable ethics laws, public officials go back and forth between government and the private sector; wherever they are, they are invariably guaranteed easy access to their former employers. Former legislators can not only walk the corridors of the Rayburn Building for eternity, they also enjoy lifetime privileges on the floors of both chambers of Congress. This makes them well worth the enormous salaries they are able to attract from their new bosses when they leave the legislative branch for their new lives as lobbyists for interest groups, law firms, industries, and associations. It also calls into question the favors that members of Congress dole out to groups when it appears that they are feathering their nests for their future "retirement" jobs.

When a Japanese civil servant leaves public service, it is called a "descent from heaven." Life after public service in the United States—with its lucrative options—is exactly the opposite. In recent years, the "revolving door" has become more partisan, and more blatant than ever, affecting job appointments from both sides of the aisle. When the Republicans took control of Congress in 1994 after forty years in the political wilderness, the infamous "K Street Project" that so infuriated Jack Valenti was launched. When the Democrats gained control of Congress, they followed suit.

As in the statehouses, many former members of Congress become lobbyists, using their contacts and knowledge of the machinery of government to benefit their new bosses. Although they cannot lobby their former colleagues for one year, they spend the interim "advising" their new employers on various strategies. They also serve as major fundraisers for congressional campaigns.

The problem of how members of Congress vote if they have their eyes on post-congressional employment also arises. Are they doing favors for companies on the assumption they will join those companies in "retirement?" What does "retirement" mean for a member of Congress or for staffers? Does the public retire a member by electing his opponent? Or do members and their staffs leave because they can get more lucrative jobs in the private sector?

Former Senate Majority Leader Tom Daschle (D-South Dakota) was hardly the first person to turn public service into private riches. His post-Senate career came to light during the 2009 nominations process, which is always useful for the revelations about how Washington's elites live. After he was defeated for reelection, Daschle made $5 million over a two-year period as a legislative "consultant." But it was his failure to pay taxes on $225,000 in income derived from a car and chauffeur that cost him the post of Secretary of Health and Human Services, to which he'd been nominated by President Barack Obama. What did his benefactor, Leo Hindery Jr., get for his money? His firm, Global Crossing, sought regulatory approval to build undersea cables to Japan, but had run into opposition from three rival firms. "Out of nowhere, Global Crossing emerged as a political powerhouse in Washington, thanks to a multi-million dollar lobbying effort and $2 million" in contributions by the company, Hindery, and two other top executives, according to a brief filed by the Center for Responsive Politics.[56]

Other former lawmakers who recently became well-heeled lobbyists include former Senators Trent Lott of Mississippi, who was the Republican leader, and John Breaux, a Louisiana Democrat. They formed their own bipartisan lobbying firm, the Breaux-Lott Leadership Group. Former Representative Billy Tauzin (R-Louisiana), who chaired the Energy and Commerce Committee, which had oversight over the pharmaceutical industry, retired to become that industry's chief lobbyist, with a pay package worth more than $2 million per year.

Former Senator Robert Torricelli (D-New Jersey) presents an intriguing picture of what a Senator-turned-lobbyist can do and how a lawmaker can prosper in the congressional hereafter. Torricelli abruptly quit his 2002 reelection campaign after being reprimanded by the Senate Ethics Committee for ethical misconduct. Two months later he became a lobbyist. During his reelection campaign he had collected $2.9 million from thousands of people, who might be surprised at how he spent a portion of the money. Forced from office in 2002, Torricelli found himself under a cloud following allegations that he had received gifts and cash from David Chang, a businessman from New Jersey who was also a major donor to the Democratic Party.[57] His gifts to Torricelli included cash, antiques, a Rolex watch, Italian-tailored suits, and an antique clock that was supposedly destined for Torricelli's ex-wife. After Torricelli's resignation, Chang went to prison and the scandal died down. Torricelli was reprimanded by the Senate Ethics Committee, and the Justice Department declined to prosecute, most likely in exchange for Torricelli's agreement not to run for public office.

Torricelli also had previously tangled with the Ethics Committee. When he was a member of the House Intelligence Committee, he fought for the right of one of his constituents, Jennifer Harbury, to inquire into the U.S. government's role in the assassination of her husband in Guatemala. Torricelli protested the involvement of the Central Intelligence Agency in training Guatemalan troops responsible for the murder of Harbury's husband, as well as the murder of an innkeeper also affiliated with the political opposition. Members of the House Intelligence Committee protested what they alleged was Torricelli's unauthorized use of classified material. Torricelli was ultimately exonerated by the House Ethics Committee, which declined to investigate further, but he received extensive publicity for his efforts, paving the way for his later run for the Senate.[58]

Fast forward five years, and to no one's surprise, Torricelli landed solidly on his well-shod feet. Guaranteed lifetime privileges on the House and Senate floors, Torricelli has become a well-paid lobbyist and political contributor. Still flush with the donations he collected during his years in Congress, Torricelli now doles out very generous contributions to political candidates who in turn serve his clients after they are elected. Sensitive to the realities of the federal system, he contributes to campaigns on the state, local, and federal levels: $10,000 to the mayor of Trenton and his candidates for city council; $10,000 to [former] Governor Rod Blagojevich of Illinois; and $4,000 to the nonvoting member of Congress from Puerto Rico. In turn, his candidates have afforded him access and influence. He has already spent about $900,000, leaving more than $2 million for a rainy day.[59]

Torricelli's lobbying enterprise, Rosemont Associates, now boasts clients that include the government of Taiwan and Cablevision. Much of the campaign money went to charities and nonprofit organizations like hospitals. But Torricelli also donated at least $65,000 to politicians and their organizations who had influence over his or his clients' business interests. This included more than $40,000 to Nevada Democratic Party organizations and candidates linked to the Senate majority leader, Harry Reid. Senator Reid arranged meetings for Torricelli with Taiwan's representative in the U.S. to discuss Taiwan's opposition to a new Chinese law that authorized the use of force if Taiwan declared independence. When governor, Rod Blagojevich placed Torricelli on the Illinois State Teachers Retirement System's list of preferred outside attorneys.[60]

Lobbying firms also follow the election results closely. When the Democrats became the majority party in 2006, Representative Rahm Emanuel and Senator "Chuck" Schumer, head of the House and Senate Democratic Campaign Committees, respectively, used some of the same strong-arm tactics they once deplored. "I've never felt the squeeze that we're under right now to give to Democrats and to hire them," said a telecom industry executive. "They've put out the word that if you have an issue on trade, taxes or regulation, you'd better be a donor and you'd better not be part of any effort to run ads against our freshmen incumbents."[61]

A year later, after Democrats won the White House and widened their congressional majorities, many Republican lobbyists found themselves out on the street. Richard Hunt, a top Republican lobbyist for the securities industry, was among the first to go, just a week after the election. Marc Racicot, president of the American Insurance Association, who had been governor of Montana and chairman of the Republican National Committee, resigned a few days later. So did Frank L. Bowman, a retired admiral and chief of the nuclear energy lobby, citing "this period of dramatic change in Congress and the White House."[62]

Because Democrats had more jobs to fill, in both the executive branch and in Congress, fewer lawmakers or their staffers were available for lobbying firms, setting off bidding wars. A Democratic staff director for an important House or Senate committee who may have earned $130,000 per year on Capitol Hill could now earn $500,000 to $800,000 per year on K Street. "There is a supply-and-demand issue with finding enough Democrats who have had senior-level positions," said Nels Olson of the recruiting firm Korn/Ferry International, adding, "It is certainly a difficult time for Republicans."[63]

To cope with such partisan contingencies, the Republican lobbying firm of Barbour, Griffith and Rogers decided to hire more Democrats and even held a fundraiser for Democratic Senator-Elect Mark Warner of Virginia. And on Election Day, they acquired the Democratic firm of Westin, Rinehart. "To go bipartisan, we rebranded the business," Ed Rogers said. "Lobbying is like a slow-motion jury trial. First you need to find out who the jury is ... So the more Democratic officeholders there are, the more you need effective, smart Democrats." Republican lobbyists' woes were exacerbated by the financial meltdown, which led lobbying firms to downsize.[64]

Twenty years ago, a witness testified before the Senate Commerce Committee on the revolving door in international trade policy.[65] At the time, the average stay of a public official negotiating trade agreements at the office of the U.S. Trade Representative or the State Department averaged eighteen months, after which time the employee was free to work for Fujitsu, Mitsubishi, Deutsche Bank, or any foreign company—including those they might have opposed on trade issues. At the time, no one seemed to care, especially because the inspector general of the State Department had pronounced the practice legal, clearing an employee who was headed for a cushy position with Fujitsu. Still, the witness testified against this practice on the grounds that no other industrialized country permitted its public employees such liberties, and in the long run this practice would hurt America's international competitiveness. But after the hearing, she was besieged by members of Congress and their staffers, protesting her testimony with arguments that focused on how restrictions of any kind would impede their efforts to get jobs when they left Capitol Hill and sought employment elsewhere.

The problem remains: How do members vote if they and their staffs are looking forward to post-congressional employment? Are they doing favors for companies on the assumption they will join those companies in "retirement?" Are they adding earmarks at midnight when no one is looking? What does "retirement" really mean for a member of Congress or for staffers?

Not everyone leaves Capitol Hill to make big bucks. From its ranks have come twenty-five of the nation's forty-four presidents and twenty-eight Supreme Court justices. President Barack Obama, a former Illinois senator, enlisted to serve in his administration Senators Hillary Clinton (D-New York) and Ken Salazar (D-Colorado), as well as Representatives Rahm Emanuel (D-Illinois), Leon Panetta (D-California), Ray LaHood (R-Illinois), and Hilda Solis (D-California). Many others become governors and big-city mayors, including New York mayors Edward Koch, John Lindsay, and Fiorello LaGuardia. Still others find other avenues for public service. Former Representative Lee Hamilton (D-Indiana), the director of the Woodrow Wilson International Center for Scholars, has been called upon to co-chair two congressional commissions: the 9/11 Commission and the Iraq Study Group. Former Representative John Brademas (D-Indiana) went on to become president of New York University, while former Senator Bob Kerrey (D-Nebraska) is president of the New School.

The same qualities of ambition, intellect, and street smarts that brought staffers to the Hill often translate into success in later life. Some go on to take their boss's place in Congress: Representative Ray LaHood (R-Illinois) was chief of staff to Representative Bob Michel (who himself took the seat of Representative Harold Velde, whom he had served as administrative assistant); Senator Roger Wicker succeeded his former boss, Trent Lott); and Representative Barbara Lee (D-California) succeeded Ron Dellums. Others who cut their political eyeteeth as Capitol Hill staffers include Speaker Nancy Pelosi (D-California) and House Majority Leader Steny Hoyer (D-Maryland), who both interned for Senator Daniel Brewster (D-Maryland).

Still other staffers become judges: Paul Michel, chief of staff to Senator Arlen Specter (R-Pennsylvania), is Chief Judge of the U.S. Court of Appeals for the Federal Circuit; Richard Eaton, former chief of staff to Senator Daniel P. Moynihan, is a judge on the U.S. Court of International Trade; while Robert Katzmann, another Moynihan protégé, is a judge on the U.S. Court of Appeals for the 2nd Circuit; as is Jon Newman, who was chief of staff to the late Senator Abraham Ribicoff. And some join the media: Chris Matthews was press secretary for Speaker O'Neill, while George Stephanopoulos had worked for Representative Richard Gephardt, as well as the Clinton White House.

Life after Congress can indeed be rewarding for both members and staffers, who use their congressional experience to advance their own careers. With their contacts and knowledge of how the institution works, they can be extremely valuable both in and out of government.

Democracy's Paradox

Citizens expect their representatives to fight the executive branch's intricate bureaucracy, get jobs for themselves or their relatives, attract companies to the region, ensure that they get a goodly proportion of earmarks in the federal budget, and keep looking for subsidies that might have proven elusive in the past. In fact, it is very hard to find an industry, profession, or group that does not receive federal subsidies either directly or indirectly. And even with the nation's current economic crisis, there is every expectation that these subsidies will increase. Most of these subsidies profess to be in the public's interests, but legislators rarely think of balancing the national interests against constituent interests, except in cases of national emergency. The average member of Congress usually spends his entire political life orbiting around the wheel of favors, negotiating with his constituents and his colleagues on the Hill for his share of the booty and comforting himself with the rationale that if he is really concerned about the public interest, he'll do everything in his power to remain in Congress.

But "pork" became a dirty word in some 2010 congressional elections. The angry Tea Party movement, alarmed by rising deficits, claimed the scalps of two congressional appropriators: Senator Robert Bennett of Utah, a longtime conservative, was defeated in the Republican primary; and Representative Alan Mollohan was defeated in the West Virginia Democratic primary. The Tea Party candidate, Rand Paul, defeated the establishment candidate, Trey Grayson, in the Kentucky Senate Republican primary. The voters opted for fiscal stability instead of projects in their districts.[66]

The fundamental question raised by America's two-constituency Congress is the degree to which the national interest suffers because of the needs of lawmakers to show their effectiveness to voters and contributors. To what extent are the lucrative military contracts necessary for national security? How about bridges to nowhere? Are billion-dollar highways critical to the future of transportation? To what extent were the Iraq, Afghanistan, and Vietnam wars extended because they provided contracts and jobs? And to what degree do soaring budgets reflect not the nation's needs, but congressional needs to bring home the bacon?

Chapter Five

Justice on eBay

"The Justice Department is probably the most political of all parts of the Federal government."

David Burnham, Associate Research Professor, Syracuse University, and Co-Director, Transactional Records Access Clearinghouse

From the Clubhouse to the Bench

Of all the discretionary powers of government, the administration of justice is the most coveted by politicians. Presidents, governors, and leaders of political machines not only select judges and prosecutors (either directly or indirectly, using the cover of judicial nominating panels, which they appoint and control) but also determine which cases will be brought and how vigorously they will be prosecuted. Despite some notable exceptions, most administrations vigorously prosecute officials of the other political party and drag their feet when confronted with misconduct by their political allies. By shaping the judiciary, they also determine the quality of decisions involving both civil and criminal law, where they also seek to help political allies, including major industries that contributed to their campaigns.

Presidents and governors traditionally select loyal supporters—many of them their campaign managers—as their attorneys general, to ward off the evil spirits and do their judicial bidding. President Kennedy's appointment of his brother Robert as attorney general, despite his lack of legal experience, was one of many examples showing how political leaders appoint prosecutors they can depend on. Robert Kennedy was also JFK's campaign manager.[1] Before the Watergate scandal dragged them both down, President Richard Nixon appointed his friend and campaign manager, John Mitchell, to the attorney general's post, and more recently, President George W. Bush selected Alberto Gonzalez, a longtime ally. Although attorneys general are supposed to represent the entire nation, Gonzalez saw his role as representing only the president, whom he steadfastly protected. Harry Daugherty was President Warren Harding's campaign manager, then attorney general; similarly, Herbert Brownell successfully managed Dwight D. Eisenhower's presidential campaign, after which he was appointed attorney general.

To his ultimate dismay, President Bill Clinton broke the rule, capitulating to his wife Hillary's demand that the cabinet reflect "EGG"—ethnicity, geography, and gender. Janet Reno was Clinton's third choice for attorney general: the first two nominees were also women, but intense scrutiny over immigration and Social Security tax problems for their household staff drew negative publicity and forced both of them out of the competition.

One little-known innovation in judicial patronage that emerged from the administration of George W. Bush involved the increased use of "deferred prosecution" and "nonprosecution" agreements in place of the previous practice of bringing criminal charges against corporate wrongdoers. Corporate malefactors were offered the choice of self-correction, and monitors were appointed to oversee their agreement to change their practices. Sound good? It was—at least to those top managers under fire. Instead of paying heavy fines and risking prison terms, corporate executives accused of wrongdoing eagerly agreed to the nonprosecution agreements, even though those agreements often required steep payments to corporate monitors. In keeping with the political necessity of punishing your enemies and rewarding your friends, it was not surprising that prosecutors—often with guidance from the White House—selected former colleagues as the monitors. In one case, John Ashcroft, President George W. Bush's first attorney general, was selected by Christopher J. Christie, the U.S. attorney for New Jersey, as a corporate monitor for a medical supply company. The job, assigned without competitive bidding, could pay Ashcroft's consulting firm up to $52 million. Of a group of 40 corporate monitors, 23 were former prosecutors, including two former U.S. attorneys. The remainder included several former judges and federally appointed commissioners.[2]

The discretionary features of the criminal justice system rose to new heights in the administration of President George W. Bush, as witness the unusual number of highly political appointments, selective prosecutions, and political control of U.S. attorneys across the nation. "Political considerations affected every facet of the department during the Bush years, from the summer intern hiring program to the dispensing of legal advice about detainee interrogations, according to reports by the inspector general and testimony from former Justice Department officials from both parties at congressional hearings."[3]

Although the appellate court eventually disagreed, the Bush administration was severely criticized for what was considered its blatantly political prosecution of former Alabama governor Don E. Siegelman, leader of the state's Democratic Party. Siegelman was prosecuted and convicted in 2006 (while governor) of taking $500,000 from Richard M. Scrushy, then chief executive of the HealthSouth Corporation, in exchange for appointing Mr. Scrushy to a seat on a state hospital licensing board. The money did not go to Siegelman, but rather was used to retire a debt that had been incurred by a Siegelman–supported campaign group advocating in favor of a state lottery. Siegelman's lawyers argued that Siegelman did not personally benefit from the contribution, nor was there any *quid pro quo* involved in the exchange. Scrushy, who was convicted along with Siegelman, had previously served on the board prior to his appointment by the governor.

Siegelman charged that the criminal charges were brought by Republicans in an effort to force him out of politics. That claim was bolstered by the sworn statement of Dana Jill Simpson, a Republican lawyer who had worked for the campaign of Bob Riley, Mr. Siegelman's Republican opponent. In her statement, Simpson swore that she had personal knowledge that Alabama Republicans talked during a conference call that year about using the Justice Department to "take care of" Siegelman. Simpson testified before the House Judiciary Committee that Rob Riley, the son of Alabama's Republican governor Bob Riley, told her that his father and Bill Canary, husband of Leura Canary, the U.S. attorney for Montgomery, Alabama, had discussed the Siegelman case with Karl Rove, the highest-ranking political operative in the White House. Rove declined to respond to a subpoena by the House Committee on Government Oversight, which sought to investigate his role in the case. He also declined to answer when asked about his role in the Siegelman case on *This Week with George Stephanopoulos,* an ABC Sunday morning news program.[4]

American political history is replete with political prosecutions, but even so, this particular case sent shockwaves through the criminal justice community, leading fifty-two former state attorneys general, both Democrats and Republicans, to sign a petition asking Congress to investigate whether politics played a role in the Siegelman case. The petition was organized by Robert Abrams, a former Democratic state attorney general from New York, who said he was startled when Siegelman was imprisoned immediately upon sentencing, well before his appeal could be heard. "There were so many suspicious circumstances surrounding the investigation, prosecution and sentencing of Don Siegelman, I felt—and the former attorneys general felt—we better ask for a full congressional inquiry to get at the facts and the truth."[5] After nine months in a federal prison, Siegelman was freed by the U.S. Court of Appeals for the 11th Circuit. The Court admitted that Siegelman had raised "substantial questions" in his appeal.[6]

One year later, however, the appeals court upheld the lower court's verdict. The conviction was upheld on all but two lesser counts involving mail fraud, and the case was remanded for resentencing. In its decision, the court agreed with the jury in the initial decision and concluded that there was sufficient evidence to convict Siegelman of bribery for appointing a campaign contributor to a state licensing board.[7]

Of course, when the evidence becomes too embarrassing to ignore, or the media storm becomes too intense, prosecutions often proceed against political loyalists. But in some cases, parties in power can occasionally help their friends even when the odds are stacked against them. Thus, the Bush administration prosecuted Senator Ted Stevens (R-Alaska), but with an inept prosecutorial team. Stevens was charged with taking $250,000 in gifts from oil tycoon Bill Allen, founder of the VECO Corporation, which specialized in home construction. Allen testified that he never billed his friend Stevens for the work done in converting a simple mountain cabin into a modern, two-story home with wraparound porches, a sauna, and a wine cellar. The construction work was never reported by Stevens either as a gift, a loan, or a fee either to the Internal Revenue Service (IRS) or to the Senate Ethics Committee. Once the scandal erupted, and the Justice Department was forced to act, the administration assigned a third-tier prosecution team that was continually reprimanded by the judge for its ineptitude, inexperience, and incompetence. Federal Judge Emmet G. Sullivan "lacerated the prosecutors for multiple problems," and in unusually strong language exclaimed that "the government knew the documents were lies." In fact, the prosecutors were so desperate at one point that they submitted fictitious timesheets—one such timesheet was supposed to prove that Stevens knowingly accepted $188,000 in free labor performed by two workers who were not even in Alaska at the time![8]

Republicans as well as Democrats agreed that Stevens's ultimate conviction said more about the quality of the evidence than the quality of the prosecution. Days after his conviction, Stevens was narrowly defeated in his reelection bid in a vote so close that it wasn't decided until two weeks after Election Day. The closeness of the race, considering that Stevens was a convicted felon at the time, was a testament to his longtime membership on the Senate Appropriations Committee (which he chaired from 1997–2005, except for an eighteen-month interlude when Democrats controlled the chamber), which meant that he enjoyed many years of funneling huge amounts of federal dollars to Alaska. President Obama's Attorney General, Eric Holder, ultimately rescinded the prosecution because of prosecutorial misconduct, and the prosecutors found themselves under internal investigation for their misconduct.

The Bush administration's politicization of the Justice Department was unequaled in modern history. Judges were often appointed more for their political allegiance than for their expertise or judicial temperament. One Midwest judge was urged by the governor of his state, a Republican, to apply for a federal judgeship. In addition to his decade on the bench, the judge had chaired a state commission and served as dean of a major law school. At his interview by a Justice Department official in Washington, he was asked if he was a member of the conservative legal group, the Federalist Society. He said he was not. "Why not?" asked the official. "Because the Federalist Society doesn't interest me," he replied. Needless to say, he didn't get the appointment.

At least one-third of the immigration judges appointed by the Bush administration since 2004 were either connected to the Republican Party or had worked for the administration, and fully half of them lacked experience in immigration law. "Immigration law is very complex," said Denise Slavin, an immigration judge who is president of the National Association of Immigration Judges. "So generally speaking, it is very good to have someone coming into this area with an immigration background. It is very difficult, for those who don't, to catch up."[9] The impact of these changes has been felt in every area of the country. The appointments, all made by the attorney general, have begun to reshape a system of courts in which judges, ruling alone, exercise broad powers. Nearly 250,000 immigrants are deported each year, following proceedings that recall Star Chamber justice, where defendants have no right to an attorney and limited rights to appeal. "The Justice Department began to jettison the civil service process that traditionally guided the selections in favor of political considerations."[10] The nation's 226 immigration judges sit in fifty-four immigration courts.

The Bush administration's conservative political litmus test for immigration judges was felt long after it was abandoned as illegal. Immigrants seeking asylum have been disproportionately rejected by those judges, according to an analysis of Justice Department data conducted by the Transactional Records Access and Clearinghouse.[11] The analysis suggested that the effects of this patronage-style selection process for immigration judges—used for three years before it was abandoned as illegal—were being felt by scores of immigrants whose fates were determined by judges installed during that period. Ultimately, what this means is that immigrants without financial resources or sometimes even basic language skills faced a system that was stacked against them. This process, coupled with the nation's ambivalence about immigration policy, also left many immigrants in legal limbo about their status—a problem that often became extremely dangerous for political refugees who faced retribution when they were forced to return to their home countries.

The immigration problem is also one of "representation," said Robert Katzmann, a federal appeals judge in New York. Immigrants often have to use defense attorneys who are burdened by too many cases; immigration judges, Katzmann added, "often have 1500 cases a year," a number that has become virtually impossible to adjudicate.

The politicization of immigration judges was part of a broad pattern at the Bush Justice Department to hire conservative loyalists for what were formerly considered career civil service positions. The Bush strategy constituted official misconduct in violation of federal civil service laws and the department's internal policies, according to a 2008 report by the Justice Department's inspector general, Glenn A. Fine, and the department's Office of Professional Responsibility. The Justice Department's policy position was led by Monica Goodling, a top adviser to Attorney General Alberto Gonzalez. Gonzalez told the inspector general that he was unaware that Goodling and other aides were using political criteria in their decisions for career positions. His successor, Attorney General Michael B. Mukasey—who took over in the winter of 2007—vowed that he would abandon these practices in future hiring, although he wasn't in office long enough for his promises to take effect. Even though Mukasey tried to limit contacts between the White House and federal prosecutors—paying frequent lip service to the importance of separating politics and law enforcement—public confidence in the judicial process will take a long time to restore.

The Firing of U.S. Attorneys

On December 7, 2006, Pearl Harbor memorials on radio and television were interrupted by newscasts broadcasting the firing of seven U.S. attorneys by their superiors in the Justice Department. Their only failure was a reluctance to pursue a political agenda. The dismissals, among nine that year, were unprecedented and were intended as an object lesson to those who forgot that they were political appointees, expected to direct their fire at members of the other party.[12]

One attorney was fired for disclosing information about an indictment; another was fired for embarrassing the Justice Department by complaining that the Central Intelligence Agency (CIA) had pressured the Justice Department not to pursue a certain case. In the past, presidents had rarely intervened after their initial appointments. President Jimmy Carter, for example, replaced U.S. Attorney David Marston at the request of two members of Congress: Representative Joshua Eilberg, a Pennsylvania Democrat whom Marston had been investigating on corruption charges, and Representative Daniel Flood, another Pennsylvania Democrat also under investigation. Although he lost his job as U.S. attorney, Marston was later vindicated because both members of Congress were eventually forced from office under ethical clouds. Eilberg lost his 1978 reelection bid and was sentenced to five years probation and a $10,000 fine, while Flood was censured by the House of Representatives for bribery, soon after which he resigned from office.

Attorney General Gonzalez's repeated denials of political retaliation didn't match the facts. In March, 2005, Kyle Sampson, Gonzalez's chief of staff, unveiled a checklist that rated each of the U.S. attorneys on the basis of criteria that included their political allegiance and their competence. He recommended retaining "strong U.S. attorneys who have … exhibited loyalty to the president and attorney general," and recommended "removing weak U.S. attorneys who have … chafed against administration initiatives." On Feb. 12, 2006, Monica Goodling, the Justice Department's liaison with the White House, sent a spreadsheet of each U.S. attorney's political activities and memberships in conservative political groups via an e-mail to senior administration officials.[13]

The nine dismissed U.S. attorneys were as follows:

- David C. Iglesias of Albuquerque, who oversaw a probe of state Democrats that Republicans didn't think was moving quickly enough.
- Daniel G. Bogden of Las Vegas, who opened an investigation related to Nevada govovernor Jim Gibbons, a Republican.
- Paul K. Charlton of Phoenix, who opened investigations of Republican Representatives Jim Kolbe and Rick Renzi.
- Bud Cummins of Little Rock, who conducted an investigation of Missouri Governor Roy Blunt, a Republican.
- Carol S. Lam of San Diego, who oversaw the bribery conviction of Rep. Randy "Duke" Cunningham, a Republican.
- John McKay of Seattle, who declined to intervene in a disputed gubernatorial election, angering the GOP.
- Margaret Chiara of Grand Rapids, whom the Chief Judge called "classy, distinguished, well-regarded."
- Todd Graves, Western Missouri, who failed to pursue what he considered politically inspired cases that the Justice Department had sought.
- Kevin P. Ryan, San Francisco, who was actively investigating a Bay Area laboratory involved in a sports doping scandal. Ryan was the only fired prosecutor to receive mostly negative job reviews.

The most highly publicized dismissal case began with an ostensibly innocent telephone call. Senator Pete V. Domenici, a distinguished and highly respected Republican from New Mexico, called David Iglesias—one of the U.S. attorneys who was later dismissed—to ask about an ongoing investigation of New Mexico Democrats on the eve of the 2006 midterm elections. Although the senator maintained that his question was not an attempt to influence the prosecutor, traditionally such senatorial requests for a "status report" are interpreted as pressure for a favorable outcome. Domenici was later "admonished" (the least-harsh sanction) by the Senate Ethics Committee, which found that he "should have known that a federal prosecutor receiving such a telephone call, coupled with an approaching election which may have turned on or been influenced by the prosecutor's actions in the corruption matter, created an appearance of impropriety that reflected unfavorably on the Senate."[14] Neither Domenici, nor any of the White House officials (including key players Karl Rove, Monica Goodling, Harriet Miers, William Kelley, and Richard Klinger) would consent to be interviewed for the Justice Department report on the firings. The White House claimed executive privilege and confidentiality as sufficient reason for both refusing to allow its officials to be interviewed and turning over what were considered internal documents.[15]

Paul Charlton, now an attorney in Phoenix, recalled that he had the opposite experience. "Senator Kyl [Senator John Kyl, Republican of Arizona] said he would intervene on my behalf," said Charlton. "I had no political pressures. I was lucky in that way." Charlton's real difficulty, he said, were "disparate views on the death penalty" between himself and his ultimate boss, Attorney General Gonzales. "The FBI policy was not to videotape confessions; they had antiquated ideas on that, which meant they were acting on laws dating back to the Code of Hammurabi. I thought they should videotape confessions to avoid false confessions as well as coerced confessions, both notable in child abuse cases. The perpetrator says it didn't happen; the victim says it did. I couldn't prosecute on that basis."[16]

Another Republican member of Congress from New Mexico, Rep. Heather Wilson, acknowledged that she also had contacted Iglesias to complain on behalf of herself and her constituents about the slow pace of the corruption investigation. Unlike Domenici, Wilson did not complain to the Justice Department and consented to be interviewed by them for their report. Justice Department officials said Domenici had complained to Attorney General Gonzalez about Iglesias three times in 2005 and 2006 and had also spoken to Deputy Attorney General Paul J. McNulty about Iglesias.[17]

The dismissed U.S. attorneys refused to take their dismissal casually. They went public, wrote articles and books about their experience, testified before Congress, spoke freely to the press, and cooperated fully with the Justice Department's Office of Professional Responsibility and inspector general. Iglesias cited Gonzalez's successor, Michael Mukasey, who called the removals "haphazard, arbitrary and unprofessional."[18] Iglesias also wrote a book about his experience.[19] Daniel G. Bogden of Las Vegas protested his poor performance review, citing the $55 million his office was able to retrieve in asset forfeitures and fine collections.[20] Carol Lam addressed the issue of prosecutorial discretion, testifying before the Senate Committee on the Judiciary that the "prosecution of individual cases must be based on justice, fairness, and compassion—not political ideology or partisan politics.

Todd P. Graves, U.S. attorney in Kansas City, Missouri, argued that he was dismissed for failing to pursue two cases that interested the Bush administration. In one case, the Justice Department's Civil Rights Division had allegedly wanted Graves to sue the state of Missouri for what federal officials thought was its failure to purge voter registration roles of people who had died, changed addresses, or left the state. Graves believed a lawsuit would not have succeeded because local governments, not the federal government, are responsible for voter registration records. Graves also testified before the Senate Judiciary Committee, acknowledging that he realized "that it was time to give another person a chance to serve," but that although the decision to fire him was made at the highest levels of government, the person calling had told him that he had "served honorably" and "performed well."[21]

After Graves's refusal to sue, the lawsuit proceeded anyway, having been authorized by Bradley J. Schlozman, then acting chief of the Justice Department's Civil Rights Division, who was named as Graves's interim successor. In Graves's case, the Department of Justice report also indicated that there was an ongoing political conflict between the state office of Senator Christopher "Kit" Bond (R-Missouri) and a close relative of Graves.[22]

Different groups of stakeholders circled the wagons. Bush loyalists viewed these lawsuits as the best possible way to combat voter fraud—especially the type of fraud that they argued benefited Democrats more than Republicans. For their part, Democratic partisans argued that the lawsuits discriminated against poor and elderly voters, who were more likely to be taken off registration rolls.[23]

The lawsuit was ultimately dismissed by a federal judge. Graves also admitted that he may have alienated Bush administration officials by giving then-candidate Claire McCaskill, a Democrat, a letter in 2004 saying there had been insufficient evidence to file charges in a case from the 1990s that involved her office manager. His replacement, interim U.S. Attorney Bradley Schlozman, disagreed and proceeded to inject the U.S. attorney's office into McCaskill's Senate campaign against Republican Jim Talent. Days before the election, Schlozman announced the indictments of four people who were registering voters for the liberal group Acorn, on charges of submitting false registration forms. Republicans turned the indictments into a campaign issue used in the 2008 presidential campaign. Justice Department guidelines prohibit election crime investigations shortly before an election for just this reason: the danger of investigations becoming campaign issues, which is exactly what happened in this case. Schlozman left his post after a year in office, and McCaskill won her election to the Senate.

The long-awaited report on the firings was finally issued on September 29, 2008. Not surprisingly, the report found that most of the firings were politically motivated and improper. The following day, Attorney General Michael Mukasey appointed a special prosecutor, Nora Dannehy, to decide whether criminal charges should be brought against Gonzales and other officials involved in the firings. But the report stopped short of resolving questions about White House involvement in the firings, primarily because of the refusal of a number of key players to cooperate, among them Karl Rove, Senator Domenici, and White House counsel Harriet Miers.[24]

The firing of the U.S. attorneys presented a new challenge for political patronage. U.S. attorneys appointed by the president are obviously not covered by civil service protections and clearly serve at the pleasure of the president. Yet there were lots of back-and-forth e-mails and conversations among White House officials, who were clearly aware that their actions could create a political "upheaval."[25] On reflection, it could be argued that the upheaval was entirely caused by political bumbling. The cover story was that the attorneys were "fired" for underperforming, when the real reasons were political. Several officials argued that the White House wanted to give others the chance to fill these jobs—in other words, for pure political patronage reasons. Attorney General Alberto Gonzalez, who delegated the whole enterprise to underlings, defended the practice as "good management."[26]

Too many reasons were offered, ranging from sheer incompetence to political disloyalty. Lists were submitted by "supervisors" to document the charge that the dismissals were based on the concept of "underperformance," although strong proof was lacking in most cases. On close scrutiny, however, the real reasons were political, both in terms of opening up more judicial patronage for the Republican Party and for addressing complaints and responding to influential senators.

"McNulty fired us for performance," recalled Charlton, angrily. "We knew that wasn't true." It also made future job possibilities more difficult if prospective employers thought they were fired for incompetence. "If they (the White House) had just articulated that they wanted more judicial jobs, that would have been O.K.; it would have been a one or two-day story; that they fired nine U.S. attorneys so that other Republicans could take their place."

"We warned them," Charlton continued. "They were extraordinarily arrogant. They thought they were bulletproof. The real reason was that a group of young Bushies wanted to move to the Southwest—to California, New Mexico, and Arizona." A group of seven fired U.S. attorneys now has an annual reunion to discuss its ongoing dispute with the Bush administration, which has grown into a full-scale investigation, led by Nora Dannehy, a career civil servant with the Justice Department. Armed with subpoena power, Dannehy hopes to retrieve the documents the White House had formerly refused to turn over to the inspector general. Rove and Miers have since agreed to testify under oath before the House Judiciary Committee, which is investigating the firings.

Since the firings, Gonzalez has had to hire an attorney. Unlike his predecessors in the attorney general post, Gonzalez was unable to settle into a lucrative position on Wall Street in New York, or K Street in Washington. A legal defense fund was created to pay his legal bills, headed by Robert H. Bork, Jr., the son of federal judge Robert H. Bork. Bork Jr. presides over a group called Bork Communications that specializes in "high-profile litigation."[27] He also serves as a spokesperson for Gonzales.[28]

The firings were also the first time in history that judicial patronage in the Justice Department was laid bare to the general public, which had always regarded the department as independent and immune from politics. The final report, which reflected this view, could change the nature of judicial patronage in this area:

> For Department officials to recommend the removal of U.S. Attorneys even in part because they do or do not have political support undermines the public's confidence that Department of Justice prosecutive decisions are based on the facts and the law and not on political considerations.[29]

Despite Mukasey's earlier pledge to end the Justice Department's politicization, examples of political preference persisted until President Bush left office in 2008.[30] The Justice Department disbanded its public corruption office in Los Angeles, ending several investigations, including that of Representative Jerry Lewis, a powerful California Republican who had directed hundreds of millions of dollars in earmarks to favored government contractors while he chaired the Appropriations Committee. Along with other Democrats, Senator Dianne Feinstein (D-California) openly expressed her fear that "political figures at the White House or Justice Department [were] behind the decision to close the office."

Judgeships: The Ultimate Reward

Judgeships are the jewel in the crown of political patronage. "Every lawyer wants to be a judge," many politicians admit: Witness the high percentage of lawyers involved in the political process. Judgeships are desirable for a variety of reasons. Scarred from continual struggles to maintain their power, politicians view the bench as a relatively secure and peaceful profession. A federal judge is appointed for life; a State Supreme Court judge in New York is elected for a period of fourteen years.[31]

Removed from the fray of ongoing political wars, judgeships also offer party veterans the dignity of being part of a high-status profession and a sense of self-esteem they sorely missed during the long years they wore the label of "politician." Many enjoy their positions as kings and queens of their courtrooms, a marked contrast to their previous positions as legislative supplicants for campaign funds. Judgeships also are attractive to politicians because of their relatively short working hours, long holidays, and secure retirement benefits. In striking contrast to the hectic pace and killing hours of political life, where weekends are often filled with an endless round of meetings, weddings, bar mitzvahs, and other events at which a politician's attendance is deemed compulsory, judges have their weekends to themselves. Also, a judge's working day often runs from about 10 a.m. to 4 p.m., including long lunch hours and recesses in between, and holidays can be enjoyed unimpeded by constituent demands. But many judges work longer hours. A federal appeals judge in New York said, "I work 85 hours a week, and have 10 days off a year."

As a group, judges draw higher salaries than any other group of professional public officials. Federal district judges earn $165,200 annually; federal appeals court judges earn $175,100; Supreme Court Justices earn $203,000; and John Roberts, the Chief Justice, earns $212,000. In New York State, trial court judges serving on the Supreme Court, Family Court, Civil Court, and Criminal Court earn $136,700. Rarely are judgeships included in the economy drives that reduce the pay of other public officials, and most of the time, judges do not have to worry about losing their jobs. During the deep recessionary period between 2008 and 2009, many judges were grateful for their jobs—although before 2008, many complained that their pay was too low, especially in comparison to the lawyers who appeared before them. As an added benefit, many judges have tenure, either through lifetime appointments or through the patronage of party leaders who can be trusted to continue to nominate them indefinitely. But some federal judges complain that their salaries are not competitive. "When a law clerk leaves my chambers, that law clerk will be making far more than I'm making," said a federal appeals judge in New York. Law professors also make more than most judges. For many years, the Chief Judge of the United States has asked Congress to raise judicial salaries, but Congress, unwilling to raise its own salaries, has usually declined.

Clearly, not all judges are political hacks. Many take their jobs very seriously and are devoted to the law. Their jobs are intellectually challenging and can require agonizing decisions, made over long hours of soul-searching in their endeavor to do justice.

When judges are elected, the key election (and thirty-nine states elect their judges) is often the primary contest, in which political machines play a significant role, particularly when the party determines who will be on the ballot. In New York, political bosses work their will through a process that can charitably be described as archaic, the most scandalous involving the process by which State Supreme Court judges are selected. The judges, who are trial-level judges (and not members of the state's highest court, the Court of Appeals) are nominated through a system known as "judicial conventions." These conventions are dominated by delegates handpicked by party bosses, who vote whichever way the bosses instruct them to vote. Independent candidates have virtually no chance of bucking the system because to win the nomination, a candidate not backed by the bosses needs to recruit more than 100 delegate candidates to run in different districts. Those candidates would then have to collect thousands of petition signatures to qualify for the ballot. Even if they finally qualify, candidates would need to conduct vast "educational" campaigns to become known because their names appear on the ballots with absolutely no identification, giving ordinary voters no way to make informed choices.[32]

Civil Court Judge Margarita Lopez Torres, who sought promotion to the Supreme Court, decided to challenge the system. She won her Civil Court judgeship in 1992, with the backing of Clarence Norman, the Brooklyn Democratic leader, and Vito Lopez, the district leader. Soon after her election, Norman and Lopez directed her to hire a person of their choosing as her law secretary. Lopez Torres interviewed the prospect and contacted his prior employer, a Brooklyn Supreme Court Justice for whom the prospect had served as law secretary. The Justice told Lopez Torres that the law secretary's work was "mediocre" and that "he had spent an enormous amount of time on the phone doing political work." With such a negative recommendation, Lopez Torres hired someone else and faced the wrath of Norman, who was "extremely upset" and told her that some day she "would want to become a Supreme Court Justice and … the party leaders would not forget this."[33]

As Norman predicted, Lopez Torres sought a promotion to the Supreme Court in 2003, but the two Democratic leaders still in power—Norman and Lopez (no relation)—refused to support her. She asked to attend a judicial convention so that she could make her case to the delegates. Her request was denied on the grounds that candidates were not allowed to participate; only delegates could attend. Jeffrey C. Feldman, Executive Director of the Kings County Democratic Committee, wrote to her, "While I am neither an attorney nor a graduate of law school, I suffer from the innocent belief that the floor of the Convention is open only to elected delegates and their successors. I am not aware of any Convention in my thirty (30) years of attendance, which permitted a nonaccredited member to be accorded the privilege of the floor."[34] Lopez Torres sued the election board in March 2004, claiming that the judicial conventions violated the First and Fourteenth Amendments to the U.S. Constitution. The brief for New York State argued that the role of political parties in elections must be respected. But the U.S. district court found that it was "virtually impossible" for a candidate lacking the support of the party to field slates of delegates at the judicial convention and upheld Lopez Torres's claim that the judicial conventions were unconstitutional.[35] The Court of Appeals for the Second Circuit concurred.

The decision was eventually reversed by the U.S. Supreme Court, in a unanimous decision. Justice Antonin Scalia delivered the opinion of the Court, which found that "a political party has a First Amendment right to limit its membership as it wishes, and to choose a candidate-selection process that will in its view produce the nominee who best represents its political platform."[36] The Supreme Court also found that Lopez Torres's complaint that the convention system did not give her a realistic chance to secure the party's nomination "says no more than that the party leadership has more widespread support than a candidate not supported by the leadership."[37] The decision sealed the fate of judicial politics. What it meant was that politics as usual would prevail, and that party bosses could keep control over the selection of judges, as well as over all the judicial patronage that flowed from the clubhouse—the hiring of judges' aides, refereeships, guardianships and other surrogate "responsibilities," administrative judgeships (such as immigration) with influence, summer internships, and corporate monitors.

Former New York Governor Eliot Spitzer tried to reform the system. He proposed that judicial candidates be allowed to speak at judicial conventions, and gain access to the primary ballot if they received 50 percent of the delegate vote and filed the necessary petitions. Spitzer also proposed public financing of judicial campaigns as well as an independent judicial qualification commission for each judicial district.[38] Unfortunately for him, Governor Spitzer was forced to resign the governorship following a widely publicized sex scandal a year after he took office; and unfortunately for judicial challengers, his plans were abandoned by his successor.

It was ever thus. Brief attempts at reform make headlines, but party leaders invariably prevail. More than forty years ago in New York, intense pressures built up over the awarding of 125 new judgeships created for Manhattan and the Bronx by the state legislature. Confronted with negative publicity over their judicial patronage practices, party leaders agreed to meet a group of "reformers" seeking to change the system. A deal was struck, and the party leaders agreed that they would nominate only candidates acceptable to the committee set up by the reform group. In retrospect, the agreement represented a promise of power-sharing between the traditional party leaders on the one hand, and newer stakeholders, including Reform Democrats; good government groups (in this case, the Citizens Union); the local bar association (the Association of the Bar of the City of New York); and a group called the VERA Foundation, which studied and lobbied in the area of criminal justice.

The original agreement promised that party leaders would submit judicial candidates to the screening committee set up by the reform group. Alas, it was an informal agreement that was immediately broken by party leaders, who nominated four candidates for Supreme Court judgeships who were rejected by the committee. One candidate was alleged to have screamed "idiot" at defendants appearing before him; another admitted under oath that he had failed to report a colleague in the state legislature for proposing to "fix" a narcotics case; a third for "reason of his age (64) and lack of recent professional and litigation experience"; and the fourth for not cooperating with the committee and for failing to prove that he had the "requisite qualifications."[39]

A fracas ensued when the reform coalition accused party leaders of double-crossing them; for their part, party leaders merely behaved as they always had and always will. They knew that they could withstand the flurry of criticism from the reformers and privately congratulated themselves for having hoodwinked their opponents into believing they were working together, while all the time keeping the patronage to themselves. What the episode showed was that "the party leaders respected the contracts they had made with each other, and with those to whom they had promised judgeships, far more than they respected their agreement with the 'good government' forces."[40]

The reformers were naïve in thinking that reason, adverse media attention, and what they considered sound arguments would ever prevail against the long-term relationships and political favors that cemented political organizations like theirs. And according to the informal but iron-bound laws of patronage politics, there was no reason why newcomers deserved instant power without coming up the hard way—the way political leaders had risen. In their world, this meant that paying political debts counted for much more than temporary spurts of reform. Although reform efforts have prevailed sporadically in different parts of the country, judicial patronage is alive and well in New York, where courthouse patronage and judgeships still go a long way to sustaining the financial health of the party organization.

Federal judicial appointments can often be as political as state judicial appointments. Candidates for the judiciary and U.S. attorneys are proposed by senators from the president's party or, in the absence of such a senator, a leading member of the House delegation. Like presidents and governors, some senators mask their intentions by working through a judicial selection committee, which they very often happen to appoint and control. Occasionally, a president will seek to name his own federal judge, but such appointments are subject to "senatorial courtesy," which is, in effect, a form of veto power exercised by senators from the state involved. Often, the courtesy system affords senators too many opportunities to exercise poor judgment, as in the case of Senator Edward M. Kennedy's (D-Massachusetts) early effort to nominate Francis X. Morrissey, a political ally of his family's, to a federal judgeship. Morrissey had a poor reputation both as a lawyer and as a judge. In a rare moment of rebellion, the U.S. Senate refused to confirm the appointment.[41]

Does it matter? "In ideologically contested cases" (such as those involving abortion, affirmative action, or race discrimination), concluded Cass R. Sunstein and his colleagues, "a judge's ideological tendency can be predicted by the party of the appointing president; Republican appointees vote very differently from Democratic appointees." This is true of the Supreme Court as well as the circuit courts, and especially "where the law is not plain ... where judicial convictions play an inevitable role ... and the differences between Republic and Democratic appointees ... significantly affects the outcomes of lawsuits and the lives of ordinary Americans."[42] But judges sometimes surprise their mentors. Justice John Paul Stevens, appointed to the Supreme Court by President Gerald Ford, became the leader of the court's liberal wing.

The Senate usually acquiesces to presidential picks. David Bunning, 35, at least fourteen years younger than the average age of the 945 federal judges appointed since 1976, was rated as "not qualified" by the judiciary committee of the American Bar Association (ABA). The committee determined that he lacked sufficient legal experience to serve as a federal judge. Bunning was the only one of President George W. Bush's sixty-four judicial nominees given the "not qualified" rating by the ABA. During his Senate confirmation hearings, Bunning was also criticized by the ABA for attending what the association considered a low-ranked law school at the University of Kentucky, where he compiled an unimpressive academic record, ranking smack in the middle of his class. Never mind. Bunning had one thing going for him: his father. Jim Bunning, a Republican U.S. Senator from Kentucky, joined with Senator Mitch McConnell, Kentucky's other senator, in recommending his son for the bench. Bunning, confirmed by the Senate, was sworn in on March 28, 2008 as Kentucky's newest federal judge.[43] Bunning epitomizes the judicial mediocrity so staunchly defended in the Nixon years by Senator Roman L. Hruska, Nebraska Republican.[44]

Federal judges serve for life; they can be removed only by impeachment—for high crimes and misdemeanors. Throughout history, only thirteen federal judges were impeached, of whom seven were convicted and lost their gavels. Mediocre judges have an impact that lasts for decades. Although 2,108 complaints were filed against federal judges from 2005 through 2007, only thirty-six resulted in corrective action. Still on the bench, for example, is Manuel Real, who serves as a U.S. district judge in Los Angeles. The subject of constant opprobrium by appellate courts, Real has been removed from cases for ignoring evidence and for failing to adequately state the reasoning behind his rulings. But those cases, involving Microsoft, Honda Motor Company, and the late President Ferdinand Marcos of the Philippines, probably represented the tip of the iceberg. The House Committee on the Judiciary held hearings in 2006 over whether to impeach Judge Real, an action spurred by allegations that he had improperly aided a woman in her bankruptcy case pending before another judge, but congressional critics couldn't muster enough votes for impeachment.[45] Lawyers are also understandably reluctant to criticize judges for a number of reasons, among them the likelihood that they may have to appear before them in the future.[46]

Judgeships on eBay: Campaign "Finance"

On the state and local level, the sale of judgeships is as old as the clubhouse. George Washington Plunkitt observed:

> The sums they pay are accordin' to their salaries and the length of their terms of office, if elected. Even candidates for the Supreme Court have to fall in line. A Supreme Court judge in New York County gets $17,500 a year, and he's expected, when nominated, to help along the good cause with a year's salary. Why not? He has fourteen years on the bench ahead of him, and ten thousand other lawyers would be willin' to put up twice as much to be in his shoes. I ain't sayin' that we sell nominations. That's a different thing altogether. There's no auction and no regular biddin'. The man is picked out and somehow he gets to understand what's expected of him in the way of a contribution, and he ponies up—all from gratitude to the organization that honored him, see?[47]

In the 1930s, the Seabury investigation found that magistrates paid $10,000, while General Sessions or Supreme Court judges paid $25,000 to $50,000. In their encyclopedic study of New York City government, Wallace S. Sayre and Herbert Kaufman described how this formula worked in 1960. The district leader decided whether to extract one or two years' salary from the judicial nominee or relied on the method of charging $50 to $100 for each election district within the judicial area. If, for example, the judicial area amounted to a municipal court district, encompassing between 145 and 180 election districts, the price would go up to about $20,000.[48] In New York City, in 1970, the going rate for a judgeship was said to be up to $80,000; in Chicago, at that time, where service counted more than money, the cost was only $7,500.[49]

One of the more bizarre cases involving the sale of judgeships occurred in the 1970s. State Senator Seymour Thaler had been elected to the State Supreme Court in New York but never took his seat. Instead, he and two others were convicted of possessing $800,000 in stolen U.S. Treasury bills, which were purchased at 25 percent of their face value. T-bills sold at a discount of 25 percent or more are presumed to be stolen. Political colleagues and law enforcement officials believed that Thaler needed the money to pay for his judgeship—then valued at an $80,000 "contribution." Oddly, Thaler was married to an heiress but apparently did not want to take her money for the judgeship. Thaler was convicted in 1972 and served a year and a day in the U.S. penitentiary in Danbury, Connecticut, from which he emerged broken in both body and spirit, according to Richard A., Brown, the current district attorney of Thaler's former political base, the county of Queens, New York.[50]

More recently, Brooklyn District Attorney Charles J. Hynes concluded a five-year investigation in 2007 on the sale of judgeships. Hynes, who got his start in the James V. Mangano Democratic Club, had occupied this position for the last 20 years and ironically was regarded by the bosses as a reliable party man. On the basis of Hynes's findings, Brooklyn Democratic leader Clarence Norman (who had earlier denied the Supreme Court nomination to Lopez Torres) and State Supreme Court Justice Gerald P. Garson were convicted and ultimately sentenced to lengthy prison terms. Norman was sentenced to three to nine years after being convicted of extorting money from judicial candidates. Garson was sentenced to three to ten years for bribery.[51] Alas, the two men failed to provide a description of how they operated. Hynes believes that the two men knew exactly how the system worked and that candidates had to pay $50,000 or more to obtain their judgeships. His estimate, though, was exceedingly low, especially because the going rate 40 years ago, according to many politicians, was $80,000.[52] Party leaders always have to cope with inflation: In 1930, the price was $10,000.[53]

The New York State Supreme Court is the highest court of original jurisdiction, while the highest appellate court is the New York Court of Appeals. "Two powerful men, Gerald Garson and Clarence Norman Jr., used the political and judicial systems to line their own pockets and the pockets of their cronies," Hynes said in an interview after the case was decided. "They both were concealing information," he added, and their failure to reveal it has cast "a pall of scandal over the honorable and decent men and women who sit as judges in Kings County." Hynes believed that the money was never delivered in hard cash. "It was always done through intermediaries. Money was sent to a lobbyist and back-doored to [party leader] Norman." What was the price of a state judgeship in Brooklyn in 2008? "It's hard to fix a dollar amount. These prosecutions are very difficult. The precise operations are very hard to unearth."

The sale of judgeships remains a mystery, couched in the arcane language of judicial "revenue." "No one knows how much judgeships go for, yet everyone knows they go for a price," concluded a law school professor who preferred to remain anonymous. "Money is the criteria for judicial nominations ... the question is how much goes into the pocket of the district leader and how much into party coffers," admitted a member of the New York City council, who also refused to be quoted by name. And "at cocktail parties you can always hear judges' wives joking about their 'debt,' referring to the money their husbands had to borrow to get on the bench," complained a judge.[54]

There are 1,250 judges on the New York state payroll. The salary of New York state Supreme Court judges is $136,700. If tradition holds, the price of a judgeship on that court is a year's salary. But there are other forms of compensation. One New York City Municipal Court judge reported that the party had give him his judgeship free of charge in order to lure him away from his seat in the state assembly, where he had been harassing party regulars. A judgeship can also be a compensation prize for a losing candidate. Former New York City Mayors Vincent Impellitteri and John Hylan ended up on the bench after being denied renomination for the mayoralty. Frank O'Connor, former New York City council president and unsuccessful gubernatorial candidate, ended up with a judgeship. Mayor John Lindsay bestowed a judgeship on William Booth in order to fire him gracefully from his chairmanship of the City Commission on Human Rights, after pressure from the city's Jewish groups, which felt Mr. Booth was ignoring their needs.[55]

Courthouse Patronage

But judicial patronage involves more than judgeships, which renders "contributions" to the local political party more than worth their weight. It also involves the largesse bestowed by judges, which includes receiverships, refereeships, guardianships, and trusteeships. Indeed, one of the reasons why young lawyers are attracted to the clubhouse is that political leaders control the kind of courthouse patronage that can be invaluable to a law practice.

In 2008, State Supreme Court Justice Milton Tingling, a candidate for the patronage-rich job of Manhattan Surrogate, which handles the estates of those who are deceased, made a startling statement. He wrote to Manhattan Democratic Leader Herman "Denny" Farrell:

> Public confidence in the integrity of the Surrogates Courts in Brooklyn and the Bronx have been undermined by allegations and reports of political favoritism in the assignment of fiduciary responsibility for cases that come before the Court. Those concerns convince me that it is imperative to do all I can to ensure residents of Manhattan that, if I am elected, politics will stop at the Courthouse door.[56]

To no one's surprise, Tingling's pledge did not sit well with Manhattan's political leaders. As a result, Tingling lost the Democratic primary and was defeated by Nora Anderson, chief clerk of the Manhattan Surrogate's Court. Anderson was familiar with the court's tradition of patronage and was trusted by party leaders to continue its practices. A month after her election, but before she was sworn in, Anderson was indicted on charges that she had concealed the source of $250,000 worth of contributions to her campaign. The state's

Court of Appeals ordered that she not be sworn in until she was absolved of the charges.[57]

What the Tingling/Anderson controversy means is that courthouse patronage is alive and well and remains the most concealed form of political patronage. When a judicial patronage controversy arises, it usually focuses on judgeships, although because public apathy usually prevails in that area as well, controversies are few and far between. But similar to the public's inattention to judicial candidates, few people care about which lawyers get refereeships, guardianships, and receiverships; and fewer still know what they are. Guardianships can divert considerable sums from an estate; after all, "it's a dead man's estate, who's to kick up a fuss?" wrote Murray Teigh Bloom, an expert on probate practices.[58]

Once again, New York emerged both as the capital of courthouse patronage and as the target of reform efforts. This kind of patronage also differs from state to state, although some states relegate these tasks to civil servants. In Georgia, for example, surrogate patronage is handled by a salaried public employee called an "ordinary," who also handles traffic violations—an indication of the relative unimportance of the surrogate function in Georgia. But probate patronage still flourishes in the richer industrial states of New Jersey, New York, Texas, Ohio, and Illinois, where estates tend to be larger than they are in Georgia. New York remains the mother lode because multimillionaires occasionally die intestate—without a will or instructions as to who should be the executor of their estates.[59] At that point, estates often fall victim to the vagaries of machine politics. A dispute over the $1.2 billion estate of tobacco heiress Doris Duke ended up in Manhattan Surrogate's Court, where many lawyers vied over what one attorney called the "world series of litigation."[60] Some politicians argue that Surrogate judges can even do some good; for example, when Judge Renee R. Roth of New York reduced the sum that hotel magnate Leona Helmsley left to her dog—a white Maltese named Trouble—from $10 million to $2 million—with the remainder going to the Helmsley charitable foundation.

Known as the "widows and orphans court," the Surrogate Court has been the bane of reform-minded politicians even way back to Mayor Fiorello LaGuardia, who called the court "the most expensive undertaking establishment in the world." He added that the Surrogate's Court of New York County did more to keep the notorious Tammany Hall political machine in business than anything else, including his own attempt to deprive the Democratic Party of city jobs, and President Franklin Roosevelt's denial of federal jobs to political hacks. The late Senator Robert Kennedy called the court a "toll booth exacting tribute from widows and orphans," but despite his own heroic efforts, served too short a time to have a real impact on changing the system. Kennedy was able, however, to put a real dent in the court, when he challenged the party's candidate for surrogate with a candidate of his own: a colorless but highly respected state Supreme

Court justice named Samuel Silverman. After a hard-fought campaign, Silverman won—a victory that was widely credited to the efforts of Senator Kennedy. Unfortunately, although Silverman remained safely ensconced in his judgeship for years, the system remained the same, showing how deeply surrogate patronage had embedded itself into the system. The biggest surprise, however, was the position of the bar associations and good government groups. In the vanguard of judicial reform, some of these groups attacked Kennedy's proposal for a salaried public guardian, leading to the conclusion that although they might disapprove of the way patronage is dispensed, they didn't want it eliminated.[61]

The problem with surrogate patronage is twofold: Even the most ardent judicial reformers cannot buck the entrenched party system, which virtually guarantees legal business to cooperative and loyal members of the party machine. When it gets really out of hand (i.e., when the fees seem disproportionately high), then brief stabs at reform quiet the criticism, and life goes on as usual. This occurred several years ago, when Brooklyn Surrogate Court Judge Michael Feinberg was removed from office for awarding nearly $9 million in guardianship fees to a close friend.

Judicial patronage has survived many attempts at reform and remains alive and well, perhaps because insiders can always count on public apathy. One recent reform effort failed to change the system, despite the horrifying data that were uncovered: In late 2001, a commission convened by Chief Judge Judith Kaye of the New York Court of Appeals reported that courthouse patronage (including guardianships, receiverships, and refereeships) were based—no surprise here— on cronyism, politics, and nepotism. The report followed a flurry of negative publicity over judicial patronage, spurred by a letter to party leaders from two Brooklyn clubhouse lawyers: Arnold Ludwig and Thomas Garry. Ludwig and Garry complained that they were getting frozen out of legal work—in particular, the lucrative receivership on the Cypress Hills Cemetery case—and were so angry they were resigning from the party. When their letter became public, people were outraged by the sense of entitlement that both lawyers felt. An inspector general combed through thousands of court files and concluded that yes, indeed, the most lucrative judicial patronage went to a small group of politically connected lawyers, most of whom had contributed their time and money to the party. In many cases, the report found, fees were extracted that were not legitimate in their view, such as a bill charging a ward of the court $1,000 for a shopping trip, or a bill for $850 to pay for a birthday cake and flowers. Other cases revealed that fees were billed without any justification for them.

Surrogate patronage often provides a comfortable retirement income for politicians who have left office. The Kaye Commission uncovered a case in which a retired Nassau County judge was appointed as a *guardian ad litem*. He hired his daughter as his counsel on the case; a retired surrogate judge as an adviser;

and another friend, the Public Administrator of Nassau County. None of his pals and relatives came cheap. Together they extracted $1.5 million from an $80 million estate: The retired judge took $424,000; his daughter, $44,000; the former surrogate, $192,000; and the administrator, $215,000.[62] Three years before Judge Kaye's report, another report by the prestigious Association of the Bar of the City of New York revealed more of the same: that campaign finance and judicial patronage went hand in hand, and that judicial campaigns were among the worst offenders. In the case of Surrogate Renee R. Roth, for example, the association charged that 66 percent of her appointments went to campaign contributors and that 38 percent of the contributions came from attorneys who received appointments either from the court or from attorneys who worked for law firms that received appointments.[63] "They didn't bother looking to see if I had appointed them long before the [re-election] campaign," Roth explained, adding, "We have a very small [surrogate] bar."

"It's a whole new world," Roth said of Manhattan Surrogate Court. "I was first elected on the platform that I was going to open up the process. This place is transparent. There is an $80,000 limit on the amount an attorney can receive over a two-year period, and all lawyers who want to be considered must take a course. County leaders no longer have any say over who is elected as a Surrogate."

Other prominent politicians also benefited from judicial largesse, among them Mario Cuomo, former governor of New York.[64]

Judge Kaye's report was stinging, in its data as well as its recommendations for reforming the system. To date, however, the report appears as if it will join other reports, languishing on dusty shelves, surfacing every now and then to join newer reform efforts—which will, based on past experience, come to naught.

Campaign Cash

"We put cash in the courtroom, and it's just wrong," Sandra Day O'Connor, the former Supreme Court justice, declared at the start of a conference on a growing threat to judicial independence: the millions of dollars that special interests are pouring into state judicial elections in an effort to buy favorable rulings.[65] John Grisham described the process in his book, *The Appeal*, which tells how a company that had lost a multimillion-dollar lawsuit put millions of dollars into the campaign of a state Supreme Court justice who would be the swing vote on an appeal. Grisham's book is a work of fiction that is grounded in facts, according to the author in a television appearance.[66]

Thirty-nine states elect at least some of their judges. Their campaigns often include fifteen- and thirty-second attack ads. Many of these contests are underwritten by stakeholders who have a vested interest in judicial decisions, often including insurance companies, tobacco firms, the building and health-care industries, unions, and trial lawyers. Justice Stephen Breyer told the same conference, at Fordham Law School, that 95 percent of the cases in the United States are handled by state courts rather than federal courts.[67]

Vernon Valentine Palmer, a law professor at Tulane University, couldn't understand how justices of the Louisiana Supreme Court could routinely hear cases involving people who had given them contributions. In a study conducted with John Levendis, an economics professor at Loyola University in New Orleans, he discovered that in nearly half of the cases they reviewed, over a fourteen-year period ending in 2006, a litigant or lawyer had contributed to the campaign of at least one justice. They found that on average, justices voted in favor of their contributors sixty-five percent of the time, and two of the justices did so eighty percent of the time. [68] Defenders of the system insisted that judges did not change their votes in response to contributions, but rather that contributors supported judges whose legal opinions they found congenial. But Professor Palmer said that after studying the judges' voting patterns, it became clear that "it is the donation, not the underlying philosophical orientation, that appears to account for the voting outcome," adding, "The greater the size of the contribution, the greater the odds of favorable outcomes."

In 2004, a total of $47 million nationwide was spent on campaigns for state Supreme Court judges, up from $29 million two years earlier. In 2006, total fundraising decreased to $34.4 million, largely owing to a decrease in the number of contested races. But the median amount raised by individual candidates in 2006 soared to nearly $244,000, from the 2004 median of about $202,000.[69] Television ads, previously a rarity in state judicial contests, have become the norm. Business groups, the biggest spenders, contributed $15 million to the eighty-eight state Supreme Court candidates who raised funds, far more than the $7 million lawyers contributed.

In Washington State, $2 million was spent in 2006 on campaigns for three seats on the State Supreme Court. "Some of the television and radio attack ads against the incumbent chief justice, Gerry Alexander, were so unfair or misleading they would have seemed out of line even if the contests were for local alderman, instead of a lofty position on the state's highest court."[70] Despite these attacks, Alexander won reelection.

In Pennsylvania, more than $5 million was spent in 2007 on election campaigns for a seat on the state's Supreme Court, while $8.2 million was spent in a contest for chief justice of the Alabama Supreme Court. The spending in large part reflects a decision by business groups to get involved in the contests. The National Association of Manufacturers announced in 2005 that it was establishing the American Justice Partnership to promote tort reform in the states.[71]

Public financing of judicial campaigns is one way to end this system, which forces too many judicial candidates into an unhealthy dependence on wealthy contributors. It also would end the incentive to reward those contributors with favorable decisions from the bench, and thereby enhance public respect for the administration of justice. At its annual mid-year meeting in February 2002, the House of Delegates of the American Bar Association urged states that hold judicial elections to finance judicial campaigns with public funds.[72] Even spending limits would help by reducing the need for financial contributions, even without public financing. Alarmed by the escalating costs of campaign finance, the Brennan Center for Justice filed *amicus* briefs and argued strongly for public financing of judicial elections. Citizens have the right to "appear before judges who are fair and impartial," which cannot occur when judges aspire to be "re-elected or to be elected to a higher court."[73] The Brennan Center released a study in the spring of 2010 indicating that the costs of winning a judicial election had escalated even higher: Three of the last five state Supreme Court elections cost more than $45 million, while in the last decade candidates for state judgeships raised more than $206 million, more than twice the cost of judicial elections in the 1990s.

In the long run, the financing of judgeships matters in much the same way stakeholders plant their feet so firmly in the political process. The problem is that until injustice happens, the public remains blissfully ignorant. Few remember the gross injustice of the Avery case—except its victims, that is. Affected were the 4.7 million policyholders in forty-eight states that were clients of the State Farm Automobile Insurance Company in a dispute involving more than $1 billion. Enter a campaign for the hotly contested race for State Supreme Court Justice. The two candidates, Illinois appellate Judge Gordon Maag and Circuit Judge Lloyd Karmeier, together raised $9.3 million, at that time the most expensive state judicial campaign in recent memory. (Illinois has no limits on campaign contributions.) The winner, Karmeier, received more than $1 million from State Farm employees, lawyers, and others involved with the company; he also benefited from contributions from other groups that included State Farm in their membership rosters. Despite these contributions and their relevance to his later success, Karmeier refused to recuse himself from State Farm's successful appeal before the Illinois Supreme Court, denying the lower court's plaintiff award of $1 billion—and the U.S. Supreme Court backed him up by refusing to grant certiorari on March, 6, 2006.[74]

The case is striking in its implications and violates the principles of due process: The petitioners were unable to remove a judge who had received money from the defendant during the same period in which the trial was taking place. Neither the U.S. Supreme Court nor the petitioners saw anything wrong with taking money from one side in a judicial proceeding; their justification was that bribes and campaign contributions should be considered separate entities, even though the effects were the same.

Another case decided quite differently by the U.S. Supreme Court involved another well-financed judge who had allegedly confused his judicial role with his campaign for office. In this case, two competing coal companies—Harman Mining and Massey Coal—fought over a $50 million jury award to Caperton (an executive with Harman). Caperton claimed that Massey Coal drove his company out of business, and the jury believed him. Immediately before the case came up for appeal, the Supreme Court Judgeship election in West Virginia pitted two rivals against each other, with attorney Brent Benjamin emerging victorious over incumbent Justice Warren McGraw. The problem? Benjamin's campaign contributions included $517,000 from an organization (And for the Sake of the Kids) directly related to the CEO, Don Blankenship of Massey Coal, the company appealing the judgment. Later reports raised the estimate of Blankenship's campaign contributions to Benjamin to $3 million. Did Benjamin recuse himself from the case? No, and not surprisingly, the newly elected judge decided against the jury award and in favor of Massey Coal. The case has roused national interest, especially because there are virtually no guidelines—except for financial interest—for recusal, and campaign contributions were not regarded in the category of personal financial interest. A flood of *amicus* briefs supported Caperton and his initial supporter, the Brennan Center for Justice, including Wal-Mart, Lockheed Martin, Pepsi, Common Cause, the League of Women Voters, and Justice at Stake, a judicial reform group concerned the unsavory role of money in judicial campaigns.[75]

A conflict of interest? A conflict with the American Bar Association's standards of recusal? Or a new pattern of justice related to campaign finance and political obligation. On June 8, 2009, the Supreme Court decided in favor of Caperton, and most important, against the improper use of campaign money in judicial elections. In other words, the Court held that the chief justice of the West Virginia Supreme Court should have recused himself from a case involving a CEO who had contributed to his recent election.[76]

The real problem with the dispute over how judges are selected—either through appointment or election—is voter ignorance and disinterest. On the one hand, raising money or having to depend on the party machine inevitably leads to the necessity to reward those responsible either for nominating or appointing a candidate for judicial office. Obviously, contributors to a judicial campaign—particularly those who fork over sizable amounts of money—look forward to more favorable outcomes than they had experienced in the past. Those who favor appointing judges argue that their method insulates judges from political pressure and from the "compromising pressures of contested elections,"[77] but surely, governors or panels of "experts" also have political agendas that sway their decisions as well. In addition, "appointments" run the risk of "incumbency protection," a real danger given the impossibility of removing judges except for "high crimes and misdemeanors."[78] Without any information, "voters lose their main cue on whom to vote for and, lacking more relevant information, rely on other factors such as ballot position or name recognition."[79] Couple all those selection methods with the typical voter's lack of information and interest, and a solution remains elusive.

The worst difficulty with public financing, or limits on campaign funding, is that without meaningful reform in the other two branches of government—the executive branch and the legislature—chances are less likely that the least-scrutinized branch, the judiciary, will get any attention. Public financing is now available (thanks to reform efforts in the past) for the presidential race, yet shrewd candidates inevitably decline this honor, preferring to raise much vaster amounts on their own. Incumbents in Congress start raising money for their next race the morning after they are reelected—especially because television time and other forms of advertising have made elections increasingly expensive. Each era brings new reforms in campaign finance, but whatever legislation emerges usually produces loopholes wide enough to make them meaningless. In this environment, the judiciary will come last—if at all.

The Massey Energy Company and its CEO later made headlines as the owner of the Upper Big Branch mine, which exploded in early April 2010, costing the lives of at least 25 miners in the worst mining disaster in the last quarter century. In retrospect, it was apparent that the judicially savvy Blankenship and his advisers decided it was cheaper to litigate than to correct safety violations, choosing to challenge all the safety violations cited by the U.S. Mine Safety and Health Administration (MSHA) instead of correcting them. Under pressure, the defanged regulatory agency, MSHA, admitted that it had cited the mine 64 times since early 2009 but neglected to follow up. The coal mine, said the agency, did not show the "pattern of violation" that would have prodded them to take further action. O'Connor followed up her strong preference for merit selection on the state level by speaking out on the issue and lending her support and name to the formation of the O'Connor Judicial Selection Initiative, an effort to involve lawyers, judges, and other stakeholders in the criminal justice system into the debate over how judges are chosen in the United States. Since the initiative was launched in 2009, Nevada abolished judicial elections in favor of a commission-based system, while similar proposals are circulating in Minnesota and Maryland. Justice Ruth Bader Ginsburg has also supported the elimination of the practice of electing judges.

Patronage and Justice for All

Many voters believe that an independent judiciary is a critical part of democracy, yet time after time their trust is breached. The real problem is that few agree on what constitutes "independence." Real campaign finance reform has not changed much since Mark Twain accused the U.S. legislature as being the "best Congress money can buy." Exhaustive analysis of judicial selection hasn't reached any consensus about whether partisan elections, nonpartisan commissions, nonpartisan elections, or any of the other systems produce judiciaries that stand out as the fairest of all.

On the surface, at least, it appears that partisan elections are "subject to manipulation and that elected officials could be captured by partisan forces."[80] Yet so-called "nonpartisan" selection processes can be captured by other groups that may have other agendas at stake, agendas that might be just as political as those of the party bosses. The ABA, for example, came out as early as 1871 against partisan judicial elections on the grounds that judges were "subject to undue and damaging political pressure."[81] Yet the ABA—which is dominated by the states and remains the leading stakeholder in this dispute—has done little to stem the tide of courthouse patronage (refereeships, guardianships, and so on) that can also politicize the system.

Waves of judicial reform throughout history from the Progressives, the Mugwumps, and the Populists—to name a few—led to very little change, largely due to resistance from the president and congress, voter apathy, and the high cost of conducting campaigns for change. Of all the reasons, voter apathy stands out as the most serious. In partisan elections, people don't usually study the candidates for judgeships before voting for them. They simply don't care, they trust the party leaders to do the selecting for them, or they fail to see the connections between the judicial system and their lives. Most citizens consider themselves law-abiding and cannot foresee themselves having any contact with a courtroom. Similarly, felons can't vote, so even though they might have definite views about the criminal justice system, there is no channel through which they can express those views. "Americans want judges who believe the constitution provides for equal justice for all," wrote Nan Aron, president of the Alliance for Justice, a group that has consistently monitored judicial appointments for the last thirty years.

As far as guardianships or receiverships are concerned, the number of voters who could make a difference is insignificant. Most people do not envision dying intestate (without a will) or probably even dying at all. Likewise, a pollster would be hard put to find voters who care about the people who will be put in charge of corporations that have fallen on hard times and are about to be put in receivership.

But close scrutiny of judicial patronage reveals huge chinks in the armor of justice. President George W. Bush's use of "deferred prosecutions" and "nonprosecutorial agreement" raised nary an eyebrow when corporate wrongdoers escaped prosecution, but much later, public anger swelled to mammoth proportions at news that AIG executives gave themselves $165 million in bonuses after their company had happily received billions of dollars from the federal government.

Is there a correlation? Years of excessive compensation for poor performance were punished by neither the marketplace nor the government; sure, "non-prosecutorial agreements" were preferable to being sued by the government, but as more than one analyst has observed, laws and regulations are useless unless the public fears them. If malfeasance can be "negotiated," no wonder existing laws and regulations governing the marketplace are worthless in a crisis.

A similar schizophrenia exists when it comes to the concept of the "rule of law." On the one hand, American democracy is distinguished by its reliance on the rule of law. Other countries may hold elections, but they can hardly be called true democracies if mob rule prevails—as occurs so often—or if running a business is impossible in the absence of business law—the case in Russia and so many other areas of the world. When the Obama administration grappled with the economic crisis in the early spring of 2008, the president and his economic advisers faced an angry American public and emphasized the importance of contract law in defending the bonuses awarded to AIG executives. Their lawyers advised them, they argued, that there was no way to stop the bonuses, undeserved as they were, because of the existence of contracts. America is a litigious society, complained former President George W. Bush. But litigation is a sign that the public regards the courts as a channel through which their grievances can be addressed; in other words, Aristotle's dictum that laws should prevail above people remains a strong principle of American life that is marred by some of the practices revealed by the political system that governs judicial patronage.

Judicial patronage runs the gamut of political rewards. The most visible are the judgeships, but a wide range of riches remains a vital part of politics. Lately, disaffected groups have highlighted some of these rewards that have largely been hidden from public view. The fired U.S. attorneys, for example, revealed the longtime and widely accepted practice of presidential patronage in the Justice Department; similarly, the historical practice of selective prosecutions came to light during the same time period. The Avery and Caperton cases stimulated a national discussion over the use of campaign contributions in judicial elections. Were these contributions fair? Should judges recuse themselves from cases involving contributors?

And what about incompetent judges? In the past, voter apathy took care of judicial elections, leaving that power largely in the hands of the political party or possibly other political leaders. But there are hopeful signs that the public is taking a greater interest in the bench, finally realizing that the quality of justice and judicial patronage are closely related to each other, and to their lives.

Chapter Six
Presidential Patronage

"When a President makes appointments with an eye to winning support for some part of his legislative program, he is not doing something *sui generis*."

Professor Stanley Kelley Jr., Princeton University

"I can't be bought, but I can be rented."

Representative (later Senator) John Breaux, (D-Louisiana), explaining why he supported President Reagan's tax bill in exchange for preservation of a sugar subsidy

Shortly after his election but before he took office, President Ronald Reagan dispatched his congressional liaison team to introduce themselves to all 535 members of Congress. "We told them, 'We're the new kids on the block,'" recalled Kenneth Duberstein, who served as Reagan's congressional liaison and later became the president's chief of staff. "We told them, 'We're here to serve you. If you need anything, don't hesitate to call us.'"

During the Reagan presidency, Duberstein said, "We tweaked legislation for them." But sometimes Reagan went further, as when passage of his first budget was very much in doubt. "Two nights before the vote, we went down [to the White House]," Duberstein recalled. "I gave Reagan a list of congressmen to call. He reached Representative John Breaux [a Louisiana Democrat] who was having dinner with several 'Boll Weevils,' southern Democrats from districts carried by Reagan. Breaux told Reagan that the sugar subsidy program was a major concern of his. [David] Stockman [the budget director] had decided to axe the program. I was tasked with explaining to Stockman that he had to back off. That was the key to the Reagan Revolution. If we had lost that vote, it [the Reagan Revolution] wouldn't have happened." The deal became known, leading Breaux to utter his now-famous quote: "I can't be bought, but I can be rented."

Reagan displayed a mastery of the care and feeding of congressmen, a key element in obtaining legislative support for his White House initiatives. He made a little patronage go a long way. A naturally gregarious man, Reagan invited members of Congress to the White House for dinner and photographs with the president, invited them to ride with him on Air Force One, and even telephoned them in their district offices. This delighted their congressional staffs, which relayed the event to the local newspapers, resulting in articles about the congressman's obvious importance in being telephoned by the president. Reagan's arch-adversary, Speaker Thomas P. O'Neill, another jovial Irish American, was a frequent White House guest with whom Reagan would dine and then retreat to the Truman balcony to swap stories and enjoy cigars. "Reagan loved people," Duberstein said. "He loved the interchange with people on the Hill."

But behind that genial smile was a tough politician. Reagan, who never had a Republican majority in the House of Representatives, used a negative threat to obtain passage of his first tax bill. He promised the Boll Weevils that he would not campaign against them the following year if they voted for the bill. Their leader, Charles Stenholm of Abilene, Texas, feared that because Reagan had carried their districts, his fellow Boll Weevils would be imperiled if he campaigned for their Republican challengers. The result: "On the tax bill, we got 48 House Democrats," Duberstein recalled. The House Republican leadership was furious, he recalled. They thought they could pick up many of those seats in the next election, with a chance of becoming the majority party. Indeed, most of those seats ultimately ended up in the Republican column.

"A President has to be revered and feared," Duberstein observed. "Reagan was both."

The president of the United States is the most powerful politician in the world. He sets the national agenda, commands armies, determines foreign policy, appoints judges, and is considered the equivalent of one-third of the members of Congress because it takes a two-thirds vote to override a presidential veto. His actions have a profound effect on the world's financial markets; in countless ways he determines which industries and companies will thrive and which will go under. A president's power to enrich one company at the expense of another was demonstrated during the financial meltdown of 2008–2009. Goldman Sachs, a politically connected investment banking house formerly chaired by then–Treasury Secretary Henry Paulson and former Treasury Secretary Robert Rubin, reaped billions in federal loans denied to Lehman Brothers, which was forced into bankruptcy, while Merrill Lynch, another Goldman Sachs competitor, was forced into an acquisition by Bank of America.

A president's "bully pulpit" gives him instant access to the American people and to the people of the world. His vast powers also make him the *de facto* leader of his party and the source of all federal political appointments. But to achieve his objectives takes an appreciation of the underpinnings of politics: what it takes to move bills through Congress, twist the arms of foreign leaders, and raise the kind of money needed to win elections.

Ironically, the Constitution provided for a weak presidency. The president's only absolute power not subject to Congress or the courts is the power to pardon, which has been used sparingly. Every other presidential power is conditional: The Supreme Court can declare a presidential action unconstitutional, as it did when President Truman seized the steel mills. Treaties require a two-thirds vote of the Senate; important appointments require Senate confirmation; and of course legislation usually travels a route from the White House (and OMB in particular) to Capitol Hill, where Congress usually reconfigures the president's initiatives. Indeed, a close reading of the Constitution reveals a weak president burdened with obligations—to "receive" foreign diplomats, "take care that the laws are faithfully executed," "shall nominate," "shall appoint," and "shall Commission all the officers of the United States."

From their perspective, the Founding Fathers' strictures on presidential power made sense. They had just won a war against a better-equipped army, a stable government, and a powerful chief executive: their nemesis, King George III. Democracy, they believed, depended on a dispersal of power, rather than a strong central authority. History, however, moved in the opposite direction, and the necessities incurred over the next 200 years by wars and wild fluctuations in the business cycle brought about the strong presidency Americans now take for granted.

But despite his enormous powers, the American president is not a dictator. By hook or crook, the president must corral enough votes on Capitol Hill to transform proposals into law. And in pursuit of those votes, he must wade into the political arena and engage in horse-trading. Enter political patronage. "It is the need to bargain that keeps presidential power as uncertain as in most respects I find it," observed the astute political scientist Richard E. Neustadt. "And the need to bargain is the product of a constitutional system that shares formal powers among separate institutions. Of these, the presidency is only one."[1]

A president's major power, Neustadt held, was the power to persuade, and to achieve that end a president has an extraordinary number of bargaining chits that revolve around his ability to reward his friends and punish his enemies. Presidents reward political allies with federal appointments, including judgeships, ambassadorships, board and commission memberships; earmarks; federal contracts; presidential pardons; appearances at campaign rallies and fundraisers; invitations to state dinners at the White House; flights on Air

Force One; and overnight stays in the White House's Lincoln bedroom. Petty as it seems, President Jimmy Carter personally presided over use of the White House tennis court.

The American people have been traditionally suspicious of power: a suspicion fueled by those who wield political power at the same time they denounce government! President Obama was the first president in modern history not to run against Washington. Beginning with President Reagan, who famously said that government was the problem, not the solution, presidential candidates of both parties blamed "faceless bureaucrats" for much of the nation's ills. But not Obama. During his campaign he pledged to increase—not decrease—the power of the federal government, to the delight of the government unions that had supported him. Obama owed more to organized labor than to the moguls who profited from privatization and outsourcing. During the first weeks of his presidency, the Obamas toured federal agencies and thanked the bureaucrats for their dedication to public service.

The U.S. president wears many hats: legislative leader, head of his party, commander-in-chief, top fundraiser, and chief administrator, to name a few. No king or queen can be called in to assume the numerous ceremonial roles of the presidency, and the president is blamed for every crisis that besets the country. In addition to all those responsibilities, the president sits atop a system with 80,000 separate jurisdictions—states, counties, municipalities, water and sewer districts—all of which look toward Washington for guidance and relief. No wonder British political scientist Harold Laski was said to have graphically described the American presidency in terms of apoplexy at the center and palsy at the limbs.[2]

But despite their enormous powers, presidents have pushed the envelope, asserting ever more powers in their efforts to confront increasingly complex problems. In the midst of the Civil War, with Congress in recess, President Lincoln suspended *habeas corpus,* summoned state militias, and placed a blockade on rebellious states. When Congress returned, Lincoln explained that his actions "whether strictly legal or not, were ventured upon under what appeared to be a popular demand and a public necessity, trusting then, as now, that Congress would readily ratify them," which Congress did.[3] During World War II, President Franklin Delano Roosevelt herded more than 100,000 Japanese Americans into "relocation centers," an action upheld by the Supreme Court despite a lone dissent by Justice Frank Murphy, who said that the president's action "bears a melancholy resemblance to the treatment accorded to the members of the Jewish race in Germany and in other parts of Europe."[4] Congress apologized to the nation's Japanese American citizens a half century later. President Harry Truman seized the steel mills as part of his effort to wage the Korean War, an action promptly struck down by the Supreme Court.[5] World War II was the last war in which a president went to Congress to obtain a declaration of war, as required by the Constitution;

the Korean, Vietnam, Afghanistan, and two wars in Iraq were fought without any congressional declaration. Although personally implicated in the Watergate scandal, President Nixon famously explained that a president was incapable of acting illegally. President George W. Bush directed illegal wiretaps on U.S. citizens and suspended *habeas corpus* for those deemed enemy combatants.

In a more recent intrusion into legislative powers that critics find constitutionally questionable, presidents have added to their power through the increasing use of "signing statements" that declare their interpretation of a bill, including which sections they will NOT enforce. Barack Obama challenged the constitutionality of this practice during his presidential campaign, but he nevertheless issued his first signing statement less than two months into his presidency. The issue involved a provision in a $410 billion spending bill that protected officials who gave Congress information about their jobs or agencies. Obama said the statute could not limit his power to control the flow of information from the executive branch to Congress. But Senator Charles Grassley, an Iowa Republican, complained that Obama's statement would "undoubtedly chill whistle-blowers who might otherwise come forward to report waste, fraud or abuse to Congress" and asked the president to fully enforce the statute. During his presidential campaign, however, Obama had criticized his predecessor's frequent use of signing statements as an abuse of power and pledged not to undermine the intent of Congress.[6]

The Carrot

Presidents have the ability to make or break political careers through their patronage powers. President Obama demonstrated the myriad ways the White House could use federal patronage to help a candidate when he mobilized his troops to help the reelection campaign of Senator Arlen Specter, a Pennsylvania Republican who became a Democrat. Specter made the switch after voting for Obama's economic stimulus package in 2009 and extracting in the process an additional $10 billion for biomedical research. Specter provided the sixtieth vote that was needed to avoid a filibuster, thereby alienating the Republican Party's right wing. He was not expected to win the Republican primary and expected a tough fight in the Democratic primary, which he ultimately lost.

Obama touched off the administration's largesse by raising $2.5 million at a Specter fundraiser. The president also singled out Specter in his speech to the national AFL-CIO convention, calling the senator "a man who came to Washington to fight for the working men and women of Pennsylvania and who has a distinguished record of doing just that."[7] Obama also appeared in several TV ads for Specter. Vice President Joe Biden also raised megabucks at several fundraisers for Specter.

The president also dispatched five cabinet secretaries to the Keystone State to demonstrate Specter's clout. Janet Napolitano, Homeland Security Secretary, announced increased funding for security at the Philadelphia airport. Ray LaHood, Transportation Secretary, broke ground on a $9.3 million project to renovate the Elizabethtown Amtrak station, pointing out that the funds came from the stimulus package that became law because of Specter's vote. Ken Salazar, Interior Secretary, had a well-publicized meeting with Somerset County Commissioners and announced the acquisition of land for a memorial for the victims of US Airways Flight 93, who had perished on 9/11. Eric Shinseki, Veterans Administration Secretary, joined Specter at two Town Hall meetings, in Philadelphia and Pittsburgh, at which he spoke of additional help for the state's veterans, and Katherine Sibelius, Health and Human Services Secretary, also joined Specter at a town hall meeting. But it was all for naught. Pennsylvania Democrats refused to accept Specter, who was handily defeated in the party's 2010 primary.

During his first year in office, Obama also rewarded scores of top Democratic donors with VIP access to the White House, private briefings with administration advisers, and invitations to important speeches and town hall meetings. One top donor described a birthday visit to the Oval Office, while another was allowed family use of the White House bowling alley. Others have been invited to golf with the president both in Washington and on Martha's Vineyard and have traveled overseas with the president.[8]

Obama's help for Specter was reminiscent of the way President Nixon showered his discretionary favors on the reelection campaign of New York City Mayor John V. Lindsay, who faced a tough Republican primary. Lindsay had pocketed a Nixon IOU at the 1968 Republican national convention in Miami by seconding the nomination of Spiro T. Agnew and by discouraging those who had urged Lindsay to contest the vice presidential nomination. When Lindsay ran for re-election as New York City's mayor in 1969, the Nixon administration directed a number of federal agencies to make public contributions to the city during the eight weeks before primary day. With much showmanship, Vice President Agnew began the flow of favors by announcing the long-sought purchase of the Brooklyn Navy Yard by the city at an advantageous price. Then the Commerce Department announced grants for job training at the Yard; the Defense Department announced the lease of the Brooklyn Army Terminal; the Interior Department announced a new federal park in Breezy Point, the Rockaways; Health, Education and Welfare announced new narcotics projects for the city; and the attorney general announced aid for the city's "war against crime." Harry S. Dent, President Nixon's special counsel and patronage dispenser, said in his soft South Carolina drawl, "The Vice President brought him here [Washington] and helped him with exposure." But all to no avail. Lindsay lost the Republican primary to a Staten Island conservative, State Senator John J. Marchi, but went on to win reelection by forming a fusion campaign, soliciting endorsements from high-profile Democrats and staying as far away as possible from the White House. Indeed, Lindsay went so far as to attack the White House and Agnew, in particular, during the 1970 congressional elections, expressing regret at having seconded Agnew's nomination. After the campaign, Dent was asked if Lindsay would lose some of the federal programs promised the city. "Punishment is counterproductive," Dent replied. "It creates sympathy for a man." But he added that thereafter federal aid to the city would be channeled exclusively through Governor Nelson Rockefeller and Senators Jacob Javits and Jim Buckley, all Republicans.[9] Lindsay formally switched parties in 1971 and ran unsuccessfully for the Democratic presidential nomination a year later.

Nixon's rise from the political ashes, after his 1960 defeat for the presidency by John F. Kennedy and his unsuccessful campaign for governor of California in 1962, was based in large part on "pre-presidential patronage." This involved Nixon's indefatigable campaigning for local candidates in his years out of office, when he was photographed with Republicans across the length and breadth of the country and was a frequent speaker at Republican fundraisers. This resurrected Nixon's moribund political career, and he later found it easy to call in IOUs when he needed them. The Nixon style was described by Governor Nelson Rockefeller in 1970, when he told a dinner meeting of the Governor's Club that the president had personally promised him full support in his reelection bid. "Confidentially," the governor related, lowering his voice, the president promised: "I will campaign for you in any way that will help, and I'll not hurt you." And for his part, Rockefeller told the group he would continue to support the president's policies "in every way I can."

Many have speculated that this strategy was later employed by 2008 GOP vice presidential candidate Sarah Palin, who resigned the governorship of Alaska to return to "private" life, where she would be free to campaign and raise funds for Republican candidates in the "lower 48" states. A proven crowd-pleaser who was known for her ability to draw large groups of the party faithful, she would later find herself in a perfect position to call in her IOUs, revive her political career as Nixon did, and run for the presidency in 2012 or 2016. She knew that if she proved successful in rebuilding the party, criticisms would soon fade away.

Sticks

Presidential patronage involves not only the carrot, but also the stick. Presidents have turned loose federal investigative agencies, including the IRS and FBI, on political foes.[10] A president can deny a member of Congress earmarks for projects previously approved by the Army Corps of Engineers, by directing the Corps to ignore the project. Presidents also have defied the custom of "senatorial courtesy" and ignored a lawmaker's judicial recommendations, as well as recommendations for appointments of regional, state, and district administrators. Such a course of action, however, may provoke retaliation by Congress. President Woodrow Wilson nominated his friend and economic adviser, Louis Brandeis, the nation's leading critic of big business and finance, to the Supreme Court in 1916, without consulting Brandeis's two home state senators, conservative Massachusetts Republicans Henry Cabot Lodge and John W. Weeks. "It was nothing less than an act of defiance, not merely of conservative senators, but more importantly, of all the powers of organized wealth in the country," wrote Arthur Link, a Wilson biographer. Link wrote that "Boston politicians, conservatives, defenders of the *status quo* and men who liked to think of themselves as devotees of constitutional government were stunned and furious ... Former President Taft almost went into trauma when he heard the news."[11]

In rare instances, presidents have even campaigned against members of Congress of their own party. Infuriated by their opposition to many New Deal programs, as well as to his court-packing scheme, President Franklin Roosevelt supported primary opponents of Democratic senators Walter George of Georgia, Millard Tydings of Maryland, and "Cotton Ed" Smith of South Carolina—all conservative Democrats who had voted against FDR's legislative initiatives. Campaigning on the caboose of what became known as the "Purge Train," Roosevelt charged during frequent stops that Tydings "had betrayed the New Deal in the past, and would again." Notwithstanding Roosevelt's opposition, or perhaps because of it, all his targets handily won their primaries and general elections.[12]

Presidents also have increasingly used recess appointments when Congress thwarted their nominees. Used sparingly by presidents since George Washington, these appointments were rare until the mid-twentieth century. They are made when Congress is in recess or cannot conduct confirmation business in a timely way, and expire at the end of a congressional session. President George W. Bush, for example, named John Bolton as United States ambassador to the United Nations in a recess appointment because he faced considerable resistance from Congress to Bolton's appointment; many in Congress objected to what they considered Bolton's intimidating and confrontational work style.

Patronage works both ways, though, and Congress occasionally asserts itself when the president goes too far in beating up his enemies. In the spring of 1937, the House of Representatives reduced from $12,000 to $10,000 the salary of President Franklin D. Roosevelt's right-hand man, Harry Hopkins, who was responsible for the nitty-gritty of what it takes to carry out the carrots and sticks of presidential power. Hopkins also headed the Works Progress Administration, an agency created during the New Deal, which put millions of Americans to work. *The Baltimore Sun* commented: "No member voiced on the floor the real reason for this feeling toward Hopkins, but there is no mystery about it. They hate Hopkins because they are afraid of him; and they are afraid of him because they think he is capable of building up an organization in their individual districts to fight them, if they do not vote according to his orders." This meant that members of Congress feared that Hopkins could use the WPA to produce a patronage army that the president could use to defeat them.[13]

Vindictiveness often comes at a high price, as President George W. Bush learned when he pointedly neglected to invite Vermont Senator Jim Jeffords to a ceremony honoring the Teacher of the Year, who happened to be a Vermonter. Bush's action was intended to punish Jeffords, a moderate Republican, for opposing many of the White House's legislative proposals. This backfired mightily, as many Republicans warned it would. Shortly thereafter, in 2001, Jeffords bolted from the Republican Party, became an Independent and caucused with the Democrats, denying Republicans their slim majority in the Senate, leading the Democrats to become the majority party.

But the president has ample tools to retaliate when irritated with members of Congress. The master of this, of course, was Lyndon Johnson, who openly used his powers over the budget to punish his enemies. "You don't want to reward Shreveport till they behave," he angrily told Senator Russell Long (D-Louisiana), who was pleading with the president to restore funding for a post office in a city that had voted for his Republican opponent. Long reminded LBJ that the post office in question was "scheduled ten years ago," and besides, he thought LBJ would carry Shreveport in the next election. "They are the meanest, most vicious people in the United States," Johnson responded, referring to comments in the city's major newspaper calling him a "thief and a thug ... Don't ask me to reward people who cut your throat."[14]

Presidents traditionally play hardball with Congress, although probably not as skillfully, directly, or thoroughly as LBJ. When John Kyl (R-Arizona) said President Obama's stimulus bill was too costly, several cabinet secretaries, ostensibly directed by the president's chief of staff Rahm Emanuel, wrote to the governor of Arizona to ask what stimulus money the state did not want.[15]

But mostly, presidents accentuate the positive and try not to use "sticks" too often or too visibly. President George W. Bush often denounced earmarks as "special interest items" that wasted taxpayer money and undermined trust in government. But to shore up political support on Capitol Hill and elsewhere, Bush requested hundreds of millions of dollars worth of earmarks in his final budget in 2008. These included $800,000 for a fish hatchery in Missouri; $1.5 million for a waterway named in honor of former Senator J. Bennett Johnston, a Louisiana Democrat; $894,000 for an air traffic control tower in Kalamazoo,

Michigan; $3 million for a forest conservation project in Minnesota; and $6.5 million for research in Wyoming on the "fundamental properties of asphalt."[16] Asked to comment on presidential earmarks, *The New York Times* reporter Robert Pear noted that "In many cases, the project was set in motion by a member of Congress," adding, "There is patronage in these projects."

Ninety-Nine Enemies and One Ingrate

Soon after he was elected president, Abraham Lincoln was afflicted with smallpox and forced to take to his bed. Outside his window, he could see the mobs of job seekers who typically besieged the White House after a presidential election.[17] On his sickbed, Lincoln summoned his secretary and told him to "Tell all the office seekers to come at once, for now I have something I can give to all," referring to his smallpox.

The number of presidential appointments is far fewer than most people imagine. Out of a total federal civilian workforce of 2.7 million, only 7,000 are noncompetitive appointments, of which about 1,100 are subject to Senate confirmation.[18] These noncompetitive appointments are mostly policymaking and confidential positions and include the Senior Executive Service and Senior Foreign Service positions; Schedule C positions are exempted from the competitive service by the president or director of the Office of Personnel Management due to the confidential or policymaking nature of the duties; and other positions at the GS-9 level and above are exempted for the same reasons. These jobs are exempted from civil service control to give the new administration its own loyal organization and flexible policymaking apparatus. (Actually, Schedule C positions were created during the Eisenhower administration. The Republicans were convinced that the bureaucracy was dominated by Democrats after twenty years of Democratic presidents.) Depending on various estimates, the president actually has between 3,100 and 3,500 patronage jobs, two-thirds of which are fairly low-level—chauffeurs, cooks, and so on—and do not require Senate confirmation.

In addition, during each two-year congressional session, approximately 4,000 civilian and 65,000 military nominations are submitted to the Senate. The overwhelming majority are routinely approved.[19] The posts filled by the president range from cabinet positions paying $191,300 per year to clerical jobs paying only $40,000. Presidential appointments include cabinet deputy and assistant secretaries, departmental speechwriters, special assistants, staff assistants, research assistants, regional directors, general and special counsels, financial officers, program analysts, public affairs specialists, and program support specialists. They also include appointments to scores of independent agencies, government corporations, boards, and commissions. Board members of the Postal Rate Commission receive an annual salary of $149,000, as do board members of the National Labor Relations Board, the National Capital Planning Commission, and most other commissions. The chairs of most commissions earn $158,500.

When a new administration arrives in Washington, copies of the "Plum Book," which lists jobs exempt from the civil service, are quickly sold out as thousands of political hopefuls scour their pages. Even though the throngs are not as ubiquitous as they were in Lincoln's time, many still hope that their expertise, or better yet, their hours of ringing doorbells and raising money, will lead to government employment. Some agencies are still known as "patronage dumping grounds" and operate accordingly, often to the detriment of their own mandates. Before foreign trade became an important part of U.S. policy, for example, certain bureaus in the Department of Commerce were well-known outposts for campaign operatives. Today, exhausted campaign workers look for other bureaus to serve as likely patronage sources.[20]

They also find fruitful patronage sources in the quasi-governmental "hybrid" organizations, those agencies that have some legal relationship or association with the federal government. Many were created because of the government's concern for protecting the interests of the taxpayers, which are often in conflict with private shareholder interests. Hybrids include quasi-official agencies, government-sponsored enterprises, federally-funded research and development corporations, agency-related nonprofit organizations, venture capital funds, and congressionally chartered nonprofit organizations. Because they remain relatively hidden from public view, appointments to hybrids are especially desirable forms of presidential patronage.[21] OPIC, the Overseas Private Investment Corporation, for example, has also been very successful in linking wealthy contributors to government largesse; OPIC subsidies for U.S. companies investing in potentially unstable parts of the world provide greater profits to those entrepreneurs seeking to take advantage of opportunities opening up around the world.[22]

Evidence exists showing that in the last fifty years, presidential appointments have increasingly extended into the career bureaucracy in order to increase presidential control, reward supporters, and deliver on campaign promises. Between 1960 and 2000, for example, there has been a fourfold increase in the number of presidential appointments requiring Senate confirmation: from 451 senior executives, political and career, in 1960, to 2,592 in 2004.[23] Paul Light, who has written extensively on this subject, argues that plunging so deeply into the bureaucracy actually weakens a president's control of government, contrary to the view that increasing patronage power actually strengthens it. It is not that government is too large; rather, it is too complex and becomes unwieldy. What Light terms the "thickening" of the bureaucracy—the introduction of new layers of authority—impedes information flow, reduces accountability, and hurts continuity—especially because the average duration of political appointees runs from eighteen to twenty-four months. The "thickened" bureaucracy includes a "number of senior title holders," such as assistant undersecretaries and deputy secretaries, many of whom represent "alter egos," or a sign of "one's importance" in the bureaucratic structure.[24]

By the time he left office in 2008, President George W. Bush had expanded his patronage power by 15 percent, due in part to the creation of the Department of Homeland Security. Even though DHS combined many executive agencies, new positions were still created. Bush's actions were reminiscent of President Franklin Delano Roosevelt's creation of new agencies during the New Deal, which were fruitful sources of presidential patronage before being "blanketed in" by the civil service.

Like previous presidents, Bush encouraged the practice of "burrowing in," by which political appointees try and sometimes succeed in converting their exempt jobs into civil service appointments. This gives them job protection when a new administration comes in. Their numbers don't amount to much—only 144 Bush appointees were converted to career positions according to a report from the GAO—but in some cases the positions were high enough, and the qualifications of the appointees limited enough, to damage morale.[25] In one egregious case sharply criticized by professional scientists, a 30-year old political appointee at the Department of Energy with an undergraduate degree in government (and significantly, the chairmanship of the Kentucky Federation of College Republicans) landed a career position at the National Oceanic and Atmospheric Administration working with "space-based science using satellites for geostationary and meteorological data." The Clinton administration also saw its share of conversions: Between 1998 and 2001, 111 political appointees landed career positions in forty-eight executive agencies.[26]

An Overseas Perspective

Presidential patronage in the United States stands out in stark contrast to other democratic, industrialized countries. Japan, the United Kingdom, France, and Germany, for example, depend largely on career civil service officials who win their posts through competitive examinations. In fact, there are usually no more than 100–200 appointees allotted to their chief executives.[27] Political power in parliamentary systems resides with the prime minister, who emerges from the legislature. The French attempted to copy the American system, but their president remains a figurehead, relegated mostly to ceremonial roles. Prime Minister Margaret Thatcher, who looked longingly across the pond at the United States, increasingly politicized the British bureaucracy by appointing "special advisers," but this practice never reached the patronage levels of the U.S. presidency. And in Japan, civil service is a large, permanent, highly competitive bureaucracy; public officials rarely leave their departments, and laws tend to emanate from government agencies, and not from the prime minister's office.

In France, as well as in the United States, high-level public officials try to supplement their salaries by taking leaves of absence and working in the private sector. The French call this practice "pantouflage," and there are signs that other nations are slowly copying this practice. But the United States still ranks the highest when it comes to personal enrichment. Before he became attorney general in the Obama administration, Eric Holder was reputed to have commanded between $800–$1,000 per hour in the eight years he spent in the private sector, following his service in the Justice Department during the Clinton administration. President Obama's chief of staff, Rahm Emanuel, also became a millionaire when he left the Clinton White House, where he was a presidential adviser. To his credit, President Clinton attempted to stop the "revolving door" in foreign trade—when public officials leave agencies to work for companies and governments with whom they had negotiated—but faced enormous resistance from Congress and his own appointees and was forced to abandon his efforts. President Obama also attempted to close the revolving door, issuing an executive order asking appointees to sign a pledge prohibiting them from receiving gifts from lobbyists and from quitting their government jobs to lobby on issues in their area of expertise. On the campaign trail, Obama promised that former lobbyists would not be allowed to "work on regulations or contracts directly . . . related to their prior employer for two years."[28] Three exceptions were announced immediately, the most important being the nomination of former Raytheon lobbyist William J. Lynn as deputy defense secretary on the grounds that he was the only person qualified for the job.

A president's ability to find employment for friends and political supporters is not limited to federal agencies, boards, commissions, and hybrids. A president also has clout in the private sector. In late 1997, for example, President Bill Clinton asked Vernon Jordan, one of his closest friends and most trusted advisers, to find a private sector job for Monica Lewinsky, the White House intern with whom Clinton had had a sexual relationship that led to his impeachment and nearly cost him the presidency. Jordan referred Lewinsky to Revlon and another company where he served on the board of directors. Jordan also had arranged a $60,000 retainer at the Revlon Corporation for Clinton's former associate attorney general Webster Hubbell, who had resigned in an investigation of alleged irregularities in his former law firm, the Rose Law Firm of Little Rock, Arkansas.[29] At the time, Jordan was a senior partner in the Washington office of the influential Texas law firm Akin, Gump, Strauss, Hauer and Feld, as well as a member of eleven corporate boards.

Presidential patronage can be a burden as well as a boon. Although voters usually know better, politicians constantly complain about the burdens. A famous apocryphal story still circulating around political circles tells of an upcoming post office job. No fewer than 100 applicants vied for the job, which finally went to a well-known political operative who had received many favors over the years, including new roads, contracts, farm subsidies, and jobs for numerous relatives. When the winner took her post, she then claimed she was "hatched," after the 1939 Hatch Act that, before it was watered down, prohibited public officials from political activity, meaning they could no longer campaign, ring doorbells, or contribute any money to politics, including the politicians responsible for getting them the job in the first place. Everyone else who applied was turned down and furious at not getting the job. So what are the politicians left with? Their complaint: "Ninety-nine enemies and one ingrate!"

Another version of the story has been attributed to former Vice President Alben Barkley, who told of Farmer Jones, a longtime constituent of Barkley's and the recipient of many favors through the years. Barkley interceded with General Pershing to bring Jones home after the armistice in World War I, intervened with the Veterans Bureau to speed up his disability compensation, helped him get loans from the Farm Credit Administration in addition to a disaster loan when his farm was flooded, and on top of everything else, engineered a job for his wife. When Barkley found himself in a tough primary fight, he learned to his astonishment that Farmer Jones was going to vote for his opponent. After asking Jones why he wasn't supporting him and reminding Jones of his many efforts on his behalf, Jones responded, "Yes, but what have you done for me lately?"[30]

Presidential Patronage Styles: FDR to Obama

Although modern presidents no longer throw everyone out of office to make room for their own supporters, transition jitters still afflict Washington on the eve of an incoming administration. Even those who have job protection show some degree of anxiety, wondering if they will be downgraded or shorn of responsibility by a new layer of government bureaucrats coming into office.

Some presidents attempted to augment their patronage by creating new government agencies—secure in the knowledge that by the time civil service "blanketed in" the jobs, they would no longer be in office. One little-known reason why President Roosevelt created all the new federal "alphabet" agencies born of the New Deal, instead of putting them in existing cabinet agencies that were covered by civil service laws, was to deliver on his patronage obligations. According to James L. Rowe, a top White House aide at the time, FDR's quiet patronage practices added an interesting historical sidelight to the social rhetoric accompanying the innovations of the New Deal. Roosevelt also "padded" existing agencies with loyalists, often using these appointments to cement his relationships with key members of Congress. The Federal Trade Commission, a more notorious example than most agencies, was run by Tennessee machine politicians, partly because Tennessee Senator Kenneth McKellar chaired the Appropriations Committee. "The FTC was loaded up with layers and layers of Tennessee lawyers," Rowe recalled. Similarly, the Justice Department was overwhelmed by Montana lawyers, although the state's Democratic Senator, Burton K. Wheeler, was not consulted about the appointments. "That's what turned him against the New Deal," Rowe observed.

Ignoring the clubhouse level of the Republican Party, President Eisenhower made his appointments from among the larger constituencies within the Republican establishment: the large Wall Street law firms, the corporate world, and the Ivy League universities.

President Kennedy required that nearly all appointees had supported him before the 1960 Democratic convention in Los Angeles. ("Were you with us before West Virginia?" was the question posed by patronage dispensers in the Kennedy administration, referring to that state's primary.) President Kennedy's antipoverty program, while serving noble social ends, also opened up an entirely new area of federal patronage in cities. Recalling Harry Hopkins's alternative patronage armies, many local politicians expressed their dismay at the potential political threat represented by all these new entrants on their turf.

President Johnson, a master of legislative patronage, considered job patronage bothersome, finding its visibility and accompanying publicity exceedingly uncomfortable. While he handled the private agreements of legislative patronage with extraordinary finesse, he lacked the resources to find highly qualified, yet politically acceptable—mostly—"men" for government positions. In fact, Johnson offended many of his party colleagues on Capitol Hill, according to an assistant, because he had appointed political enemies to career positions. Another aide recalled an argument he had with Johnson, warning the president that if he persisted in "picking career men, he would have to pick his own workers for the 1968 campaign." Johnson countered with a memo, arguing that "if we pick career men, or military men, we won't get in trouble. Every time we've gone outside we've gotten into trouble." He cited problems he had in staffing the regulatory agencies with appointees who had earned the confidence of industry and labor, yet were not at the same time owned by the private sector. "I needed an appointee for the Federal Power Commission. Because I'm a Texan, I had to get a fellow who couldn't spell 'oil.' I finally found someone, a solicitor for the railroads from Illinois. After I appointed him, the newspapers charged him with sitting in on a segregationist meeting back in Illinois regarding real estate."[31]

Sensitive to presidential slights when he was in the Senate, Lyndon Johnson directed all administration officials to return telephone calls from members of Congress within ten minutes, an admirable if impractical goal before the invention of cell phones. Johnson wanted to demonstrate his respect for the institution that spawned him. When it came to rewarding his friends, no president could take a back seat to Lyndon Johnson.

As a young congressman, Johnson benefited from presidential patronage when the Federal Communications Commission increased the wattage—and reach—of KTBC in Austin, Texas, a radio station owned by his wife. "In few businesses was the role of government as crucial as in radio, for not only were the very licenses which allowed the use of the airwaves granted, and periodically renewed, only at the sufferance of the Federal Communications Commission, but the FCC possessed virtually unchallengeable authority over every aspect of a station's operations."[32] The station provided the cornerstone of a network of radio and television stations and the foundation of the Johnson fortune.

Patronage played a major role in passage of key elements of the Great Society. "Patronage was very important to him," recalled Senator William Proxmire, a Wisconsin Democrat, referring to LBJ. "He didn't retaliate. He knew that a man who opposed you on some issues might turn up as your useful friend in others." A master of legislative politics (Johnson spent twelve years in the Senate, six as majority leader and one year as minority leader, and twelve years in the House), Johnson was able to engineer through Congress many of the New Frontier bills formulated by his predecessor, John F. Kennedy. Johnson took great pride in delivering the nation's first strong civil rights bill, a strong housing bill, meaty social welfare legislation that included Medicare and Medicaid, and a Model Cities Act. Working on the theory that you build up favors for future use, Johnson piled up his patronage chits slowly, without immediately stating the *quid pro quo,* so that at any time he could collect on his due bills and draw on the huge reservoir of congressmen already under obligation to him for past favors. Johnson was not above using threats, but Johnson's threats were usually implicit, rarely carried on publicly, and therefore all the more effective, leading one of his former aides to describe patronage politics under Johnson as "war carried on by nonviolent means ... with never an end to the conflict." The aide continued, "Johnson exercised dominance over legislators primarily through cooperation—a series of temporary accommodations—but the conflict continues."[33] But Johnson was human, and his irritation occasionally flared publicly. When Senator Frank Church, who chaired the Senate Foreign Relations Committee, cited an article by columnist Walter Lippman to explain his opposition to the Vietnam War, the piqued president countered, "The next time you want a dam for Idaho, you go ask Walter Lippman."

One of the best examples of how Johnson structured a network of mutual cooperation among legislators was in the enactment and execution of the Model Cities Act, whose grants were given not on the basis of need but of political criteria, formulated to reward towns represented by key committee chairmen. The original sixty-three cities chosen for initial grants varied in size from Smithville, Tennessee (population 2,300) to New York City (population 8 million). New York City received three grants, but neither Cleveland nor Los Angeles received grants even though both cities had experienced serious racial disturbances. Because the purpose of Model Cities was to provide federal funds for a coordinated attack on the social as well as the physical causes of urban blight, the inclusion of Smithville appears baffling until one realizes that the city was represented by Representative Joe L. Evins, a Democrat who was chairman of the Housing and Urban Development Subcommittee. Four other cities whose representatives supported the program in a crucial subcommittee vote were also immediately rewarded by the program: Texarkana, Arkansas (population 221,000), represented by David Pryor, a Democrat; Manchester, New Hampshire (population 90,000), represented by Louis C. Wyman, a Republican; New Haven, Connecticut (population 150,000), represented by Robert N. Giamo, a Democrat; and Springfield, Massachusetts (population 166,000), represented by Edward P. Boland, a Democrat. President Johnson also rewarded two House Democrats who had played major roles in salvaging the administration's antipoverty program with Model Cities' funds. These were Pikeville, Kentucky (population 5,000), represented by Carl D. Perkins, a Democrat who was chairman of the Education and Labor Committee; and Tampa, Florida (population 166,000), represented by Sam M. Gibbons, a Democrat.

Not forgetting his original constituency, President Johnson gave Model Cities' funds to four communities in his home state of Texas: Eagle Pass (population 14,000), San Antonio (population 645,000), Texarkana (population 32,000), and Waco (population 105,000). Two of these communities were represented by House chairmen—Texarkana by Wright Patman, chairman of Banking and Currency, and Waco by W.R. Poage, chairman of Agriculture. The president attempted to give the program a nonpolitical caste, however, by funding Charlotte, North Carolina, which was represented by one of the most vigorous House opponents of the Model Cities program, GOP Representative Charles Raper Jonas.[34]

At the presidential level, collecting on patronage debts means more than a simple exchange following a private political contract. Legislators have constituencies and obligations of their own, and only occasionally can the president reasonably expect them to vote for or against issues that will cause them trouble back home. Moreover, the president most often finds it in keeping with his own interests to help cooperative legislators from his own party remain solidly entrenched, not only to ensure their reelection but to also free them from the rigors of intraparty warfare so that their energies can more constructively be channeled back into legislative business. Nixon expected the impossible from senators, especially those from states with large black populations and strong labor unions, when he demanded party loyalty above political survival. Johnson, on the other hand, understood the dangers inherent in forcing congressmen to commit political hara-kiri and preferred other methods of arm-twisting.

Johnson employed the skills he had developed as a congressional leader. When he wanted a congressman's vote on an issue he knew would be political suicide, he would set up the issue to make it more palatable, enabling legislators to vote for the bill, yet justify their vote and return home without having to face retribution. As majority leader, for example, Johnson managed the tricky feat of engineering through the legislature a public housing bill for the construction of 250,000 units. Homer Capehart, an Indiana Republican, knew he had the votes for an alternative bill allowing for the much lower figure of 35,000 units requested by President Eisenhower. But Johnson simply set up the bill's wording so that congressmen who opposed public housing could nevertheless vote for the bill, yet save face with the voters. What Johnson did was talk to the southerners, who were mostly against public housing, into voting against the Capehart amendment, so that they could go home and say they had voted against public housing. Without the help of the southerners, the Capehart amendment lost, and the Johnson bill was enacted with its original high public housing figure.

President Nixon was more flexible than many of his predecessors. Nixon, who expended a great deal of energy on antipatronage rhetoric, nevertheless set up an elaborate screening process. In contrast with Kennedy's patronage requirements, Nixon did not demand preconvention loyalty for many top-level jobs, owing perhaps to his need for talent, his own uneven party career, and his desire to unite the Republican Party. Nixon installed Henry Kissinger as his national security adviser and Robert L. Kunzig as administrator of the General Services Administration even though both men had worked for Nelson Rockefeller, New York's governor and competitor for the Republican presidential nomination, until shortly before Nixon won the nomination.

Nixon's patronage process was described by George Bell, who ran the program, as a six-step filter process, ending with a security check and divided into distinctly political categories. These ranged from "U" ("failure to appoint would result in adverse political consequences to the administration") to "Z" ("applicant not compatible with the Nixon administration and should not be appointed to public office"). Categories in between included "Y" ("no political importance to the administration") and "V" ("played a prominent role in the campaign; recommended in the highest terms by a member of the House or Senate leadership"). Nixon's predecessors and successors have had similar systems.[35]

The elaborate nature of the screening process showed how valuable these patronage jobs were to the administration in terms of unifying the party at its local and legislative levels. If a candidate opted for a job with the Department of the Interior (important also because of the patronage that department controls, particularly in Western states), a White House aide would telephone the ranking Republican on the corresponding committee in both the House and Senate to assure that the candidate was acceptable. If the job was important enough, the aide might continue his check with the House and Senate Interior Appropriations subcommittees, with the checking process also serving the useful purpose of increasing the contacts between the president and key legislators, who took for granted the president's willingness to check with them before making appointments within their jurisdiction. Once a candidate reached the stage in which he was seriously considered for a top-level government patronage job, such as (at that time) a civil service classification of G.S. 16 or above, additional members of the White House staff would run further checks before he was actually appointed. But Nixon used sticks as well as carrots. He created an "enemies list," and used government agencies—including the IRS and FBI—to investigate the designated offenders.

In selecting their White House staffs, most presidents have appointed aides from their home state who had worked closely with them on their campaigns. Kennedy gave us the "Massachusetts Mafia," Johnson and George W. Bush were surrounded by Texans, Nixon and Reagan by Californians, Carter by Georgians, Clinton by FOB (Friends of Bill) from Arkansas, and Obama by Chicagoans.

Carter's disdain for patronage became evident early in his presidency. He didn't think he'd have to bargain with members of Congress, regarding Congress as he had viewed the Georgia legislature: a body that could easily be steamrolled. Punishment was swift, and the patronage lessons clear: Carter lost a succession of battles with Congress, beginning before the president even assumed office, by allowing his top aide to deny extra tickets to the inauguration gala to Tip O'Neill, the Speaker of the House—which held up legislation from the White House for two years. Carter also attempted to cancel pork barrel water projects much beloved by members of Congress, which also turned out to be a political disaster.[36]

Carter thought that if he worked hard enough on a bill, Congress would be compelled to recognize the bill's intrinsic merits and pass it intact. "Carter sent his energy bill to the Hill fully expecting it to pass as is," recalled Robert Hanfling, an energy expert who served in the Carter administration. "He was furious when they sent it back."

Carter also showed his contempt for Congress on election night, 1980, when he ignored Speaker O'Neill's plea and conceded the election to Ronald Reagan while the polls were still open in the West. O'Neill joined political experts in believing that Carter's early concession cost many western Democrats their seats in the House and Senate because Democratic voters thought it was futile to vote and stayed home.

President Clinton initially found it difficult to translate his political skills into legislation, even when his own party held the majority. The president ignored Congress by putting his wife in charge of his healthcare initiative, which was worked out behind closed doors that excluded knowledgeable and influential members of Congress. Congress "reciprocated" by rejecting the initiative.

Relying on the "merits" of his legislation, Clinton pressured Representative Marjorie Margolies-Mezvinsky (affectionately known as 3M), a Pennsylvania Democrat, into voting for a budget that they both knew was highly unpopular back home. The bill passed by a single vote—Margolies-Mezvinsky's. But that vote became the major issue in her campaign for reelection, and she was soundly defeated. Adding insult to injury, Mezvinsky, who fell on her sword for Clinton, was not offered a significant administration job to salve her wounds. It is safe to assume that President Johnson would have found a suitable way to reward such loyalty. Later in his presidency, Clinton spoke the language of patronage, which accounted for his success with NAFTA and other legislation. Clinton insisted on an increased number of women in his administration, particularly in cabinet posts that had traditionally gone to men: Madeleine Albright at State, Janet Reno at Justice, and Donna Shalala at Health and Human Services.

In his presidential appointments and in the administration of his office, President George W. Bush, prodded by Vice President Richard Cheney, created the most politicized federal government in modern history. One could argue that because he had won the White House, he was entitled to put his political imprimatur wherever he wanted. But some government functions are best performed when they are not politicized, and when administrators are selected for their talent and competence rather than political loyalty. Bush's poll ratings began to decline after Hurricane Katrina and the tepid response of the Federal Emergency Management Agency, well-known as a patronage dumping ground.

But Bush was hardly the first president to place loyalty above competence. President Kennedy engaged in several efforts to put family cronies in public positions. President Nixon appointed John Mitchell attorney general, and President Carter appointed Bert Lance OMB director. And who can forget the shortcomings of Alberto Gonzalez, Bush's attorney general?

Another patronage mistake that came to light under Bush was the appointment of Daniel Troy, who had previously represented drug and tobacco companies, as chief counsel of the Food and Drug Administration. (Traditionally, the post had gone to a career employee who had come up through the ranks of the FDA.) Not surprisingly, Troy tried to restrict the agency's power, first stalling its efforts to investigate ephedra, an herb used in a dietary supplement that was suspected as a factor in causing at least 100 deaths. He also held dozens of private meetings with drug companies and others regulated by the FDA, but kept no notes of those meetings. Troy favored less rigorous enforcement of regulations for some products and was lenient about scrutinizing advertising claims by companies.[37]

The head of the Bush White House procurement office was David Safavian, whose procurement experience consisted of twenty months as chief of staff of the General Services Administration. Safavian was convicted in 2006 of lying to investigators and obstructing justice in connection with a land deal involving Jack Abramoff, a lobbyist now serving prison time in a corruption case. Julie Myers, head of the Immigration and Customs Enforcement agency, was married to the chief of staff of Homeland Security Secretary, Michael Chertoff. She replaced an acting agency head, John Clark, who had twenty-five years of experience in the field. Myers, the niece of General Richard Myers, chairman of the Joint Chiefs of Staff, was previously chief of staff to an assistant attorney general at the Justice Department. Bush tapped Jay Hallen, age twenty-four, to reopen the Iraqi stock exchange, although Hallen had no background in finance. Ellen Sauerbrey, the Maryland chairman of Bush's 2000 presidential campaign, was appointed assistant secretary of State for Population, Refugees and Immigration, although she had "no experience in dealing with refugees and has been antagonistic to mainstream population efforts."[38] Sauerbrey's appointment represented another important function of presidential patronage: a consolation prize for defeated members of the president's party. (Sauerbrey had run unsuccessfully for governor on the Republican ticket against Parris Glendening in 1998.)

George W. Bush's political alter ego was Karl Rove, a political strategist who had played a key role in his elections both as governor and as president, and whose fingerprints were visible in Bush's policy and patronage decisions. But Rove overdid it. In filling administration jobs, Rove placed loyalty above competence, often to the detriment of the president. The resulting disasters, including the financial meltdown of 2008–2009, were also the result of a strong tilt toward the business community that had provided his major support. The Bush administration accelerated deregulation and reduced the size and scope of government agencies, creating problems—like the poor response to Hurricane Katrina—that the reduced government was unable to remedy. Another source of support, known as the "Christian right," representing evangelical Christians and conservative Republicans, was rewarded with bans on stem cell research; support of teaching "creationism" in the schools; and the appointment of two Supreme Court justices, John Roberts and Samuel Alito, both committed to the erosion and eventual repeal of a woman's right to an abortion.

A president will be "remembered in history more by the accomplishments of his administration than by the ideological purity of his appointments," concludes

James Pfiffner, a well-known presidential scholar, although the president has to achieve a balance between politics and good management.[39]

The Mother of Necessity

That balance teetered in the early months of the Obama presidency. During his presidential campaign, Obama had vowed to veto any legislation that contained earmarks—favors to lawmakers in exchange for their votes. In effect, that would mean that members of Congress would no longer be able to "bring home the bacon" to their districts and reap the ensuing rewards. This new "purity" would have unraveled more than 200 years of traditional legislative practice. Predictably, it was not to be. Shortly after Obama was sworn in, Congress completed the previous year's appropriations bill, which to Obama's alleged dismay contained 9,000 earmarks, of which 40 percent were inserted by Republicans. He nevertheless signed the bill, saying that it merely completed the previous year's work. But his action led many in Congress to question whether Obama could get what he wanted from Congress without giving members something they wanted in return. To enact healthcare reform, he approved earmarks including the "Louisiana Purchase," worth more than $100 million, to obtain the vote of Senator Mary Landrieu and the "Cornhusker Kickback" to win the vote of Senator Ben Nelson. Both Landrieu and Nelson were Democrats. Landrieu boasted back home that the appropriation would really be worth $300 million.

President Obama still had more faith in rationality than arm-twisting. To sell his stimulus plan, Obama went on the road, singling out devastated areas that had supported his presidential campaign. The first stop was Fort Myers, Florida, a town known as ground zero for home foreclosures; Fort Myers was located in Lee County, which had voted for a Democratic presidential candidate in 2008 for the first time in 60 years. His visit was expected to lift not only the residents' spirits but also their real estate values. His next stop was Elkhart, Indiana, a town in a state long considered a Republican stronghold, which also had voted for Obama. The new president relied on the public's demand that Washington ease the severity of the financial crisis to override the demands of politics as usual. But the bill also contained a $70 billion tax break for the upper middle class, considered a swing vote in presidential elections and, therefore, vigorously wooed by both parties. The tax break would spare millions of well-to-do Americans from paying the alternative minimum tax. Ironically, the leading advocates of hands-off government—the banks, insurance companies, and industrial giants that had long fought government intervention—became supplicants in their efforts to avoid bankruptcy. In addition to the economic stimulus bill, the Obama administration poured billions into the automobile industry and initiated a $2.5 trillion public-private rescue plan for the financial system, a combination of loans to banks and incentives intended to bring private capital into the banking system. Despite his campaign rhetoric, all the new president's attempts to pass and sell the stimulus package relied on the age-old levers of patronage: trading votes for favors.

The financial crisis of 2008–2009 raised a host of questions. Why did it happen? Where were the regulators? Where was congressional oversight? Where were the media watchdogs? Why were some companies, such as AIG, bailed out, and others, such as Lehman Brothers, left to flounder and die? Why were no conditions initially attached to these multibillion-dollar "loans?" The discretionary powers of government were never more apparent.

Cronyism is as old as the republic. The presidency is first and foremost a political position, reached with the support of a majority of voters. The strength of a presidency, therefore, relies as much on political factors as on rational choices, which is why presidents need aides who are loyal to them. Woodrow Wilson leaned heavily on Colonel Edward House, a political strategist who had helped elect him. Franklin Delano Roosevelt's alter ego was Harry Hopkins, who had established his loyalty and political acumen when Hopkins worked for Roosevelt when he was governor. John Kennedy's closest adviser was his brother Robert, whom he appointed attorney general, while Bill Clinton's wife, Hillary, was known as his closest political confidant.

Patronage-savvy presidents know they have a better chance of persuading a congressman to vote against his or her constituency by promising something concrete to neutralize the political hostility back home. "It is very much like a ballet," said James L. Rowe, who served two Democratic presidents: Roosevelt and Johnson. "When FDR was looking for votes, certain senators said that the legislation was against their constituents, but that they would go along if they could have something to show for it." One example was the 1940s vote on the extension of the draft, which was approved by a single vote, the most expensive vote Mr. Rowe said he could recall in all his years in government: "Rayburn and McCormack yelled for help and the voted turned on Representative Levy of Spokane, Washington. He had lots of problems, he told us. One thing he wanted was a judgeship. He also wanted a military airport in Spokane. I got Justice [the Justice Department] to offer him a judgeship, which he took. We called Harry Stimson [Secretary of War] and Hap Arnold [general in the U.S. Army Air Force] and they said, 'You can flip a coin. You can put it in Spokane or someplace else.' I said, 'Mr. Secretary, the coin just came down Spokane.'" [40]

Such swaps are typical of effective presidencies. "When a President makes appointments with an eye to winning support for some part of his legislative program, he is not doing something *sui generis*," wrote Professor Stanley Kelley. "The trading of favors is a practice that pervades the legislative process. Members of Congress, heads of administrative agencies, and lobbyists continually do unto others in the hope that others will do at least as well by them. The president as a manager of patronage is simply one trader in a market system."[41]

Considering it beneath the dignity of the office of chief executive, presidents usually do not handle their patronage tools directly. Instead, patronage is handled by the White House congressional liaison, who also works with Congress on the content of legislative proposals. President Kennedy's chief special assistant for congressional affairs, Lawrence O'Brien, was also his patronage dispenser. Kennedy worked out an elaborate scheme whereby John Bailey (then Democratic National Chairman) was given official responsibility for patronage, while O'Brien took charge of actually dispensing the patronage. In this way Bailey could take the blame while O'Brien got the credit, enabling him to continue to further Kennedy's legislative agenda. O'Brien expanded the practice of allowing members of Congress to announce federal grants and contracts in their districts, while letting the blame fall on federal agencies whenever pet projects failed to materialize. In the Clinton administration, the congressional liaison was Howard Paster, while Nick Calio performed the job for Bush I and II. Phil Schiliro, a former congressional staffer, is President Obama's representative on Capitol Hill.

In addition to his congressional liaison staff, a president usually builds up patronage relationships with selected interest groups, who then serve him as extra channels to Capitol Hill, adding their own valuable clout to the president's. Understood in the patronage agreement Johnson forged with the AFL-CIO was that in exchange for presidential support for its legislation, the union would refrain from attacking the president, except under extreme circumstances. Staff members from the AFL-CIO routinely went over head counts with Johnson to see if they, through their political arm Committee on Political Education (COPE), could then work with the more marginal members of Congress to gain their support on important votes.

Similarly, President George W. Bush built up a patronage relationship with conservative groups, such as the Federalist Society, which had a major voice in his selection of both judges and Justice Department officials. Many of these groups, including those from the Christian Right, lobbied members of Congress on behalf of conservative legislation, developing power comparable to that of party whips in other countries—from the English term "whipper in," used in fox hunting to refer to the practice of keeping the hunting dogs in line. They also appeared on radio, television, and newspapers on the president's behalf.

Follow the Money

But patronage has its limitations. Johnson could not understand why a revolutionary foe like Ho Chi Minh, a man who spent his life fighting for Vietnamese independence, could not be won over by the promise of a dam. Johnson was unable to understand an alien political culture—in good company with the nation's foreign policy apparatus, which has always found it easier to deal with traditional regimes that speak the language of political rewards than with revolutionary ones. Nixon learned the limits of patronage early in his presidency with his inability to send Clement Haynsworth and G. Harrold Carswell to the Supreme Court. Similarly, Clinton's mastery of patronage could not save his health reform legislation; neither could George W. Bush's political skills revive his proposal to replace Social Security with private investment.

For the most part, presidential patronage has thrived in the shadows. Big decisions supposedly emanated from groups of "wise men,"[42] who ostensibly decided the fate of the nation on the basis of principles not politics. In reality, however, patronage factors enter into every important presidential decision, from Supreme Court and Cabinet appointments, to life-changing legislation, like healthcare. Sonia Sotomayor, Obama's first Supreme Court appointee, was clearly qualified, but her appointment also shored up support from the increasingly politically potent Hispanic community.

Every president's political appointments are carefully scrutinized to determine what they portend. Did President Obama's appointees represent real change? "Change we can believe in," to quote his campaign promise? Or did they represent other factors? The president appointed an economic team that many thought were responsible for the economic crisis in the first place. Cabinets have traditionally been used by presidents to reward key constituencies (regions of the country, ethnic groups, economic interests, and occasionally, the other party). The Department of the Interior, for example, has traditionally been reserved for a Westerner; the Department of Labor for a union leader; and Commerce for an industrialist. One of the key attributes of Governor Bill Richardson, Obama's original choice for Commerce Secretary, was that he was Hispanic; more important, Richardson had endorsed Obama for president over Obama's chief rival, Senator Hillary Clinton, even though he had been appointed to the Cabinet by her husband, President Bill Clinton. Clinton was the first president to appoint Hispanics to the cabinet: San Antonio Mayor Henry Cisneros, to the Department of Housing and Urban Development, and Denver Mayor Federico Peña to the Department of Transportation.

President George W. Bush's first cabinet followed Clinton's tradition in attempting to showcase gender and ethnic diversity: He appointed four women, two Asian Americans, two blacks, and one Hispanic. Unfortunately, Bush's Hispanic appointee, Attorney General Alberto Gonzales, left office under a cloud of controversy involving his now-notorious memo supporting the use of torture as official U.S. policy in direct violation of the Geneva Conventions. But despite Obama's efforts to follow the traditions of his predecessors to appoint a cabinet—as Clinton said—that looks like America, it took him some time to learn the mores of Capitol Hill, and he faced some unusual opposition even from members of his own party. The appointment, for example, of Leon Panetta to head the CIA brought unusually sharp criticism from Senator Dianne Feinstein (D-California). Feinstein publicly opposed Panetta for his lack of intelligence experience; more likely, she spoke out against the appointment because as the chairman of the Senate Intelligence Committee, she was not consulted on the appointment. A breach of protocol? An oversight?

At the base of presidential patronage is the unique U.S. system of campaign finance. Jerry Maguire's client challenged his agent to "show me the money," while Deep Throat's advice to "follow the money" turned out to be equally true of political decisions. Before the Watergate scandals unmasked routine political practices before a horrified public, campaign contributions from individuals—often delivered in paper bags filled with cash—in return for substantial government favors were typical. After Watergate, election reforms during the 1970s prohibited large contributions from individuals, but nature abhors a vacuum, and today lobbyists and other favor seekers can skirt election laws by holding large fundraisers, "bundling" the money, and delivering the large sums to the politicians from whom they later seek favors. What this meant was that a new class of political operatives—primarily lobbyists—now held the power that was previously wielded by the party's "fat cats"—wealthy contributors who later gained admission to the exclusive "Presidents Clubs" of yore—which gave them all kinds of special favors: easy access to the White House, coveted White House dinner invitations, pictures with the president and first lady, *ad infinitum*.

Several of President Obama's nominees ran into trouble with money problems. Treasury Secretary Timothy Geithner survived questions about his taxes; former Senator Tom Daschle, Obama's choice for Secretary of Health and Human Services, did not. Was this politics as usual? Were the media more vigorous in pursuing activities that would have been regarded as typical a few years before? And why did some cabinet choices, like Daschle, lose their appointments, while others, like Geithner, survived?

Governor Bill Richardson, for example, withdrew his nomination—some say he was pushed—until the dust cleared over an investigation of a $1.48 million contract allegedly awarded in exchange for a generous political contribution. In this case, the governor was accused of influencing a state agency to hire a California firm, CDR Financial Products, to advise the state government on interest rate swaps and the refinancing of funds related to transportation bonds. The firm and its president, David Rubin, gave $100,000 to two Political Action Committees formed by Richardson. In retrospect, many criticized Obama's transition team for not vetting Richardson more thoroughly and for not knowing that a grand jury in Albuquerque was looking into the arrangement to see whether there was any correlation between the contract and the political contributions. Richardson was exonerated of any charges eight months later.[43]

When political scandals arise, the rule of thumb is often to "*cherchez* the losers." The initial selection of CDR drew the attention of other firms bidding for the contract that considered themselves more qualified. Most likely, they spurred the FBI investigation, which ultimately led straight to Richardson's office. The question is whether this represented politics as usual or a distortion of the process.

How different is the awarding of ambassadorships or contracts in exchange for campaign contributions, for example, from the attempted sale of President Obama's Senate seat by Illinois Governor Roy Blagojevich's "pay to play" scheme? This, too, drew FBI attention, not because of the link between campaign contributions and political office, but by the exaggeration of the practice. Blagojevich allegedly put the seat out for bid, asking how much individuals were willing to "contribute"; he also added another dimension by requesting guarantees of jobs and board positions for himself and his wife.

Money plays the biggest role when it comes to awarding ambassadorships. What's not to like? Embassies come staffed with cooks, butlers, and all manner of aides; not to mention a social schedule filled with parties, galas, and prime tickets to cultural and sporting events. In the old days, ambassadors were expected to use their own money to refurbish embassies and pay for parties and staffs. With the foreign service increasingly professionalized, longtime officers can now look forward to promotions as high as ambassador, but not to the more desirable postings: an appointment to the Court of St. James comes with a price; Mogadishu does not. A comparison of Presidents Clinton and Obama shows marked differences between the two Democrats, with Clinton tending to pick more ambassadors with public policy experience, even for the most desirable posts. Obama picked Louis B. Susman as ambassador to Great Britain, for example; Clinton chose William J. Crowe, Jr. Susman had raised $735,000 for Obama, while Crowe, the former chairman of the Joint Chiefs of Staff, raised nothing. John V. Roos was selected for Japan; a Silicon Valley attorney, he had raised $545,000 for Obama. Clinton's pick was former vice president Walter F. Mondale, who had only raised $12,500 for his presidential bid.[44]

Money and past political associations also played a large role during the presidency of George W. Bush, who exceeded both his father and President Clinton in the percentage of noncareer ambassadorial appointments. Thirty-six percent of ambassadorial nominations in the Bush administration went to friends and contributors, compared to 29 percent for Clinton and 31 percent for George Herbert Walker Bush.[45] Supporters of patronage appointees contend that they have better access to the president than those who come up through the foreign service and are therefore better able to do their jobs.

Does presidential patronage produce better public policy than parliamentary systems that rely more heavily on professionalized civil servants? Many students of politics believe that the patronage system is too corrupt; that agencies laden with political appointees cannot possibly deliver sound public policy. On the other hand, professionals argue that "if only the president would leave us alone, we would emerge with more rational solutions to our problems."

But voters usually elect presidents on the basis of their promises of change. "Change we can believe in" was Barack Obama's campaign slogan. Shouldn't he have the opportunity to deliver on that promise? Political appointees are naturally more sensitive to the goals of a new administration and to a president who has appointed them to positions of authority.

In the final analysis, presidential patronage remains a balancing act. Correctly used, patronage enhances efficiency and enables a president to translate his vision into reality. Like all patronage, however, it is highly susceptible to waste, fraud, and abuse. Thus, the value of patronage depends on the president. President George W. Bush relied too heavily on favoritism over competence and paid a heavy price. President Clinton, after a faltering start, used patronage to great effect. President Barack Obama's legacy is yet to be written. There is no question, however, that all three presidents benefited greatly from the explosion of pinstripe patronage, the ballooning of government grants, contracts, and quasi-government agencies. And there is also no doubt that their successors will fare even better.

Chapter Seven
Pinstripe Patronage

Outsourcing Government

"I have never met a contractor who, if not watched, would not leave
the government holding the bag."[1]
> President Harry S Truman, while senator from Missouri

"This is the new face of government. This isn't companies gouging the
government. This *is* the marketplace."[2]
> Stan Soloway, president of the Professional Services Council

While America Slept

Nearly every president in recent memory has run against government. Government is the problem, they said; if only government would get out of the way
profits would soar, businesses would thrive and ice cream wouldn't melt. President Ronald Reagan transported this theme to its highest peak and promised
the American people that he would get government off their backs once and for
all; government is not the solution, he said, but the problem. Even Democrats
climbed the antigovernment bandwagon, most notably President Bill Clinton,
who declared that the "era of big government is over." President Barack Obama's
approach contrasted sharply with that of Reagan; indeed, Obama was the first
president in recent history not to run against government.

The argument for "minimal government" recurred throughout America's
political history, going back to the first half of the nineteenth century and South

Carolina's Senator John Calhoun, who stuck resolutely to his argument that the best form of government was one that "governed the least." Later that century, Henry David Thoreau began his famous essay *Civil Disobedience* with an echo of Calhoun: "That government is best which governs the least," adding "that government is best which governs not at all."[3]

Because most Americans identify government first and foremost with taxes, retribution comes swiftly to politicians who ignore this lesson. "Read my lips; no new taxes," was the broken promise that cost President George H. W. Bush his reelection bid in 1992. His loss traumatized his son, George W. Bush, the nation's forty-third president, who repeatedly lowered taxes—in spite of the high cost of the war in Iraq and the country's ballooning budget deficits. Tax themes have resonated with Americans ever since colonial times, when farmers greeted "revenuers" with pitchforks to keep them from collecting taxes on their corn crops. The Whiskey (corn also produced moonshine) and Shays rebellions were tax revolts, successors to the American Revolution's rallying cry of "taxation without representation." The pitchfork-wielding farmers of yore and the Tea Party activists today both failed to see the relationship between taxes and their well-being, no doubt accounting for the fact that the United States remains the lowest-taxed nation in the industrialized world.

Smaller government, less regulation, and more outsourcing does indeed mean greater profits for business, especially contractors, often handpicked, who perform work previously done by government. But this combination has often left the public in the lurch. Sadly, public expectations of government and the harsh realities of daily life often find themselves at odds. At the site of every tragedy, angry citizens call for government intervention, and there is usually hell to pay for politicians who ignore their needs—just look at the aftermath of Katrina, the mother of all hurricanes; train wrecks; plane crashes; forest fires; tornadoes; bridge collapses; space accidents; and offshore oil spills. Americans always take for granted that the government will be there for them when they need it. But they forget about what comes in between, for in the final analysis there is no way to "get the government off the backs of the people" and be able to meet trouble when it does come.

And come it does. Frequently. Over the years, for example, FEMA was steadily denuded of funds, while its leadership became notorious as a convenient repository for political hacks without real management credentials. "You're doing a heck of a job, Brownie," President George W. Bush famously said, commending Michael Brown, the head of FEMA, after the Katrina disaster. Alas, Brown's mismanagement of the crisis only compounded the disastrous effects of what turned out to be the nation's worst natural disaster in history. And small wonder: His management experience prior to leading FEMA was sparse to the point of nonexistent—he was president of an association (the International Arabian Horse Association) whose sole purpose was the promotion of Arabian horses in America. Brown's primary qualification for the job was his friendship with Joe Allbaugh, Bush's campaign director in 2000, who was the head of FEMA in 2001. Brown's chief of staff, Patrick Rhode, had been the president's advance man. To no one's surprise, the president replaced Brown very quickly, but too late to spare the thousands of New Orleans residents who were left homeless, ill, and destitute in the wake of the hurricane.

The myth lives on, with Democrats as well as Republicans competing on the campaign trail with their visions of smaller government—more efficient, leaner, and more responsive to the citizenry. A subtle subtheme of contempt for government often accompanies the rhetoric. President Reagan easily won his first presidential election, no doubt partly on the slogan of getting the government off the backs of the people; he also promised that his top appointees would be people who didn't need government jobs. President Bill Clinton, a Democrat, boasted that he had reduced government by reducing the federal work force, forcing people off the welfare rolls, and eliminating the budget deficit. Clinton even joined the deregulatory bandwagon, with his economic advisers refusing to regulate derivatives and hedge funds—a decision that came to haunt Americans during the economic crisis of 2008–2010. Indeed, all presidents in recent memory have vowed to slim down government and have convinced the public that this was the right thing to do. They counted on voters equating government solely with public employees, forgetting about the vast armies of contractors hired for the express purpose of filling in the yawning gaps left in the wake of downsized government.[4]

But candidate Obama took the opposite tack, praising the federal work force and pledging to beef up government programs and give new power to bureaucrats. His campaign reflected the sad fact that people tend to look to government when times are hard. Also, Obama owed less to the (mostly Republican) contractors who had received billions of dollars in government spending through outsourcing and more to working people who had supported him. Specifically, Obama promised to scale back on contracts to private firms engaged in government work, strengthen the Department of Housing and Urban Development to restore confidence in the housing market, increase the staff at the Social Security Administration to erase the backlog of disability claims, enhance the Department of Labor's enforcement powers, and help employees of the new Transportation Security Administration obtain the same bargaining rights and workplace protections as other federal workers.[5] Less than two weeks after her husband was sworn in as the forty-fourth president, Michelle Obama began a "Thank You" tour of government agencies. "My task here is to thank you," she told hundreds of employees at the Department of Education. "I am a product of your work. I wouldn't be here if it weren't for the public schools that nurtured me and helped me along."[6]

Who's in Charge?

State and local public officials are also often singled out for criticism—sometimes justifiably; sometimes not. Almost everyone who has encountered a rude clerk at the tax bureau or been ticketed for speeding by an angry state trooper blames government "bureaucrats" for all problems great and small. And if unchallenged, local officials can wield considerable power at the grassroots level. A clerk at the motor vehicle bureau in Montgomery, County, Maryland, tried to convince a 25-year-old woman to remove "organ donor" from her license application.

"It just means Mickey Mantle (the baseball player) will get a liver, and he didn't deserve it because he drank all his life," she said. "Well, my brother never had a drink in his life, and he's waiting for a double-lung transplant," answered the applicant. "I'm sorry," said the clerk. "I'll never say that again."

Does the clerk at that Maryland motor vehicle bureau represent government? Or does the firefighter who rescues a child from a burning building? The helicopter pilot who pilots his craft over raging rivers to save victims from drowning? The ambulance driver who drives a heart attack victim to the emergency room in time to save his life? No matter. Government is still painted with a broad brush, all strokes leading to the political movements that have captured the public imagination in the last quarter century: deregulation, the free market, and privatization. Critics all shared the same contempt for government—just get government out of the way, and everything will improve. Did these concepts work? Sometimes they did; sometimes they didn't. But few questioned their utility, and fewer still made the connection between the quality of their daily lives and the slow but steady takeover of these theories. Americans are still wielding antitax pitchforks—that is, until they need help.

The tainted dog food incident of March 2008 still stands out as a perfect example of the consequences of lax regulation. After a number of household pets across the country got sick or died, investigators started looking into the cause. It turned out that the toxic substance in dog food came from a tainted source in China. Many wondered where the government was while all this was going on; still others asked what the government could have done to prevent this crisis. It was the perfect storm: a combination of deregulation, privatization, and globalization. None of the dozen or so agencies in charge of international trade held itself responsible for checking the safety of products that were imported into the country. Neither, it seems, did the high-profile agencies that Americans expected to be watching out for them. The Food and Drug Administration

(FDA) had neither the capacity nor the inclination to inspect dog food, and the Consumer Product Safety Commission (CPSC) claimed it lacked the mandate to inspect dog food. And because the Federal Trade Commission (FTC) and the Justice Department had long since deregulated antitrust, monopolistic behavior was no problem, either. It appeared that only one company, located in Canada, manufactured most brands of dog food, albeit under different names. Out of the legal reach of even the neutered U.S. regulatory agencies, no one knew what to do with that one Canadian company, which had unknowingly added the same contaminated ingredient to a wide variety of canned dog foods. Meanwhile, major television networks had a field day televising the "product safety" lab at the CPSC, which occupied half of a small office, with one investigator in a white lab coat in charge!

After years of labeling government the problem, a self-fulfilling prophecy occurred. Many agencies were forced into a permanent condition of paralysis, powerless to cope with such crises as arthritis drugs whose side-effects produced heart attacks; hurricanes with gale-force winds that damaged life, limb, and property; climate changes producing more frequent and more ferocious floods and forest fires; mysterious *E. coli* bacteria contaminating the U.S. food supply from sources around the globe; and the giant oil spill in the Gulf of Mexico at a British Petroleum rig in April 2010. The Minerals Management Service, the Interior Department agency charged with regulating the oil industry, found that from 2001–2007 there were 1,443 serious drilling accidents in offshore operations, leading to 41 deaths, 342 injuries, and 356 oil spills, and had urged the industry to install backup systems to control the giant undersea valves. In spite of its warnings, the federal agency allowed the industry to police itself.[7]

As the financial crisis deepened in the fall of 2008, questions finally arose about the regulation of investment banks. Who are the regulators? Where were the regulators? And why weren't they more vigorous in preventing the housing crisis? The questions kept coming. Were there regulations on the books that were not enforced? Which companies were saved, and which were not? And why? And who came to the rescue? The buyer of last resort, of course: the federal government. The Treasury Department bought failing banks, the Federal Reserve kept lowering interest rates, and Congress eventually forked over considerable taxpayer funds to save the ailing and unprofitable auto industry, as well as banks and insurance companies.

Specifically, the U.S. Treasury purchased $125 billion worth of bank stocks, making a government agency one of the largest stockholders in the world: $25 billion was invested in Citigroup, JPMorgan Chase, and Wells Fargo; another $15 billion was invested in Bank of America; and $10 billion went to the brokerage firm of Merrill Lynch, which was later acquired by Bank of America. The fact that very few conditions were attached to these purchases, called "loans," became all too clear when *The New York Times* columnist Joseph Nocera eavesdropped on an "employee-only" conference call four days after JPMorgan Chase's CEO accepted a $25 billion bailout from the taxpayers. Although the bankers were fully aware that they were supposed to use the bailout funds to jumpstart the American economy by making loans, the "JPMorgan executive ... moderating the employee conference call" indicated that the bank had no intention of helping the economy with invigorated lending policies; on the contrary, bank policy was to expand its acquisitions of "banks who are still struggling." Nocera called the U.S. Treasury's policy a "fig leaf ... [used] to encourage more bank mergers" and contrasted U.S. policies unfavorably with similar British policies: "Unlike the British government, which is mandating lending requirements in return for capital injections, our government seems afraid to do anything except plead." Angered on behalf of taxpayers, Nocera argued that in the United States the money was just a gift, with no strings attached; the British were smarter in retaining control over how the money was to be spent.[8] (Actually, British taxpayers countered with the argument that strings didn't matter; the banks simply ignored them.) Several days later, the editorial page of *The New York Times* attacked the banks' response: "... with $250 billion [out of the $700 billion] in bailout funds committed to dozens of large and regional banks, it turns out that many of the recipients of this investment from taxpayers are not all that interested in making loans."[9]

Why were "conditions" off the table? How did the government go from regulation to outright ownership? From free market capitalism to timid socialism? Three months later, the banks dug in, eager to accept bailout money but still reluctant to use the money as it was intended. "Make more loans?" said John C. Hope III, chairman of Whitney National Bank in New Orleans. "We're not going to change our business model or our credit policies to accommodate the needs of the public sector as they see it."[10]

Bailouts without enforceable conditions meant Americans were still ambivalent about the roles of government and the free market, and the interchangeability of both. When should government intercede? At what point in market failure? And for how long? Although many looked to government as a savior in emergencies, evidence existed that still showed considerable public support for the imminent return of market discipline and supremacy, and smaller government.

Conditioned by a quarter of a century of deregulation, privatization, and an almost religious faith in free markets, America found itself unable to conduct a real rescue—with life jackets, lifelines, and the ability to save its economy from disaster. Only when the automakers' CEOs came courting Congress for bailouts (in private jets on their first visit) did policymakers catch on and start talking about "conditions." When Congress finally emerged with a $15 billion bailout for General Motors and Chrysler, vague "conditions" finally accompanied cash, including strong statements from members of Congress criticizing the business executives who drove the industry into near-bankruptcy and suggesting that they be replaced. Several months later, the Obama administration, heeding public anger, finally set strict conditions for the auto bailout, which included the resignation of the Chairman and CEO of General Motors, "Rick" Wagoner.

What Is Government?

The economic debacle of 2008–2010 brought government back as a major player. But before the crisis struck, government as we knew it had changed, with few aware of the tectonic movements that have accompanied these changes. Today, government contractors and hybrid agencies far exceed what we used to think of as government, their functions ranging far beyond what the Founding Fathers envisaged, even considering how different life is today from what it was in 1789. Contractors collect income taxes and work on agency budgets. They take notes at meetings on war and peace, have a role in intelligence gathering, and fulfill all kinds of security needs in Iraq. In fact, government is so "lean" that it is forced to hire contractors—some of them under a cloud themselves—to conduct studies on their competitors, all too often with predictable results. And during the war in Iraq, observers were shocked to find that the number of government contractors exceeded public employees.

Contractors work hand-in-glove with hybrid agencies, public-private partnerships, which have only recently come to public attention. Most of them operated happily in relative obscurity until the housing crisis revealed the role of two hybrids, Fannie Mae and Freddie Mac. Fannie and Freddie played key roles in granting the shaky loans that led to the nation's financial disaster. Indeed, how many of these hybrids have run amok before coming to public attention?

The real problem is that all too many of these "subgovernments" function largely out of public view, out of the reach of any kind of scrutiny or oversight. And most important of all: They present new and ever better opportunities for political patronage. Jobs for White House chauffeurs pale next to lucrative government contracts or a seat on the advisory board of a hybrid "agency." How many of these new hybrids, besides Fannie Mae and Freddie Mac, serve as fertile patronage sources—particularly for the president?[11]

The quasi-governmental, or hybrid, organizations are usually defined as those that have some legal relationship or association with the federal government. Many were created because of the government's concern for protecting the interests of the taxpayers, which could be in conflict with the interests of private shareholders. Hybrids include quasi-official agencies, government-sponsored enterprises, federally funded research and development corporations, agency-related nonprofit organizations, venture capital funds, and congressionally chartered nonprofit organizations.

Government-sponsored enterprises include the Federal National Mortgage Association (Fannie Mae), the Federal Home Loan Mortgage Corporation (Freddie Mac), and the Federal Agricultural Mortgage Corporation (Farmer Mac). They started small and were considered an appropriate response to a defined problem. Then they took on a life of their own, providing benefits to certain groups and risks to others. Today, they are viewed by many as too big and powerful to be effectively regulated and supervised.[12]

Quasi-official agencies include the Legal Services Corporation, the Smithsonian Institution, the State Justice Institute, and the U.S. Institute for Peace. The first federally funded research and development centers included RAND, created by the Air Force in California, the Mitre Corporation, and the Institute for Defense Analysis.

"The American Revolution was ignited, in no small measure, by the practices of an early quasi-governmental hybrid entity, the British East India Company," observed Ronald Moe, the preeminent scholar of hybrids. "With broad authority from Parliament, the company collected taxes according to its own rules. The citizenry of Boston in 1773 staged a 'tea party' to express their opposition to this type of public management. While we do not anticipate another tea party, there is, nonetheless, sufficient evidence today of non-accountable activity going on in the quasi government to give pause to any concerned citizen."[13]

Circular A-76

The antigovernment ball started rolling with a rather dry memo sent down from the Budget Office during the Eisenhower administration. Essentially, the memo argued for the slow replacement of parts of the public sector with private companies, and read: "It is the general policy of the Federal government that it will not start or carry on any commercial activity to provide a product or service for its own use if such a product or service can be procured from private enterprise through ordinary business channels."[14]

The Eisenhower edict was replaced in 1983 by the Reagan administration's famous OMB Circular A-76, attributed to Budget Director David Stockman, which virtually restated what had been said before. Only this time, it took on a new urgency, and since that time has been variously credited and blamed for the increasing privatization of government on the federal, state, and local levels.[15]

Although each new administration has felt compelled to reinvent the wheel and give different names to similar "reorganizing" efforts, it was clear that the basic principles of A-76 would remain entrenched, regardless of who was in power. Circular A-76, revised in 1999, provided that government functions must be performed in the most efficient and cost-effective way, whether by government employees or private contractors. The implication was that the private sector would perform these jobs in a more efficient and less costly manner than government. For the half century following the Eisenhower administration, a steadily increasing number of government functions were contracted out. It was argued that contracting out government functions to the private sector made good sense on paper and in practice. Theoretically, government would no longer be competing with business, putting the public sector in a better position of helping American businesses to flourish, grow, and pay taxes. But unspoken was the hidden agenda: the flourishing of "pinstripe patronage," or the opportunity for doling out lucrative contracts to political supporters in lieu of jobs that few seemed to want or need. Although government contracts usually go to political allies, the difference today is that doors are now open to activities previously unheard of. From garbage collection to foreign policy, government as we knew it no longer exists. Instead, a vast array of opportunities awaits those with the influence and knowledge to take advantage of them.

Circular A-76 led to a revolution that began with local government and has affected every layer of government since. Politically, all candidates great and small were able to boast that big government is a thing of the past. Although it is true that fewer civilian federal employees worked for the government in 2008 than at its peak in 1954, the number of government contractors at all levels of government has risen exponentially.

Today, the federal civilian work force has leveled off at 1.9 million permanent, full-time civil servants, about the same as it was in 1960, but an additional 7.6 million contract employees were on the federal payroll, according to Max Stier, president and CEO of the nonpartisan Partnership for Public Service. In other words, it is easier to hide an expanding government with contract employees because they do not appear on official civil service lists, and their jobs do not appear in the Plum Book: a listing of policy-level appointments to be chosen by the incoming president. But the nation's population has increased substantially during that same time period (from about 179 million in 1960 to almost 304 million in 2008), which means there is a lot more for government to do.

Circular A-76 also means that you can fool the public most of the time. Politicians can boast that they have reduced government, but no one asks them who is going to do the work that still needs to get done. A-76 also led to a sea change in state and local governments, which followed the federal example in rhetoric but not in reality. While the federal government was reducing its workforce, state government employment tripled during that same time period, while no fewer than 80,000 entities—including states, counties, special water districts, and sewer districts—picked up the slack. Data points to a dramatic increase in contracting;

indeed some studies indicate that contracting out has increased by more than 100 percent in the last decade.[16] The truth is elusive and curious at the same time, and because no government agency collects this data, it is difficult to draw conclusions, except from isolated examples. The results beg the question: Why does no central data source collect information that is so vital? While information is not forthcoming, it can be retrieved at times by agency or by function (such as "intelligence"), but at present no central source is responsible for the big picture.

The Costs of Contracting Out

Privatization has affected everything from local garbage collection to state prison and hospital administration—and even the prosecution of war. But reality crept in as quickly as the toxins in dog food, and although the workforce has been reduced, the functions of government have failed to keep pace. Instead of big government, there are big contracts, and instead of reduced expenditures, budgets have soared, as government contracts out functions that were previously allotted to the public sector.

The mixed results ranged from increased efficiency to wasteful spending. Outsourcing costs sometimes dwarfed what those services would cost if performed by government. A secretarial position that might have cost the government about $40,000 per year, including benefits, can now cost triple that amount if those functions are released to a private contractor, who justifies the increase with charges for overhead and profit. Congressional conferees estimated that the average civilian employee cost the government "$126,500 annually in salary and benefits, while a core contractor [is] estimated to cost an average of $250,000 annually."[17]

The current confusion is really over who is in charge. Does the government oversee these contracts? Do the companies make policy on the spot? Who decides when conflicts arise? Are contracts let to the cheapest bidder? To the best performer? To the most effective manufacturer? To the politically connected?

The answer, unsatisfactory as it is, is this: It depends. If the task is sexy enough, congressional committees may conduct oversight hearings, which catapult the issue into the public spotlight. All too often, a full-blown crisis must emerge before the public pays attention. In the case of Pentagon contractors, for example, former Government Accountability Office (GAO) head David Walker testified that oversight was sadly lacking. In most cases, oversight is uneven, primarily because hybrid agencies and contracts function virtually without transparency, accountability, and clear-cut mandates.[18]

The road to hell, and all that. A-76 was initiated with the best intentions, but the results turned out to be very different from the original plans. Government

contracts appeared to represent just one more opportunity for political patronage, and the very direct relationship between contracts and public policy often
left the beneficiaries bereft and without recourse.[19]

The trailers in New Orleans were a recent casualty of privatization without
oversight. Sixty thousand trailer homes ordered by FEMA to provide shelter
to those left homeless by Hurricane Katrina turned out to have high levels of
formaldehyde, a dangerous carcinogen that affected not only the residents of
the trailers, but also the government workers and contract employees who tested
them. It turned out that the trailers were supplied by a private manufacturer,
Gulf Stream Coach, a company that won this lucrative $500 million government
contract on a no-bid basis! Gulf Stream Coach neglected to inform FEMA when
it became aware of the toxicity of its product, while FEMA, in turn, failed to act
speedily when it found out the trailers were dangerous.

FEMA's failure to provide relief for the stranded victims of Hurricane Katrina
could be isolated into many different pieces, but one of the worst was the fact
that the agency had become a patronage dumping ground, and therefore the
target of the most flagrant kind of politicization. Close political connections
between the companies providing the trailers and officeholders in Louisiana
were revealed during the height of the crisis.

The plunder turned out to be bipartisan. A firm owned by two brothers
related to the treasurer of the Louisiana Democratic Party subcontracted with
Gulf Stream Coach to provide the 60,000 trailers for those left homeless by the
hurricane. One of the biggest contract winners for hurricane relief was married
to a nephew of Mississippi Governor Haley Barbour, a Republican. Certified
by the Small Business Administration as a disadvantaged small business owner,
Rosemary Barbour headed a company that received $6.4 million in federal con-
tracts, many of them "won" without competitive bidding.[20]

Unfortunately, the formaldehyde-tainted trailers represented only a small
piece of the patronage pie; many other companies also won contracts worth
hundreds of millions of dollars for tasks with such vague mandates as disaster
clearing, environmental cleaning, and site management. Democrats finally re-
belled against the gigantic rip-off these contracts were inflicting on the hapless
victims of Katrina as well as on the taxpayers. Representative Henry Waxman
and then–Minority Leader Nancy Pelosi, both California Democrats, joined in
2005 to introduce the "Hurricane Katrina Accountability and Clean Contracting Act," attacking the "greed, mismanagement, and cronyism" that squandered
"billions of taxpayer dollars." But their attempt to reform the system failed. The
bill would have established an independent commission to investigate and make
recommendations on ending waste, fraud, and abuse in the federal response to
Hurricane Katrina. The bill never made it out of the House committee, and the
patterns persist to this day.[21]

Representative Waxman tried repeatedly to force Congress to pay attention to the pitfalls of contract practices under the Bush administration. His committee on government reform issued annual reports estimating that between 2000 and 2005, "procurement spending" had increased by 80 percent. He charged that contracts were being awarded without competitive bidding, leading to massive— and unreported—"contract mismanagement ... rising waste, fraud and abuse." Ironically, Hurricane Katrina was not only one of the worst domestic disasters to strike the nation; others soon presented new and hidden opportunities for pinstripe patronage.[22]

Why Privatization Matters[23]

One of the worst examples of privatization and outsourcing occurred under the radar: the neglect and substandard care of war veterans returning for medical treatment from service in Iraq. The appalling conditions at Walter Reed Hospital, once known as the "crown jewel of military medicine" were revealed in riveting detail by reporters Dana Priest and Anne Hull of the *Washington Post*. They won a Pulitzer Prize for their efforts to detail the mouse droppings, mold, bureaucratic delays, and outright medical neglect that had become commonplace. More than 700 veterans suffering from "brain injuries, severed arms and legs, organ and back damage, and various degrees of post-traumatic stress" faced serious neglect, and as one soldier put it, conditions "nearly as chaotic as the real battlefields they faced overseas."[24]

The public shock and outrage at conditions at Walter Reed led to the high-profile firings of Major General George W. Weightman, who had served as Walter Reed's commander, and Army Secretary Francis J. Harvey. But another scandal involved the steady privatization of many of the functions at Walter Reed Hospital, scheduled for closure in 2011. No one knows what happened behind closed doors, but ultimately a private company, International American Products, Inc. (IAP), won a $120 million contract to maintain and operate Walter Reed, despite a recommendation from the Army that these functions should remain in-house. After OMB protested the Army's recommendation, the Army "cooperated" and revised its figures, which left IAP in charge of providing housekeepers, computer analysts, and clerks at Walter Reed. The company also provided services to New Orleans after Hurricane Katrina, in Iraq, and—no surprise—was politically connected to the Bush administration through ties to former Treasury Secretary John Snow. IAP also won lucrative awards as a defense contractor in Iraq and Afghanistan, winning $628,421.62 in contracts between 2002 and 2004. The substitution of private contractors for federal workers was vigorously protested by the American Federation of

Government Employees (AFGE).[25] The private contractor for Walter Reed, IAP, is a subsidiary of Cerberus Capital Management, whose ranks—in addition to former Treasury Secretary John Snow—are heavily larded with influential Republicans. Former Vice President Dan Quayle sits on the corporate board, while President Bush's former Defense Secretary, Donald Rumsfeld, was a major investor.

Forever Quango: Learning About the Hybrids

With apologies to Dickens, "hybrids" represent the worst of capitalism and the worst of socialism. On the surface, they looked very much like the savings and loans, at least in terms of some of their protections. S&Ls suffered many of the same problems after they were deregulated in the early 1980s. Bank presidents could offer depositors certificates of deposit paying interest rates of a whopping 16 percent, while government insurance afforded those very same depositors protection against loss for accounts that totaled up to $100,000.[26] A lethal combination, tantamount to government encouraging bankers to take risks without any fear that the marketplace would keep them in check.

Thousands of hybrid organizations were created during this period, and many tasks previously thought of as public were quietly entrusted to the private sector. In this way, the hybrids—also called "quagos" and "quangos" for quasi-governmental organizations—would not be hampered by unwieldy civil service regulations in the selection of personnel and the implementation of policy. Not to mention pay scales: Hybrids can often pay employees twice (or more) what comparable federal workers would get for the same task. As for the pay scales of board members and top executives, the sky's the limit. Perhaps most important of all: Hybrids do not have to abide by Hatch Act–type rules prohibiting political activity because employees can contribute money, electioneer, and support candidates as freely as they like, unrestricted by the cobweb of rules and laws governing their colleagues in traditional agencies.[27]

What happens when the inevitable question of oversight arises? Who supervises, oversees, or regulates the hybrids? Not only is congressional oversight spotty, but the hybrids also function virtually without any meaningful regulation or scrutiny that would affect their governance. The esteemed government scholar Harold Seidman raised the issue of accountability with the creation of new agencies, with no visible effect. Also echoing Dickens, he wrote of the danger inherent in creating agencies that would inevitably "privatiz[e] profits and socialize losses."[28]

Fannie Mae and Freddie Mac, two hybrid agencies set up to insure homeowners against mortgage losses, stood out dramatically as test cases in failure. Many people who lacked adequate assets or stable jobs were encouraged to buy homes and investment properties in the expectation that prices would keep going up. They were told not to worry: Fannie and Freddie would come to their rescue with dollars supplied by the taxpayers. More than half of the country's mortgages, for example, are held by those two hybrids: Freddie Mac and Fannie Mae. Were those entities regulated to protect the public's interests? Or were they yet another patronage receptacle for political leaders who owed their major supporters jobs after the campaign season?[29] Reams of copy finally riveted the public's attention on these agencies, which wielded considerable power over homeownership—a basic tenet of U.S. public policy since World War II. They were also protected from public and congressional scrutiny, thanks to protections guaranteed by their hybrid status: They are government-chartered, but shareholder-owned. That means that although these hybrids contributed heavily to the nation's sub-prime lending crisis, to be fair, the government quietly pressed them to award mortgages to lower income—and higher risk—purchasers with uncertain credit histories. A worthy public policy goal but, as it turned out, more costly to the taxpayer in the long run, for although the government was finally forced to take over Fannie Mae and Freddie Mac in September 2008, the status of the hybrids was left deliberately murky.

To the hybrid agencies before the government takeover, it was the best of all possible worlds. Chartered by the government, Fannie Mae and Freddie Mac enjoy a line of credit from the Treasury Department, as well as a blanket exemption from state and local income taxes, except for property taxes. These advantages, argued their defenders, made it easier for the agencies to buy home loans from banks and other real estate lenders and repackage them into securities that could then be sold to other investors. The lobbyists from Fannie Mae and Freddie Mac were extraordinarily successful at preventing the kind of rigorous oversight that might have avoided financial meltdowns at both agencies when even their combined portfolios of nearly $1.5 trillion couldn't prevent the accounting scandal that befell Freddie Mac in 2003 and the federal bailout of the bankrupt Fannie Mae in 2008.[30] Both Fannie Mae and Freddie Mac were put into a conservatorship in 2008 under the aegis of a "regulatory agency," the Federal Housing Finance Agency.[31]

The patronage benefits of Fannie and Freddie didn't come to light until the 2008 economic crisis struck, and their activities became widely scrutinized. James Johnson, a former aide to Democratic presidential candidate Walter Mondale, was appointed to head Fannie Mae, which he did without meaningful public scrutiny for seven years, from 1991 to 1998. When candidate Barack Obama picked James Johnson to head his vice-presidential selection committee during the 2008 presidential primary, Johnson's role at Fannie Mae came to light, and Johnson was forced to quit both positions. At Fannie Mae, he was paid $21 million per year, not including annual bonuses. Following Johnson as CEO was Daniel H. Mudd, the forty-eight-year-old son of Roger Mudd, the retired anchor of NBC and CBS News. His annual salary of $986,923 paled next to Johnson's, but far exceeded the salaries of cabinet secretaries; so did his benefits, one of which was the payment of the initiation fee and annual membership costs for a private country club.[32] Mudd's formal compensation was deceptive, however, because he stood to earn far more than $986,000. The docile (politically appointed) Board of Directors voted Mudd a compensation package that raised his base salary to a whopping $14,449,947 million—just for 2006! The board could be counted on each year to add hefty "bonuses" and "long-term incentive awards" to salary packages.[33]

Richard Syron, chairman of Freddie Mac, received compensation of $19.8 million in 2007, including a $1.2 million salary, $3.5 million in bonuses, $14.3 million in stocks and options, and $771,585 in other compensation. Henry Edelman, chairman of Farmer Mac, made a total of $2.7 million.

Lucrative positions were not relegated to top officials. Rahm Emanuel, former member of Congress from Chicago and aide to President Bill Clinton, held a year-long appointment to the Freddie Mac board of directors—deemed a "going-away present" from Clinton—which paid him $292,774 for one-year's service.[34] Rahm was the first appointee to the administration of President Barack Obama—as the White House chief of staff.

Other board members with past political service included Louis J. Freeh, head of the Federal Bureau of Investigation (FBI) under President Clinton; Henry Kissinger, secretary of state under Presidents Ford and Nixon; H. Patrick Swygert, president of Howard University; Jamie Gorelick, a private attorney who had served as deputy attorney general under President Clinton; Floyd H. Flake, a Democratic member of Congress from New York City; Robert E. Rubin, secretary of the Treasury also under President Clinton; Duane Duncan, former chief of staff to Representative Richard H. Baker (R-Louisiana); and Richard N. Haass, president of the Council on Foreign Relations.[35]

Board members also thrive financially. In 1997, Farmer Mac's directors began awarding themselves options. By 2002, the fifteen board members (all politically connected) had holdings averaging $816,249 each. Nine board members made millions more selling shares. Without spending a dime buying stock, they owned 13 percent of the company by 2002—all from stock options and restricted stock grants.[36]

Republicans as well as Democrats joined the lucrative patronage party offered by the hybrids. One board member of Fannie Mae, Warren Erdman, was the former chief of staff for Governor Kit Bond and managed Bond's 1986 Senate campaign. He went on to serve as regional chairman of the Bush-Cheney reelection campaign in 2004 and was then appointed to the board of the Kansas City

Economic Development Corporation. When appointed to Fannie Mae, he was executive vice president of the Kansas City Southern railroad.

Fannie Mae and Freddie Mac couldn't lose. Chartered in 1968 and 1970, both agencies provided banks with loans guaranteed by Congress. It worked rather simply: Banks originated loans to home purchasers; then sold the loans to Fannie Mae and Freddie Mac, enabling them to use the proceeds from that sale to offer new loans. Fannie and Freddie then financed their own purchases by issuing mortgage-backed securities. In the process, homeownership was increased, and both "agencies" became thriving corporations. Together they turned a $10 million profit in 2001, earning a prominent place on *Fortune* magazine's list of the most profitable corporations—Fannie Mae ranked thirteenth; Freddie Mac ranked eighteenth. The whole house of cards tumbled down in 2008, when the real enabler of this scheme—the U.S. government—was forced to buy all the securities, many of which had turned sour by then, contributing mightily to the economic disaster that followed.

The gravy train jumped its tracks with the economic collapse of 2008. John Koskinen, non-executive chairman of the board of Freddie Mac, now receives a compensation package totaling $290,000, far short of the $19 million received by his predecessor in 2007. Board members now receive $160,000 per year, somewhat less than the $292,000 received by Rahm Emanuel. In addition, the agency now has a government overseer, Ed DeMarco, who is acting director of the Federal Housing Authority. "The regulator must approve the hiring of senior executives, their compensation, and can require us to take actions that we think are too costly or not required," Koskinen said. In addition, former Washington, D.C. Mayor Anthony Williams is the only politician on the board, Koskinen said, and he was appointed because he is an expert on housing.

But hybrids have retained some privileges not granted to civil servants, namely the right (some say obligation) to make political contributions. The advisory boards of both agencies revealed prominent Republicans as well as Democrats—reason enough to contribute to both parties. Contrast this with the debates over the Hatch Act and how ridiculous they now seem in light of the political freedom of the hybrids and their executives: Were the prohibitions against political activity by government employees, for example, a violation of their First Amendment rights to free speech? In retrospect, the debate over whether low-level Commerce Department employees had the right to attend political rallies seems frivolous in light of all the influence-peddling allowed the hybrid agencies over the years.

An important issue that should give pause to free market purists is the extent to which hybrids play with a stacked deck at the expense of their competitors in the private sector. The income of Fannie Mae and Freddie Mac, for example, is only taxed at the federal level, which leaves them exempt from state and local corporate taxes. How many private companies enjoy this privilege? In addition, they are exempt from registration fees charged by the Securities and Exchange Commission (SEC). They can also borrow unlimited amounts of money at lower interest rates from the credit market and from the Treasury Department—at the Treasury's discretion. In other words, many of these privileges give them enormous advantages over their competitors in the private sector.[37]

The bailout of Freddie Mac and Fannie Mae in October 2008 proved their extensive lobbying efforts highly successful. Under pressure from Congress and the White House to save the failing housing market, the Treasury Department bought worthless stock in both agencies. Their favorable treatment by the government related directly to the fact that both hybrids spent more than $170 million in the previous decade to lobby the government to forestall the very regulations that might have prevented the need for such a bailout in the first place.

"Don't be too hard on Fannie Mae and Freddie Mac," said a political activist from Washington, D.C. The reason? Both agencies not only spend money to lobby the government, but they also contribute some of their excess funds to charities, often at the direction of members of Congress. When the Museum of the City of Washington was launched in 2003, Fannie Mae contributed $1 million to the effort. Unfortunately, the museum went out of business a year later.

No market discipline, and no shame either. Even in the face of scandals and the worst economic crisis since the Depression, both Fannie and Freddie planned to continue their lobbying activities, dooming legislation submitted in 2008 by Senator Jim DeMint (R-South Carolina) to prevent both companies from lobbying and making political donations.[38] Too many members of Congress benefited from the hybrids' lavish political and charitable contributions, golf outings, and other blandishments. In one year's time, from 2007–2008, Fannie Mae spent $5.6 million on lobbying, while Freddie Mac spent $8.5 million, according to the Center for Responsive Politics. Their defenders argue that as long as the groups have shareholders and are publicly traded companies, they have every right to political representation to influence political decisions that can affect them.

Members of Congress who had questioned the favored tax treatment accorded Fannie Mae and Freddie Mac were ignored, although now they are regarded as prophetic. Representative Pete Stark (D-California) introduced legislation in 2003 (the "Secondary Mortgage Market Fair Competition Act") that specifically targeted the hybrid agencies, which he called "corporations." Citing figures from the Congressional Budget Office, Stark charged that federal loan guarantees and the privileged status of Fannie Mae and Freddie Mac "translated into a subsidy of $13.6 billion a year." At a time when states were struggling with their own fiscal crises, Stark was particularly concerned about unfair competition. "Let's be true to states' rights and allow the states to determine the tax treatment of these corporations," he argued, and not "shelter Fannie and Freddie from the rigors of the marketplace indefinitely."[39]

Because many hybrids are ostensibly self-sustaining and do not require government funding, there has been scant congressional oversight, according to Kevin Kosar, of the Congressional Research Service. In the wake of the financial meltdown, however, Congress created a new agency, the Federal Housing Finance Agency, to regulate Fannie Mae and Freddie Mac. In a bow to the past, its chairman, James B. Lockhart, is a presidential appointee.

Signs appeared in 2009 that indicated a glimmer of congressional interest in what is now called "insourcing": bringing back the same lower-level jobs that agencies had been contracting out. The 2008 Defense Authorization Act, for example, directed the Pentagon to switch back to federal employees any work that had previously been outsourced. Other agencies, such as the Internal Revenue Service, followed suit, indicating the beginning of a trend that was greeted enthusiastically by the unions that represented government workers.[40]

Outsourcing, Bush Style

To reward the business community, President George W. Bush took outsourcing to new heights: Fifty percent of all federal functions, out of a total of $415 billion, were awarded to a total of 176,172 companies, mostly without competitive bidding. More than half those funds were spent on defense.[41] By the end of 2008, more than 170,000 contract employees worked in Iraq, more than the 147,000 American troops stationed in that country. Only about 17 percent were Americans, according to administration figures. About half were Iraqis, and one-third were workers from other countries. Initially contractors were given legal immunity, but that immunity ended at the behest of the Iraqi government.[42] Among their duties, the contractors provided food, tents (often moldy), shower water (often contaminated), laundry services (at $100 per laundry bag), and mechanics for tanks and helicopters; as well as police training, private security, truck drivers, and prisoner interrogators (including those at the now-notorious Abu Ghraib prison). Some GIs complained that they had to train contractors to do their jobs and then were themselves relegated to guard duty.[43]

Kellogg, Brown and Root, a subsidiary of Halliburton, a corporation formerly led by Vice President Richard Cheney, received the most money—more than $11 billion through July 2004, mostly for contracts to "rebuild" Iraq. Halliburton executives contributed millions to (mostly Republican) political campaigns from 2000–2002.[44] Representative Henry Waxman (D-California) charged that "Halliburton's unsupported bills exceeded $1 billion." But the Republican-controlled Congress held not a single hearing to determine how the contracts were awarded or executed. This was not surprising because the major contractors provided hundreds of millions of dollars for Bush and for Republican candidates running for Congress and the statehouses.[45]

Privatizing Foreign Policy

Public attention finally focused on government contracting when it became apparent that private companies are involved in defense and foreign policy. These include intelligence-gathering, combat, interrogation, and the protection of diplomats. Even General David Petraeus, the Commanding General of the Multi-National Force in Iraq, confessed that he was not protected by his own military forces, but by private security contractors hired by the Department of State.

An outstanding example of the privatization of foreign policy was revealed during the Iran-Contra scandal. This involved the Israeli sale of weapons to Iran, with the proceeds going to fund the anti-Sandinista rebels—or Contras, as they were known—in Nicaragua. The Israelis were then resupplied by the U.S. This aid to the Nicaraguan rebels defied an act of Congress, specifically the Boland amendment attached to the 1984 Appropriations Bill, which prohibited U.S. assistance to the Contras if their purpose was to overthrow the recently elected Nicaraguan government.

In fact, the Contras did oppose the left-wing Sandinista regime and appeared to be financed in part by nonappropriated money allocated to the National Security Council.[46] The scandal that eventually ensued, the Iran-Contra affair, forced the nation to focus on the larger issue of the privatization of foreign policy. Robert "Bud" McFarlane, who was President Reagan's national security adviser, was in charge of selling the arms. He journeyed to Iran and brought its leader, Ayatollah Khomeini, a birthday cake containing a hidden key. The key was meant to be symbolic but turned out to be just plain ludicrous. Although the fiasco had the trappings of a comic opera, it was deadly serious: On stage were public officials, all attached to the White House, directing funds to a group of rebels attempting to overthrow the popularly elected government of a sovereign nation, however inimical that nation was to American interests.

President Reagan was not formally implicated, but the scandal resulted in a number of convictions, including Defense Secretary Caspar Weinberger, McFarlane, and Lieutenant Colonel Oliver North, who had engineered the transfers of funds. They were later pardoned by President George H. W. Bush, whom some believe also was involved in the scandal when he was vice president. The pardons thus represented self-protection for Bush, as well as generosity toward those who were probably following the White House's directives.

Today, the privatization of foreign policy not only continues to thrive, but has greatly expanded its reach. Private security firms abounded in Iraq. The incentives to privatize were enormous. With the true costs of the war hidden, it was easier to cut through bureaucratic red tape and to move troops and materiel much faster than it would have been otherwise. Significantly, the blame for policies gone awry was dispersed, often laid at the feet of invisible and unaccountable corporations. In addition to support services—such as laundry, meals, and gasoline deliveries—private contractors were also engaged in roles traditionally reserved for the military and intelligence services, such as interrogating prisoners at the notorious Abu Ghraib prison. This work was done by CACI International, a private company that provides interrogation support and analysis work for the U.S. Army in Iraq.[47] An army investigation led by Major General Antonio M. Taguba accused CACI of being complicit in the physical abuse of prisoners.

Private contractors also filled the gap left open by America's diminishing allies. Absent a draft, troops were inevitably stretched thin as the United States found itself fighting on two major fronts, Iraq and Afghanistan. International cooperation in both wars has been woefully inadequate, which meant that the greatest burdens were carried by U.S. troops. The failure to recruit more allies turned out to be one of the greatest disappointments of the Bush presidency, particularly to President George W. Bush and his vice president, Richard Cheney. They would certainly also have liked more help in paying for the astronomical cost of the wars, which tallied (according to the best estimates) up to nearly $10 billion per month, and turned out to be a major source of voter dissatisfaction in the 2008 presidential primaries. The all-volunteer army, the absence of a draft in wartime, and the appalling insufficiency of such necessities as adequate body armor to protect the troops have all worked to create a yawning gap between America's responsibility as a "superpower" and the grim realities of war.

Private contractors were involved in training the Iraqi Army and police force; analyzing intelligence; treating wounded soldiers (at the partly privatized Walter Reed Army Hospital); and, of course, providing security for military convoys, the Baghdad Airport, and the Green Zone. Few paid attention to this development until Blackwater, a security firm advertised as the most "comprehensive professional, military, law enforcement, security, peacekeeping and stability operations company in the world," found several of its employees accused of violating Iraqi law. Until then, no one had given much thought to this vast army of contractors, who worked side by side with American troops and were subject to the same pressures and dangers. What was the level of training that these contractors brought to the job? More important: Who is in charge when employees of an American firm violate the law of another country? The Department of Defense? The Iraqi judicial system? American courts? No one knew at the time, making the situation even more difficult for all the parties involved. Many years passed before a decision was finally rendered that made private contractors working in a war zone subject to military law, specifically the U.S. Uniform Code of Military Justice (UCMJ).[48]

The Blackwater case involved several of its employees, who killed seventeen Iraqi civilians in the course of providing security to the American troops fighting in the Iraq War.[49] The incident occurred on September 16, 2007, and the Iraqi government quickly announced that it was forwarding criminal charges to its own courts. "The murder of citizens in cold blood ... by Blackwater is considered a terrorist action against civilians just like any other terrorist organization," said a report from the government of Iraq, reflecting the findings of the Iraqi Interior Ministry. In its only official statement, Blackwater defended its employees, saying that they were acting in self-defense, no doubt recalling an ambush three years before, in 2004, which resulted in the deaths of four men whose bodies were publicly hung from a bridge over the Euphrates River in the city of Fallujah.

The legal problem remained unresolved until 2009, despite the ongoing controversy. Blackwater stood firmly by an order written by L. Paul Bremer, former head of the Coalition Provisional Authority (CPA), which exempted all contractors and all Americans associated with the CPA from being subject to Iraqi law.[50] The State Department, which was responsible for security in Iraq, reacted to Iraqi pressure by rewriting its rules for security contracts. State required video surveillance equipment on all Blackwater armored vehicles and promised to place its own security agents alongside those contracted to provide the service. Distrustful of the Iraqi courts, State also granted contractors immunity from prosecution in Iraq. The situation was finally resolved in early 2010, when a federal district judge dismissed the indictments of five Blackwater employees on the grounds that their rights had been violated by prosecutorial misconduct. The Iraqi government strongly protested the ruling, and especially the fact that the defendants were prosecuted under American law, not Iraqi law.

During the time period before the ruling, the contracting issues emerged in sharp relief. What would happen, many asked, if a Blackwater employee became inebriated and shot an innocent civilian who lived in a war zone? Typically, the employee was quietly packed off on an airplane and shipped home, where he or she could count on *de facto* immunity from U.S. criminal law, civilian law, and, before 2008, military law. Now in the absence of clear rules of accountability, there are still virtually no mechanisms to call contractors to account for abuses that range from waste and fraud to assault, torture, and murder.

The largest of the three private security firms serving the State Department's security needs in Iraq, Blackwater considered itself fortunate to win a $750 million contract from the State Department. At its state-of-the-art facility in Moyock, North Carolina, the company trains more than 50,000 consultants to be "deployed anywhere in the world."[51] Ninety percent of Blackwater's contracts come from the U.S. government, two-thirds of which are no-bid contracts.

(No-bid means there is no competition; this practice is justified by the fact that in wartime there is no time for the long, drawn-out process of competitive sourcing.) Although these contracts have expanded exponentially from their initial $21 million contract to guard L. Paul Bremer in 2003, the company's mandate still remains vague: to guard officials and installations, train Iraq's new army and police force, and provide support for the troops. According to some estimates, Blackwater has received more than $1 billion in contracts since 2002, most of them with the Bureau of Diplomatic Security, the State Department's security and law enforcement arm. No one is quite sure about where to place the responsibility for security: with the Pentagon or the State Department? The problem becomes even more confusing when the two functions are as intertwined as they are now, with the State Department in charge of providing security to U.S. military forces.

The author of a riveting book on Blackwater, Jeremy Scahill, argues that the magnitude of Blackwater's activities is much greater than the public or the government is willing to admit: Americans are under the impression that the United States currently has about 145,000 active-duty troops on the ground in Iraq. What is seldom mentioned is the fact that there are at least 126,000 private personnel deployed alongside the official armed forces. These private forces effectively double the size of the occupation force, largely without the knowledge of the U.S. taxpayers that foot the bill.[52]

In addition to the legal ambiguities of contractors such as Blackwater, other disparities have surfaced that are especially galling to U.S. soldiers, especially the disparities in pay. "How can I get soldiers to reenlist offering them a $2,000 bonus, when they can go to Blackwater and draw beginning salaries of $80–100,000?" complained one high-ranking army official. "What does my $60,000 salary mean next to the $250,000 pulled down by my counterpart at Blackwater?" said another. A House-Senate conference committee reporting on the use of private contractors in intelligence work estimated that the average civilian employee (in all sixteen intelligence agencies) cost the government $126,500 annually in salary, while the cost of a "core contractor" hovered at $250,000.

Then there is the issue of transparency. The families of the four contractors who were killed in Fallujah sued Blackwater for wrongful death, alleging that the company showed a callous disregard for safety. They also raised general questions about the company's lack of transparency, accountability, and public oversight.

For their part, Blackwater and other contractors argue that companies like theirs offer expertise that is sorely needed in the regular armed forces. They are not mere mercenaries; rather, their ranks are filled with retired American military and intelligence officers with years of experience behind them. According to experts, private contractors are professionals, and those who award contracts to them are tapping the wisdom and expertise of elder statesmen in the combat-arms community who are respected by military commanders in the field. Two striking examples: Cofer Black, Blackwater's vice-chairman, who was director of the CIA's Counterterrorist Center and ambassador-at-large for the State Department from 2001–2003 before he joined Blackwater; and Joseph Schmitz, a former Pentagon inspector general, whose responsibilities included oversight of Blackwater.

The ambiguities involved in the privatization of war and foreign policy pale in contrast to the political opportunities afforded to companies fortunate enough to take advantage of this new policy. Many of the discussions are reminiscent of the debates over the quagos. While everyone is debating the merits and disadvantages of privatization, the real story is often lost in the shuffle: in this case, the steady expansion of rewards to political supporters. In the case of Blackwater, the company's political credentials more than matched its contributions to the war effort. Erik Prince, the company's founder and current owner, is—along with his family—a major financial supporter of the Republican Party. His sister chaired the Michigan Republican Party from 1996–2000 and from 2003–2005, and his family donated more than $325,000 over the past decade primarily to Republican candidates and committees. Prince spent part of his inherited wealth—from his father's billion-dollar auto parts company—to create Blackwater, which prides itself on its state-of-the-art training facility and corporate headquarters. An intern in George H.W. Bush's White House and a former Navy SEAL, Prince served in Haiti, Bosnia, and the Middle East, where he acquired his knowledge of military as well as regional needs for those areas. Officials of competing contracting firms accused Prince of meeting with government contracting officers—a practice, which they alleged, that was highly unusual for a chief executive officer.[53]

Other Republican ties surfaced when the company found itself on the defensive and needed public relations and legal help. Kenneth D. Starr, who served as the longtime independent counsel on the Whitewater investigation, and Fred Fielding, a White House counsel in the administration of George W. Bush, were hired by Blackwater to handle the company's legal troubles. Public relations advisors included Mark Corallo, who had worked for Attorney General John Ashcroft. The company's chief spokesperson was Anne E. Tyrrell, the daughter of R. Emmett Tyrrell, the editor of the conservative magazine *American Spectator*. Lobbying help came from Paul Behrends, whose former firm had close ties to the convicted lobbyist Jack Abramoff.

Blackwater remains only one of an accelerating number of military contractors conducting vital functions that have been in government hands since the beginning of the republic. The danger inherent in allocating "vital state functions to private actors" arises when "public goods," in this case national defense, are handed over to contractors whose major goal is "profit."[54] There is also the question of the chain of command: Who's the boss? Who really governs in a theater of war? Theoretically, U.S. troops could be left vulnerable if Iraq implodes and contractors decide to go home. Who would remain to deliver ammunition, fuel, and food supplies? Unfortunately, more questions than answers fill the information gap. Reacting to negative publicity over its activities in Iraq, Blackwater changed its name to Xe Services in 2009.

Similar relationships colored Halliburton's relationship with the White House. Before joining the administration of George W. Bush as vice president, Richard Cheney had served for five years as the CEO of Halliburton. Although Cheney was very careful to sever his ties with the company when he became vice president, Halliburton was still given more than 70 percent of the contracting business in Iraq. Before that, Halliburton had similar contracts in the Balkans, and its performance in that part of the world was sufficient reason to continue that relationship—according to some observers. They argued that the "Halliburton subsidiary of Kellogg, Brown and Root (KBR)" was "indispensable to the Balkan intervention" and their "bases in Bosnia and Kosovo ... [became] templates for those in Iraq and Afghanistan."[55]

Halliburton's ties go back much further than Kosovo. The Texas-based company's "grandfather," Brown & Root, has a long political history. George Brown, along with numerous members of his family, contributed to President Lyndon Baines Johnson's President's Club, as well as to his numerous political campaigns. It was no coincidence that Brown & Root won a lucrative contract from the National Science Foundation and landed the franchise—along with three other firms—to build airfields and other military installations in South Vietnam during the ten-year war between the United States and North Vietnam.[56] The problem lies with the inexorability of these contracts and the uncomfortable questions that arise from them. What was the relationship, for example, between the contracts for building airfields in South Vietnam and the length of the war?

Halliburton is only one of numerous defense contractors whose livelihood and existence depends on the generosity of the taxpayers. The top military contractor, Lockheed Martin, won $141,742,357,277 in 2002, but spent a great deal of money ($47,249,780) on "lobbying expenditures"; $7,338,676 on campaign contributions; and much more on individual contributions, PAC contributions, and "soft money" to influence the hearts and minds of politicians with budget influence.[57] While billions of dollars are spent in what has grown to be the very big business of contracting out, no one seems to know how much of that money goes to the actual defense of the nation and how much goes toward rewarding political allies. During the 2008 economic crisis, many economists argued for the bailouts of large investment banks and insurance companies on the rationale that they were "too big to fail." The same philosophy has become true of large defense corporations that have become too big to fail thanks to their government benefactors.

Governing the "Quango," Outside Contracts, and Other Hybrids

Given the frequent revelations of mismanagement, waste, fraud, and abuse, it is finally time to question the current federal structure that means so much to American lives. "The federal contracting system," observed Max Stier, "is in serious disrepair, and has become a losing proposition for our government, for the American taxpayers, and even for the contractors who have to navigate through these dysfunctional waters."

In the final analysis, government is neither the solution nor the problem. When trouble strikes, government appears on the starting line—where the Founding Fathers intended it to go. But when things look good, private companies step in, absorbing an increasing share of the functions that used to be the job of government. Aggravated by the war in Iraq, federal spending on federal contracts has more than doubled during the presidency of George W. Bush: from $207 billion in 2000 to more than $500 billion in 2008. Even when rules that prevent contracting out for security reasons—such as intelligence collection—are ignored, hardly any protests are heard. Few are looking over the government's shoulder, and fewer still care.

As government keeps shrinking, hardly anyone is left to guard the public. It is no longer a question of the fox guarding the henhouse; the foxes have moved right in. In one of the most ironic cases of all, a government contractor—CACI International—was chosen to review cases of incompetence and fraud among contractors. It didn't matter that CACI itself had just escaped a suspension from federal contracting, or that under the contract company employees would be allowed to look into the files of their competitors.

No problem for a government in which contracting has become virtually a "fourth branch of government," or that in the words of Scott Amey, general counsel at the Project on Government Oversight, reflected "a government that's run by corporations."[58] The problem, continued Amey, is that "the real politics of contracting out is less about contracting than it is about campaign contributions." Amey estimated that in FY 2008, the government spent $531 billion for contracts, with 60 percent of those contracts for services. In the past, contracts were supposed to be short-term and flexible. "Now they go for 50 years," he added.

At the start of the financial meltdown in September 2008, the government bailed out AIG, the nation's largest insurance company, rescuing the company by providing it with an $85 billion stake. Soon afterward, the executives of AIG sought to recover from the strain of the bailout by taking themselves at company expense to a California spa. The spa tab of over $400,000 was miniscule, especially compared to the $700 billion bailout plan that the Treasury Department convinced Congress was necessary to rescue the nation. But it rankled nonetheless as just another example of unregulated excess. A few months later, undaunted by the negative publicity over the spa holiday and flush with federal bailout money, AIG awarded the hefty sum of $165 million in "bonuses" to selected executives.

The real problem with outsourcing is that it "leads to the corruption of our bureaucracy, at least of its politically appointed members," and ultimately to the "demoralization" of civil servants.[59] If a no-bid contract for hurricane disaster relief goes to a campaign contributor, it is tainted almost before work begins. But what about the argument that emergencies—like Katrina or the war in Iraq— leave no time for competitive bidding? True enough, but that doesn't explain the exponential growth of this practice, which has gone well beyond emergency relief to virtually dominate the conduct of government in many other areas that are not considered emergencies. As always, transparency is key, and transparency is the very quality that appears to be disappearing forever.

Gone are the Christmas turkeys. And jobs as sewer inspectors no longer look as attractive as they did fifty years ago. In their place are billion-dollar "defense" contracts, board seats on Fannie Mae, and government bailouts for politically connected corporations. Political leaders no longer need armies of people ringing doorbells, when the Internet, cable TV, and other forms of new media are more successful at penetrating the voting public. What they need is more money and lots of it. Whole new sets of stakeholders now feed at the government trough, and they expect different and more lucrative kinds of rewards.

CHAPTER EIGHT
HARBINGER OF CHANGE

For good and for ill, political patronage has always been a harbinger of change. The skillful use of patronage has ushered in new political eras—from the New Deal to the Great Society to President Obama's campaign slogan of "Change we can believe in." Patronage was a key factor in enactment of the 2009 stimulus package that eased the worst financial crisis since the Great Depression, as well as in passage of healthcare reform in 2010. On the local level, patronage was used by Washington's Mayor Adrian Fenty to wrest control of education from a moribund school board, by New York's Mayor Michael Bloomberg to ban smoking in public places, and by Mayor Richard M. Daley to beautify downtown Chicago. Substantial change—from Social Security to Medicare to healthcare reform—has always met strong resistance, which patronage has blunted.

Patronage facilitated the ascent of ethnic groups, from Irish immigrants in the nineteenth century, to blacks and Hispanics in the twentieth, whose own political machines have imitated both the successes and flaws of their predecessors. As a young district leader in Cambridge, Massachusetts, Tip O'Neill handed out "snow buttons" that authorized jobless men to remove snow from the city's streets. Years later, as Speaker of the House, O'Neill handed out committee assignments and a host of other favors to party loyalists.

But snow buttons and committee assignments have been eclipsed by pinstripe patronage, including global billion-dollar contracts that reward the party faithful, those who have poured millions of dollars into both Democratic and Republican coffers. Many contractors who "win" these grants have a corrupting influence on the American political system, which has been distorted by their outsized political contributions. Their reach extends well beyond our borders, and their arrogance has undermined America's prestige around the world. One striking example stands out in Iraq, where Blackwater security forces—under contract with the U.S. government—killed Iraqi civilians. Immune from prosecution in Iraq, their acquittal in a U.S. court further fueled international resentment. Indeed, their general disregard for the rights of Iraqis has made them poster children for the recruitment of the very terrorists they are fighting.

Although five U.S. Supreme Court decisions have virtually outlawed patronage in the awarding of jobs and contracts, political favors are bigger and better than ever. The soaring growth of government in the last century has meant a proliferation of jobs, contracts, and all the coveted positions that fill out the ranks of the hybrids, which make Tammany Hall look like an Elysian field. Government's increased reach has geometrically increased the power of politicians to make or break those they govern.

The roots of pinstripe patronage run deep in America's soil. Big donors need big rewards, such as an ambassadorial appointment, or an appointment to the board or the corporate hierarchy of Fannie Mae—or for that matter to any of the new "quangos" or "quagos" that have long flourished under the radar. One recent CEO of Fannie Mae, for example, took home an annual salary of $21 million, plus bonuses; the Chairman of Freddie Mac did not lag far behind, with an annual compensation package of $19.8 million in 2007. What a contrast with sewer inspectors!

The new rewards still follow the old patterns: Bread cast upon the political waters comes back as an eighteen-layer cake. At the same time, a new set of influential stakeholders has arrived on the political scene, most of them with outsized demands.

The real problem is that outsourcing and the hybrids represent an abdication of government. No one knows who is really in charge or who is accountable for the myriad problems that beset the public. Who protects the public against the *E. coli* bacteria that periodically appear in the food supply—in oysters, dog food, or raw spinach? And who pays for these new forms of governance? Inflated salaries link arms with all kinds of hidden escalating costs for the taxpayer. One very minor example: It costs more than twice as much to pay a contract worker than it does to pay a public employee. Does outsourcing really represent increased efficiency or wasteful spending? Deficits? Small wonder America has become the land of the free and the home of the deficits: budget, trade, and current account (America's debt to foreign investors).[1]

Like deficits, the real problem with pinstripe patronage is its link to policy— one particularly important development is the privatization of foreign policy. Beginning with the Iran-Contra scandal in the mid-1980s, American foreign and defense policy found itself increasingly in the hands of politically connected private companies. In fact, private contractors far outnumbered public employees in Iraq. Today, these firms find themselves doing tasks far more important than washing army fatigues and providing food: They gather intelligence, train foreign soldiers, protect military and civilian VIPs, and interrogate prisoners. It almost goes without saying: They are politically connected. Halliburton, formerly led by Vice President Richard Cheney, reaped many of the contracts in Iraq.

What happens when vital public functions—like defense—are turned over to private firms whose major goals are profit? And who is the boss? The CEO of the company or the U.S. president? Who really governs in wartime? The four-star general or the CEO of Halliburton? Who cleans up after Hurricane Katrina or rescues the desperate citizens of New Orleans from flood and famine? The government or the manufacturers of faulty trailer homes? And who is responsible for controlling the vast oil spill that threatens the people, the businesses, and the wildlife along the coast of the Gulf of Mexico? British Petroleum or the U.S. government, which has since acknowledged its failure to regulate the industry?

On the plus side, patronage has brought many previously disaffected groups into the political process. Lyndon Johnson used patronage to overcome resistance in Congress to the Voting Rights Act, which led to the enfranchisement of southern blacks; the election of African American officials on the local, state and national levels; and the election of a black president in 2008.

But in 2009, the soaring deficits gave rise to an organized movement of angry conservatives, called the Tea Party. The following year, in the midterm congressional elections, the movement struck pay dirt by defeating longtime members of Congress who prided themselves on bringing home the bacon. Although the issue of deficits was the Tea Party's first priority, members were also angry at the massive government financial bailouts and what they perceived to be the arrogance of Washington and Wall Street. It is ironic that although government's regulatory powers had been eviscerated over the last quarter century, leading to the financial collapse of 2008 and government's inability to cope with crises such as the BP oil spill and poisoned food, the Tea Party movement wanted still less government and lower taxes.[2]

At its best, patronage has changed the nation's culture, thanks to the forces of identity politics and the political necessity for both political parties to incorporate new groups into their orbits. In the 1950s, the nation's capital was a Jim Crow town with separate bathrooms, drinking fountains, and restaurants for whites and African Americans. Fortunately, things have changed, albeit rather slowly, over the last half of the twentieth century. President Barack Obama's election was preceded by two black Secretaries of State, two black Supreme Court justices, several black congressional chairmen, and numerous black officials holding lesser public positions. As late as the 1970s, Congress was ruled by southern reactionaries, mostly bigots, who chaired the key committees and held their power very closely. Today a black legislator is the House Majority Whip and other African

Americans chair the House Ways and Means Committee, the House Judiciary Committee, and the Homeland Security Committee.

Women also have made gains in the political system, although they remain underrepresented. Thanks in large measure to the women's movement, women now enter the political system through the front door, rather than (as in the old days) succeeding their husbands in the statehouses and on Capitol Hill. In 1975, there were no women in the Senate and a smattering of women governors and House members. In 2008, there were fifteen women senators and seventy-five women members of the House; in addition, Nancy Pelosi, the Speaker of the House, was the first woman to hold that post. Nor was anti-Semitism unknown on Capitol Hill. Today, Jewish Senators chair the House Financial Services committee as well as the Energy and Commerce, Foreign Affairs, and Veterans' Affairs committees. In a dramatic shift from the past, two Jewish women occupy both Senate seats in the state of California.

These changes attest to the remarkable adaptability of the U.S. political system. At the heart of that system is political patronage, still thriving—although in many different forms—more than thirty years after it was doomed by the Supreme Court. Like feudal kings who gave their subjects titles and power in exchange for their fealty and funds, political leaders have given titles, resources and power in exchange for political loyalty, votes, and campaign contributions. This holds true not just for women and African Americans but also for all groups now entering the political system, including Hispanics, one of whom—Sonia Sotomayor—now sits on the Supreme Court, while another, Alberto Gonzalez, served as attorney general. Bill Richardson, who served as U.N. Ambassador, Energy Secretary and governor of New Mexico, also claims Latino roots. As with the feudal kings, those beneficiaries occasionally amass enough power to oust their benefactors.

Patronage remains essential to party discipline because those who oppose party initiatives are denied the political favors that most politicians covet. Some find themselves facing primary battles initiated by the party leadership. Other independent-minded souls also are denied their well-established perks, even at times when the retaliation can seem petty.

Not everyone covets political favors. Some people enter politics to champion an issue. The issue of abortion, for example, has passionate advocates: those who favor freedom of choice, and those who believe abortion is tantamount to murder. Similarly, gun control advocates face off against hunters, while the hotly debated issue of gay marriage continues in statehouses, Congress, and street corners all over the country. It is hard to believe that only a little over 100 years ago, people actually debated whether or not to allow maggots on the meat; thankfully for today's food shoppers, the Pure Food and Drug Act of 1906 rendered that issue moot—but not without a fight. Others enter politics to identify with groups that reinforce their beliefs—Jews, Asian Americans, Cuban Americans; they find the solidarity of numbers a sufficiently compelling reason to catch the attention of lawmakers, which it often does. Many issue-based activists find European and Israeli politics more congenial to their style: They can vote for many more candidates and political parties than their American counterparts, who are forced to make a choice in single-member districts; and they can be assured that their votes count for something. Unfortunately, multiple parties often make strange bedfellows when organized into one government, many of them forced into unstable coalitions that inevitably fall apart. American idealists, on the other hand, often find themselves flattened by the steamroller of American pragmatism: When an idea proves sufficiently attractive to the voters, either or both political parties adopts it as its own, preventing over the last 200 years the formation of third parties. This was the experience of Populists, Progressives, Greenbackers, and most recently the Reform Party headed by Ross Perot. Perot's attention to the budget deficit—a major factor in his capture of 19 percent of the presidential vote in 1992—was adopted by both the Democratic and Republican Parties, ultimately leaving Perot's Reform Party in the dust. Similarly, the Green Party, headed by consumer activist Ralph Nader, focused attention on environmental issues.

To some extent, patronage thrives because voters don't seem to care. Too caught up with the practicalities of industrial and technological achievement, Americans seldom respond over the long term to the political philosophies of any era. Or even to the mundane functions of day-to-day politics. Who cares where government banks its money or buys its furniture, or who installs heating systems in public buildings? Few paid attention to the nation's burgeoning foreign debt, which topped nearly $1 trillion in 2009, up from a mere $35 billion in 1985. State contracts attract public attention when losing companies complain about the bidding process. Are they complaining about the rigged bids or their own exclusion? The strongest opposition to leasing highways came not from drivers who stood to lose the most from rising tolls, but from politicians who feared the loss of patronage jobs, construction contracts, and restaurant leases.

In general, American politics is more about cooperation than confrontation, more about patronage than ideology, despite a marked increase in issue polarization since the late 1970s. Although a passionate group of believers on the right or left can sometimes initiate or block legislation, most of the time patronage politics prevails. Lawmakers' complaints about a lack of collegiality and the lack of civility in public discourse reached a low point in September 2009, when President Obama's address to a joint session of Congress on healthcare was interrupted by a Republican heckler, Representative Joe Wilson of South Carolina, who shouted, "You lie." Wilson apologized after being scolded by both Democrats and Republicans.

Because the U.S. political system runs on consensus, heated rhetoric often masks the truism that success almost always requires compromise. The sixty votes needed to end a Senate filibuster, for example, means that enactment of a bill usually requires bipartisan support. Senate Democrats voted 29–21 to support President George W. Bush's call for the Iraq War, while House Democrats were also divided. At the same time, President Bush, a conservative Republican, partnered with Senator Edward M. Kennedy, a liberal Democrat, to enact the No Child Left Behind Act. In the Senate, much of the work is still done by unanimous consent. In the House each week there is a "suspension of the rules," which allows Democrats and Republicans to join together to enact legislation by a two-thirds majority. Committee chairs and ranking members of the opposition party often work together to fashion legislation. "When you campaign you try to destroy your opponent," said Kenneth Duberstein, President Reagan's chief of staff. "And that's become the legislative process now as well. But when you govern you need to try to find ways to become affectionate with your opponent." Most recently, patronage politics was bared in full view, when a deal giving Senator Mary Landrieu, Democrat of Louisiana, $100 million for her state was struck just for her vote that allowed the Senate to debate the all-important health reform bill. No wonder it was called the "Louisiana Purchase." In addition, Senator Ben Nelson, a Democrat from Nebraska, was given more than $100 million in Medicaid funds for his state, a sum that became notorious as a symbol of back-room dealing. The "Cornhusker Kickback," as it was known, was deleted from the final health reform bill. Political leaders remain wedded to patronage as the most efficient form of cooperation: Patronage rewards hold the party together and cement loyalties up and down the line. To the surprise of few, many of the rewards are perfectly legal. Indeed, the problem is not what is illegal, but what is legal; all too often, the differences are more rhetorical than substantive. "Earmarks" today have a negative connotation, although members of Congress have always been judged by the "pork" they could bring home to their districts. Notwithstanding the "Bridge to Nowhere," earmarks have grown exponentially on every level of politics, with nary a peep from the voters: In New York City, they have grown from $35 million to $175 million in one year alone. Again, apathy reigns. There is also nothing illegal about privatization: Who cares what company picks up the garbage, runs the prisons and hospitals, or protects American generals in Iraq?

Yet all kinds of patronage still exist, and when one form reaches scandalous proportions, another takes its place—usually under an assumed name. When people have some degree of freedom of choice—and most politicians do—incentives can make a big difference in their decisions. Patronage also exists because of the necessity of political leaders to ensure the loyalty of their subordinates, with ideology making only occasional appearances. A recent British scandal consisted of members of parliament abusing their government expense accounts by charging personal items; in one case, the construction of a moat around a castle. But patronage is not simply a phenomenon of democracies. Soviet bureaucrats enjoyed governmental favors denied to most citizens, including special clinics and other health facilities, special stores stocked with foods not available to ordinary citizens, and vacation homes. Similarly, Minxin Pei, a China scholar at the Carnegie Endowment for International Peace, found that, "The real glue that has held the Chinese Communist Party together is a vast patronage system that has been underwritten by a long period of economic growth." He added: "China's non-ideological ruling elites have stuck with the party because it has been paying them off."[3] Even more than America's political bosses, the world's authoritarian leaders need to buy loyalty to ensure their longevity in office.

Traditional patterns of American democratic pluralism—the inclusion of new groups through patronage favors—are alive and well in twenty-first century America. Those groups believe they earned the right to those favors through the ballot box, often achieved after years of struggle that resulted not only in increased appointments but also in system changes. In theory and in practice, American politics has never developed a genuine alternative to the patronage system. It never had to. Developed to correct the worst abuses of patronage, the civil service system still in place after 125 years has not yet succeeded in becoming a truly viable alternative. With a reputation for sluggishness and stagnation, the U.S. Civil Service has failed at times to work well, primarily because it lacks the most basic advantage of a well-run patronage system: clear-cut rewards in return for good service and unquestioned loyalty. Civil Service augments the patronage system, but its jobs have never risen to the status of the ripest fruits closely guarded by patronage dispensers. Although critics attribute this failure to the absence of "threat power"—the ability to fire bad workers without going through endless red tape—the real problem with civil service is that the system lacks the kind of substantial rewards needed to motivate workers toward better performance. In fact, teachers' unions and other interest groups have long opposed financial incentives for performance; only recently have New York City and Washington resisted the unions in order to experiment with ways to reward good teachers and discharge poor ones. In addition, the United States is the only country with such a large network of presidential appointees directing merit-based (civil service) appointees, while top leaders in other industrialized democracies must content themselves with only a small fraction of loyalists. In theory, this guarantees an adherence to the president's policies not found anywhere else.

At the same time, the quiet development of hybrids virtually guarantees the undermining of the civil service. True, they are more flexible than government agencies, but they are fraught with questions: Who governs them? Who makes policies? To whom are they accountable on a regular basis? And most important of all: What damage do they do to the budget?

As with the hybrids, patronage power eludes reformers because the real rewards still lurk in the shadows of public awareness. As long as they can preserve the judgeships, contracts, high-level jobs, subsidies, and grants, political leaders continue to ignore groups that advocate what is euphemistically called "good government." Presidents Roosevelt, Kennedy, and Johnson greatly enhanced their power by exempting large swaths of public employees from civil service. At the same time they publicly extolled civil service, these presidents quietly and with great skill expanded patronage rewards in areas they knew would pay off, directing favors to individuals and groups they knew would reciprocate with their support. On lower levels, local politicians know how little it matters if city planners work within a civil service system as long as they can still control zoning patterns by "political contract." Similarly, governors and other politicians do not seem overly concerned that their judicial nominees are subject to a screening process by an "independent" board because they appoint the board's members and control its decisions.

Where it counts, the patronage system is secure. Sound planning almost always takes second place to political necessity, while the real rewards of government are bestowed on those with the most "clout." Patronage reform, when it does surface, is usually a phony issue, often failing because it comes in an empty vessel. In the end, many reformers just want some of the patronage for themselves and rarely leave in their wake concrete programs (such as more incentives for civil servants, mandated rational planning for cities, or more stringent competitive bidding for discretionary contracts) to correct the abuses of patronage they fought against so bitterly. When the reformers succeed in gaining more patronage for themselves, there remains the nagging question of whether they really represent an improvement over the original patronage-dispensers. Are the bar associations, who want more power over the selection of judges, better judges of judges than local party leaders?

Patronage determines not only the real power structure but also who enters and who succeeds in politics. Lawyers and businessmen dominate Congress and the state legislatures because government's rewards are critical to their endeavors. Chances are that the young lawyer speaking on a soap box today, extolling the virtues of a Democratic or Republican candidate, will be sitting on the bench tomorrow. Legislators from the arts, the sciences, skilled and unskilled labor, health professions, or the academic world rarely get elected; they are forced by the system and by their own inclinations to influence government one step removed from its inner circles.

Political rewards also determine who stays active in politics. Regardless of how a member of Congress stands on the issues of the day, a lawmaker who fails to satisfy his or her district with speeded-up Social Security checks, contracts, and other constituent services will have a harder time getting reelected than his colleagues who have mastered the art of patronage. Even more certain is the unhappy fate of the lower court judge—no matter how brilliant his opinions—who fails to send refereeships and guardianships back to party leaders. That judge could look forward to poor judicial assignments, trouble in processing his cases, and trouble obtaining clerical help, and most certainly would find obstacles in the path to renomination.

Patronage has a life of its own, ranging from dispensing fairly simple favors—such as a photograph with a mayor, governor, or president—to the more munificent rewards that come with contracts and earmarks. Although a necessary tool of government, patronage also presents many dangers and often lends itself to corruption and waste. The beneficiaries of the dark side of patronage have included incompetent judges, inept bureaucrats, unneeded expenditures, and prolonged wars.

Patronage is uniquely susceptible to corruption. If you need medical attention, try to avoid a physician who received his medical degree from the University of Medicine and Dentistry of New Jersey. If one must appear before a judge, try to avoid one whose chief qualification is his closeness to a political machine. Patronage can be especially susceptible to corruption when lots of money is involved. Witness the flagrant attempt by the former Illinois governor to auction off the vacant senate seat of President Barack Obama. Not only was Blagojevich attempting to raise campaign funds for the party, he was trying at the same time to feather his own and his wife's future professional nests. Does this go on in other states? And at other times? Certainly. But not as crassly and not as carelessly as it was in Blagojevich's case. As U.S. Attorney Patrick Fitzgerald explained: He was not trying to interfere with the normal horse trades of politics; he was only concerned with politicians who were clearly enriching themselves in the process. But here is where professional and personal enrichment clash, often blurring the line between the two. What is the real difference, for example, between a campaign contributor appointed Ambassador to the Court of St. James in exchange for his hefty donation to a presidential campaign, and a governor trying to get a job for himself after his retirement from public service? Or a lawmaker who brings back an earmark for the sirex woodwasp and reelection to office? They are all advancing professionally, which shows how easy it is to cross the line.

Patronage also breeds waste. Unneeded weapons systems and huge public works projects are approved because they provide jobs in the congressional districts of powerful lawmakers. The F-22 fighter plane, coproduced by Boeing and Lockheed Martin, survived strong opposition from the military as well as from the Clinton and two Bush administrations because it provided 30,000 jobs in thirty-three states. After authorizing production of 187 aircraft, Congress finally ended the program at the behest of the Obama administration, but only after a hard-fought battle.

Patronage also has led to the appointment of incompetents, those whose talents are more political than managerial. But presidents, governors, and mayors who appoint incompetents often pay a price at the polls. FEMA's incompetent handling of Hurricane Katrina led to President Bush's decline in the polls, much as some mayors have discovered that their failure in snow removal has shortened their public careers.

The most insidious impact of patronage is on policy, and the exclusion of those unable to reciprocate political support. This often means the exclusion of the poor, who cannot contribute financially to political campaigns and who often don't vote; the medically uninsured; minority groups, whom custom has excluded from many traditional rewards; in short, anyone barred by a political system geared to satisfying only its own maintenance needs. Parceling out rewards on the basis of a political cost-benefit ratio often fails to meet the demands of these groups, whose leaders are routinely excluded from the inner world of political decisions. All too often, these groups have real needs that must be addressed by government. If not, the political system must answer for the ensuing alienation, apathy, and occasional violence that stem from their frustration.

The real lesson of patronage politics is that those who control patronage usually control policy, unless an overriding issue captures the public's attention. The goal, really, is to harness government's enormous rewards on behalf of rational planning and on behalf of the public interest. Of course, what constitutes rational planning and the public interest is invariably in the eye of the beholder.

Government of the future seems loaded with patronage practices, with many of them hidden from public view. Political leaders over the last quarter-century have deluded themselves as well as their constituents with visions of smaller government—leaner, more efficient, and more responsive to public demands. In keeping with their dreams, government has succumbed to the increasing privatization of everything from sewer repair to foreign policy and has actually shrunk in size. But at the same time regulatory agencies have been neutered—many beyond repair—quagos, quangos, and other hybrids have quietly crept in, loaded with political appointees and mostly out of reach of public control. The SEC knew about Bernard Madoff's Ponzi scheme in the late 1990s, for example, but the agency was so eviscerated by then, it could do little to stop him. For years, the National Highway Traffic Safety Administration (NHTSA) turned a blind eye to numerous reports that Toyota vehicles had significant safety problems. Fleshing out the current patronage system will lead to even more links to current crises and the current inability of government to deal with them. For although the workforce of government has been downsized, many of government's functions have expanded; in fact, the cost of government continues to escalate, funded by the very taxpayers who are handed false impressions of what they are being asked to pay for.

Americans yearn for political leaders who are "above politics," but they forget that politics also produces leaders with the experience and judgment to weather the crises that inevitably confront the nation. Indeed, those who consider themselves above politics often act as if democracy is beneath them.

Now more than ever it behooves both public servants and private citizens to increase their vigilance, bring hidden practices out into the open, and subject more public policies to a patronage litmus test that asks the vital questions that voters want to know. Does it work? Does it work in the long run? What will it cost today and tomorrow? And how will it affect the nation's integrity at home and abroad?

Gifts of Christmas turkeys and jobs as sewer inspectors actually produced more accountability than current practices allow. After all, the old patronage was transparent. The turkeys could be roasted, and the jobs were highly visible, as street car conductors clanged their bells and sewer inspectors emerged cold and wet from the city's lower depths. District leaders were quickly removed from office if taxes rose too high, the trains failed to run on time, or a party worker's nephew remained unemployed for long.

But the new pinstripe patronage is different. And the stakes are much higher. No one sees the country club fees; in fact, country clubs have very secure gates to exclude prying eyes. Or lavish bonuses for Fannie Mae executives. And few Americans care who does the laundry in Iraq, guards the generals, or influences foreign policy. Fewer still care about picking up the garbage, constructing hospitals, or building prisons. As long as everything gets done and taxes remain low, very few voters look under the swelling dark underbelly of political favoritism. Perhaps it is time they did.

In the final analysis, political patronage is as messy and unpredictable as democracy itself. The key is to understand it, force it to bend in the direction of the public good, and weed out leaders who succumb to its temptations. For all its flaws, patronage is an inextricable part of politics and government, and those who regard it with disdain do so at their peril.

RESOURCE A
JUDGESHIPS IN THE UNITED STATES OF AMERICA

	Supreme Court		Court of Appeals	
State	**Number of Judges**	**Method of Selection**	**Number of Judges**	**Method of Selection**
Alabama*	9	Partisan election	10	Partisan election
Alaska	5	Gubernatorial appointment	3	Gubernatorial appointment
Arizona	5	Gubernatorial appointment	22	Gubernatorial appointment
Arkansas	7	Nonpartisan election	12	Nonpartisan election
California	7	Gubernatorial appointment	105	Gubernatorial appointment
Colorado	7	Gubernatorial appointment	16	Gubernatorial appointment
Connecticut	7	Gubernatorial appointment	9	Gubernatorial appointment
Delaware	5	Gubernatorial appointment	5	Gubernatorial appointment
District of Columbia			9	Presidential appointment
Florida	7	Gubernatorial appointment	62	Gubernatorial appointment
Georgia	7	Nonpartisan election	12	Nonpartisan election
Hawaii	5	Gubernatorial appointment	6	Gubernatorial appointment
Idaho	5	Gubernatorial appointment	3	Gubernatorial appointment
Illinois	7	Partisan election	42	Partisan election
Indiana	5	Gubernatorial appointment	15	Gubernatorial appointment
Iowa	7	Gubernatorial appointment	9	Gubernatorial appointment
Kansas	7	Gubernatorial appointment	12	Gubernatorial appointment
Kentucky	7	Nonpartisan election	14	Nonpartisan election
Louisiana	7	Partisan election	53	Partisan election
Maine	7	Gubernatorial appointment		
Maryland*			20	Gubernatorial appointment
Massachusetts	7	Gubernatorial appointment	25	Gubernatorial appointment
Michigan	7	Partisan nomination/ nonpartisan election	28	Nonpartisan election
Minnesota	7	Nonpartisan election	16	Nonpartisan election
Mississippi	9	Nonpartisan election	10	Nonpartisan election
Missouri	7	Gubernatorial appointment	32	Gubernatorial appointment

Superior Court		District/Circuit Court		Observations	
Number of Judges	Method of Selection	Number of Judges	Method of Selection	Number of Judges	Method of Selection
		143	Partisan election	162	Election
40	Gubernatorial appointment			48	Appointment
174	Nonpartisan election/ gubernatorial appointment			201	Appointment or election
118	Nonpartisan election			137	Election
1,498	Nonpartisan election			1,610	Appointment or election
		148	Gubernatorial appointment	171	Appointment
180	Gubernatorial appointment			196	Appointment
19	Gubernatorial appointment			29	Appointment
59	Presidential appointment			68	Appointment
		592	Nonpartisan election	661	Appointment or election
201	Nonpartisan election			220	Election
		33	Gubernatorial appointment	44	Appointment
		40	Gubernatorial appointment	48	Appointment
		513	Partisan election	562	Election
196	Partisan election	102	Partisan election		Appointment or election
		116	Gubernatorial appointment	132	Appointment
		163	Gubernatorial appointment	182	Appointment
		146	Nonpartisan election	167	Election
		217	Partisan election	277	Election
17	Gubernatorial appointment			24	Appointment
		153	Gubernatorial appointment	173	Appointment
82	Gubernatorial appointment			114	Appointment
		221	Nonpartisan election	256	Election
		288	Nonpartisan election	311	Election
		51	Nonpartisan election	70	Election
		141	Partisan election	180	Appointment or election

State	Supreme Court		Court of Appeals	
	Number of Judges	**Method of Selection**	**Number of Judges**	**Method of Selection**
Montana	7	Nonpartisan election		
Nebraska	7	Gubernatorial appointment	6	Gubernatorial appointment
Nevada	7	Nonpartisan election		
New Hampshire	5	Nominated by governor, appointed by executive council		
New Jersey	7	Gubernatorial appointment	34	
New Mexico	5	Partisan election	10	Partisan election
New York**	7	Gubernatorial appointment	60	Gubernatorial appointment
North Carolina	7	Nonpartisan election	15	Nonpartisan election
North Dakota	5	Nonpartisan election		Chosen from among active retired district judges
Ohio**	7	Partisan primaries, nonpartisan election	68	Partisan primaries, nonpartisan election
Oklahoma*	9	Gubernatorial appointment	17	Gubernatorial appointment
Oregon	7	Nonpartisan election	10	Nonpartisan election
Pennsylvania**	7	Partisan election	15	Partisan election
Rhode Island	5	Gubernatorial appointment		
South Carolina	5	Legislative election	9	Legislative election
South Dakota	5	Gubernatorial appointment		
Tennessee**	5	Gubernatorial appointment	24	Gubernatorial appointment
Texas	9	Partisan election	89	Partisan election
Utah	5	Gubernatorial appointment	7	Gubernatorial appointment
Vermont	5	Gubernatorial appointment		
Virginia	7	Legislative election	11	Legislative election
Washington	9	Nonpartisan election	22	Nonpartisan election
West Virginia**	5	Partisan election		
Wisconsin	7	Nonpartisan election	16	Nonpartisan election
Wyoming	5	Gubernatorial appointment		

Source: This chart comes from data collected in part by the American Judicature Society. http://www.judicialselection.us/judicial_selection/methods/selection_of_judges.cfm?state=, accessed October 14, 2008.

Notes: *Court of appeals category includes different courts, such as criminal, civil, and special appeals. **In these cases, the name of the courts is different from the categories.

Superior Court		District/Circuit Court		Observations	
Number of Judges	Method of Selection	Number of Judges	Method of Selection	Number of Judges	Method of Selection
		43	Nonpartisan election	50	Election
		55	Gubernatorial appointment	68	Appointment
		64	Nonpartisan election	71	Election
22	Nominated by governor, appointed by executive council			27	Appointment
371	Gubernatorial appointment			412	Appointment
		84	Partisan election	99	Election
324	Partisan election	125	Partisan election		Appointment or election
95	Nonpartisan election			117	Election
		42	Nonpartisan election	47	Election
391	Partisan primaries, nonpartisan election			466	Election
		75	Nonpartisan election	101	Appointment or election
		173	Nonpartisan election	190	Election
9	Partisan election	439	Partisan election	470	Election
22	Gubernatorial appointment			27	Appointment
		46	Legislative election	60	Election
		39	Nonpartisan election	44	Appointment or election
		153	Partisan election	182	Appointment or election
		433	Partisan election	531	Election
		70	Gubernatorial appointment	82	Appointment
12	Gubernatorial appointment	17	Gubernatorial appointment	34	Appointment
		157	Legislative election	175	Election
186	Nonpartisan election			217	Election
		66	Partisan election	71	Election
		241	Nonpartisan election	264	Election
		21	Gubernatorial appointment	26	Appointment

Observations: Total number of judges in each state ranges from 24 (Maine) to 1610 (California). Judges at all levels are elected in 23 states, appointed in 19 states. In the remaining 9 states, judges are appointed at higher court levels and elected at lower court levels.

Resource B
Defense Contributions

**Postwar Contractors Ranked by Total Contract Value
in Iraq and Afghanistan from 2002 through July 1, 2004**

Contractor	Contract Total
KBR, Inc. (Halliburton)	$11,431,000,000
Parsons Corp.	$5,286,136,252
Fluor Corp.	$3,754,964,295
Washington Group Intl.	$3,133,078,193
Shaw Group/Shaw E&J	$3,050,749,910
Bechtel Group	$2,829,833,859
Perini Corp.	$2,525,000,000
Contrack Intl. Inc.	$2,325,000,000
Tetra Tech Inc.	$1,541,947,671
USA Environmental Inc.	$1,541,947,671

Source: Center for Public Integrity

RESOURCE C
CONTRACTORS' POLITICAL CONTRIBUTIONS
AND CONTRACT EARNINGS

Campaign Contributions of Postwar Contractors from 1990 through Fiscal Year 2002

Contractor	Contract Total
General Electric Co.	$8,843,884
Vinnell Corp. (Northrop Grumman)	$8,517,247
BearingPoint Inc.	$4,949,139
Science Applications Intl. Corp.	$4,704,909
Fluor Corp.	$3,624,173
Bechtel Group	$3,310,102
KBR, Inc. (Halliburton)	$2,379,792
American President Lines Ltd.	$2,185,303
Dell Marketing L.P.	$1,774,971
Parsons Corp.	$1,403,508

Source: Center for Public Integrity

Postwar Contractors Ranked by Total Government Earnings: All Federal Contracts from 1990 through Fiscal Year 2002

Contractor	Contract Total
General Electric Company	$43,736,487,000
Vinnell Corp. (Northrop Grumman)	$42,414,198,000
Science Applications Intl. Corp.	$16,194,431,000
DynCorp (Computer Sciences Corp.)	$15,809,649,000
Bechtel Group	$11,742,537,000
Unisys Corp.	$10,772,003,000
Fluor Corp.	$8,544,917,000
United Defense Industries L.P.	$7,299,691,000
KBR, Inc. (Halliburton)	$5,686,006,000
Dell Marketing L.P.	$2,714,952,000

Source: Center for Public Integrity

RESOURCE D
A BRIEF HISTORY OF PATRONAGE*

The Bible is rife with examples of "To the victor belong the spoils of the enemy," providing even the most devout worshippers with horrifying accounts of conquering armies looting the vanquished and taking their lives, their property and their women. Although barbaric to modern eyes, our ancestors provided the template for today's victorious politicians, who swiftly oust their opponents from their jobs, contracts, and special privileges and replace them with their allies, who in turn reap the rich benefits of government rewards.

Early patronage involved the marketing of public offices by bankrupt rulers, whose actions predated the rise of the Roman Empire, circled the globe, led to the rise and fall of empires, and influenced the development of almost every political institution known today. Monarchs in China, England, Spain, Italy, the Netherlands, and the Ottoman Empire grew tired of relying on noblemen and the clergy for support and discovered that selling titles was the most convenient way to build up national treasuries.

The ancient Chinese, for example, in response to natural disasters such as war, flood, and famine, bartered government jobs in exchange for agricultural produce. As early as 243 B.C., those who gave a certain amount of grain to the state were rewarded with one rank in the official hierarchy. During the Ming Dynasty (1368–1644), the government resorted to selling offices to shore up its resources whenever barbarians from the north threatened to invade the country. Ironically, while China claimed the first known patronage system, it also initiated the first merit system. Mandarin status, the highest in the civil service, could not be bought for any sum of money and was achieved only by passing a long and difficult examination requiring years of preparation and a talent for rote memory.

Curiously, the Catholic Church was the only institution that sanctioned patronage by law, and references to it in canon law describe the practice as the benevolent exercise of privilege. (The term "patronage" also was used to describe the transfer of power by the Pope to his natural sons, euphemistically called nephews—hence nepotism—and to his other relatives.) "Juspatronatus," the sum of privileges according to canon law, was derived from the Roman system, which contained within itself an entire class of free men who were not citizens, who nonetheless attached themselves to "patrons." Translated into canon law, the "patron" was someone who financed the building of a church in return for the privilege of controlling the lives of those involved with the church. Also called the "founder" of the church, the patron enjoyed the right to appoint some members of the lower clergy and, more often, to assign candidates who would take part in church ceremonies and enjoy certain of its privileges. To augment its income, the church also sold "indulgences," which provided some relief from temporal sins—for a price, of course. The system of selling indulgences became so corrupt that it provided some of the richest fodder for Martin Luther's protest against the Catholic Church and the subsequent rise of Protestantism.

After the Middle Ages, the ability of the Church to retain its patronage depended on its power vis-à-vis the monarchy. Thus early in its development, patronage became an index of the power of political institutions.

As patronage bailed out bankrupt governments and brought them to solvency, its excesses grew greater, as rulers discovered the unlimited possibilities patronage held for making money. Patronage politics was an avenue to untold wealth as early as the fourteenth-century Ottoman Empire, when sultans auctioned off the governorships of Egypt and Syria for 60,000 gold ducats apiece, an investment that yielded returns of millions of gold ducats in annual tributes. Under the Ottoman emperors, patronage was profitable but fraught with danger, for officeholders who had purchased their power with credit were often tempted to extort, borrow, or steal in order to pay back their creditors. When all other attempts to repay their loans failed, governing pashas occasionally resorted to hanging more persistent creditors on the palace door. Creditors with more luck were sometimes paid back with influence, just as wealthy party contributors are rewarded today; in fact, many Greek financiers took positions as "executive aides" to the very public officials whose careers they had financed.

The going rate under the English Stuarts for the office of secretary of state ranged from 6,000 to 10,000 pounds, and by the eighteenth century it had become common practice to purchase seats in Parliament. The practice of patronage, perfected and coined by the French as the *vénalité des offices,* reached its peak in the seventeenth century and involved the sale of nearly all offices—political, civil, and military. Selling offices without regard to their usefulness created vast bureaucracies laden with what the French called *offices imaginaires*; as expected, they tended to drain the economy. Worse, most offices were hereditary and treated as stock on the open market. Louis XVI, destined to be decapitated in 1793 by an angry public, was saddled with paying the salaries of "wig inspectors" and "inspectors of hogs' tongues," useless jobs that had helped produce revenue for the depleted treasury of his great-grandfather but no longer helped his own flagging economy.

Short-sighted monarchs, anxious for solvency and riches, sold offices with abandon, unaware of the drastic consequences that were soon to change the political structure of the Western world. They failed to understand that although those who owed their offices to them would usually remain loyal, no guarantee existed that they would support their successors. By creating a situation in which political power could be purchased, they brought new classes of untitled but moneyed people into government, people who were not content to remain on the fringes of power and who began to demand power commensurate with their financial investments. Sir Walter Raleigh was the first to warn the Tudors that their patronage policies would encourage the British masses to revolt against the aristocracy.

Money brought the middle class into the ruling class. Ironically, European royalty unintentionally signed its own death warrant, as bourgeois-led revolutions gripped England, France, and the Americas. Patronage practices, which were invented with the simple but basic motive of making money, indirectly contributed to the democratization of the Western world by having caused the initial expansion of the ruling class.

No group ever justifies its attempts at revolution by articulating the real reason: the desire for power. Many revolutionaries seized on the abuses of patronage power for their rhetoric, as Martin Luther did, using the issue as an immediate cause for overthrowing the existing order. Patronage practices under the Stuarts, for example, increased the British public's already intense feelings against them and led to a civil war. The great jurist, Sir Edward Coke, blamed the corruption at the Court of St. James on patronage, which survived a brief reform movement during the Interregnum (1642–1660), but returned in full force with the restoration of the Stuart monarchy.

Perhaps the worst abuses of the patronage system occurred in the British colonies of North America, stirring revolutionary feelings there as they had in Europe. The colonies provided a distorted mirror image of the European patronage system, where no-show officeholders made little pretense of public service, and graft and inefficiency flourished. The practice of selling offices in the colonies of Maryland, Virginia, and North and South Carolina galled the colonists who saw the proceeds from the sale of offices returned to the crown and the profits of office similarly sent back across the seas.

As distasteful to the colonists as the outflow of capital was their lack of a meaningful voice in the selection of their governors. When the citizens of Vera

Cruz, Mexico, protested to King Philip of Spain because he had appointed a treasurer and controller without consulting them, Philip shrugged off their complaints with the excuse that he had no choice—he needed the money.

The most basic flaw in the system, and the one most likely to produce revolution, was that those most able to pay for offices were not necessarily the best able to govern. Filling public offices with inept and arbitrary administrators often resulted in rebellion, depending on the relative strength and awareness of the subject populations.

Patronage became part of the fabric of the American political system soon after the birth of the Republic, despite George Washington's disclaimer that government jobs should be filled by "those who seem to have the greatest fitness for public office." When Thomas Jefferson became president in 1801, he found himself engulfed by Federalists, who had previously dominated the government. President Jefferson replaced enough Federalists with Republicans from his own party, to ensure—he said—a more even distribution between the two parties. He wrote that he would "return with joy to that state of things when the only questions concerning a candidate shall be, 'Is he honest? Is he capable? Is he faithful to the constitution?'"

A quarter of a century later, Andrew Jackson went on to develop and justify that very system that allowed victors *carte blanche* in appointing whomever they wished to political office. Known as "King Caucus," Jackson's contribution to patronage was that he was the first to articulate, legitimize, and translate the spoils system into the American experience, although William Learned Marcy, then governor of New York, heralded the era by proclaiming: "To the victor belong the spoils of the enemy."

Ironically, Jackson himself won the presidency largely by accusing his predecessor, John Quincy Adams, of dastardly patronage practices during his administration. The first time Jackson ran for the presidency against Henry Clay and John Q. Adams (in 1824), the election was stalemated and thrown into the House of Representatives. Holding the balance of power with only three states in his hand, Clay cast his electoral votes for Adams, who won by the narrow margin of one state. Adams rewarded Clay with the post of secretary of state, leading Jacksonian Democrats to charge Adams with making a "corrupt bargain." On the hustings, Jackson men charged Adams—a rather dour and straitlaced man—with gross immorality, highly inconsistent with Adams's character. They also accused Adams of purchasing "gambling tables and gambling furniture" with public funds. Near the close of the campaign, Adams was even accused of pimping for the Emperor of Russia!

Elections are not courts of law. Voters too often accept accusations of corruption without demanding proof. So it was with Adams, who went down to defeat thoroughly disgraced by Jackson's supporters. Thus began what was to become a familiar pattern in American politics: gaining political mileage by equating patronage with political corruption.

The spoils system developed at a time when revenues had to be found to support the increased activities of political parties. With the broadening of suffrage and the use of elections to choose large numbers of officials, political parties began to assume heavy campaign costs. With great relish, Jackson insisted on overseeing all patronage appointments personally. Encouraged by the promise that Jackson would see them all, great hordes of men thronged to Washington to demand jobs. One man asked for anything that would yield $300 to $3,000 per year, except for a clerkship because he couldn't write. Jackson did see them all, or nearly all, holding court at his temporary lodging, Gadsby's tavern.

Patronage, Jackson believed, could give the common man the opportunity to participate in government. He was galled by the fact that only one social class—the aristocracy—had monopolized public office for so long. When doling out his Cabinet appointments, Jackson ignored the upper classes and refused to appoint a New Englander or a Virginian on the grounds that those states fostered exclusiveness in government. Neither of these sections of the country, it might be added, had contributed to his victory.

Jackson changed the structure of government by admitting new classes as participants in it—reminiscent of the way in which patronage in Europe fostered the growth of the bourgeoisie. In Europe, however, the bourgeoisie had wrested power from the upper classes; Jacksonian democracy, more revolutionary in its outlook, professed to have brought the lower classes into government, to the shock and dismay of the middle classes who themselves had monopolized power for only a short while.

Despite all the publicity Jackson gave to patronage, in actual fact he removed very few officeholders. No office with judicial functions was touched, and out of the 612 executive positions, only 252 were removed. Approximately 600 postmasters out of 8,000 were removed to make way for Jackson appointees. During Jackson's entire tenure of office, it is estimated that only one-tenth to one-third of all federal officeholders were changed, indicating that even then, in matters of patronage, rhetoric bore little resemblance to reality.

Lacking a tradition of professionalism, the spoils system became a battlefield on which several vicious struggles for power were waged. Jackson's administration (which contended with a Whig Senate balanced off against a Democratic House) spent the better part of its time dealing with patronage controversies that barely concealed the political conflicts surging beneath. Challenging Jackson from the Senate floor were John Tyler, who had lost the position of secretary of state to Martin Van Buren, and John Calhoun, who was rapidly falling out of presidential favor. Calhoun conducted a formal inquiry into the extent of federal patronage and "the practicability of reducing the same" after leading the battle to refuse confirmation of some of Jackson's appointments. Calhoun's inquiry professed that patronage made government too big: If this practice continued, he warned, states would be crushed under the force of an ever-expanding federal bureaucracy. His investigation revealed the shocking fact that the 60,294 employees of the federal government, together with their dependents and other pensions, made up a payroll of more than 100,000 people dependent on the federal treasury. (Today, the government employs 2.7 million people.) According to Calhoun, this constituted a governmental machine of frightful proportions, and he recommended a drastic reduction of federal patronage as a means of economizing.

Calhoun was the first to recognize and call the public's attention to the scope of federal patronage. In his recommendations to Congress, Calhoun requested the elimination of the practice of offering public land to be handled by an army of receivers, registers, and surveyors, all appointees of the president. He also opposed giving the president the power to select banks as public depositories, which obligated them to the president.

Needless to say, while the Senate formulated bills to correct these abuses of federal power, the issue really represented an attack on Jackson, for the Whig Senate certainly knew that its legislation would be rejected by the lower house. The battles over the spoils system masked the real war, fought between two political parties, over parceling out government power. Many felt it was during this period that the two-party system developed into its modern form.

Although Jackson achieved historical notoriety for the spoils system, Lincoln practiced it far more extensively. Lincoln's removal, after his first victory in 1860, of 1,195 out of 1,520 presidential appointees to make room for his own supporters was the most sweeping use of the patronage power to date. Lincoln showed how necessary patronage was in order to keep together the diverse elements of his party and to attract the allegiance of those supporting the Union who were outside the party. Patronage was the secret ingredient by which Lincoln secured a power base for a second term, for many federal officeholders participated in the movement to secure Lincoln's renomination. Lincoln was criticized at the time for spending too much of his time on patronage questions, but historians have later admitted that the Union was held together through his strategic use of this power.

Patronage grew to full maturity concurrently with the growth of the American political system. When Lincoln became president, it was impossible for one man to sit in a tavern and personally take charge of all appointments. Members of Congress and party leaders were gradually entrusted with some of these powers, and by the time of the Civil War, legislators had complete charge of post office appointments.

After the Civil War, Presidents Johnson and Grant attempted with considerably less skill to use patronage power as Lincoln had used it. Their ineptitude encouraged a reform movement, composed primarily of dissident Republicans who had not themselves reaped the spoils of victory.

The National Civil Service League, founded in 1881, led a reform movement that succeeded, in 1883, with enactment of the Pendleton Act, which provided for creation of a Civil Service Commission and merit system.

With the spotlight on jobs, American politicians began to exploit the patronage possibilities of other discretionary powers of government. Mark Twain boasted with humor: "I think I can say, and say with pride, that we have legislatures that bring higher prices than any in the world." The legislators earned their fees by voting legislative gifts to railroad, oil, coal, and timber interests. These special franchises were opposed by a handful of men, including Hiram Johnson, who ran for governor of California on the forthright platform: "Kick the corporations out of politics." Patronage abuses were uncovered by "muckrakers": Ida M. Tarbell exposed how legislatures were wooed by the Standard Oil Company of New Jersey, and Lincoln Steffens wrote of corrupt municipal governments—Minneapolis, St. Louis, Pittsburgh, Philadelphia, Chicago, and New York. The muckrakers achieved limited success in reforming government, but their writings planted an image in the public mind firmly linking patronage to the shadowy, illegitimate side of government.

By 1939, all states were compelled to initiate merit systems for employees engaged in programs aided by federal funds. By 1950, 75 percent of all American cities had some type of formal merit system, but only 25 percent of the cities covered all employees. Almost half of the reporting cities with populations of fewer than 25,000 had no formal civil service system.

Ironically, modern reformers have now begun to question the growth of a civil service system that has allowed the public very little recourse against administrative abuses. They note that under the present civil service system, there is little hope of removing a public servant who—through indolence, ineptitude, or design—sabotages the express wishes of elected officials.

---

*Some of the historical material from Resource D was adopted from our earlier work, *To the Victor: Political Patronage from the Clubhouse to the White House,* New York: Random House, pp. 319–328.

Notes

Chapter One

1. Tyler Grimm, "John Murtha's Airport for No One," *Wall Street Journal,* September 4, 2009, A15.

2. Pat Choate, *Dangerous Business: The Risks of Globalization for America* (New York: Alfred A. Knopf, 2008), 128–129.

3. Robert Caro, *Power Broker: Robert Moses and the Fall of New York* (New York: Knopf, 1974), 391.

4. See the most corrupt states compiled by the *Corporate Crime Reporter,* October 8, 2007, http://corporatecrimereporter.com/corrupt100807.htm. The figures are based on data from the Justice Department's Public Integrity Section's 2006 report. The study included the 35 most populous states. The 15 states with populations under 2,000,000 were not included in the analysis, which based its rankings on the number of public corruption convictions per 100,000 residents from 1997 to 2006.

5. Elrod v. Burns, 509 F. 2d 1133.

6. Branti v. Finkel, 445 U.S. 507.

7. Rutan v. Republican Party of Illinois, 42 U.S. 62.

8. Board of County Commissioners Wabaunsee County, Kansas v. Umbehr, 518 US 668 (1996).

9. O'Hare Truck Service v. Northlake, Ill. 518 US 712 (1996).

10. Each of the previously mentioned decisions cited the authors' previous book: Martin and Susan Tolchin, *To the Victor: Political Patronage from the Clubhouse to the White House* (New York: Random House, 1971).

11. Citizens United v. Federal Election Commission, 558 U.S. 2010.

12. Robert O'Harrow, "Federal No-Bid Contracts on Rise," *Washington Post,* August 22, 2007, 1.

13. Testimony before Congress's Joint Economic Committee's Defense Procurement Subcommittee, January 20, 1960.

14. See Chapter 7.

15. Speech before a Coalition of New York Lawyers Against the War, reported in *The New Yorker,* May 30, 1970, 24.

16. Warren Weaver, Jr., "Carswell Nomination Attacked and Defended as Senate Opens Debate on Nomination," *The New York Times,* March 17, 1970, A21. See also Martin and Susan Tolchin, op. cit., 12.

17. See Chapter 5.

18. Clarence N. Stone, "Urban Political Machines: Taking Stock," *PS: Political Science & Politics* 29, no. 3 (September 1996): 446–450.

19. "Real Judicial Elections," *The New York Times,* editorial, October 2, 2007.

20. Amy Goldstein and Dan Eggen, "Immigration Judges Often Picked Based on GOP Ties," *Washington Post,* June 11, 2007, 1.

21. John P. Martin and Jeff Whelan, "Ex-Newark Mayor Sharpe James Sentenced to 27 Months," *Star Ledger,* July 29, 2008, 1.

22. See Chapter 4.

Chapter Two

1. Elrod v. Burns, 427 U.S. 347 (1976).

2. Branti v. Finkel, 445 U.S. 508 (1980); Rutan v. Republican Party of Illinois, 497 U.S. 62 (1990); Board of County Commissioners Wabaunsee County, Kansas v. Umbehr, 518 U.S. 668 (1996); and O'Hare Truck Service v. Northlake, Ill. 518 U.S. 712 (1996).

3. Gretchen Ruethling, "Chicago Officials Convicted in Patronage Arrangement," *The New York Times,* July 6, 2006, online. The Federal Court of Appeals affirmed the conviction in April 2008. See United States Court of Appeals for the Seventh Circuit, Case Nos.: 06–4251, 06–4252, 06–4254.

4. Ibid.

5. Dan Mihalopoulos and Todd Lightly, "City Agrees to Ban Patronage," *Chicago Tribune,* March 22, 2007, online.

6. "Daley's Choice, Sorich's Guilt," editorial, *Chicago Tribune,* July 7, 2006.

7. Anne Freedman, *Patronage: An American Tradition* (Chicago: Nelson-Hall, 1994), 35–36.

8. Ibid., 49. See also Lana Stein, "Merit Systems and Political Influence: The Case of Local Government," *Public Administration Review* 37, no. 3 (May–June 1987): 263–271.

9. See Chapters 3 and 4.

10. Martin and Susan Tolchin, *To the Victor: Political Patronage from the Clubhouse to the White House* (New York: Random House, 1971), 59.

11. Ibid., 55–59.

12. Ibid., 59.

13. Ibid., 62.

14. Mary Pat Flaherty and Cheryl W. Thompson, "County Requires Donations but Fails to Collect," *Washington Post,* July 6, 2008, A11.

15. Martin and Susan Tolchin, *To the Victor,* op. cit., 28.

16. Stephen Kinzer, "Letter from Chicago: A Prized Project, a Mayor and Persistent Criticism," *The New York Times,* July 13, 2004, online.

17. Dick Simpson, Ola Adeoye, Daniel Bliss, Kevin Navratil, and Rebecca Raines, "The New Daley Machine: 1989–2004," a paper by political scientists at the University of Illinois at Chicago, 2004.

18. Martin and Susan Tolchin, *To the Victor,* op. cit., 29.

19. Ibid., 52–55.

20. Ray Rivera, "New York Candidates Awash in Real Estate Cash," *The New York Times,* February 1, 2009, A21.

21. Elrod, op. cit., 5.

22. Ibid.

23. Branti, op. cit.

24. Ibid.

25. Kenneth J. Meier, "Ode to Patronage: A Critical Analysis of Two Recent Supreme Court Decisions," *Public Administration Review* 41, no. 5 (September/October 1981): 558–563.

26. Ibid., 560.

27. Rutan v. Republican Party of Illinois, 497 U.S. 62 (1990).

28. Board of County Commissioners Wabaunsee County, Kansas v. Umbehr, 518 US 668 (1996).

29. O'Hare Truck Service v. Northlake, Ill. 518 US 712 (1996).

30. Colbert I. King, "What D.C.'s Elves Do with Your Taxes," *Washington Post,* May 17, 2008, A17.

31. Nikita Stewart, "Housing Authority Contracts Illegal," *Washington Post,* October 24, 2009, B1.

32. Clay Risen, "The Lightning Rod," *The Atlantic,* November 2008, 82.

33. Cheryl W. Thompson and Mary Pat Flaherty, "Sweetheart Deals," *Washington Post,* July 6, 2008, 1.

34. Martin and Susan Tolchin, *Glass Houses: Congressional Ethics and the Politics of Venom* (Boulder, CO: Westview Press, 2004), 66.

35. Doug Donovan, "Baltimore Mayor Indicted in Theft and Perjury Case," *The New York Times,* January 10, 2009, A8.

36. "While Corruption Flourishes, the State Naps," editorial, *The Star-Ledger,* January 12, 2003.

37. Mark Naymik and John Caniglia, "Jimmy Dimora, Frank Russo and Local Businesses Are Under Federal Investigation," *The Plain Dealer,* July 28, 2008.

38. Women didn't even have the vote when Plunkitt was in politics! Plunkitt represented the 15th Senate District of New York City. See William L. Riordan, *Plunkitt of Tammany Hall,* originally published in 1905 (Bedford Books of St. Martin's Press, New York, 1994 edition), 69.

39. Ibid.

40. Michael Parrish, "Sheriff, Wife and Another Are Indicted," *The New York Times,* October 31, 2007, A19.

41. Richard Benfield, "The City Boss Becomes the Country Boss," *The New York Times,* January 2, 2008, A20.

42. Michael Barbaro, "Push for 3d Term Alienates Some Bloomberg Supporters," *The New York Times,* October 23, 2008, A24. See also Joyce Purnick, *Mike Bloomberg: Money, Power, Politics* (New York: Perseus Books, 2009).

43. Ben McGrath, "The Untouchable," *New Yorker,* August 24, 2009, 43.

44. Nicholas Confessore and Michael Barbaro, "Mayor Deprives Rival of Black Clergy's Support," *The New York Times,* October 29, 2009, A21.

45. Michael Barbaro, "A Mayor Who Discarded Political Parties Now Woos Them," *The New York Times,* February 19, 2009, A21.

46. Diane Cardwell, "Longtime Practice of City Council Financing Lands on Speaker's Shoulders," *The New York Times,* May 11, 2008, 25.

47. Monserrate was elected to the New York State Senate in 2008, but in December of that year he was arrested and charged with assault in connection with an injury to his girlfriend. See Ray Rivera, "Group Spent City Cash, but Hasn't Shown How," *The New York Times,* October 19, 2008, 28; and Ray Rivera and Sewell Chan, "Queens Councilman is Charged with Assault," *The New York Times,* December 19, 2008, online.

48. Jonathan P. Hicks, "Barron Calls Brooklyn Democratic Gathering Too Scripted," *The New York Times,* September 16, 2008, online.

49. Jonathan P. Hicks, "Judge Finds vs. Rivera's Bronx Democrats," *The New York Times,* December 1, 2008, online.

50. Michael Barone and Richard E. Cohen, *Almanac of American Politics, 2006: The Senators, the Representatives, and the Governors: Their Records and Election Results, Their States and Districts* (Washington, D.C.: National Journal, 2005), 1174. See also National Association of Counties, "A Brief Overview of County Government," revised, August 2003.

51. See Chapter 4.

Chapter Three

1. See Chapter 2 for a discussion of the five major U.S. Supreme court decisions that changed political patronage on the state and local levels.

2. Martin and Susan Tolchin, *To the Victor: Political Patronage from the Clubhouse to the White House* (New York: Random House, 1971), 118.

3. See state employment in *The Book of the States 2008*, 458–459, and *The Book of the States 2009*, 438–439, both published by the Council of State Governments.

4. Alan Ehrenhalt, "Patronage Trap Flap," Governing.com, December 15, 2005.

5. Jane Mayer, quoted in "Homer Simpson Has What the Bancrofts Want," by Jack Shafer, *Slate Magazine*, July 13, 2007.

6. "Missouri's Fee-office System: A Relic Calling Out for Reform," editorial, Kansascity .com, October 1, 2008.

7. "Company that Leases Parkway Erred in Political Donations," *Richmond Times Dispatch*, July 3, 2008, B-1.

8. Factiva, Abertis and Citi: Pennsylvania Turnpike, October 1, 2008.

9. NW Financial Group LLC Report, "Then There Were Two ... Indiana Toll Road vs. Chicago Skyway," November 1, 2006.

10. "Giuliani is Selling Investment Firm," editorial, *The New York Times*, March 6, 2007, A18.

11. Bethany McLean, "Would You Buy a Bridge from This Man?" *Fortune Magazine*, October 2, 2007.

12. Bruce Wallin, "The Need for a Privatization Process: Lessons from Development and Implementation," *Public Administration Review* 57, no. 1 (January–February 1997): 11–20.

13. See David M. van Slyke, "The Mythology of Privatization in Contracting for Social Services," *Public Administration Review* 63, no. 3 (May–June, 2003): 296–315. See also Elliot Sclar, *You Don't Always Get What You Pay For: The Economics of Privatization* (Ithaca, NY: Cornell University Press, 2000).

14. Jocelyn M. Johnston and Barbara Romzek, "Contracting and Accountability in State Medicaid Reform: Rhetoric, Theories, and Reality," *Public Administration Review* 59, no. 5 (September–October 1999): 383–399.

15. Alan Greenblatt, "Tougher than Wall Street," *Governing Magazine*, December 2007.

16. Josh Margolin and Kelly Heyboer, "UMDNJ Scandal: With Campus Attorney's Exit, a Star is Done," *Newark Star-Ledger*, December 30, 2005. See also Bob Ingle and Sandy McClure, *The Soprano State: New Jersey's Culture of Corruption* (New York: St. Martin's Press, 2008).

17. Ingle and McClure, 9–18.

18. Ibid., 79–82.

19. Nick Baumgarten, "The Humbling of Eliot Spitzer," *New Yorker Magazine*, December 10, 2007, 77.

20. Joyce Purnick, "Assembly's Speaker Keeps Power Intact and Options Open," *The New York Times*, June 20, 2007, A21.

21. See Chapter 2.

22. Jeremy W. Peters, "Joblessness was Brief for a Retired Politician," *The New York Times*, July 23, 2008, A21.

23. Mike McIntire and Jeremy W. Peters, "Longtime New York GOP Leader Indicted by U.S. on Corruption Charges," *The New York Times*, January 24, 2008, A15.

24. Martin and Susan Tolchin, op. cit., 23.

25. Carrie Johnson, "FBI Says Illinois Governor Tried to Sell Senate Seat," *Washington Post*, December 10, 2008, 1.

26. Rutan et al. v. Republican Party of Illinois, et al., 1990. U.S. Supreme Court Reports 111 L. Ed. 2nd.

27. David Hamilton's research concludes that real reform in hiring can occur only with a change in philosophy and procedures. See David Hamilton, "The Staffing Function in Illinois State Government after Rutan," *Public Administration Review* 53, no. 4 (July–August, 1993): 381–386.

28. See the most corrupt states compiled by the *Corporate Crime Reporter,* October 8, 2007 (http://corporatecrimereporter.com/corrupt100807.htm). Compiled from data collected by the Public Integrity Section of the Department of Justice.

29. Adam Nossiter, "Fear, Paranoia and, Yes, Some Loathing in Alabama's Hallowed Halls," *The New York Times,* April 6, 2008, 12.

30. Ibid.

31. "Judge Says Governor Can't Be Tried in Office," *Associated Press,* August 12, 2006. See also John David Dyche, "Their Own Worst Enemy," *Weekly Standard,* October 29, 2007, 16.

32. Gary Fineout, "Florida Speaker Steps Down, Citing Corruption Investigation," *The New York Times,* January 31, 2009, A14.

33. Robert Penn Warren, *All the King's Men* (New York: Harcourt Brace & Co., 1946).

34. Bret Schulte, "A Troubling Bayou Tradition," *US News,* October 2, 2005, online.

35. The reporter was also the coauthor, Martin Tolchin.

36. California Public Employees Retirement System, which manages the pension and health benefits for 1.6 million public employees in the state of California.

37. Danny Hakim and Louise Story, "Obama Adviser Said to Be Tied to Pension Deal," *The New York Times,* April 17, 2009, 1. See also Louise Story, "Quadrangle Facing Questions over Pension Funds," *The New York Times,* April 21, 2009, online.

38. "Ex-New York Political Boss Pleads Guilty in Pension Fund Case," *The New York Times,* October 7, 2009, A23.

39. Michael J. de la Merced, "Four Firms Agree to Settlement in New York Pension Fund Inquiry," *The New York Times,* September 19, 2009.

40. Many laughed, for example, when candidate Ross Perot appeared at debates with charts of the United States budget deficit, but the issue propelled a relatively unknown political candidate to national prominence. To everyone's surprise, he captured 19 percent of the vote in the 1992 presidential election, costing President George H. W. Bush a second term in office. Both Democratic and Republican parties adopted the issue as their own very quickly, forging a consensus over the budget deficit; together with President Clinton, by 2000 the budget was not only balanced, but there was a small surplus.

41. See *Corporate Crime Reporter 2007,* op. cit., endnote 41.

42. Sarah Laskow, "State Lobbying Becomes Billion Dollar Business," *Center for Public Integrity,* December 20, 2006.

43. Walker v. Cheney, 230 F. Sup.2d 51(D.C.C. 2002).

44. Evan Halper and Nancy Vogel, "Nunez Used a Charity to Funnel Donations," *Los Angeles Times,* November 2, 2007, 1.

45. Ibid.

46. Kevin Bogardus, "Statehouse Revolvers," *Center for Public Integrity,* October 12, 2006.

47. Ibid.

48. Elspeth Reeve, "It's All Relative," *Center for Public Integrity,* December 20, 2006.

49. Ibid.

50. Nadine Elsibal, "From Lobbyist to Legislator," *Center for Public Integrity,* October 12, 2006.

51. Jay Root, "Lax State Laws Allow Cozy Lobbyist-Lawmaker Ties," *Associated Press,* October 6, 2008.

52. There were two Hoover Commissions—one met between 1947 and 1949; the other between 1953 and 1955. They both issued reports. See United States Committee on the Organization of the Executive Branch, *The Hoover Commission Report on the Organization*

of the Executive Branch (New York: McGraw-Hill, 1949). Later, many states followed the federal pattern and established "Little Hoover Commissions."

53. Martin and Susan Tolchin, op. cit., 98.

54. The Governor obliged, and delivered another public message, "Yes, John," he said, "you go on home." Ibid., 93.

Chapter Four

1. See Chapter 7.

2. Matt Kelley, "The Congressman & the Hedge Fund," *USA Today,* January 19, 2006, online.

3. Ibid.

4. See Chapter 5.

5. Martin and Susan Tolchin, *To the Victor: Political Patronage from the Clubhouse to the White House* (New York: Random House, 1971), 3.

6. Vice President Richard Cheney refused to identify the lobbyists who prepared energy legislation.

7. Ed Henry, *CNN Wire,* May 8, 2008.

8. Jack Valenti, *This Time, This Place* (New York: Harmony Books, 2007), 435.

9. See Chapter 1.

10. Barbara Sinclair, *Unorthodox Lawmaking: New Legislative Processes in the U.S. Congress* (Washington, D.C.: Congressional Quarterly Press, 3rd ed., 2007), 76–77, 111, 25.

11. Ibid.

12. Walter Kravitz, *Congressional Quarterly's American Congressional Dictionary* (Washington, D.C.: Congressional Quarterly Press, 1993), 260.

13. Robert Caro, *Master of the Senate: The Years of Lyndon Johnson* (New York: Alfred A. Knopf, 2002). See also Robert Dallek, *Flawed Giant: Lyndon Johnson and His Times* (New York: Oxford University Press), 1998.

14. Martin and Susan Tolchin, *To the Victor,* op. cit., 195.

15. She later wrote a book about her experiences, titled *Unbossed and Unbought,* which later became a documentary film. The book was published by Houghton Mifflin in 1970.

16. Martin and Susan Tolchin, *To the Victor,* op. cit., 187.

17. Lee Hamilton, *How Congress Works, and Why You Should Care* (Bloomington: Indiana University Press, 2004), 63.

18. Speech to the electors of Bristol, November 3, 1774, in Ross J. S. Hoffman and Paul Levak, eds., *Burke's Politics: Selected Writings and Speeches of Edmund Burke on Reform, Revolution, and War* (New York: Alfred A. Knopf, 1949), 115–116.

19. Council for Citizens Against Government Waste, *2008 Congressional Pig Book* (Introduction).

20. Walter Kravitz, *Congressional Quarterly's American Congressional Dictionary* (Washington, D.C.: Congressional Quarterly Press, 1993), 96.

21. William Safire, *Safire's Political Dictionary* (New York: Oxford University Press, 2008), 205.

22. From data compiled by the Taxpayers for Common Sense and Robert O'Harrow, Jr., "Earmark Spending Makes a Comeback," *Washington Post,* June 13, 2008, A1, A17.

23. Council for Citizens Against Government Waste, *2008 Congressional Pig Book.*

24. Alexander Bolton, "Democratic Leaders Shower Pork on Freshmen," *The Hill,* February 14, 2008, 8.

25. James D. Savage, "The Administrative Costs of Congressional Earmarking: The Case of the Office of Naval Research," *Public Administration Review* (May–June 2009): 448–449. Savage cites the Congressional Research Service reports, "Earmarks in Appropriations Acts: FY 1994, FY 1998, FY 2000, FY 2002, FY 2004, FY 2005, January 26, 2006," CRS-12.

26. Robert G. Kaiser, "Citizen K Street," *The Washington Post*, March 19, 2007.

27. Council for Citizens Against Government Waste, *2008 Congressional Pig Book*.

28. Tony Newmeyer and Kate Ackley, "Puttin' On the Ritz," *Roll Call*, February 11, 2008, online.

29. Ibid.

30. John R. Wilke, "How Lawmaker Rebuilt Hometown on Earmarks," *Wall Street Journal*, October 30, 2007, A1.

31. Representative Murtha was one of the champions of earmarks, having secured more than $200 million in funds in the past decade to fund an airport in his district that is underutilized by both the airlines and passengers. Its name? The John Murtha Johnstown-Cambria County Airport.

32. Martin and Susan Tolchin, *To the Victor*, op. cit., 201.

33. From data compiled by the Taxpayers for Common Sense and Robert O'Harrow, Jr. "Earmark Spending Makes a Comeback," *Washington Post*, June 13, 2008, A1, A17.

34. James Savage, op. cit., 448.

35. The First Tee website, http://www.thefirsttee.org/club/scripts/view/view_insert .asp?IID=13109&NS=PUBLIC.

36. Paul Kane, "Congress May Seek Criminal Probe of Altered Earmark," *Washington Post*, April 17, 2008.

37. Roger H. Davidson and Walter J. Oleszek, *Congress and Its Members* (Washington, D.C.: Congressional Quarterly Press, 2000), 299.

38. Robert Pear, "From Bush, Foe of Earmarks, Similar Items," *The New York Times*, February 2, 2008.

39. Mike McIntire, "Nuclear Leaks and Response Tested Obama in the Senate," *The New York Times*, February 3, 2009, online.

40. Mostly for his positions on campaign finance issues and for opposing President George W. Bush and Vice President Richard Cheney on torture.

41. David D. Kirkpatrick and Jim Rutenberg, "A Developer, His Deals and His Ties to McCain," *The New York Times*, April 22, 2008, 1. See also Martin and Susan Tolchin, *Glass Houses: Congressional Ethics and the Politics of Venom* (Boulder, CO: Westview Press, 2004), 49–60.

42. Robert Pear, "Lawmakers Put Out New Call for Earmarks," *The New York Times*, February 14, 2008, 18.

43. Hal Bernton and David Heath, "Palin's Earmark Requests: More Per Person Than Any Other State," *Seattle Times*, September 3, 2008.

44. Aaron Latham, "Will Rogers is Running for President," *New York Magazine*, December 1974, 74–86. See also Morris K. Udall, Bob Neuman, and Randy Udall, *Too Funny to be President*, New York: Henry Holt, 1988.

45. Jonathan Rauch, "A Stubborn Senator Who Matters," *National Journal*, November 17, 2007, 19.

46. Rahm Emanuel, "Don't Get Rid of Earmarks," *Washington Post*, August 24, 2007. See an insightful new book that defends earmarks: Scott A. Frisch and Sean Q. Kelly, *Cheese Factories on the Moon: Why Earmarks Are Good for American Democracy*, Boulder, CO: Paradigm Publishers, 2010.

47. Full disclosure: Coauthor Susan Tolchin testified on behalf of obtaining those funds.

48. Richard F. Fenno, Jr., *When Incumbency Fails: The Senate Career of Mark Andrews*, Washington, D.C.: *Congressional Quarterly Press*, 1992, 92.

49. Joseph Nocera, "Anxiety on Economy Wins Out," *The New York Times*, October 4, 2008, D1.

50. Cecilia Kang, "Rescue Sweetened With Tax Incentives," *Washington Post*, October 4, 2008, D1, 2.

51. David Kocieniewski, "Rangel Pushed for a Donation, Insurer Pushed for a Tax Cut," *The New York Times*, January 2, 2009, 1.

52. David Kocieniewski, "The Congressman, the Donor and the Tax Break," *The New York Times*, November 25, 2008, 1.

53. Eric Lipton and Raymond Hernandez, "A Champion of Wall Street Reaps Benefits," *The New York Times*, December 13, 2008, 1.

54. Ibid.

55. Jeffrey M. Jones, "Confidence in Congress: Lowest Ever for Any U.S. Institution," http://www.gallup.com/poll/108142/Confidence-Congress-Lowest-Ever-Any-US-Institution.aspx, accessed September 13, 2008. See also Ken Dilanian, "Congress Ratings Plunge in Poll," *USA Today*, July 16, 2008, 1.

56. R. Jeffrey Smith, Cecilia Kang, and Joe Stephens, "Old Ways Doomed New Job for Daschle," *Washington Post*, February 4, 2009, 1.

57. Prior to the election of President Bill Clinton in 1992, Chang had contributed to the Republicans, but quickly switched his allegiance to match political reality.

58. Martin and Susan Tolchin, *Glass Houses*, op. cit., Ch. 7.

59. Raymond Hernandez and David W. Chen, "Now Lobbyist, an Ex-Senator Uses Campaign Money," *The New York Times*, August 24, 2007, online.

60. Ibid.

61. Stephen Moore, "Comfy with K Street," *Wall Street Journal*, October 19, 2007, A19.

62. David D. Kirkpatrick, "For Lobbyists, No Downturn, Just a Turnover," *The New York Times*, November 25, 2008, 1.

63. Ibid.

64. Ibid.

65. Full disclosure: Susan Tolchin, the coauthor, testified on Foreign Investment in the United States, the results of the data in Martin and Susan Tolchin, *Buying into America: How Foreign Money is Changing the Face of Our Nation* (New York: Alfred A. Knopf, 1988).

66. For a more detailed discussion of the roots of American political anger, see Susan J. Tolchin, *The Angry American: How Voter Rage Is Changing the Nation* (Boulder, CO: Westview Press, 1996).

Chapter Five

1. JFK initially fought against the appointment of his brother as attorney general because of the appearance of cronyism, but eventually succumbed to the insistence of his father, Joseph Kennedy. He even sent an emissary, Clark Clifford, up to New York to plead with his father, but the mission proved unsuccessful.

2. Eric Lichtblau and Kitty Bennett, "30 Ex-Government Officials Got Lucrative Posts as Corporate Monitors," *The New York Times*, May 23, 2008, A21.

3. Carrie Johnson, "Obama Team Faces Major Task in Justice Department Overhaul," *Washington Post*, November 13, 2008, A2.

4. "Mr. Rove Talks, but Doesn't Answer," *The New York Times*, June 2, 2008, A20.

5. Ibid.

6. Adam Nossiter, "Alabama Ex-Governor Ordered Freed Pending Appeal of Bribery Conviction," *The New York Times*, March 28, 2008, A14.

7. In the United States Court of Appeals for the Eleventh Circuit, No. 07-13163, United States of America versus Don Eugene Siegelman, Richard Scrushy, D.C. Docket No. 05-00119-CR-F-N, March 6, 2009.

8. Neil A. Lewis, "Using Disclosure Rules as a Defense for a Senator," *The New York Times*, October 13, 2008, A13.

9. Amy Goldstein and Dan Eggen, "Immigration Judges Often Picked Based on GOP Ties," *Washington Post*, June 11, 2007, 1.

10. Ibid.

11. TRAC, Federal Criminal Enforcement, an organization that studies and compares the actions of federal judges and prosecutors, http://tracfed.syr.edu/results/w64494148a.38 .html.

12. U.S. Department of Justice, *An Investigation into the Removal of Nine U.S. Attorneys in 2006*, Joint Report by the Office of the Inspector General and the Office of Professional Responsibility, September 2008.

13. Ibid., 18.

14. Paul Kane, "Domenici Rebuked for Call to U.S. Attorney Before Election," *Washington Post*, April 25, 2008, A7.

15. Department of Justice, op. cit., 1–7, and reiterated throughout the report.

16. For an interesting discussion on the importance of taped interviews, see Thomas P. Sullivan, "Recording Federal Custodial Interviews," *American Criminal Law Review* 45, no. 4 (Fall 2008): 1297–1349.

17. Paul Kane and Dan Eggen, "Second Lawmaker Contacted Prosecutor," *Washington Post*, March 6, 2007, A1.

18. David C. Iglesias, "Dangerous New Turn in Justice Department Investigation, *The Huffington Post*, www.huffingtonpost.com, February 21, 2009.

19. David C. Iglesias, *In Justice: Inside the Scandal that Rocked the Bush Administration* (Hoboken, NJ: John Wiley & Sons, 2008).

20. Adrienne Packer, "U.S. Attorney Rebuts Claim Performance Led to Firing," *Las Vegas Review Journal*, February 8, 2007.

21. Ibid., 15. The Judiciary Committee found White House Chief of Staff Joshua Bolten and former White House Deputy Chief of Staff Karl Rove in contempt of Congress "because of their continuing non-compliance with the Committee's subpoenas." Ibid., 21.

22. Ibid., 99–114.

23. Eric Lipton, "Missouri Prosecutor Says He Was Pushed to Resign," *The New York Times*, May 10, 2007, A22.

24. Department of Justice, op. cit., 356–357.

25. Ibid., 47.

26. Ibid., 64.

27. http://www.bork.com.

28. Zachary Roth, "Gonzo's Lawyer Quits Civil Case," March 5, 2008, http:// tpmmuckraker.talkingpointsmemo.com.

29. Ibid., 331.

30. "The Political Specter at Justice," *The New York Times*, editorial, March 21, 2008, A22.

31. See Resource A for a state-by-state list of methods of appointing and electing judges.

32. Ibid.

33. Lopez Torres v. New York State Board of Elections, U.S. Court of Appeals for the 2d Circuit, August 30, 2006, Docket No. 06-0635-cv, 22.

34. Ibid., 25.

35. Lopez Torres v. New York State Board of Elections, 411 F Supp 2d, 212.

36. New York State Board of Elections v. Lopez Torres, decided January 10, 2008, no. 06-766, 1.

37. Ibid.

38. "Governor Spitzer Proposes Sweeping Court Reforms," Press Release from the New York State Executive Chamber, April 26, 2007.

39. Martin and Susan Tolchin, *To the Victor: Political Patronage from the Clubhouse to the White House* (New York: Random House, 1971), 133.

40. Ibid., 134.

41. Ibid., 171.

42. Cass R. Sunstein, David Schkade, Lisa M. Ellman, and Andres Sawicki, *Are Judges*

Political? An Empirical Analysis of the Federal Judiciary (Washington, D.C.: The Brookings Institution, 2006).

43. Patrick Crowley, "Judge Bunning Takes Bench," *Cincinnati Enquirer,* March 28, 2002, online.

44. Martin and Susan Tolchin, op. cit., 12.

45. Nathan Koppel, "For 'Maverick' Federal Judges, Life Tenure Is Largely Unfettered License," *Wall Street Journal,* August 8, 2008.

46. There is also a question about whether their criticism is legally protected. See Monroe H. Freedman, "The Threat to Judicial Independence by Criticism of Judges—A Proposed Solution to the Real Problem," *Hofstra Law Review* 25, no. 3: 1–15.

47. William Riordan, *Plunkitt of Tammany Hall* (New York: McClure & Phillips & Co., new paperback edition, 1994), 88.

48. Herbert Mitgang, *The Man Who Rode the Tiger: The Life and Times of Judge Samuel Seabury* (Philadelphia: J.P. Lippincott, 1963), 161; Wallace S. Sayre and Herbert Kaufman, *Governing New York City* (New York: Russell Sage Foundation, 1960), Chapter 14, "Courts and Politics."

49. Martin and Susan Tolchin, op.cit., 145.

50. United States Court of Appeals, Second Circuit, 475 F.2d, United States of America, Appellee v. Herbert R. Jacobs etc., Defendants-Appellants, March 5, 1973.

51. Daniel Wise, "N.Y. DA Says Former Judge, Assemblyman, Hold Keys to Probe of Buying and Selling Judgeships," *New York Law Journal*: April 23, 2007.

52. Martin and Susan Tolchin, op. cit., 145.

53. Richard Tofel, *Vanishing Point: The Disappearance of Judge Crater and the New York He Left Behind* (Chicago: Ivan R. Dee), 2004.

54. Martin and Susan Tolchin, op. cit., 144.

55. Martin and Susan Tolchin, op. cit., 147.

56. Azi Paybarah, "The Anti-Patronage Pledge from a Surrogate's Candidate," *New York Observer,* September 8, 2008, online.

57. John Eligon, "Judge-Elect Facing Criminal Charges Will Be Suspended," *The New York Times,* December 30, 2008.

58. Murray Teigh Bloom, *The Trouble with Lawyers* (New York: Simon & Schuster, 1968), 233–263.

59. For a more detailed discussion of surrogate patronage, see Martin and Susan Tolchin, op.cit., 150–160.

60. Gary Tilzer, "The Surrogate's Court and Why It Should Go," *Gotham Gazette,* July 4, 2005.

61. Martin and Susan Tolchin, op. cit., 158–160.

62. *Citizens for Judicial Accountability,* "Patronage: A Feast for Lawyers, Report from the New York Court," February 24, 2009. See also Recommendations on Fiduciary Appointments in New York, December 2001, *Report of the Commission on Fiduciary Appointments.*

63. Association of the Bar of the City of New York, "Contributions to Campaigns of Candidates for Surrogate, and Appointments by Surrogates of Guardians Ad Litem," Report of the Committee on Government Ethics of the Association of the Bar of the City of New York, July 1998.

64. Tilzer, op. cit.

65. Dorothy Samuels, "The Selling of the Judiciary: Campaign Cash 'in the Courtroom'," *The New York Times,* April 15, 2008, A22.

66. John Grisham, *The Appeal* (New York: Doubleday, 2008).

67. See Resource A, op. cit. See also David K. Hamilton, "The Continuing Judicial Assault on Patronage," *Public Administration Review* 59, no. 1 (January–February 1999): 54–62.

68. Valentine Palmer and John Levendis, "The Louisiana Supreme Court in Question: An Empirical Study of the Effect of Campaign Contributions on the Judicial Function,"

Tulane Law Review 82 no.2 (2008): 1291–1314. See also Adam Liptak, "Looking Anew at Campaign Cash and Elected Judges," *The New York Times,* January 29, 2008, A14.

69. "The Best Judges Business Can Buy," *The New York Times,* June 18, 2007, A20.

70. "Judicial Politics Run Amok," *The New York Times,* September 19, 2006, online.

71. Robert Barnes, "Judicial Races Now Rife with Politics—Corporate Funds Help Fuel Change," *Washington Post,* October 28, 2007, 1.

72. Deborah Goldberg, "Public Funding of Judicial Elections: The Roles of Judges and the Rules of Campaign Finance," *Brennan Center for Justice,* July 2, 2002, 9. A newer publication, "The New Politics of Judicial Elections 2006," updates the earlier study, as does the study in 2010.

73. Ibid., 6.

74. No. 05-842, Michael E. Avery, et al., on behalf of themselves and all others similarly situated, Petitioners v. State Farm Mutual Automobile Insurance Company, Respondent. See also James Sample, David Pozen, and Michael Young, "Fair Courts: Setting Recusal Standards," *Brennan Center for Justice,* April 1, 2008; James Sample, "The Campaign Trial: The True Cost of Expensive Court Seats," *Brennan Center for Justice,* March 6, 2006.

75. Robert Barnes, "Case May Define When a Judge Must Recuse Self," *Washington Post,* February 2, 2009, 1, 14.

76. U.S. Supreme Court, 200 U.S. 321, Caperton et al. v. A.T. Massey Coal Co., Inc., et al., June 8, 2009.

77. Deborah Goldberg, "Public Funding of Judicial Elections: The Roles of Judges and the Rules of Campaign Finance," *Brennan Center for Justice* (July 2, 2002): 22. She also recommends "voter guides," but there is no guarantee that they will be read (most likely, they will not be).

78. Ibid., 18. For an excellent discussion of the upshot of the Caperton-Massey case, the regulatory role in the mine blast that killed 25 miners, see Steven Mufson, Kimberly Kindy, and Ed O'Keefe, "Mine Avoided Harsh Penalties Despite Violations," *Washington Post,* April 9, 2010, A1.

79. Judith L. Maute, "Selecting Justice in State Courts: The Ballot Box or The Back Room," *41 S. Texas Law Review* (2000): 1198–1246.

80. F. Andrew Hanssen, "Learning about Judicial Independence: Institutional Change in the State Courts," *Journal of Legal Studies,* 22 (June 2004): 431–473.

81. Ibid., 450.

Chapter Six

1. Richard Neustadt, *Presidential Power: The Politics of Leadership, with Reflections on Johnson and Nixon* (New York: John Wiley & Sons, 1976), 12.

2. Harold Laski was a very famous British political scientist who wrote and commented prodigiously on the subject of American government and politics. See an essay of Laski's in Harold J. Laski, ed., *The Foundations of Sovereignty and Other Essays* (New York: Harcourt Brace & Co., 1921), vii; and Harold J. Laski, "The French Elections," *The Fortnightly* 164, N.S. 158 (December 1945): 359.

3. Louis Fisher, *Constitutional Conflicts between Congress and the President* (Lawrence: University Press of Kansas, 2007), 253.

4. Kiyoshi Hirabayashi v. United States, 320 U.S. 81 (1943).

5. Youngstown Sheet & Tube Co. v. Sawyer, 343 U.S. 579 (1952).

6. Charlie Savage, "Obama Undercuts Whistle-Blowers, Senator Says," *The New York Times,* March 17, 2009, A17.

7. Jonathan Martin and Carol E. Lee, "Obama Bets the House on Specter," *Politico,* September 16, 2009, 1.

8. Matthew Mosk, "Top Donors Rewarded with White House Perks," *Washington Times,* October 28, 2009, 1.

9. Martin and Susan Tolchin, *To the Victor: Political Patronage from the Clubhouse to the White House* (New York: Random House, 1971), 251–252.

10. On presidential abuse of the IRS, see David Burnham, *A Law Unto Itself: Power, Politics, and the IRS* (New York: Random House, 1990).

11. Arthur S. Link, *Wilson: Confusions and Crisis, 1915–1916* (Princeton, NJ: Princeton University Press, 1964), 323–325.

12. Marian Cecilia McKenna, *Franklin Roosevelt and the Great Constitutional War* (New York: Fordham University Press, 2002), 545–552.

13. Robert E. Sherwood, *Roosevelt and Hopkins: An Ultimate History* (New York: Harper & Bros., 1948), 90–91.

14. The Johnson tapes, Scripps Library, January 12, 1995, http://millercenter.org.

15. Peter Baker and Jeff Zeleny, "Obama's Chief of Staff Wields Power Freely, and Faces the Risks," *The New York Times,* August 16, 2009, 16.

16. Robert Pear, "From Bush, Foe of Earmarks, Similar Items," *The New York Times,* February 10, 2008, online.

17. The Pendleton Act, which created the Federal Civil Service, was enacted in 1883 in response to public anger at the assassination of President Garfield by a disappointed office seeker.

18. See "Summary of Positions Subject to Noncompetitive Appointment in United States Government Policy and Supporting Positions" (Plum Book), 2008, http:www.gpoaccess.gov/plumbook/2008/index.html.

19. Don Wolfensberger, "A Primer on Presidential Nominations and the Senate Confirmation Process," Woodrow Wilson International Center for Scholars, paper delivered March 16, 2009.

20. Committee on Government Reform, U.S. House of Representatives, *U. S. Government: Policy and Supporting Positions* (Plum Book), 110th Congress, 2d Session.

21. See Chapter Seven.

22. Jim McTague, "Embattled Bankroller," *Barron's,* September 16, 1996.

23. G. Calvin Mackenzie, "The State of the Presidential Appointments Process," in G. Calvin Mackenzie, ed., *Innocent Until Nominated: The Breakdown of the Presidential Appointments Process* (Washington, D.C.: The Brookings Institution, 2001). See also Joel D. Aberbach and Bert A. Rockman, "The Appointments Process and the Administrative Presidency," *Presidential Studies Quarterly* 39, no. 1, (March 2009): 38–59.

24. Paul Light, "Fact Sheet on the Continued Thickening of Government," Washington: *The Brookings Institution,* July 23, 2004. Paul Light, "The Tides of Reform Revisited: Patterns in Making Government Work, 1945–2002," *Public Administration Review* (January–February 2006). See also Paul Light, *The Tides of Reform: Making Government Work, 1945-1995* (New Haven, CT: Yale University Press, 1997); and *A Government Ill Executed: The Decline of the Federal Service and How to Reverse It* (Cambridge, MA: Harvard University Press, 2008).

25. The term "burrowing in" is sometimes used to describe a status conversion from a political appointment on the federal level to a career position protected by the Civil Service. See Barbara L. Schwemle, "Federal Personnel: Conversion of Employees from Appointed (Noncareer) Positions in the Executive Branch," Congressional Research Service Report for Congress, October 14, 2008. See also U.S. Government Accountability Office, "Personnel Practices: Conversions of Employees from Noncareer to Career Positions May 2001–April 2005," May 2005.

26. Christopher Lee, "Political Appointees 'Burrowing In'," *Washington Post,* October 5, 2007, A19; Juliet Eilperin and Carol D. Leonnig, "Top Scientist Rails Against Hirings," *Washington Post,* November 22, 2009, A3; U.S. Government Accountability Office, *Personnel Practices: Conversions of Employees from Noncareer to Career Positions May 2001–April*

2005. GAO-06-381 (Washington: GAO, May 2006); and Gregg Carlstrom, "Bush Appointees Burrow In," *Federal Times,* December 8, 2008, http://www.federaltimes.com/index .php?S-3841535.

27. David Lewis, "Revising the Administrative Presidency: Policy, Patronage, and Agency Competence," *Presidential Studies Quarterly,* 39, no. 1 (March 2009): 68. See also Joseph C.N. Raadschedlers and Kwang-Hoon Lee, "Between Amateur Government and Career Civil Service: The American Administrative Elite in Cross-time and Comparative Perspective," *Jahrbuch Fur Europaische Verwaltungsgeschichte* 17: 201–222.

28. OMB Watch, "Obama Strengthens Revolving Door Restrictions," http://www .ombwatch.org/blog/234/all/all?page3); and Angie Drobnic Holan, "Former Lobbyist in the White House? It's Okay If They Say It's Okay," *St. Petersburg Times,* http://www .politifact.com/truth-o-meter.

29. "Key Player: Vernon E. Jordan Jr," *Washington Post,* October 5, 1998, http://www .washingtonpost.com/wp-srv/politics/special/clinton/players/jordan.htm.

30. Martin and Susan Tolchin, op. cit., 207; and Donald Matthews, *U.S. Senators and Their World* (Chapel Hill: University of North Carolina Press, 1960), 219.

31. Martin and Susan Tolchin, op. cit., 259.

32. Robert A. Caro, *The Years of Lyndon Johnson: Means of Ascent* (New York: Knopf, 1990), 82 and supra.

33. Martin and Susan Tolchin, op. cit., 288.

34. "Fact Sheet on Model City Grants," *Congressional Quarterly* (November 27, 1967): 1–4.

35. Martin and Susan Tolchin, op. cit., 256.

36. James P. Pfiffner, *The Strategic Presidency: Hitting the Ground Running* (Lawrence: University Press of Kansas, 2nd ed., 1996), 120–122.

37. Stacey Schultz, "Mr. Outside Moves Inside," *U.S. News,* March 16, 2003, online.

38. *Minneapolis Star Tribune,* January, 12, 2006, online.

39. James P. Pfiffner, op. cit., 72.

40. Martin and Susan Tolchin, op. cit., 292.

41. Stanley Kelly, Jr. "Patronage and Presidential Legislative Leadership," unpublished paper, 1968.

42. The title of an excellent book about the six men who ran the government after World War II. See Evan Thomas and Walter Isaacson, *The Wise Men: Six Friends and the World They Made* (New York: Touchstone, 1986).

43. Michael D. Shear and Carol D. Leonnig, "Commerce Pick Richardson Withdraws, Citing N.M. Probe," *Washington Post,* January, 5, 2009, A1, 4.

44. Al Kamen, "Dollar Signs Point to Many a U.S. Embassy," *Washington Post,* June 10, 2009, A17.

45. Denny, Dr., "Bush's Patronage Appointments to Ambassador Exceed Father's, Clinton's," posted June 25, 2007 at Scholars and Rogues, http://scholarsandrogues .wordpress.com/2007/06/25/bushs-patronage-appointments-to-ambassador-exceed-fathers-clintons/.

Chapter Seven

1. Scott Shane and Ron Nixon, "In Washington, Contractors Take on Biggest Role Ever," *The New York Times,* February 4, 2007.

2. Ibid.

3. He also wrote that "when men are prepared for it, that will be the kind of government which they will have. Government is at best but an expedient; but most governments are usually, and all governments are sometimes, inexpedient." See *Respectfully Quoted: A Dictionary of Quotations* (Library of Congress, No. 753). See also Ralph Waldo Emerson, "Politics,"

in Essays: Second Series, in the *Complete Writings of Ralph Waldo Emerson* (Vol. 1, 1929), 302.

4. See U.S. Census Bureau, "Procurement Data 1983–2009" in *Consolidated Federal Funds Report for Fiscal Year 2008.*

5. Carol D. Leonnig, "Obama Wrote Federal Staffers About His Goals," *Washington Post,* November 17, 2008,1.

6. CBS News, February 2, 2009.

7. Eric Lipton and John M. Broder, "Regulators' Warnings weren't Acted On," *The New York Times,* May 8, 2010, 12.

8. Joseph Nocera, "So When Will Banks Give Loans?" *The New York Times,* October 25, 2008, B1.

9. Joseph Nocera, "Loans? Did We Say We'd Do Loans?" *The New York Times,* October 28, 2008, www.nytimes.com/2008/10/29/opinion/29wed1.html.

10. Mike McIntire, "Bailout Is a No-Strings Windfall to Bankers, if Not to Borrowers," *The New York Times,* January 18, 2009, 1.

11. No one knows for sure, but the hybrids offer a fertile field for new and probing research.

12. See also Julie Kosterlitz, "Siblings Fat and Sassy: Now That Fannie Mae and Freddie Mac have ballooned into Multibillion-Dollar Players in the Nation's Financial Markets, Critics Say These Government-Created Companies Are Too Big and Too Powerful," *National Journal,* 32 no. 20 (2000): 1498–1507.

13. Ronald C. Moe, "The Emerging Federal Quasi Government Issues of Management and Accountability," *Public Administration Review,* 61, no. 3 (May–June 2001), 290–312. No one knows for sure how many hybrids exist today, but Moe's article remains the best source.

14. The *Bureau of the Budget,* the agency that preceded OMB, issued *Bulletin Number 55-4,* which stated: "It is the general policy of the administration that the Federal Government will not start or carry on any commercial activity to provide a service or product for its own use if such product or service can be procured from private enterprise through ordinary business channels."

15. The circular was revised in 1999. See www.whitehouse.gov/omb/circulars/aO76 .pdf.

16. Ronald D. Utt, "Cutting the Deficit and Improving Services by Contracting Out," *Heritage Foundation,* March 10, 1995, 4, http://www.heritage.org/Research/Reports/1995/03/Cutting-the-Deficit-and-Improving-Services-By-Contracting-Out-U.

17. See the House Senate conference report on the FY 2008 intelligence authorization bill, cited in Walter Pincus, "Conferees Want Hard Look at Contractors," *Washington Post,* December 17, 2008, A19.

18. GAO, *Securing, Stabilizing, and Rebuilding Iraq: Key Issues for Congressional Oversight,* GAO-07-308SP, Washington, D.C., January 9, 2007.

19. The latest directive on A-76 was issued by OMB on May 29, 2003, see Executive Office of the President, Office of Management and Budget, "Circular No. A-76 (Revised)," with attachments A and B.

20. James Varney, "Trailer Dealer May Avoid Fine, Taxes," *Times-Picayune,* September 19, 2006; Eric Lipton, "Governor's Relative Is Big Contract Winner," *The New York Times,* December 7, 2006; Sue Sturgis, "Katrina Trailer Contractor Failed to Act on Known Health Risks," *Southern Studies,* July 10, 2006, http://www.southernstudies .org/2008/07/katrina-trailer-contractor-failed-to.html; and Katrina Information, "Key Corporations Cited by House Oversight Committee," http://www.katrinaaction.org/Katrina_contractors.

21. Taxpayers for Common Sense, http://www.taxpayer.net/budget/katrinaspending/contracts. See also House of Representatives Committee on Government Reform, Minority

Staff Special Investigations Division Report, *Waste, Fraud, and Abuse in Hurricane Katrina Contracts,* http://oversight.house.gov/Documents/20060824110705-30132.pdf.

22. House Committee on Oversight and Government Reform, *More Dollars, Less Sense: The 2007 Report; Dollars, Not Sense: The 2006 Report;* and *Searchable Database of Problem Contracts,* http://www.oversight.house.govfeatures/more dollars/less sense.

23. Although privatization, outsourcing, and contracting out are somewhat different conceptually, they will be used interchangeably in this chapter because there appears to be considerable overlap. Also, they do seem to correlate with each other from a patronage point of view.

24. Dana Priest and Anne Hull, "Soldiers Face Neglect, Frustration at Army's Top Medical Facility," *Washington Post,* February 18, 2007, A1.

25. Philip Mattera, "Outsourcing Walter Reed," www.tompaine.com/print/outsourcing-walter_reed, March 6, 2007; IAP, "Who We Are," www.lapws.com/who/heritage.asps, letter from Jacqueline Simon, Public Policy Director, to Clay Johnson, Deputy Director for Management, Office of Management and Budget, March 20, 2007; and Steve Vogel and Renae Merle, "Privatized Walter Reed Workforce Gets Scrutiny," March 10, 2007, www.washingtonpost.com.

26. Fearful of another run on the banks, such as the one experienced during the Depression in 1929, Congress raised depositor protection to $250,000 in the 2008 bailout.

27. "Quagos" are "essentially a government organization that is assigned some, or many, of the attributes normally associated with the private sector." Quangos, another type of hybrid, are "essentially [private organizations] ... assigned ... attributes normally associated with the governmental sector.... the Legal Services Corporation, for example, would be a quago, while the Red Cross is a quango." See Kevin Kosar, "The Quasi Government: Hybrid Organizations with Both Government and Private Sector Legal Characteristics," CRS Report for Congress, Congressional Research Service, February 13, 2007, 2–3.

28. Harold Seidman, *Politics, Position and Power* (New York: Oxford University Press, 1998), 213.

29. David S. Hilzenrath and Zachary A. Goldfarb, "Mortgage Giants' Mess Falls to Their Regulator," *Washington Post,* September 11, 2008, D1 and D3.

30. Annys Shin, "Examining Fannie Mae—How a Former Chief Helped Shape the Company's Political Culture," *Washington Post,* May 24, 2006, D1.

31. For more information on Fannie Mae, see Federal National Mortgage Association Charter Act, http://www.fhfa.gov/GetFile.aspx?FilID+29, and FEDERAL HOME LOAN MORTGAGE CORPORATION ACT, 12 U.S.C. 1452m /sec. 303. (a) (2); and also the official Freddie Mac website, http://www.freediemac.com/governance/pdf/charter.pdf.

32. The initiation fee for one of his clubs, the Chevy Chase Club outside Washington, D.C., came to $80,000.

33. "Fannie Mae Board Establishes 2007 Compensation for President and Chief Executive," Reuters, http://www.reuters.com/article/pressRelease/idUS264637+30-Jan-2008+PRN20080130.

34. Steve Hendrix and Michael D. Shear, "The Chief's Chief," *Washington Post,* November 7, 2008, C4.

35. "Senior Government Officials Turned Current or Former Contractor Executives, Directors or Lobbyists 1997 through 2004," by Project on Government Oversight (POGO), "The Politics of Contracting," Washington, D.C.: June 24, 2004. POGO also issues an annual report covering this material.

36. Alison Leigh-Cowan, "Big-City Paydays at 'Farmer Mac'," *The New York Times,* April 28, 2002, 1, Sunday Business Section.

37. Kevin Kosar, "The Quasi Government: Hybrid Organizations with Both Government and Private Sector Legal Characteristics," CRS Report for Congress, Congressional Research

Service, February 13, 2007, 12. Kosar also calls quagos GSEs (for Government Sponsored Enterprises), a larger category that encompasses quagos.

38. "DeMint Statement on Fannie Mae & Freddie Mac," September 7, 2008.

39. "Stark Statement Introducing Bill to Allow States to Draw on Fannie Mae and Freddie Mac Profits," http://www.house.gov/stark/news/108th/fmfmreformst.htm.

40. Elise Castelli, "The Case for Insourcing," *Federal Times,* September 21, 2008.

41. David Wallechinsky, Lyric Wallwork Winik, and Daryl Chen, "Who Gets Your Money," Parade.com, http://www.parade.com/articles/editions/2007/edition_10-14-2007/Intelligence_Report.

42. James Risen, "End of Immunity Worries U.S. Contractors in Iraq," *New York Times,* December 1, 2008, A14.

43. *CBS-TV News,* "Iraq for Sale: The War Profiteers," 2006.

44. "Despite Being Under an Investigative Cloud, Halliburton Gets $4.3 Billion in 2003," *The Center for Public Integrity,* August 18, 2004. See also "The Corporate Invasion of Iraq Profile of U.S. Corporations Awarded Contracts in U.S./British-Occupied Iraq," prepared by *U.S. Labor Against the War* (USLAW) for The Workers of Iraq and International Labor Movement.

45. See Resources B and C.

46. Initially submitted as H.R. 2968, the bill authorized appropriations for fiscal year 1984 for intelligence and intelligence-related activities. Named were the U.S. government, intelligence community staff, and the Central Intelligence Agency Retirement and Disability System. Rep. Edward Boland (D-Massachusetts) introduced the bill on May 11, 1983, and on December 9, 1983, it became Public Law No. 98-215. See http://thomas.loc.gov/cgi-bin/bdquery/z?d098:HRO2968.

47. Ellen McCarthy, "CACI Contract: From Supplies to Interrogation," *Washington Post,* May 17, 2004, E1.

48. Secretary of Defense, "Memorandum for Secretaries of the Military Departments, Chairman of the Joint Chiefs of Staff, Under Secretaries of Defense, Commanders of the Combatant Commands," March 10, 2008.

49. Actually the estimates range from 8–21, but most accounts put the figure at 17.

50. Order #17, written two days before Bremer left Iraq in June, 2004.

51. Rosa Brooks, "Outsourcing Foreign Policy," *Los Angeles Times,* September 21, 2007.

52. Jeremy Scahill, "Blackwater," *The Nation,* May 11, 2007. The book is called *Blackwater: The Rise of the World's Most Powerful Mercenary Army* (New York: Nation Books, 2007). See also, P. W. Singer, *Corporate Warriors: The Rise of the Privatized Military Industry,* revised ed., (Ithaca, NY: Cornell University Press, 2003).

53. See Brian Bennett, "Victims of an Outsourced War," *Time,* July 19, 2008; and John M. Broder and James Risen, "Blackwater Logs Most Shootings of Firms in Iraq," *New York Times,* September 27, 2007, A1 and A14. See also Government Accountability Office, "Contingency Contracting—DOD, KState, and USAID Contracts and Contractor Personnel in Iraq and Afghanistan," October 2008.

54. Janine Wedel, "The Shadow Army," *Boston Globe,* September 30, 2007. See also Janine Wedel, *Shadow Elite: How the World's New Power Brokers Undermine Democracy, Government, and the Free Market* (New York: Basic Books, 2009).

55. Robert Kaplan, "Outsourcing Conflict," The Atlantic.com, July 19, 2008.

56. Martin and Susan Tolchin, *To the Victor: Political Patronage from the Clubhouse to the White House* (New York: Random House, 1971), 275.

57. See Resources B and C.

58. Scott Shane and Ron Nixon, "In Washington, Contractors Take on Biggest Role Ever," *The New York Times,* February 4, 2007.

59. Paul L. Verkuil, *Outsourcing Government: Why Privatization of Government Functions Threatens Democracy and What We Can Do About It* (New York: Cambridge University Press, 2007), 6.

Chapter Eight

1. For a further discussion of the origins of deregulation, see Susan J. Tolchin and Martin Tolchin, *Dismantling America: The Rush to Deregulate* (Boston: Houghton Mifflin, 1983). On the subject of political anger, see Susan J. Tolchin, *The Angry American: How Voter Rage Is Changing the Face of Our Nation* (Boulder, CO: Westview Press, 1996).

2. Gerald F. Seib, "Where Have All the Deal Makers Gone?" *Wall Street Journal,* August 27, 2009, A4. For a further discussion of misbegotten trade and deficit policies, see Martin and Susan J. Tolchin, *Selling Our Security: The Erosion of America's Assets* (New York: Alfred A. Knopf, 1992); and Martin and Susan Tolchin, *Buying Into America: How Foreign Money Is Changing the Face of Our Nation* (New York: Times Books/Random House, 1988).

3. Minxin Pei, "Will the Chinese Communist Party Survive the Crisis?" *Carnegie Endowment for International Peace,* posted on the *Foreign Affairs* website, March 12, 2009.

Bibliography

Books

Adams, Henry Brooks. *Democracy: An American Novel,* New York: Modern Library Paperback Edition, 2003.

Auerswald, Philip et al. *Seeds of Disaster, Roots of Response: How Private Action Can Reduce Public Vulnerability.* New York: Cambridge University Press, 2006.

Axelrod, Donald. *Shadow Government: The Hidden World of Public Authorities—And How They Control Over $1 Trillion of Your Money.* New York: John Wiley & Sons, 1992.

Barone, Michael, and Richard E. Cohen. *The Almanac of American Politics, 2006: The Senators, the Representatives, and the Governors: Their Records and Election Results, Their States and Districts,* Washington, D.C.: National Journal, 2005.

Bloom, Murray Teigh. *The Trouble with Lawyers.* New York: Simon & Schuster, 1968.

Burnham, David. *A Law Unto Itself: Power, Politics, and the IRS.* New York: Random House, 1990.

Camm, Frank, and Victoria A. Greenfield. *How Should the Army Use Contractors on the Battlefield? Assessing Comparative Risk in Sourcing Decisions.* Santa Monica, CA: RAND, 2005.

Cannon, Lou. *President Reagan: The Role of a Lifetime.* New York: Public Affairs, 2000.

Caro, Robert A. *The Power Broker: Robert Moses and the Fall of New York.* New York: Knopf, 1974.

___. *The Years of Lyndon Johnson: Means of Ascent.* New York: Knopf, 1990.

Chisholm, Shirley. *Unbossed and Unbought.* Boston: Houghton Mifflin, 1970.

Choate, Pat. *Dangerous Business: The Risks of Globalization for America.* New York: Alfred A. Knopf, 2008.

Davidson, Roger H., and Walter J. Oleszek. *Congress and Its Members.* Washington, D.C.: Congressional Quarterly Press, 2000.

Dean, Alan L., and Harold Seidman. *Considerations in Establishing the Patent and*

Trademark Office as a Government Corporation. Washington, D.C.: National Academy of Public Administration, 1998.

DiIulio, John Jr., ed. *Deregulating the Public Service: Can Government Be Improved?* Washington, D.C.: Brookings Institution Press, 1994.

Dillaway, Diana. *Power Failure: Politics, Patronage, and the Economic Future of Buffalo, New York.* Amherst, N.Y.: Prometheus Books, 2006.

Edgeworth, Maria. *Patronage,* introduced by Eva Figes. London and New York: Pandora, 1986.

Erie, Steven P. *Rainbow's End: Irish Americans and the Dilemmas of Urban Machine Politics.* Berkeley: University of California Press, 1988.

Fenno, Richard F. Jr. *When Incumbency Fails: The Senate Career of Mark Andrews.* Washington, D.C.: Congressional Quarterly Press, 1992.

Fisher, Louis. *Constitutional Conflicts between Congress and the President.* Lawrence: University Press of Kansas, 2007.

Flinders, Matthew V. "Setting the Scene: Quangos in Context," in *Quangos, Accountability and Reform,* edited by Matthew V. Flinders and Martin J. Smith. New York: St. Martin's Press, 1999.

Freedman, Anne E. *Patronage: An American Tradition.* Chicago: Nelson-Hall, 1994.

Frisch, Scott, and Sean Q. Kelly. *Cheese Factories on the Moon: Why Earmarks Are Good for Democracy.* Boulder, CO: Paradigm Publishers, 2011.

Genovese, Michael A. *The Power of the American Presidency: 1789–2000.* New York: Oxford University Press, 2001.

Goodsell, Charles T. *The Case for Bureaucracy,* 4th ed. Washington, D.C.: Congressional Quarterly Press, 2004.

Grisham, John. *The Appeal.* New York: Doubleday, 2008.

Guttman, Dan. "Inherently Governmental Functions and the New Millennium: The Legacy of Twentieth-Century Reform," in *Making Government Manageable: Executive Organization and Management in the Twenty-First Century,* edited by Thomas H. Stanton and Benjamin Ginsberg. Baltimore: Johns Hopkins University Press, 2004.

Guttman, Dan, and Barry Wilner. *The Shadow Government.* New York: Random House, 1976.

Hamilton, Lee H. *How Congress Works and Why You Should Care.* Bloomington: Indiana University Press, 2004.

Hamilton, Lee H. *Strengthening Congress.* Bloomington: Indiana University Press, 2009.

Heclo, Hugh. "The In-and-Outer System," in *The In-and-Outers: Presidential Appointees and Transient Government in Washington,* edited by G. Calvin Mackenzie. Baltimore: Johns Hopkins University Press, 1987, pp. 207–211.

Hoffman, Ross J. S., and Paul Levak, eds. *Burke's Politics: Selected Writings and Speeches of Edmund Burke on Reform, Revolution, and War.* New York: Knopf, 1949.

Iglesias, David C. *In Justice: Inside the Scandal that Rocked the Bush Administration.* Hoboken, NJ: John Wiley & Sons, 2008.

Ingle, Bob, and Sandy McClure. *The Soprano State: New Jersey's Culture of Corruption.* New York: St. Martin's Press, 2008.

Jones, Charles O. *The Presidency in a Separated System.* Washington, D.C.: Brookings Institution Press, 1994.

Jones-Correa, Michael. *Between Two Nations: The Political Predicament of Latinos in New York City.* Ithaca, NY: Cornell University Press, 1998.

Kaufman, Herbert. *Red Tape.* Washington, D.C.: Brookings Institution Press, 1977.

Kettl, Donald F. *The Regulation of American Federalism.* Baton Rouge, LA: Louisiana State University Press, 1983.

Kettl, Donald F. *Sharing Power: Public Governance and Private Markets.* Washington, D.C.: Brookings Institution Press, 1993.

Koppell, Jonathan G. S. *The Politics of Quasi-Government: Hybrid Organizations and the Dynamics of Bureaucratic Control.* Cambridge: Cambridge University Press, 2003.

Kravitz, Walter. *Congressional Quarterly's American Congressional Dictionary.* Washington, D.C.: Congressional Quarterly, Inc, 1993.

Laski, Harold J., ed. *The Foundations of Sovereignty and Other Essays.* New York: Harcourt Brace, 1921.

Lewis, David E. *The Politics of Presidential Appointments: Political Control and Bureaucratic Performance.* Princeton, NJ: Princeton University Press, 2008.

Light, Paul C. *A Government Ill Executed: The Decline of the Federal Service and How to Reverse It.* Cambridge, MA: Harvard University Press, 2008.

Light, Paul C. *Thickening Government: Federal Hierarchy and the Diffusion of Accountability.* Washington, D.C.: Brookings Institution Press, 1995.

Light, Paul C. *The Tides of Reform: Making Government Work, 1945–1995.* New Haven, CT: Yale University Press, 1997.

Light, Paul C. *The True Size of Government.* Washington, D.C.: Brookings Institution Press, 1999.

Link, Arthur S. *Wilson: Confusions and Crisis, 1915–1916.* Princeton, NJ: Princeton University Press, 1964.

Lynn, Barry C. *Cornered: The New Monopoly Capitalism and the Economics of Destruction.* New York: John Wiley & Sons, 2010.

Mackenzie, G. Calvin, ed. *Innocent until Nominated: the Breakdown of the Presidential Appointments Process.* Washington, D.C.: Brookings Institution Press, 2001.

Mackenzie, G. Calvin. *The Politics of Presidential Appointments.* New York: Free Press, 1981.

MacManus, Susan A. *Doing Business with Government,* New York: Paragon House, 1992.

Madrick, Jeff. *The Case for Big Government.* Princeton, NJ: Princeton University Press, 2009.

Matheson, Scott M. *Presidential Constitutionalism in Perilous Times.* Cambridge, MA: Harvard University Press. 2009.

Matthews, Donald. *U.S. Senators and Their World.* Chapel Hill: University of North Carolina Press, 1960.

Mayhew, David. *Divided We Govern: Party Control, Lawmaking, and Investigations, 1946–2002.* New Haven, CT: Yale University Press, 2005.

McKenna, Marian C. *Franklin Roosevelt and the Great Constitutional War: The Court-packing Crisis of 1937.* New York: Fordham University Press, 2002.

Mitgang, Herbert. *The Man Who Rode the Tiger: The Life and Times of Judge Samuel Seabury.* Philadelphia: J.P. Lippincott, 1963.

Nathan, Richard P. *The Plot That Failed: Nixon and the Administrative Presidency.* New York: John Wiley & Sons, 1975.

Neustadt, Richard E. *Presidential Power: The Politics of Leadership with Reflections on Johnson and Nixon.* New York: John Wiley & Sons, 1976.

Olesek, Walter J. *Congressional Procedures and the Policy Process* 7th ed. Washington, D.C.: Congressional Quarterly Press, 2007.

Pfiffner, James P. *The Strategic Presidency: Hitting the Ground Running,* 2nd ed. Lawrence: University Press of Kansas, 1996.

Pritchett, C. Herman. *The Tennessee Valley Authority: A Study in Public Administration.* Chapel Hill: University of North Carolina Press, 1943.

Purnick, Joyce. *Mike Bloomberg: Money, Power, Politics.* New York: Perseus Books, 2009.

Respectfully Quoted: A Dictionary of Quotations. Washington, D.C.: Library of Congress, 1989.

Riordon, William L. *Honest Graft: The World of George Washington Plunkitt,* 2nd ed. New York: Bedford Books of St. Martin's Press, 1994.

Riordon, William L. *Plunkitt of Tammany Hall.* New York: McClure & Phillips & Co, 1905.

Roland, Gerard, ed. *Privatization: Successes and Failures.* New York: Columbia University Press, 2008.

Safire, William. *Safire's Political Dictionary.* New York: Oxford University Press, 2008.

Savas, Emanuel S. *Privatization and Public-Private Partnerships.* New York: Chatham House, 2000.

Sayre, Wallace S., and Herbert Kaufman. *Governing New York City.* New York: Russell Sage Foundation, 1960.

Scahill, Jeremy. *Blackwater: The Rise of the World's Most Powerful Mercenary Army.* New York: Nation Books, 2007.

Sclar, Elliot. *You Don't Always Get What You Pay For: The Economics of Privatization.* Ithaca, NY: Cornell University Press, 2000.

Seidman, Harold. "Government-Sponsored Enterprise in the United States," in *The New Political Economy: The Public Use of the Private Sector,* edited by Bruce L. R. Smith. New York: John Wiley & Sons, 1975.

Seidman, Harold. *Politics, Position and Power: The Dynamics of Federal Organization.* New York: Oxford University Press, 1998.

Seidman, Harold, and Robert Gilmour. *Politics, Position and Power: From the Positive to the Regulatory State,* 4th ed. New York: Oxford University Press, 1986.

Sherwood, Robert E. *Roosevelt and Hopkins: An Ultimate History.* New York: Harper & Bros., 1948.

Sinclair, Barbara. *Unorthodox Lawmaking: New Legislative Processes in the U.S. Congress,* 3rd ed. Washington, D.C.: Congressional Quarterly Press, 2007.

Singer, Peter Warren. *Corporate Warriors: The Rise of the Privatized Military Industry.* Ithaca, NY: Cornell University Press, 2003.

Skowronek, Stephen. *Building a New American State: The Expansion of National Administrative Capacities, 1987–1920.* New York: Cambridge University Press, 1982.

Skowronek, Stephen. *The Politics That Presidents Make: Leadership from John Adams to Bill Clinton.* Cambridge, MA: Harvard University Press, 1997.

Smillie, Ian, ed. *Patronage or Partnership: Local Capacity Building in Humanitarian Crises.* Bloomfield, CT: Kumarian Press, 2001.

Stanger, Allison. *Empire of the Willing: The Privatization of American Power.* New York: Basic Books, forthcoming.

Stanger, Allison. *One Nation Under Contract: The Outsourcing of American Power and the Future of Foreign Policy.* New Haven, CT: Yale University Press, 2009.

Stanton, Thomas H. *A State of Risk: Will Government-Sponsored Enterprise Be the Next Financial Crisis?* New York: Harper Business, 1991.

Sunstein, Cass R., David Schkade, Lisa M. Ellman, and Andres Sawicki. *Are Judges Political? An Empirical Analysis of the Federal Judiciary.* Washington, D.C.: The Brookings Institution, 2006.

Tangri, Roger. *The Politics of Patronage in Africa.* Trenton, NJ: Africa World Press, 1999.

Thomas, H. Stanton. *Government Sponsored Enterprises: Mercantilist Companies in the Modern World.* Washington, D.C.: American Enterprise Institute Press, 2002.

Tofel, Richard. *Vanishing Point: The Disappearance of Judge Crater and the New York He Left Behind.* Chicago: Ivan R. Dee, 2004.

Tolchin, Martin, and Susan Tolchin. *Buying into America: How Foreign Money Is Changing the Face of Our Nation.* New York: Alfred A. Knopf, 1988.

Tolchin, Martin, and Susan Tolchin. *Clout: Womanpower and Politics.* New York: Coward, McCann & Geoghegan, 1974.

Tolchin, Martin and Susan Tolchin. *Dismantling America: The Rush to Deregulate.* Boston: Houghton Mifflin, 1983.

Tolchin, Martin, and Susan Tolchin. *Glass Houses: Congressional Ethics and the Politics of Venom.* Boulder, CO: Westview Press, 2001.

Tolchin, Martin, and Susan Tolchin. *Selling Our Security: The Erosion of America's Assets.* New York: Alfred A. Knopf, 1992.

Tolchin, Martin, and Susan Tolchin. *To the Victor: Political Patronage from the Clubhouse to the White House.* New York: Random House, 1971.

Tolchin, Martin, and Susan Tolchin. *A World Ignited: How Ethnic, Religious and Racial Hatreds Are Torching the Globe.* Lanham, MD: Rowman & Littlefield, 2006.

Tolchin, Susan. *The Angry American: How Voter Rage Is Changing the Nation.* Boulder, CO: Westview Press, 1996 and 1998.

Valenti, Jack. *This Time, This Place: My Life in War, The White House, and Hollywood.* New York: Harmony Books, 2007.

Verkuil, Paul R. *Outsourcing Sovereignty: Why Privatization of Government Functions Threatens Democracy and What We Can Do about It.* New York: Cambridge University Press, 2007.

Wallace-Hadrill, Andrew. *Patronage in Ancient Society.* London: Routledge, 1989.

Walsh, Annmarie H. *The Public's Business: The Politics and Practices of Government Corporations.* Cambridge, MA: MIT Press, 1978.

Warren, Robert Penn. *All the King's Men.* New York: Harcourt Brace & Co., 1946.

Wedel, Janine. *Shadow Elite: How the World's New Power Brokers Undermine Democracy, Government, and the Free Market.* New York: Basic Books, 2009.

Weko, Thomas J. *The Politicizing Presidency: The White House Personnel Office, 1948–1994.* Lawrence: University of Kansas Press, 1995.

Newspaper and Periodical Articles, Monographs, Speeches, Book Chapters, and Dissertations

"The Best Judges Business Can Buy." *The New York Times,* June 18, 2007, p. A20.

"Company That Leases Parkway Erred in Political Donations." *Richmond Times Dispatch,* July 3, 2008, p. B-1.

"Daley's Choice, Sorich's Guilt." *Chicago Tribune,* July 7, 2006, editorial.

"Despite Being Under an Investigative Cloud, Halliburton Gets $4.3 Billion in 2003." *The Center for Public Integrity,* August 18, 2004.

"Ex-New York Political Boss Pleads Guilty in Pension Fund Case." *The New York Times,* October 7, 2009, p. A23.

"Fact Sheet on Model City Grants." *Congressional Quarterly,* November 27, 1967, pp. 1–4.

"Giuliani is Selling Investment Firm." *The New York Times,* March 6, 2007, editorial, p. A18.

"Judicial Politics Run Amok." *The New York Times,* September 19, 2006, online.

"Judge Says Governor Can't Be Tried in Office." *Associated Press,* August 12, 2006.

"Key Player: Vernon E. Jordan Jr." *Washington Post,* October 5, 1998, http://www.washingtonpost.com/wp-srv/politics/special/clinton/players/jordan.htm.

"Loans? Did We Say We'd Do Loans?" *New York Times,* October 28, 2008, online.

"Missouri's Fee-office System: A Relic Calling Out for Reform." KansasCity.Com, October 1, 2008, editorial.

"Mr. Rove Talks, but Doesn't Answer." *The New York Times,* June 2, 2008, p. A20.

"The Political Specter at Justice." *The New York Times,* March 21, 2008, editorial, p. A22.

"While Corruption Flourishes, the State Naps." Newark, NJ: *Star-Ledger,* January 12, 2003, editorial.

Aberbach, Joel D., and Bert A. Rockman. "The Appointments Process and the Administrative Presidency." *Presidential Studies Quarterly,* Vol. 39, No. 1, March 2009, pp. 38–59.

Aman, Alfred C. Jr. "Privatization, Prisons, Democracy, and Human Rights: The Need to Extend the Province of Administrative Law." *Indiana Journal of Global Legal Studies,* Vol. 12, 2005.

Baker, Peter, and Jeff Zeleny. "Obama's Chief of Staff Wields Power Freely, and Faces the Risks." *New York Times,* August 16, 2009, p. 16.

Barbaro, Michael. "A Mayor Who Discarded Political Parties Now Woos Them." *The New York Times,* February 19, 2009, p. A21.

Barbaro, Michael. "Push for 3d Term Alienates Some Bloomberg Supporters." *The New York Times,* October 23, 2008, p. A24.

Barnes, Robert. "Case May Define When a Judge Must Recuse Self." *Washington Post,* 2/2/09, pp. 1, 14.

Barnes, Robert. "Judicial Races Now Rife with Politics—Corporate Funds Help Fuel Change." *Washington Post,* October 28, 2007.

Baumgarten, Nick. "The Humbling of Eliot Spitzer." *New Yorker Magazine,* December 10, 2007, p.77.

Bawn, Kathleen. "Political Control versus Expertise: Congressional Choices about Administrative Procedures." *American Political Science Review,* Vol. 89, No. 1, 1995, pp.62–73.

Bearfield, Dominic A. "What Is Patronage? A Critical Reexamination." *Public Administration Review,* Vol. 69, 2009, pp. 64–76.

Benfield, Richard. "The City Boss Becomes the Country Boss." *The New York Times,* January 2, 2008, p. A20.

Bennett, Brian. "Victims of an Outsourced War." *Time,* July 19, 2008.

Bernton, Hal, and David Heath. "Palin's Earmark Requests: More Per Person Than Any Other State." *Seattle Times,* September 3, 2008.

Bertelli, Anthony, and Sven E. Feldmann. "Strategic Appointments." *Journal of Public Administration Research and Theory* 17, 2007, pp. 19–38.

Bogardus, Kevin. "Statehouse Revolvers." *Center for Public Integrity,* October 12, 2006.

Bolton, Alexander. "Democratic Leaders Shower Pork on Freshmen." *The Hill,* February 14, 2008, p. 8.

Boyne, George A. "Bureaucratic Theory Meets Reality: Public Choice and Service Contracting in U. S. Local Government." *Public Administration Review,* Vol. 58, No. 6, 1998, pp. 474–484.

Broder, John M., and James Risen. "Blackwater Logs Most Shootings of Firms in Iraq." *The New York Times,* September 27, 2007, pp. A1, A14.

Broder, John M., and James Risen. "Blackwater Mounts a Defense with Top Talent from Capital." *The New York Times,* November 1, 2007, pp. A1, A8.

Brooks, Rosa. "Outsourcing Foreign Policy." *Los Angeles Times,* September 21, 2007.

Brownings, Lynnley. "I.R.S. Use of Private Debt Collectors Is Criticized." *The New York Times,* January 10, 2007, p. C3.

Burstein, Rachel, and Janice C. Shields. "A probe not taken: Congress takes a look at OPIC's taxpayer-backed sweetheart deals. We Did." *Mother Jones,* July/August, 1997, p. 44.

Cardwell, Diane. "Longtime Practice of City Council Financing Lands on Speaker's Shoulders." *The New York Times,* May 11, 2008, p. 25.

Carlstrom, Gregg. "Bush Appointees Burrow In." *Federal Times,* December 8, 2008, http://www.federaltimes.com/index.php?S-3841535.

Castelli, Elise. "The Case for Insourcing." *Federal Times,* September 21, 2008.

Chappell, Howard W. Jr., Thomas M. Havrilesky, and Rob Roy McGregor. "Partisan Monetary Policies: Presidential Influence through the Power of Appointment." *Quarterly Journal of Economics,* Vol. 108, 1993, pp. 185–201.

Clingermayer, James C., Richard C. Feiock, and Christopher Stream. "Governmental Uncertainty and Leadership Turnover: Influences on Contracting and Sector Choice for Local Services." *State & Local Government Review,* Vol. 35, No. 3, 2003, pp. 150–160.

Coffey, Matthew B. "A Death at the White House: The Short Life of the New Patronage." *Public Administration Review,* Vol. 34, No. 5, September–October 1974, pp. 440–444.

Confessore, Nicholas, and Michael Barbaro. "Mayor Deprives Rival of Black Clergy's Support." *The New York Times,* October 29, 2009, p. A21.

Crowley, Patrick. "Judge Bunning Takes Bench." *Cincinnati Enquirer,* March 28, 2002, online.

Daniel, Christopher. "Curbing Patronage without Paperasserie." *Public Administration Review,* Vol. 53, No. 4, June–August 1993, pp. 387–390.

de la Merced, Michael J. "4 Firms Agree to Settlement in New York Pension Fund Inquiry." *The New York Times,* September 19, 2009.

Dickinson, Laura A. "Public Law Values in a Privatized World." *Yale Journal of International Law,* Vol. 31, 2006, pp. 383–426.

Dilanian, Ken. "Congress Ratings Plunge in Poll." *USA Today,* July 16, 2008, p. 1.

Dilger, Robert Jay, Randolph R. Moffett, and Linda Struyk. "Privatization of Municipal Services in America's Largest Cities." *Public Administration Review,* Vol. 57, No. 1, 1997, pp. 21–26.

Dimock, Marshall E. "Government Corporations: A Focus of Policy and Administration, I." *American Political Science Review,* Vol. 43, No.5, 1949, pp. 899–921.

Doig, Jameson W. "Expertise, Politics, and Technological Change: The Search for Mission at the Port of New York Authority." *Journal of the American Planning Association,* Vol. 59, No. 1, 1993, pp. 31–44.

Donovan, Doug. "Baltimore Mayor Indicted in Theft and Perjury Case." *The New York Times,* January 10, 2009, p. A8.

Denny, Dr., "Bush's Patronage Appointments to Ambassador Exceed Father's, Clinton's," posted June 25, 2007 at Scholars and Rogues. http://scholarsandrogues.wordpress.com/2007/06/25/bushs-patronage-appointments-to-ambassador-exceed-fathers-clintons/.

Dyche, John D. "Their Own Worst Enemy." *Weekly Standard,* October 29, 2007, p. 16.

Edwards, George C. III. "Why Not the Best? The Loyalty-Competence Trade-Off in Presidential Appointments." *Brookings Review,* Vol. 19, 2001, pp. 12–16.

Ehrenhalt, Alan. "Patronage Trap Flap." Governing.Com, December 15, 2005.

Eilperin, Juliet, and Carol D. Leonnig. "Top Scientist Rails Against Hirings." *Washington Post,* November 22, 2009, p. A3.

Eligon, John. "Judge-Elect Facing Criminal Charges Will Be Suspended." *The New York Times,* December 30, 2008.

Elsibal, Nadine. "From Lobbyist to Legislator." *Center for Public Integrity,* October 12, 2006.

Emanuel, Rahm. "Don't Get Rid of Earmarks." *Washington Post,* August 24, 2007.

Emerson, Ralph W. "Politics," in *Essays: Second Series,* in the Complete Writings of Ralph Waldo Emerson, Vol. 1, 1929.

The Federalist Papers, *The Federalist,* 1787–1788.

Feeney, M. K., and G. Kingsley. "The Rebirth of Patronage: Have We Come Full Circle?" *Public Integrity,* Vol. 10, 2008, pp. 165–176.

Feiock, Richard C., James C. Clinger, Manoj Shrestha, and Carl Dasse. "Contracting and Sector Choice across Municipal Services." *State & Local Government Review,* Vol. 39, No. 2, 2007, pp. 72–83.

Feldman, Ron. "Estimating and Managing the Federal Subsidy of Fannie Mae and Freddie Mac: Is Either Task Possible?" *Journal of Public Budgeting, Accounting and Financial Management,* Vol. 11, No. 1, 1999, pp. 81–116.

Fineout, Gary. "Florida Speaker Steps Down, Citing Corruption Investigation." *The New York Times,* January 31, 2009, p. A14.

Flaherty, Mary P., and Cheryl W. Thompson. "County Requires Donations but Fails to Collect." *Washington Post,* July 6, 2008, p. A11.

Freddoso, David. "When Murtha Asks, Defense Contractors Give." *Roll Call,* February 11, 2008, p. 1.

Freedman, Anne. "Commentary on Patronage." *Public Administration Review,* Vol. 54, No. 3, May–June 1994, p. 313.

Freedman, Anne. "Doing Battle with the Patronage Army: Politics, Courts, and Personnel Administration in Chicago." *Public Administration Review,* Vol. 48, No. 5, September–October 1988, pp. 847–859.

Freedman, Monroe H. "The Threat to Judicial Independence by Criticism of Judges— A Proposed Solution to the Real Problem." *Hofstra Law Review,* Vol. 25, No. 3, pp. 1–15.

Freeman, Jody. "The Private Role in Public Governance." *New York University Law Review,* Vol. 75, No. 101, 2000.

Garrett, R. Sam, James A. Thurber, A. Lee Fritschler, and David H. Rosenbloom. "Assessing the Impact of Bureaucracy Bashing by Electoral Campaigns." *Public Administration Review,* Vol. 66, 2006, pp. 228–240.

Gilmour, John B., and David E. Lewis. "Political Appointees and the Competence of Federal Program Management." *American Politics Research,* Vol. 34, 2006, p. 41.

Goldberg, Deborah. "Public Funding of Judicial Elections: The Roles of Judges and the Rules of Campaign Finance." *Brennan Center for Justice,* July 2, 2002.

Goldstein, Amy, and Dan Eggen. "Immigration Judges Often Picked Based on GOP Ties." *Washington Post,* June 11, 2007, p.1.

Greenblatt, Alan. "Tougher Than Wall Street." *Governing Magazine,* December 2007.

Guttman, Dan. "Governance by Contract: Constitutional Visions; Time for Reflection and Choice." *Public Contract Law Journal,* Vol. 33, No. 2, 2004.

Guttman, Daniel. "Public Purpose and Private Service: The Twentieth Century Culture of Contracting Out and the Evolving Law of Diffused Sovereignty." *Administrative Law Review,* Vol. 52, 2000, pp. 859–926.

Hakim, Danny, and Louise Story. "Obama Adviser Said to Be Tied to Pension Deal." *The New York Times,* April 17, 2009, p. 1.

Halper, Evan, and Nancy Vogel. "Nunez Used a Charity to Funnel Donations." *Los Angeles Times,* November 2, 2007, p. 1.

Hamilton, David K. "The Continuing Judicial Assault on Patronage." *Public Administration Review,* Vol. 59, No. 1 (January–February 1999), pp. 54–62.

Hamilton, David K. "The Staffing Function in Illinois State Government after Rutan." *Public Administration Review,* Vol. 53, No. 4 (July–August 1993), pp. 381–386.

Hansen, Susan B. "Governors' Job Performance Ratings and State Unemployment: The Case of California." *State & Local Government Review,* Vol. 31, No. 1, 1999, pp. 7–17.

Hanssen, F. Andrew. "Learning about Judicial Independence: Institutional Change in the State Courts." *Journal of Legal Studies,* Vol. 22, June 2004, pp. 431–473.

Hendrix, Steve, and Michael D. Shear. "The Chief's Chief." *Washington Post,* November 7, 2008, p. C4.

Hernandez, Raymond, and David W. Chen. "Now Lobbyist, an Ex-Senator Uses Campaign Money." *The New York Times,* August 24, 2007, online.

Hicks, Jonathan P. "Barron Calls Brooklyn Democratic Gathering Too Scripted." *The New York Times,* September 16, 2008, online.

Hicks, Jonathan P. "Judge Finds vs. Rivera's Bronx Democrats." *The New York Times,* December 1, 2008, online.

Hilzenrath, David S., and Zachary A. Goldfarb. "Mortgage Giants' Mess Falls to Their Regulator." *Washington Post,* September 11, 2008, pp. D1 and D3.

Holan, Angie D. "Former Lobbyist in the White House? It's Okay If They Say It's Okay." *St. Petersburg Times,* http://www.politifact.com/truth-o-meter.

Iglesias, David C. "Dangerous New Turn in Justice Department Investigation." *The Huffington Post,* www.huffingtonpost.com, February 21, 2009.

Ingraham, Patricia W. "Building Bridges or Burning Them? The President, the Appointees, and the Bureaucracy." *Public Administration Review,* Vol. 47, No. 5 (September–October 1987), pp. 425–435.

Jacobson, Arthur J. "The Private Use of Public Authority: Sovereignty and Associations in the Common Law." *Buffalo Law Review,* Vol. 29, 1980, pp. 599–665.

James, Scott C. "Patronage Regimes and American Party Development from 'The Age of Jackson' to the Progressive Era." *British Journal of Political Science,* Vol. 36, 2006, pp. 39–60.

Johnson, Carrie. "FBI Says Illinois Governor Tried to Sell Senate Seat." *Washington Post,* December 10, 2008, p. 1.

Johnson, Carrie. "Obama Team Faces Major Task in Justice Department Overhaul." *Washington Post,* November 13, 2008, p. A2.

Johnson, Ronald N., and Gary Libecap. "Patronage to Merit and Control of the Federal Government Labor Force." *Exploration in Economic History,* Vol. 31, 1994, pp. 91–119.

Johnston, David Cay. "I.R.S. Enlists Outside Help in Collecting Delinquent Taxes, Despite the Higher Costs." *The New York Times,* August 20, 2006.

Johnston, Jocelyn M., and Barbara Romzek. "Contracting and Accountability in State Medicaid Reform: Rhetoric, Theories, and Reality." *Public Administration Review,* Vol. 59, No. 5 (September–October 1999), pp. 383–399.

Jones, Jeffrey M. "Confidence in Congress: Lowest Ever for Any U.S. Institution." http://www.gallup.com/poll/108142/Confidence-Congress-Lowest-Ever-Any-US-Institution. aspx, accessed September 13, 2008.

Kaiser, Robert G. "Citizen K Street." *Washington Post,* March 19, 2007.

Kamen, Al. "Dollar Signs Point to Many a U.S. Embassy." *Washington Post,* June 10, 2009, p. A17.

Kane, Paul. "Congress May Seek Criminal Probe of Altered Earmark." *Washington Post,* April 17, 2008.

Kane, Paul. "Domenici Rebuked for Call to U.S. Attorney Before Election." *Washington Post,* April 25, 2008, p. A7.

Kane, Paul, and Dan Eggen. "Second Lawmaker Contacted Prosecutor." *Washington Post,* March 6, 2007, p. A1.

Kang, Cecilia. "Rescue Sweetened With Tax Incentives." *Washington Post,* October 4, 2008, pp. D1, 2.

Kaplan, Robert. "Outsourcing Conflict." *The Atlantic.com,* July 19, 2008.

Kelley, Matt. "The Congressman & the Hedge Fund." *USA Today,* January 19, 2006, online.

Kelly, Stanley Jr. "Patronage and Presidential Legislative Leadership." Unpublished paper, Princeton, 1968.

Kennedy, Duncan. "The Stages of the Decline of the Public/Private Distinction." *University of Pennsylvania Law Review,* Vol. 130, p. 1882.

Khademian, Anne M. "Reinventing a Government Corporation: Professional Priorities and a Clear Bottom Line." *Public Administration Review,* Vol. 55, No.1, 1995, pp. 17–28.

King, Colbert I. "What DC's Elves Do With Your Taxes." *Washington Post,* May 17, 2008, p. A17.

Kinzer, Stephen. "Letter from Chicago: A Prized Project, a Mayor and Persistent Criticism." *The New York Times,* July 13, 2004, online.

Kirkpatrick, David D. "For Lobbyists, No Downturn, Just a Turnover." *The New York Times,* November 25, 2008, p. 1.

Kirkpatrick, David D., and Jim Rutenberg. "A Developer, His Deals and His Ties to McCain." *The New York Times,* April 22, 2008.

Kocieniewski, David. "The Congressman, the Donor and the Tax Break." *The New York Times,* November 25, 2008, p. 1.

Kocieniewski, David. "Rangel Pushed for a Donation, Insurer Pushed for a Tax Cut." *The New York Times,* January 2, 2009, p.1.

Kopecki, Dwan. "When Outsourcing Turns Outrageous." *Business Week,* July 31, 2006.

Koppel, Nathan. "For 'Maverick' Federal Judges, Life Tenure Is Largely Unfettered License." *Wall Street Journal,* August 8, 2008.

Koppel, Ted. "These Guns for Hire." *The New York Times,* May 22, 2006, p. A21.

Kosterlitz, Julie. "Siblings Fat and Sassy: Now That Fannie Mae and Freddie Mac Have Ballooned into Multibillion-Dollar Players in the Nation's Financial Markets, Critics Say These Government-Created Companies Are Too Big and Too Powerful." *National Journal,* Vol. 32, No. 20, 2000, pp. 1498–1507.

Kulish, Nicholas, and Jacob M. Schlesinger. "How Fannie Mae Beat Effort by Adversaries to Rein It In." *The Wall Street Journal,* July 5, 2001. Online at http://interactive.wsj.com/.

Laski, Harold J. "The French Elections." *The Fortnightly,* Vol. 164, no. 158, December 1945, p. 359.

Laskow, Sarah. "State Lobbying Becomes Billion Dollar Business." *Center for Public Integrity,* December 20, 2006.

Latham, Aaron. "Will Rogers Is Running for President." *New York Magazine,* December 1974, pp. 74–86.

Lee, Christopher. "Political Appointees 'Burrowing In.'" *Washington Post,* October 5, 2007, pp. A19.

Leigh-Cowan, Alison. "Big-City Paydays at 'Farmer Mac.'" *The New York Times,* April 28, 2002, p. 1, Sunday Business Section.

Leonnig, Carol D. "LaHood Sponsored Millions in Earmarks." *Washington Post,* January 14, 2009, p. A2.

Leonnig, Carol D. "Obama Wrote Federal Staffers About His Goals." *Washington Post,* November 17, 2008, p. 1.

Lewis, David E. "Revisiting the Administrative Presidency: Policy, Patronage, and Agency Competence." *Presidential Studies Quarterly,* Vol. 39, 2009, pp. 60–73.

Lewis, David E. "Staffing Alone: Unilateral Action and the Politicization of the Executive Office of the President, 1988–2004." *Presidential Studies Quarterly,* Vol. 35, No. 3, pp. 496–514.

Lewis, Neil A. "Using Disclosure Rules as a Defense for a Senator." *The New York Times,* October 13, 2008, p. A13.

Lichtblau, Eric, and Kitty Bennett. "30 Ex-Government Officials Got Lucrative Posts as Corporate Monitors." *The New York Times,* May 23, 2008, p. A21.

Light, Paul C. "Fact Sheet on the Continued Thickening of Government." *The Brookings Institution,* July 23, 2004.

Light, Paul C. "The Tides of Reform Revisited: Patterns in Making Government Work, 1945–2002." *Public Administration Review,* Vol. 66, 2006, pp. 27–54.

Liptak, Adam. "Looking Anew at Campaign Cash and Elected Judges." *The New York Times,* Jan 29, 2008, p. A14.

Lipton, Eric. "Governor's Relative Is Big Contract Winner." *The New York Times,* December 7, 2006.

Lipton, Eric. "Missouri Prosecutor Says He Was Pushed to Resign." *The New York Times*, May 10, 2007, p. A22.

Lipton, Eric, and Raymond Hernandez. "A Champion of Wall Street Reaps Benefits." *The New York Times*, December 13, 2008, p.1.

Mackenzie, G. Calvin. "The State of the Presidential Appointments Process," in *Innocent Until Nominated: The Breakdown of the Presidential Appointments Process*, edited by G. Calvin Mackenzie. Washington, D.C.: Brookings Institution, 2001.

Maranto, Robert, and Karen M. Hult. "Right Turn? Political Ideology and the Higher Civil Service, 1987–1994." *American Review of Public Administration* Vol. 34, 2004, pp. 199–221.

Margolin, Josh, and Kelly Heyboer. "UMDNJ Scandal: With Campus Attorney's Exit, a Star Is Done." *Newark Star-Ledger*, December 30, 2005.

Martin, Jonathan, and Carol E. Lee. "Obama Bets the House on Specter." *Politico*, September 16, 2009, p. 1.

Mattera, Philip. "Outsourcing Walter Reed." www.tompaine.com/print/outsourcing-walter_reed, March 6, 2007.

Maute, Judith L. "Selecting Justice in State Courts: The Ballot Box or the Back Room." *41 S. Texas Law Review* 11098, 1206 (2000).

McCarthy, Ellen. "CACI Contract: From Supplies to Interrogation." *Washington Post*, May 17, 2004, p. E1.

McCarty, Nolan, and Rose Razaghian. "Advice and Consent: Senate Responses to Executive Branch Nominations, 1885–1996." *American Journal of Political Science*, Vol. 43, 1999, pp. 1122–1444.

McGrath, Ben. "The Untouchable." *New Yorker*, August 24, p. 43.

McIntire, Mike, and Jeremy W. Peters. "Longtime New York GOP Leader Indicted by U.S. on Corruption Charges." *The New York Times*, January 24, 2008, p. A15.

McIntire, Mike. "Bailout Is a No-Strings Windfall to Bankers, if Not to Borrowers." *The New York Times*, January 18, 2009, p. 1.

McIntire, Mike. "Nuclear Leaks and Response Tested Obama in the Senate." *The New York Times*, February 3, 2009, online.

McLean, Bethany. "Would You Buy a Bridge from This Man?" *Fortune Magazine*, October 2, 2007.

McTague, Jim. "Embattled Bankroller." *Barron's*, September 16, 1996.

Meier, Kenneth J. "Ode to Patronage: A Critical Analysis of Two Recent Supreme Court Decisions." *Public Administration Review*, Vol. 41, No. 5, 1981, pp. 558–563.

Mihalopoulos, Dan, and Todd Lightly. "City Agrees to Ban Patronage." *Chicago Tribune*, March 22, 2007, online.

Minow, Martha L. "Outsourcing Power: How Privatizing Military Efforts Challenges Accountability, Professionalism, and Democracy." *46 Boston College Law Review* 989, 2005.

Moe, Ronald C. "The Emerging Federal Quasi Government Issues of Management and Accountability." *Public Administration Review*, Vol. 61, No. 3 (May–June 2001), pp. 290–312.

Moe, Ronald C., and Thomas H. Stanton. "Government-Sponsored Enterprises as Federal Instrumentalities: Reconciling Private Management with Public Accountability." *Public Administration Review,* Vol. 49, No. 4, 1989, pp. 321–329.

Moe, Terry M. "Regulatory Performance and Presidential Administration." *American Journal of Political Science,* Vol. 26, 1982, pp. 197–224.

Moore, Stephen. "Comfy with K Street." *Wall Street Journal,* October 19, 2007, p. A19.

Mosk, Matthew. "Top Donors Rewarded with White House Perks." *Washington Times,* October 28, 2009, p.1.

Naymik, Mark, and John Caniglia. "Jimmy Dimora, Frank Russo and Local Businesses Are Under Federal Investigation." *The Plain Dealer,* July 28, 2008.

Newland, Chester A. "Imperium, Sacerdotium, Collegium? Bicentennial Leadership Challenges." *Public Administration Review,* Vol. 47, 1987, pp. 45–56.

Newmeyer, Tony, and Kate Ackley. "Puttin' On the Ritz." *Roll Call,* February 8, 2008, online.

Nocera, Joseph. "Anxiety on Economy Wins Out." *The New York Times,* October 4, 2008, p. D1.

Nocera, Joseph. "So When Will Banks Give Loans?" *The New York Times,* October 25, 2008, p. B1.

Nossiter, Adam. "Alabama Ex-Governor Ordered Freed Pending Appeal of Bribery Conviction." *The New York Times,* March 28, 2008, p. A14.

Nossiter, Adam. "Fear, Paranoia and, Yes, Some Loathing in Alabama's Hallowed Halls." *The New York Times,* April 6, 2008, p.12.

O'Harrow, Robert Jr. "Earmark Spending Makes a Comeback: Congress Pledged Curbs in 2007." *Washington Post,* June 13, 2008, p. A1.

Packer, Adrienne. "U.S. Attorney Rebuts Claim Performance Led to Firing." *Las Vegas Review Journal,* February 8, 2007.

Palmer, Valentine, and John Levendis. "The Louisiana Supreme Court in Question: An Empirical Study of the Effect of Campaign Contributions on the Judicial Function." *Tulane Law Review,* Vol. 82, No. 2, 2008, pp. 1291–1314.

Parrish, Michael. "Sheriff, Wife and Another Are Indicted." *The New York Times,* October 31, 2007, p. A19.

Paybarah, Azi. "The Anti-Patronage Pledge from a Surrogate's Candidate." *New York Observer,* September 8, 2008, online.

Pear, Robert. "From Bush, Foe of Earmarks, Similar Items." *The New York Times,* February 10, 2008, online.

Pear, Robert. "Lawmakers Put Out New Call for Earmarks." *The New York Times,* February 14, 2008.

Pei, Minxin. "Will the Chinese Communist Party Survive the Crisis?" *Carnegie Endowment for International Peace,* posted on *Foreign Affairs* website, March 12, 2009.

Peters, Jeremy W. "Joblessness Was Brief for a Retired Politician." *The New York Times,* July 23, 2008, p. A21.

Pfiffner, James P. "The Public Service Ethic in New Public Personnel Systems." *Public Personnel Management,* Vol. 28, 1999, p. 551.

Pfiffner, James P. "Recruiting Executive Branch Leaders." *Brookings Review* Vol. 19, 2001, p. 4.

Pincus, Walter. "Conferees Want Hard Look at Contractors." *Washington Post,* December 17, 2008, p. A19.

Priest, Dana, and Anne Hull. "Soldiers Face Neglect, Frustration at Army's Top Medical Facility." *Washington Post,* February 18, 2007, p. A1.

Pritchett, C. Herman. "The Government Corporation Control Act of 1945." *American Political Science Review,* Vol. 40, No. 3, 1946, pp. 495–509.

Purnick, Joyce. "Assembly's Speaker Keeps Power Intact and Options Open." *New York Times,* June 20, 2007, p. A21.

Raadschedlers, Joseph C. N., and Kwang-Hoon Lee. "Between Amateur Government and Career Civil Service: The American Administrative Elite in Cross-Time and Comparative Perspective." *Jahrbuch Fur Europaische Verwaltungsgeschichte,* Vol. 17, pp. 201–222.

Rauch, Jonathan. "A Stubborn Senator Who Matters." *National Journal,* November 17, 2007, p 19.

Reeve, Elspeth. "It's All Relative." *Center for Public Integrity,* December 20, 2006.

Rehfuss, John. "Contracting out and Accountability in State and Local Governments: The Importance of Contracting Monitoring." *State & Local Government Review,* Vol. 22, No. 1, 1990, pp. 44–48.

Rehm, Barbara. "Put-Up Time for White House on Supervision of the GSEs." *American Banker,* mortgage 1, July 16, 2001.

Risen, Clay. "The Lightning Rod." *The Atlantic,* November 2008.

Risen, James. "End of Immunity Worries U.S. Contractors in Iraq." *New York Times,* December 1, 2008, p. A14.

Rivera, Ray. "Group Spent City Cash, but Hasn't Shown How." *New York Times,* October 19, 2008, p. 28.

Rivera, Ray. "New York Candidates Awash in Real Estate Cash." *New York Times,* February 1, 2009, p. A21.

Rivera, Roy, and Sewell Chan. "Queens Councilman Is Charged with Assault." *New York Times,* December 19, 2008, online.

Root, Jay. "Lax State Laws Allow Cozy Lobbyist-Lawmaker Ties." *Associated Press,* October 6, 2008.

Rosenbloom, David H., and Suzanne J. Piotrowski. "Outsourcing the Constitution and Administrative Law Norms." *American Review of Public Administration,* Vol. 35, 2005, pp. 103–121.

Roth, Zachary. "Gonzo's Lawyer Quits Civil Case." March 5, 2008, http://tpmmuckraker .talkingpointsmemo.com.

Ruethling, Gretchen. "Chicago Officials Convicted in Patronage Arrangement." *New York Times,* July 6, 2006, online.

Sample, James. "The Campaign Trial: The True Cost of Expensive Court Seats." *Brennan Center for Justice,* March 6, 2006.

Sample, James, David Pozen, and Michael Young. "Fair Courts: Setting Recusal Standards." *Brennan Center for Justice,* April 01, 2008.

Samuels, Dorothy. "The Selling of the Judiciary: Campaign Cash 'in the Courtroom'." *New York Times*, April 15, 2008, p. A22.

Sanghera, Sathnam. "Fannie Mae and Freddie Mac Come Up Against Their Lobbying Match: The Companies May Face an Overhaul in Regulation." *Financial Times* (London), Vol. 4, June 15, 2000.

Savage, Charlie. "A Donor's Gift Soon Followed Clinton's Help." *New York Times*, January 4, 2009, p. 1.

Savage, Charlie. "Obama Undercuts Whistle-Blowers, Senator Says." *New York Times*, March 17, 2009, p. A17.

Savage, James D. "The Administrative Costs of Congressional Earmarking: The Case of the Office of Naval Research." *Public Administration Review*, May/June 2009, pp. 448–449.

Savas, E. S. "Competition and Choice in New York City Social Services." *Public Administration Review*, Vol. 62, No. 1, 2002, pp. 82–91.

Scahill, Jeremy. "Blackwater." *The Nation*, May 11, 2007.

Schmidt, Diane E. "The Presidential Appointment Process, Task Environment Pressures, and Regional Office Case Processing." *Political Research Quarterly* 48 (1995), pp. 381–401.

Schulte, Bret. "A Troubling Bayou Tradition." *U.S. News*, October 2, 2005, online.

Schultz, Stacey. "Mr. Outside Moves Inside." *U.S. News*, March 16, 2003, online.

Seib, Gerald F. "Where Have All the Washington Deal Makers Gone?" *Wall Street Journal*, August 27, 2009, p. A4.

Seidman, Harold. "The Government Corporation: Organization and Controls." *Public Administration Review*, Vol. 14, No. 3, 1954, pp.183–192.

Seidman, Harold. "The Theory of the Autonomous Government Corporation: A Critical Appraisal." *Public Administration Review*, Vol. 12, No.2, 1952, pp. 89–96.

Seiler, Robert S. Jr. "Fannie Mae and Freddie Mac as Investor-Owned Public Utilities." *Journal of Public Budgeting, Accounting & Financial Management*, Vol. 11, No.1, 1999, pp. 117–154.

Shafer, Jack. "Homer Simpson Has What the Bancrofts Want." *Slate Magazine*, July 13, 2007.

Shane, Scott, and Ron Nixon. "In Washington, Contractors Take on Biggest Role Ever." *New York Times*, February 4, 2007.

Shear, Michael D., and Carol D. Leonnig. "Commerce Pick Richardson Withdraws, Citing N.M. Probe." *Washington Post*, January, 5, 2009, pp. A1, A4.

Shin, Annys. "How a Former Chief Helped Shape the Company's Political Culture." *Washington Post*, May 24, 2006, p. D1.

Smith, R. Jeffrey, Cecilia Kang, and Joe Stephens. "Old Ways Doomed New Job for Daschle." *Washington Post*, February 4, 2009, p.1.

Sorauf, Frank J. "The Silent Revolution in Patronage." *Public Administration Review*, Vol. 20, 1960, pp. 28–34.

Stevenson, Richard. "Government May Make Private Nearly Half of Its Civilian Jobs." *New York Times*, November 15, 2002, p. A1.

Stewart, Nikita. "Housing Authority Contracts "Illegal." *Washington Post,* October 24, 2009, p. B1.

Stone, Clarence. "Urban Political Machines: Taking Stock." *PS: Political Science & Politics,* Vol. 29, No. 3, September 1996, pp. 446-450.

Story, Louise. "Quadrangle Facing Questions over Pension Funds." *New York Times,* April 21, 2009, online.

Sturgis, Sue. "Katrina Trailer Contractor Failed to Act on Known Health Risks." *Southern Studies,* July 10, 2006, http://www.southernstudies.org/2008/07/katrina-trailer-contractor-failed-to.html.

Sullivan, Thomas P. "Recording Federal Custodial Interviews." *American Criminal Law Review,* Vol. 45, No. 4, Fall 2008, pp. 1297–1349.

Thompson, Cheryl W., and Mary Pat Flaherty. "Sweetheart Deals." *Washington Post,* July 6, 2008, p. 1.

Tilzer, Gary. "The Surrogate's Court and Why It Should Go." *Gotham Gazette,* July 4, 2005.

Utt, Ronald D. "Cutting the Deficit and Improving Services by Contracting Out." *Heritage Foundation,* March 10, 1995, p. 4, http://www.heritage.org/Research/Budget/upload/89314 1.pdf.

van Slyke, David M. "The Mythology of Privatization in Contracting for Social Services." *Public Administration Review,* Vol. 63, No. 3 (May–June, 2003), pp. 296–315.

Varney, James. "Trailer Dealer May Avoid Fine, Taxes." *Times-Picayune,* September 19, 2006.

Verkuil, Paul R. "Public Law Limitations on Privatization of Government Functions." *North Carolina Law Review,* Vol. 84, 2006.

Vernon, Rebecca. "Battlefield Contractors: Facing the Tough Issues." *Public Contract Law Journal,* Vol. 33, No. 2 (Winter), 2004, pp. 369–421.

Vogel, Steve, and Renae Merle. "Privatized Walter Reed Workforce Gets Scrutiny." *Washington Post,* March 10, 2007, online.

Wallechinsky, David, Lyric Wallwork Winik, and Daryl Chen. "Who Gets Your Money?" *Parade.com,* http://www.parade.com/articles/editions/2007/edition_10-14-2007/Intelligence_Report.

Wallin, Bruce. "The Need for a Privatization Process: Lessons from Development and Implementation." *Public Administration Review,* Vol. 57, No. 1 (January–February 1997), pp. 11–20.

Warner, Mildred, and Robert Hebdon. "Local Government Restructuring: Privatization and Its Alternatives." *Journal of Policy Analysis and Management,* Vol. 20, No. 2, 2001, pp. 315–336.

Wedel, Janine. "The Shadow Army." *Boston Globe,* September 30, 2007.

Weingrod, Alex. "Patrons, Patronage, and Political Parties." *Comparative Studies in Society and History,* Vol. 10, 1968, pp. 377–400.

Wilke, John R. "How Lawmaker Rebuilt Hometown on Earmarks." *Wall Street Journal,* October 30, 2007, p. A1.

Wilson, David. "Quangos in the Skeletal State," in *The Quango Debate,* edited by F. F. Ridley and David Wilson. New York: Oxford University Press. 1995.

Wise, Daniel. "N.Y. DA Says Former Judge, Assemblyman, Hold Keys to Probe of Buying and Selling Judgeships." *New York Law Journal,* April 23, 2007.

Wolfensberger, Don. "A Primer on Presidential Nominations and the Senate Confirmation Process." Woodrow Wilson International Center for Scholars, paper delivered March 16, 2009.

Government Documents, Reports, and Congressional Hearings and Testimony

"Governor Spitzer Proposes Sweeping Court Reforms." Press release from the New York State Executive Chamber, April 26, 2007.

"Testimony April 13, 1994, Henry Cisneros, Secretary of Housing and Urban Development, Senate Banking: GSE Housing Goals." *Federal Document Clearing House Congressional Testimony.* April 13, 1994.

Bureau of the Budget, Bulletin Number 55-4.

Committee on Government Reform, Minority Staff, Special Investigations Division (prepared for Henry A. Waxman, June 2006). *Dollars, Not Sense: Government Contracting under the Bush Administration.*

Committee on Government Reform, U.S. House of Representatives. *U. S. Government: Policy and Supporting Positions.* (Plum Book) 110th Congress, 2d Session.

Committee on Oversight and Government Reform, U.S. House of Representatives. *United States Government Policy and Supporting Positions 2006* (Plum Book).

Congressional Budget Office. *Assessing the Costs and Benefits of Fannie Mae and Freddie Mac.* Washington, D.C.: Government Printing Office, 1996.

Congressional Budget Office. *Controlling the Risks of Government-Sponsored Enterprises.* Washington, D.C.: Government Printing Office, 1991.

Congressional Research Service. *Administering Public Functions at the Margin of Government: The Case of Federal Corporation,* by Ronald C. Moe. 1983.

Congressional Research Service. *Earmarks in Appropriations Acts: FY 1994, FY 1998, FY 2000, FY 2002, FY 2004, FY 2005.* January 26, 2006, CRS-12.

Congressional Research Service. *US Attorneys Who Have Served Less Than Full Four-Year Terms, 1981–2006.* February 22, 2007.

Cotterman, Robert F., and James E. Pearce. "The Effects of the Federal National Mortgage Association and the Federal Home Loan Mortgage Corporation on Conventional Fixed-Rate Mortgage Yields." in U.S. Department of Housing and Urban Development, Office of Policy Development and Research. *Studies on Privatizing Fannie Mae and Freddie Mac.* Washington, D.C., 1996.

Council for Citizens Against Government Waste, *2008 Congressional Pig Book,* Introduction.

Executive Office of the President, Office of Management and Budget. "Circular No. A-76 (Revised), with attachments A and B."

Federal Home Loan Mortgage Corporation Act, 12 U.S.C.–1452m /sec, 303. (a) (2).

General Accounting Office. *Government Corporations: Profiles of Existing Government Corporations.* GAO/GGD-96-14. Washington, D.C.: Government Printing Office, 1995.

General Accounting Office. *Government-Sponsored Enterprises: A Framework for Limiting the Government's Exposure to Risks.* GAO/GGD-91-90. Washington, D.C.: Government Printing Office. 1991.

Government Accountability Office. *High-Risk Series: An Update.* Washington, D.C., 2007, pp. 71, 73, 75.

Government Accountability Office. Comptroller General of the United States. *Suggested Areas for Oversight for the 110th Congress.* Washington, D.C., 2006.

House Committee on Government Reform, Minority Staff. *Dollars, Not Sense: Government Contracting under the Bush Administration.* Committee print, 2006.

House Committee on Oversight and Government Reform. U.S. House of Representatives. *More Dollars, Less Sense: The 2007 Report; Dollars, Not Sense: The 2006 Report;* and *Searchable Database of Problem Contracts.* http://www.oversight.house.govfeatures/more dollars/less sense.

House of Representatives. Committee on Government Reform—Minority Staff Special Investigations Division Report. *Waste Fraud, and Abuse in Hurricane Katrina Contracts.* http://oversight.house.gov/Documents/20060824110705-30132.pdf.

H. R. 2968, http://thomas.loc.gov/cgi-bin/bdquery/z?d098:HR02968.

Kosar, Kevin. "The Quasi Government: Hybrid Organizations with Both Government and Private Sector Legal Characteristics." CRS Report for Congress. Washington, D.C.: Congressional Research Service, February 13, 2007.

Letter from Charles A. Bowsher, Comptroller General, to Hon. David Pryor (December 29, 1989), in Use of Consultants and Contractors by the Environmental Protection Agency and the Department of Energy. Senate Committee on Government Affairs, Hearing before Subcommittee on Federal Services, Post Office, and Civil Service, 101st Cong. S. 1. 1989.

Office of Management and Budget. Circular No. A-76 revised 1999, http://www.whitehouse.gov/omb/rewrite/circulars/a076/a076.html.

Office of Management and Budget. *Competitive Sourcing: Report on Competitive Sourcing Results Fiscal Year 2003.* May 2004, available at http://www.whitehouse.gov/results/agenda/cs_omb_647_report_final.pdf.

Order #17, written by L. Paul Bremer in Iraq in June, 2004.

Presidential Appointee Initiative. *Staffing a New Administration: A Guide to Personnel Appointments in a Presidential Transition.* Washington, D.C.: Brookings, 2000.

Secretary of Defense. "Memorandum for Secretaries of the Military Departments, Chairman of the Joint Chiefs of Staff, Under Secretaries of Defense, Commanders of the Combatant Commands." March 10, 2008.

Taylor, Andrew. "Bill Establishing New Overseer for Fannie, Freddie Clears." *Congressional Quarterly Weekly Report,* vol. 3, October 10, 1992, p. 138.

U.S. Census Bureau. *Consolidated Federal Funds Report for Fiscal Year 2008.*

U.S. Congress. Senate. Committee on Homeland Security and Government Affairs. 2006.

Hurricane Katrina: A Nation Still Unprepared. 109th Congress, 2nd Session, http://hsgac.senate.gov/index.cfm?Fuseaction=Links.Katrina.

U.S. Department of Justice. *An Investigation into the Removal of Nine U.S. Attorneys in 2006.* Joint Report by the Office of the Inspector General and the Office of Professional Responsibility. September 2008.

U.S. General Accounting Office. *Commercial Activities Panel: Improving the Sourcing Decisions of the Government: Final Report,* 2002.

U.S. General Accounting Office. *Competitive Sourcing: Great Emphasis Needed on Increasing Efficiency and Improving Performance.* GAO-04-367, 2004, available at http://www.gao.gov/new.items/d04367.pdf.

U.S. Government Accountability Office. *Contract Management: Opportunities to Improve Surveillance on Department of Defense Service Contracts.* GAO-05-274 March 2005, available at http://www.gao.gov/cgi-bin/getrpt? GAO-05-274.

U.S. Government Accountability Office. *Personnel Practices: Conversions of Employees from Noncareer to Career Positions May 2001–April 2005.* GAO-06-381, Washington, D.C., May 2006.

U.S. Government Accountability Office. *Securing, Stabilizing, and Rebuilding Iraq: Key Issues for Congressional Oversight,* GAO-07-308SP, Washington, D.C., January 9, 2007.

U.S. Office Of Personnel Management. *The Fact Book: Federal Civilian Workforce Statistics.* October 2004, available at http://www.opm.gov/feddata/factbook/2004/factbook.pdf.

United States Committee on the Organization of the Executive Branch. *The Hoover Commission Report on the Organization of the Executive Branch.* New York: McGraw-Hill, 1949.

United States Government Policy and Supporting Positions. (Plum Book 2008), http://www.gpoaccess.gov/plumbook/2008/index.html.

U.S. House of Representatives. Committee on Banking, Finance and Urban Affairs. *Government-Sponsored Housing Enterprises Financial Safety and Soundness Act of 1991: Report Together with Additional and Dissenting Views (to accompany H.R. 2, 900).* House Report 102–206. Washington, D.C.: Government Printing Office. 1991.

U.S. Senate Committee on Banking, Housing and Urban Affairs. *Legislative Proposals to Ensure the Safety and Soundness of Government-Sponsored Enterprises.* 102nd Congress, 1st session, May 10 and July 11. Washington, D.C.: Government Printing Office. 1991.

Reports, Monographs, Court Cases, and Other Sources

American Judicature Society. *Methods of Judicial Selection.* http://www.judicialselection.us/judicial_selection/methods/selection_of_judges.cfm?state=, accessed October 14, 2008.

Center for Responsive Politics. http://www.opensecrets.org/industries/indus.php?cycle=2008&ind=D.

"The Corporate Invasion of Iraq—Profile of U.S. Corporations Awarded Contracts in U.S./British-Occupied Iraq." *U.S. Labor Against the War* (USLAW), prepared for The Workers of Iraq and International Labor Movement.

The Council of State Governments. *The Book of the States 2008.*

The Council of State Governments. *The Book of the States 2009.*

DC Corporate Crime Reporter. October 8, 2007, http://corporatecrimereporter.com/corrupt100807.htm.

"Fannie Mae Board Establishes 2007 Compensation for President and Chief Executive." *Reuters,* http://www.reuters.com/article/pressRelease/idUS264637+30-Jan-2008+PRN20080130.

"Iraq for Sale: The War Profiteers." *CBS-TV News,* 2006.

Project on Government Oversight (POGO). *The Politics of Contracting.* Washington, D.C., June 24, 2004.

"Stark Statement Introducing Bill to Allow States to Draw on Fannie Mae and Freddie Mac Profits." http://www.house.gov/stark/news/108th/fmfmreformst.htm.

Appeals for the 2d Circuit, Docket No. 06-0635-cv. August 30, 2006, p. 22.

Army Field Manual No. 3-100.21. *Contractors on the Battlefield.* January 3, 2003, available at http://www.globalsecurity.org/military/library/policy/army/fm/3-100-21/index.html.

Association of the Bar of the City of New York. "Contributions to Campaigns of Candidates for Surrogate, and Appointments by Surrogates of Guardians Ad Litem." Report of the Committee on Government Ethics of the Association of the Bar of the City of New York, July 1998.

Board of County Commissioners, Wabaunsee County. Kansas v. Umbehr, 518 US 668 (1996).

Branti v. Finkel, 445 U.S. 508 (1980).

CBS News. February 2, 2009.

Center for Public Integrity. "Contracts and Reports." http://www.publicintegrity.org/wow/resources.aspx?act=resources.

Center for Public Integrity. "Windfalls of War." http://publicintegrity.org/wow/.

Citizens for Judicial Accountability. "Patronage: A Feast for Lawyers."

Coalition Provisional Authority Order No. 17 (Revised) at 4, June 27, 2004. Available at http://www.iraqcoalition.org/regulations/20040627_CPAORD_17_Status_of_Coalition_Rev_with_Annex_A.pdf.

Constitutional Limits on "Contracting Out" Department of Justice Functions under OMB. Circular A-76, 14 Op. Off. Legal Counsel 94, 1990 (William P. Barr, Assistant Attorney General).

DC Docket No. 05-00119-CR-F-N. March 6, 2009.

DeMint, Jim, U.S. Senator of South Carolina. "DeMint Statement on Fannie Mae & Freddie Mac." September 7, 2008.

Elrod v. Burns, 427 U.S. 347 (1976).

Factiva, Abertis and Citi: Pennsylvania Turnpike. October 1, 2008.

Federal National Mortgage Association Charter Act. http://www.fhfa.gov/GetFile.aspx?FilID+29.

First Tee website. http://www.thefirsttee.org/club/scripts/view/view_insert.asp? IID=13109&NS=PUBLIC.

Freddie Mac website. http://www.freediemac.com/governance/pdf/charter.pdf.

Henry, Ed. *CNN Wire,* May 8, 2008.

The Iraq Study Group Report (James A. Baker III, and Lee H. Hamilton, co-chairs), 2006.

The Johnson tapes. Scripps Library, January 12, 1995, http://millercenter.org.

Katrina Information. "Key Corporations Cited by House Oversight Committee." http://www.katrinaaction.org/Katrina_contractors.

Kiyoshi Hirabayashi v. United States. 320 U.S. 81 (1943).

Letter from Jacqueline Simon, Public Policy Director, to Clay Johnson, Deputy Director for Management, Office of Management and Budget, March 20, 2007.

Lopez Torres v. New York State Board of Elections, 411 F Supp 2d, 212.Mariner, Joanne. "Private Contractors Who Torture." May 10, 2004, available at http://writ.news .findlaw.com/mariner/20040510.html.

New York State Board of Elections v. Lopez Torres, Decided, No. 06-766, January 10, 2008.

No. 05-842, Michael E. Avery, et al., on behalf of themselves and all others similarly situated, Petitioners v. State Farm Mutual Automobile Insurance Company, Respondent.

NW Financial Group LLC Report. "Then There Were Two ... Indiana Toll Road vs. Chicago Skyway." November 1, 2006.

Office of Senator Charles Schumer. *Press Release: Multi-Billion Dollar Company That Operates NYC Port to Be Taken Over by United Arab Emirates Government-Owned Firm Today.* February 13, 2006, available at http://schumer.senate.gov/SchumerWebsite/ pressroom/press_releases/2006/PR60.NYC%20Port%20Security.021306.html.

O'Hare Truck Service v. Northlake, Ill. 518 US 712 (1996).

OMB Watch. "OMB Watch Launches FedSpending.org." October 11, 2006, available at http://ombwatch.org/article/articleview/3613/1/82.

OMB Watch. "Obama Strengthens Revolving Door Restrictions." http://www.ombwatch .org/blog/234/all/all?page3.

Recommendations on Fiduciary Appointments in New York. *Report of the Commission on Fiduciary Appointments.* December 2001.

Report from the New York Court. February 24, 2009.

Rutan et al. v. Republican Party of Illinois, et al., 1990. U.S. Supreme Court Reports 111 L. Ed. 2nd.

Rutan v. Republican Party of Illinois, 497 U.S. 62 (1990).

Simpson, Dick, Ola Adeoye, Daniel Bliss, Kevin Navratil, and Rebecca Raines. "The New Daley Machine: 1989–2004." University of Illinois, Chicago, 2004.

Taxpayers for Common Sense. http://www.taxpayer.net/budget/katrinaspending/ contracts.

TRAC. "Federal Criminal Enforcement: An Organization That Studies and Compares the Actions of Federal Judges and Prosecutors." http://tracfed.syr.edu/results/ w64494148a.38.html.

United States Court of Appeals for the Eleventh Circuit, No. 07-13163, United States Court of Appeals, Second Circuit, 475 F.2d, United States of America, Appellee, v. Herbert R. Jacobs etc., Defendants-Appellants, March 5, 1973.

United States Court of Appeals for the Seventh Circuit, Case Nos.: 06-4251, 06-4252, 06-4254.

United States of America v. Don Eugene Siegelman and Richard Scrushy, Case No. 07-13163-B.

Walker v. Cheney, 230 F. Sup.2d 51 (DCC. 2002).

Youngstown Sheet & Tube Co. v. Sawyer, 343 U.S. 579 (1952).

INDEX

About the Authors

Martin Tolchin capped a forty-year career at *The New York Times,* where he reported on Congress and politics, by becoming founder, publisher, and editor-in-chief of *The Hill* newspaper. He also was the founding senior publisher and editor of *Politico.* He is now a senior scholar at the Woodrow Wilson International Center for Scholars.

Susan J. Tolchin is University Professor of Public Policy at George Mason University and the author of *The Angry American: How Voter Rage Is Changing the Nation* (1996 and 1998) and *Women in Congress: 1917–1976.*

Together the Tolchins have written seven previous books: *A World Ignited: How Apostles of Ethnic, Religious, and Racial Hatred Torch the Globe* (2006); *Glass Houses: Congressional Ethics and the Politics of Venom* (2004); *Selling Our Security: The Erosion of America's Assets* (1992); *Buying Into America: How Foreign Money Is Changing the Nation* (1988); *Dismantling America: The Rush to Deregulate* (1983); *Clout: Womanpower and Politics* (1974); and *To the Victor: Political Patronage from the Clubhouse to the White House* (1971), which has been cited in five U.S. Supreme Court decisions.